France and Women 1789–1914
Gender, Society and Politics

Subtly conceived, elegantly written, a fresh and important study of how French women thought, acted and were imagined in the nineteenth century.
Robert Gildea, University of Oxford

France and Women is a winner! James McMillan is a consummate master of the art of distilling what is significant and distinctive. His crisp and lucid prose will delight both experts and beginners.
Pamela Pilbeam, Royal Holloway, University of London

James McMillan has brilliantly achieved his aim of writing a comprehensive, near 'total' history of women in France between the Revolution and the First World War. A book not to be missed.
Roger Price, University of Wales, Aberystwyth

James McMillan takes on the whole modern history of French women – the first work in English to do so as a continuous, comprehensive narrative. An essential part of every reading list, it is more that just a textbook – it has a clear thesis, and one that will raise patriotic republican blood pressure.
Robert Tombs, Cambridge University

James McMillan is Richard Pares Professor of History at the University of Edinburgh. He has published extensively on the political, social and religious history of modern France. His books include *Twentieth Century France: Politics and Society 1898–1991* (1992) and *Napoleon III* (1991).

France and Women 1789–1914

Gender, Society and Politics

James F. McMillan

London and New York

First published 2000
by Routledge
11 New Fetter Lane, London EC4P 4EE

Simultaneously published in the USA and Canada
by Routledge
29 West 35th Street, New York, NY 10001

Routledge is an imprint of the Taylor & Francis Group

Transferred to Digital Printing 2003

Typeset in Perpetua and Franklin Gothic by Prepress Projects, Perth, Scotland

British Library Cataloguing in Publication Data
A catalogue record for this book is available from the British Library

Library of Congress Cataloging in Publication Data
McMillan, James F., 1948–
France and women, 1789–1914 : gender, society and politics/James F. McMillan
p. cm.
Includes bibliographical references and index.
ISBN 0-415-22602-3 – ISBN 0-415-22603-1 (pbk.)
1. Women–France–History. 2. Women–France–Social conditions. I. Title.
HQ1613.M38 2000
305.4'0944 21–dc21   99-042213

Printed and bound by Antony Rowe Ltd, Eastbourne

FOR DONATELLA, AS ALWAYS

Contents

Contents

Contents

Tables

Preface

Writing books as a lone scholar is a solitary activity, but it is one in which authors are likely to incur many obligations. I have certainly been no exception to this rule and I am happy to acknowledge my debts here.

I am grateful to successive History editors at UCL Press and Routledge who have shown great patience at repeated delays to their publishing schedules. The initial approach from UCL Press invited me to produce a revised version of my out-of-print *Housewife or Harlot: The Place of Women in French Society 1870–1940* (1981). That was a tempting offer since, in a field which has expanded enormously over the past twenty years, newcomers sometimes appear to need reminding of work which was carried out in more pioneering days. On reflection, however, I decided that, because of the increasingly sophisticated conceptual and methodological approaches to the subject as well as the sheer volume of recent work, I needed to take on the challenge of writing an entirely new book. Perhaps a fifth of *Housewife or Harlot* survives in these pages in some shape or form, but *France and Women* is decidedly a book of the 1990s rather than of the 1970s.

Nevertheless, I would still like to pay tribute primarily to the work carried out by my own generation of researchers, and in particular to a cohort of American scholars whose research, begun in the early 1970s, helped to create a new historical discipline. The monographs of such as Chips Sowerwine, Steve Hause, Patrick Bidelman and Claire Moses, along with the articles and invaluable documentary collections of Karen Offen, have been indispensable to the realisation of the present project. Similarly, the work of the likes of Joan Scott, Michelle Perrot and Alain Corbin has been inspirational. The full range of my intellectual debts, is, I hope, acknowledged in the notes – though of course none of the people named either here or there shares any responsibility for what I have ultimately written.

Another debt of gratitude is to the staff of the many archives and libraries where I have worked over the years, above all in Paris. In particular, I should mention the Archives Nationales, the Bibliothèque Nationale, the Bibliothèque Historique de la Ville de Paris, the Bibliothèque Marguerite Durand, the Musée Social and the Arsenal.

Preface

In Glasgow, invaluable help has been provided by the staff responsible for the Inter-Library Loan desk of the Library at the University of Strathclyde and I also have the good fortune of access to the superb collections of the University of Glasgow. It is a pleasure, too, to record debts of a different kind, namely to those institutions which have helped to fund my research, and more especially my research trips abroad. My thanks go especially to the Carnegie Trust for the Universities of Scotland and to the Caledonian Foundation and the Royal Society of Edinburgh, who in 1993–94 awarded me a European Visiting Research Fellowship. The University of Strathclyde was likewise strongly supportive of my research, in terms both of making available funds for travel and field research and of allowing time to write. My final debt is to the book's dedicatee, simply for being there.

Glasgow
October 1999

Introduction

My interest in the history of French women and in the politics of gender in France goes back thirty years, to my time as a graduate student in Oxford working under the direction of the late and much lamented Richard Cobb. My focus then was on the impact of the First World War on women's situation, a problematic which likewise governed my approach in the book of the thesis, *Housewife or Harlot: The Place of Women in French Society 1870–1940* (1981). In order to assess the significance of the period 1914–18, I was obliged to make comparisons with the nineteenth-century background, and my task would have been made altogether simpler had there been a single authoritative volume available for consultation. At that time, though I discovered many interesting and long-forgotten monographs from around the turn of the century, there was nothing approaching a synthesis. Some thirty years later, students may be surprised to learn that this remains one of the glaring gaps in French historiography. Despite the production of a massive scholarly literature devoted to virtually all aspects of women's condition over the 'long nineteenth century', general works remain essentially multi-authored collections of essays rather than integrated histories or genuine overviews. The originality of *France and Women* is to provide the first attempt by a single author to relate the history of French women in the period in a continuous and coherent historical narrative.

Telling that story poses many methodological and conceptual challenges. The fundamental difficulty, of course, lies in the category 'women' itself. How can one write about 'women' when the term embraces more than half of the French population and is made up of individuals from many different walks of life? It is self-evident that the aristocratic salon lady of the Ancien Régime lived in a different universe from that of a poor, landless labourer, and that the *grande bourgeoise* of the *belle époque* did not share the status of her chambermaid or her dressmaker. *France and Women*, in the first instance, is about people – female persons – and in that regard it is a work of social history, portraying French women both as individuals and as members of different social classes and regional and cultural communities. Chapters 4 and 10 are explicitly about upper-class and bourgeois women, while

Chapters 5 and 11 concentrate on the condition of the rural and urban labouring classes. The private sphere – the object of much of the research into the female condition in the late 1970s and early 1980s – is neither privileged nor neglected. Rather, the emphasis here is on the overlap and interaction between public and private.

Discursively, 'women' were also 'Woman', the cultural construct who fired the imaginations of writers and artists, and about whom intellectuals (most of them, but not all of them, male) speculated endlessly in an ongoing debate on what came to be called the 'woman question'. To write the history of women is necessarily also to write about how 'woman' has been constructed in discourses on 'womanhood' and 'femininity'. The period from the late eighteenth century through to the First World War was remarkable for the degree to which a particular vision of woman as a morally superior and domestically oriented being came to be accepted as authoritative by the educated elites in France (as elsewhere). It had not always been thus. A major part of our story, therefore, is concerned with the efforts which went into defining – and refining – a gender order which prescribed social roles for both men and women on the basis of their biological sex. The theme is a pervasive one, but is dealt with explicitly in Part 1 and especially in Part 3, which is entirely devoted to nineteenth-century discourses on 'woman'. In that sense, *France and Women* is as much a cultural history as it is a social history.

Ultimately, however, the book is a political history. Systematically, it tells the story of French women's unsuccessful quest for citizenship over the course of the nineteenth century, from the time of the French Revolution, when the likes of Olympe de Gouges sought to apply the doctrines of the 'Rights of Man' to the situation of women, through to the eve of the First World War, when the political masters of the Third Republic, in an age of mass politics and so-called 'universal' suffrage, refused to concede the vote to women despite the best efforts of organised feminist groups. Chapters 2, 6, 9 and 12, along with the Epilogue, offer a comprehensive account of the history of French feminism in this period, though they also have much to reveal about the neglected subjects of anitfeminism and misogyny in France.

In short, *France and Women* aspires to be an example of 'total' history, not in the sense of saying the last word (no one is more aware than the author of the book's omissions and limitations), but in the sense that it seeks to provide a comprehensive master narrative which does justice to the many dimensions of its subject. In the process, it hopes to stimulate a re-reading of nineteenth-century French history. Its aim has been not just to produce a more inclusive account of the past, in which the place of women is more clearly visible. Rather it has been also to present the past in a different light. From the perspective of gender, many of the myths of progress associated with the dominant Republican tradition and the coming of 'modernisation' begin to lose much of their credibility.

Part I (1789–1815)

Redefining women's sphere

Chapter 1

Defining womanhood

The legacy of the Enlightenment

The eighteenth century was in many respects a good time to be a woman – at least for a female elite. As the Goncourt brothers suggested in a classic work, never before, perhaps, had women appeared to be so powerful or so sexually liberated.[1] At Court and in the world of the Parisian salons, brilliant society women wielded immense influence in their aristocratic and upper-class milieu. Royal mistresses such as Mme de Pompadour and Mme du Barry, or society hostesses such as the wealthy Mme du Deffand or the scandalous Mme du Tencin, mother of the philosophe d'Alembert, were only the most obvious examples: and to these could be added independent women who succeeded in earning their own living as writers, like the Marquise de Châtelet, the translator of Newton's *Principia* and friend of Voltaire, or as artists, like the painter Elizabeth Vigée-Lebrun. Just as men were known (if not expected) to indulge in extra-marital affairs, so too in polite society female sexual infidelity was tolerated, provided it was not flaunted and the honour of a husband not impaired. The French aristocracy undoubtedly practised birth control, which was the main reason that the birth rate in the families of the nobility fell from 6.5 in the seventeenth century to 2 in the eighteenth century, and this in turn could only have diminished women's fears of the dangers of childbirth, as well as of male sexual aggression.[2] In practice, if not in theory, the double standard of morality no longer applied to many women of the French upper classes.

Yet, as the Goncourts also recognised, women simultaneously appeared in another and less flattering light in the period. Anti-woman prejudice remained strong in the eighteenth century, and in many ways the unconventional behaviour of women of the elite succeeded only in making it stronger, as we shall see. The birth of a female child was not necessarily greeted as good news in eighteenth-century France. In the words of the Goncourts, families regarded the new arrival as 'a blessing which they accept as a disappointment'. Maternal love was not to be wasted on the little girl: she would be sent away to a wet nurse, then, on her return home, consigned to a governess and later dispatched to board at a convent school. As soon as possible, she would be married off to a husband chosen for her by her family.[3] The inference from such usages seems plain enough: under the Ancien Régime, women were regarded as a 'second sex' whose inferiority to men could scarcely be doubted.

Redefining women's nature: medical discourse and the female body

In this regard, the eighteenth century was the inheritor of a misogynistic tradition which had come down from the ancient and medieval worlds and which, in a body of texts about women (all of them written by men), defined women as 'other' and affirmed their subordination. The occasional dissentient female voice of a Christine de Pisan in the early fifteenth century or of a Marie Jars de Gournay in the early seventeenth century struggled to be heard.[4] Neither the intellectual changes associated with the Renaissance and the Reformation eras nor the Scientific Revolution of the seventeenth century had contributed to any substantial re-evaluation of women's position. Scientific opinion, which questioned many of the theses of medieval and classical authors, reinforced rather than undermined assumptions about women's inferiority. Seventeenth-century champions of Aristotle may have clashed with contemporary disciples of Galen on points of detail concerning the female anatomy, but all were agreed that women were the dangerous sex, driven by more powerful sexual urges than men. Some leading doctors still subscribed to Plato's theory of the 'wandering womb' (the idea that the womb 'wandered' when not sufficiently activated by sexual intercourse and reproduction, thus giving rise to disturbed behaviour and 'hysteria').[5]

What had happened in the early modern period, it would seem, was that in many quarters, convictions about women's inferiority actually hardened. The celebrated preacher Bishop Bossuet was not alone in regarding childbirth as women's punishment for the sin of Eve in leading Adam astray: 'Fecundity is the glory of woman', he affirmed: but 'that is where God inflicts his punishment: it is only at the peril of her life that she is fertile ... the child cannot be born without putting its mother in danger. Eve is wretched and accursed in all her sex'.[6] Likewise, the saintly François de Sales, without being quite so brutal, encouraged pregnant women to pray to God with the words: 'At my confinement, fortify my heart to support the pains which accompany it and which I accept as the effects of your justice on my sex, for the sin of the first woman'.[7] For both Catholic and Protestant authorities of the period, the ideal woman was the pious and submissive spouse who accepted her husband's authority without question and spent the greater part of her time in prayer.[8] Jesuits and Jansenists, at odds on so many other issues, concurred about women's role in society. The Jesuit Father Desmothes, in a work dedicated to Mme de Maintenon, wrote that women's foremost duty was to be well informed about their religion. Young girls should shun worldly pleasures, especially dancing ('a school of prostitution'), in favour of domestic cares. The less they were seen in society, the

4

higher they would be esteemed.[9] The Jansenist abbé Duguet counselled likewise, advising women 'to set no store by amusements and pleasure, or to engage in them only through necessity, and because you have need of them for your health'.[10]

The originality of the eighteenth-century Enlightenment was to shift the centuries-old debate on womanhood on to a new plane. Breaking both with the limitations of the older *querelle des femmes*, which debated women's qualities in terms of their moral worth, and with appeals to the authority of Christianity, of whatever variety, Enlightenment thinkers addressed themselves to the question of women's 'otherness' and attempted to explain the essence of sexual difference in the light of the advanced thinking and scientific discoveries of the day.[11] For medical science in particular, the difference between the sexes was a subject of endless fascination in the late eighteenth century. Men such as Pierre Roussel, author of *Système physique et moral de la femme* (1775) which went through five editions before 1809 and continued to be cited as an authority throughout the nineteenth century, and Pierre Cabanis, who published *Rapports du physique et du moral de l'homme* (1802), sought to identify and clarify the elements of a specifically feminine nature which rendered women distinctive as human beings.[12]

Rejecting time-honoured beliefs about the similarities between men's and women's genitalia and about women's voracious sexual appetites, the doctors now pronounced the sexual organs of men and women to be entirely different. The key to women's nature lay in their reproductive function, which gave them not only their sexual identity but also their social identity. According to Julien-Joseph Virey, a prolific populariser of the medical discourse of the Enlightenment, woman's existence was only a fraction of that of man's. She lived not for herself alone but for the multiplication of the species, in conjunction with man. This was the single goal which nature, society and morality prescribed for woman. It followed, therefore, in Virey's logic, that woman 'is only a being naturally subordinated to man on account of her needs, her duties, and above all because of her physical constitution'. Because nature decreed that woman should be submissive in the sexual act, she was born for sweetness, tenderness, patience and docility, and obliged to submit to constraints without protest, for the sake of peace and concord in the family.[13] In the view of Cabanis, 'woman is rightly frightened of those labours of the mind which cannot be carried out without long and deep meditation; she chooses those which demand more tact than science, more vivacity of conception than of strength, more imagination than reason, those in which a facile talent, so to speak, can lightly remove the surface of the objects'.[14] Such ideas found a resonance in the writings of the philosophes. No less a person than Diderot, editor of the *Encyclopédie*, stated that woman was at bottom in thrall to her uterus, 'an organ subject to terrible spasms, which rules her and rouses up in her phantoms of every sort'. It was because women were governed by their reproductive organs that they were weak, sensitive creatures, unfit for intellectual endeavours.[15]

But the doctors insisted further that women differed from men not just because of their reproductive organs but on account of their entirely distinctive anatomy and physiology. Roussel affirmed that the essence of sexual difference was not confined to a single organ, but spread to all aspects of the body.[16] Likewise Virey, in his *De la femme sous ses rapports physiologique, moral et littéraire* (1823), insisted that 'sexual differences between men and women are not limited solely to their generative organs: but all parts of their bodies, even those which seem undifferentiated in the sexes, come under their influences'.[17] Eighteenth-century doctors inferred such differences from simple comparisons of male and female skeletons.[18] Thus, in medical discourse, women were represented as above all sexual creatures, 'the Sex', victims of their own bodies and of biology, which determined all aspects of their behaviour, physical and moral. At the same time, however, their sexuality had been completely redefined: for, if medical science confirmed some traditional notions of sexual difference – men were rational, orderly, masterful, whereas women were irrational, disorderly and emotional – it no longer supported the view that women were more highly sexed than men. In opposition to the discourse which, down the centuries, had made women out to be the dangerous sex, the Enlightenment proclaimed them to be more spiritual than sexual, and not so much a sexual threat as in need of protection against male sexual aggression. The ideology of separate spheres, which identified women primarily as wives and mothers whose destiny was domesticity and the reproduction of the species, was now legitimised by the authority of science and the best philosophical opinion of the day.

The philosophes and women

Of course, medical discourse on its own was not responsible for a universally accepted redefinition of femininity. For a start, doctors still disagreed among themselves about female sexuality, as was evident from their disputes over '*maladies des femmes*', those disorders which supposedly derived from women's sexuality, such as hysteria. At a popular level, too, traditional beliefs about gender difference persisted well into the nineteenth century.[19] The new medical ideas would only become dominant later, in the wake of considerable political, economic and social upheaval, as we shall see. Nevertheless, it is legitimate to underline the degree to which the Enlightenment transformed the debate on women's nature, not only raising it to a new level but providing a new language and a new frame of reference within which to discuss what would thereafter be known as the 'woman question'. Here the contribution of the philosophes was fundamental. Seeking to reshape government and society by the application of reason to human affairs, they addressed themselves to the question of the proper social role for women both explicitly and implicitly. For some, indeed, the status accorded to women was the measure of how far a given society had evolved. In the *Persian Letters* (1721) Montesquieu employed the metaphor of the seraglio to denounce despotic rule in general and the exploitation of women in particular. In the *Spirit of the Laws* (1748), he went on to argue that both men and women should have the right to divorce, though, ominously, he also expressed fears about the pernicious effects of 'licentious' behaviour on the part of women which, he thought, might be detrimental to the common good. Diderot attacked the legal disabilities to which women were subjected by male legislators, while Jaucourt in his article for the *Encyclopédie* argued for equality within marriage. Male dominance, in his view, was a consequence not of nature but of man-made laws.[20]

Yet it would be a mistake to exaggerate the degree to which Enlightenment thinkers devoted themselves to the issue of ending women's subordination. On the contrary, in the vast *oeuvre* of Voltaire, for instance, there is only the odd reference to women. He supported divorce, but more out of his deep-seated animus against the Church than out of any genuine feminist sympathies. A number of philosophes were overtly misogynous. Helvétius, for example, (who was known to the police of the Ancien Régime as a sexual pervert with a taste for flagellation) was in favour of placing women's bodies at the disposition of the state.[21] Nor did the *Encyclopédie* speak with one voice on the subject of women (any more than it did on other matters). In contrast to Jaucourt, the dramatist and associate of Voltaire Demahis penned an entry on 'Woman, Morality', which repeated hoary shibboleths about women's alleged weakness, timidity and duplicity.[22] Barthez, who wrote on 'Woman, Anthropology', discussed with all seriousness the extent to which a woman was an imperfect man (*un homme manqué*), though he graciously conceded that, after all, women might not necessarily be as feeble-minded as their detractors made them out to be.[23]

Some modern scholars have suggested that the recycling of traditional misogynous opinion in the *Encyclopédie* was a cunning strategy to deceive the censors, and that, just as it sought to undermine orthodox attitudes to religion and custom, so too it wanted to subvert conventional wisdom about man's alleged superiority over woman. The plates, as opposed to the texts, of the *Encyclopédie* represented women positively in active occupations, and articles not ostensibly dealing with women such as Le Roi's 'Man, Morality' made the point that women's arrested cultural development could be attributed to male jealousy and control.[24] Enlightenment thinkers undoubtedly broke with the past in their willingness to speculate in new and daring ways about human nature. According to Paul Hoffmann, it is unfair to accuse the authors of the Age of Light of being antifeminist since merely by recognising the concept of femininity they were refuting the Aristotelean and Christian idea that 'the mind has no sex'. Their understanding of women's liberation may have been one which involved individual temperament and outlook rather than political rights, he suggests, but it was no less real for all that.[25]

Anachronism is one of the cardinal sins of historical scholarship and Hoffmann's point about the dangers of applying labels such as 'feminist' and 'antifeminist' to thinkers of an era where the concept of feminism had yet to be invented is salutary. He overstates a good case, however. The fact remains that the great majority of Enlightenment thinkers viewed woman as an inferior creature not simply because of their oppression by man-made laws but because nature had so ordained. Entirely representative was Antoine Thomas, author of *Essai sur le caractère, les moeurs, et l'esprit des femmes* (1772), which recognised that women's inferiority was attributable, at least in part, to the laws and customs of different societies. Thus in Periclean Athens women were unable to participate in the rich intellectual life of the age, since the Athenian ideal prescribed a secluded role for wives and deemed their greatest achievement to be invisibility, so that they went unnoticed either to receive praise or blame. On the other hand, according to Thomas it was unthinkable that women could ever be men's intellectual equals: their minds were 'more pleasing than strong'. Such was the will of nature.[26] Diderot, who in his own essay *Sur les femmes* (1772) taxed Thomas with underestimating women's feelings, sufferings and emotions, did not dispute Thomas's gendered representation of the natural order. For Diderot, woman was more delicate and spiritual than man, but also less cerebral.[27] Indeed, as he elaborated in his *Supplément au voyage de Bougainville* (1772, published 1796), there was much of the savage about women, which could only be held in check by conventional codes of civilised behaviour.[28] Diderot educated his own daughter entirely in conformity with received wisdom.[29] Even in the most enlightened circles – and Diderot was the epitome of enlightened thought – women's otherness and inferiority were taken for granted.

Salon women and their enemies

Glaringly absent from the eighteenth-century philosophical (and medical) discourse on women's nature was any significant contribution by women themselves. France did not produce a female philosophe, and in that sense it is possible to claim that for French women the Enlightenment – like the Renaissance – was a non-event.[30] Such a verdict, however, ignores the larger context within which philosophical debate took place. The Enlightenment project of changing existing ways of thinking required the creation of an intellectual community dedicated to the spread of Enlightenment ideals – a new Republic of Letters. Central to the exchange of ideas was a forum where philosophes could meet. In France that forum was provided by the Parisian salon, and the salon was a quintessentially feminine institution, presided over by a literary hostess, or *salonnière*, who was responsible for ensuring the success of her gatherings.[31]

Dating from the time of the Marquise de Rambouillet in the late sixteenth century, the salon acquired celebrity in the course of the seventeenth century thanks to the *précieuses* – self-consciously intellectual ladies who forsook marriage and domesticity to dedicate themselves to culture, learning and the pursuit of a model of *civilité* altogether at odds with that which emanated from the Court at Versailles (for their pains they were made the butt of Molière's humour in two of his plays, *Les Précieuses ridicules* (1659) and *Les Femmes savantes* (1672)).[32] But whereas seventeenth-century *salonnières* cultivated aristocratic and leisure ideals, those of the eighteenth century sought to bring together leading intellectuals and members of the elite who shared a commitment to the ideals of the Enlightenment. The salon, though still a private space, simultaneously developed into what Jurgen Habermas has called an 'authentic public space', that is a forum in which criticism could be voiced, even of the monarchy. No longer simply an outlet for civilised leisure, the salon was transformed into a serious working environment where the business of the Enlightenment got done.

This transformation was brought about by women like Mme Geoffrin, Mlle de Lespinasse and Mme Necker, for whom running a salon was a career in which it was possible to obtain the kind of education that was conventionally denied to women. A *salonnière* needed to have considerable organisational skills: exhaustive preparation and planning went into making the weekly or twice weekly sessions a success. Conversation was not haphazard but structured, with the hostess setting the agenda. Wealth was also a prerequisite, and it was of course only a minority of women who were able to establish themselves as successful *salonnières*. Such women, however, undoubtedly did participate in the Enlightenment, facilitating the diffusion of ideas by means of a unique form of feminine sociability.[33]

Some male intellectuals, however, were uncomfortable with the high profile which women enjoyed in the salons, which, especially when combined with a considerable degree of sexual freedom, contradicted their notions of womanhood and reversed their idea of the natural order. One of the more indignant was the social commentator, novelist and pornographer Restif de la Bretonne, who in *Les Gynographes* (1777) detected the undermining of paternal authority everywhere in Europe and called for its restoration.[34] Another was Jean-Jacques Rousseau (1712–78), arguably the most influential, though certainly not the most typical, of the philosophes. As is apparent from his *Confessions*, Rousseau was a man of many contradictions. The son of a Swiss watchmaker, he lost his mother in infancy and never knew that maternal love which he so extolled in his writings. By profession a moralist of strongly didactic views, he achieved fame after opportunistic switches of loyalty between friends and religion. Yet for all his success, he was never comfortable in the world of the Parisian salons, suffering from insecurity while always remaining a supreme egotist. An apologist for the joys of marriage, he himself married late after many sexual liaisons and betrayed and abandoned his illiterate wife, the domestic servant Thérèse Le Vasseur, along with their five children, whom he had placed in a home. A self-proclaimed admirer of women, he continually insisted on their inferiority. In a society which remained overwhelmingly patriarchal, Rousseau was always ready to exaggerate female influence.[35]

Hence Rousseau, like Restif, was adamant that nature intended women to inhabit a different world from that of men, as the ancient Greeks and the city fathers of his native Geneva had understood. Whatever the new philosophy might say, he wrote to fellow philosophe d'Alembert in 1759, sex differences were more than a matter of the law and education since they derived from nature itself. The amiable and virtuous daughters of Geneva, he alleged, practised a comely domesticity in contrast to the behaviour of the 'loose women' of the salons and the cities. The prominent position occupied by salon women, each the sponsor of a coterie of tame male intellectuals, represented an intolerable confusion of sex roles. As he told d'Alembert, there was a danger that women, unable to make themselves into men, would make men into women, which in turn would undermine the state itself.[36]

For Rousseau, women had no business participating in the affairs of the world beyond the home. In his epistolatory novel *La nouvelle Héloïse* (1761), the heroine Julie, beautiful and virtuous daughter of an aristocratic family, repents of her illicit love for her tutor Saint-Preux and renounces him for a husband chosen by her father. Her feminine goodness is confirmed by her tragic death (brought on by a cold contracted as a result of trying to save her child from drowning) which made her a martyr for motherhood. In *Emile* (1762), his influential treatise on education, Rousseau depicted the kind of education required for the acquisition of the responsible citizenship of the kind he outlined in the *Social Contract*, published the same year. Emile is raised in the countryside under the guidance of a tutor (the wise Jean-Jacques!) who allows the boy to learn for himself through experience, though his education is completed by the 'natural religion' taught to him by the Vicar of Savoy. By contrast, Emile's future wife, Sophie, is educated entirely with the objective of making her a suitable helpmeet for her spouse. Whereas Emile learns to be independent, Sophie is taught by her mother to be submissive and pleasing to men and to be prepared for the assumption of her responsibilities as a wife and a mother. The sexes were complementary, but sexual differences were profound. Man was strong and active, woman weak and passive. The inescapable law of nature was that woman had been made to please man. There was no corresponding obligation on man to please woman, since his virtue resided in his superior power.[37]

If distrust of intellectual and educated women was one lasting legacy of the French Enlightenment, so too was suspicion of powerful women at Court, royal mistresses who allegedly controlled the destiny of the state behind the scenes. Montesquieu's *Persian Letters* had already alluded to the influence wielded by the likes of Mme de Maintenon in the reign of Louis XIV, but the high profile of mistresses of Louis XV such as Mme de Pompadour and Mme du Barry, and their associations with unpopular policies and ministers, furnished juicier and more explicit subject matter for the scandal-mongers and gutter journalists who operated at the lower end of Enlightenment publishing, and did much to bring the monarchy into disrepute by the time of Louis XV's death in 1774.[38] To be sure, it was difficult to convict the much more sober and possibly undersexed Louis XVI of dissipation and of submission

10

to the whims of licentious women: one of his first acts on becoming king was to dispatch Mme du Barry to a nunnery. Louis's misfortune, however, was that the target of journalistic abuse was not a royal mistress but his own wife, Marie-Antoinette, brother of Joseph II of Austria, a country that, despite the 'diplomatic revolution' effected during the Seven Years War, remained for many Frenchmen the traditional enemy. In the 1780s the Queen was vilified in outrageous pornographic attacks which represented her as a monster of depravity possessed of an insatiable sexual appetite who took lovers of both sexes and even taught perversions to her own son. Filth such as the *Essai historique sur la vie de Marie-Antoinette*, a purportedly autobiographical and confessional account of her sex romps, was first published in 1781 and ran through many subsequent editions. This and similar *libelles* became prized items of a clandestine pornographic literature which inflicted massive damage on the reputation of royalty. Come the Revolution, republicans would remember Rousseau's dictum about men being needed in a Republic.[39]

Female journalism and nascent feminism

The allegation that women were responsible for the corruption of the nation's morals did not go entirely unanswered. On the eve of the French Revolution, Marie-Armande-Jeanne Gacon-Dufour (1753–1835) published a pamphlet which argued that women were more sinned against than sinning. Already known as a female intellectual sympathetic to the ideals of the Physiocrats, she was also a member of the Société d'Agriculture de Paris who conducted agricultural experiments and a novelist. In her pamphlet, without challenging the need to educate girls differently from boys, Gacon-Dufour blamed fathers for marrying off their daughters to unsuitable husbands at a young age and cited the example of Richardson's heroine Clarissa as a prime example of what could go wrong. Bad marriages were the real problem, and the blame for these rested squarely with men because mothers, having often themselves been the victims of constraint, and knowing 'all the dangers and all the evils of a forced marriage', were less likely to pressure their daughters into a match which they did not want.[40]

Gacon-Dufour's was by no means the sole voice of female protest. Between 1759 and 1778, the monthly *Journal des Dames* not only contested established institutions such as the academies, the theatre and the state-sponsored press but also articulated specifically feminine grievances, including its objections to statements about women on the part of prominent philosophes like Desmahis and Rousseau. Originally intended by its male founder to be a source of amusement and light entertainment for society ladies, the review fell into the hands of a succession of feisty women and maverick male editors (Louis Sebastian Mercier being the most famous of the latter) who made it into an opposition journal which frequently incurred the wrath of the Old Regime censor. Both female and male editors of the

Journal, unlike the *salonnières*, who were jealous of their elite status and who shared the horror of the masses felt by most philosophes, attempted to reach out to a wide public by raising issues of political and social concern, including the rights of women. With a subscription list of between 300 and 1000, the paper would have reached a much larger audience.

The feminist tone was set by the first woman editor Mme de Beaumer, who took control of the *Journal* in 1761. Almost certainly a Huguenot and possibly a Freemason, Mme de Beaumer was an outspoken advocate of women's rights as well as a strong sympathiser with the cause of the poor, the downtrodden and the victims of religious persecution. After an abortive attempt in 1759 to start up a journal entitled *Lettres curieuses, instructives et amusantes* for circulation in France from a base at The Hague, she acquired the *Journal des Dames* in 1761. In her first editorial she encouraged women to be bold and to 'prove that we can think, speak, study, and criticise as well as [men]', announcing that she awaited this revolution with impatience and that she would do all in her power to precipitate it. When Desmahis, author of the derogatory article 'Femme' in the *Encyclopédie*, died in 1763 she showed no regret at the passing of one of the 'enemy', writing that death could hardly detract from his reputation since his life had failed to add to it. She also claimed that 'men everywhere are being forced to recognise that Nature made the two sexes equal'. Having provoked the censor Marin, who regarded her as a disgrace to the female sex, Mme de Beaumer was obliged to flee to Holland, relinquishing the *Journal* to the more tactful and well-connected Mme de Maisonneuve, who moved in the circle of the Duc de Choiseul, the King's then chief minister. Albeit in a less strident tone, she too, however, made no secret of her support for women's rights. Taking issue directly with Rousseau, she insisted that experience proved 'that women can learn, reflect, meditate, think profoundly, that they can read fruitfully, that they can equal men . . . There is no real difference between the two sexes. Thousands upon thousands of examples contradict the partisans of a modern philosophe [Rousseau] who argues that the mental faculties were not equally distributed' (July 1764). A firm champion of improving women's minds by better education (perhaps by way of protest at the life of enforced idleness she had hitherto endured), Mme de Maisonneuve argued that there was no reason why the future should not see the emergence of a female Virgil, Descartes or Rubens.[41]

Other women writers, without confronting Rousseau head-on, attempted to adapt his ideas to their own ends. It is important to appreciate that many eighteenth-century women were less ready to convict Rousseau of misogyny than twentieth-century feminists have been. Rationalism was by no means the only powerful intellectual current in France at the end of the Ancien Régime: a cult of sensibility also enjoyed considerable vogue, not least on account of the writings of Rousseau himself, since they explored the workings of the human heart and stressed the importance of emotions and feelings. Rousseau's model of femininity stirred many women into a positive re-evaluation of their own role as wives and mothers. Some were clearly attracted to the thesis propounded in *La nouvelle Héloïse* that the role of the family in the moral regeneration of the citizen was crucial: Sophie was therefore a role model not of feminine inadequacy but of the enormous potential of motherhood as a social influence on the next generation.[42]

The likes of Mme de Montbart, Mme Roland and Mme de Genlis all developed Rousseau's theme of the inspirational – and breast-feeding – mother, herself educated to a full comprehension of her role and in her turn the educator of her children, ensuring that sons grew up conscious of their civic responsibilities and daughters aware of their maternal duties. Madame de Genlis, for example, in her widely read *Adèle et Théodore* (1782), showed how aristocratic children could be reared on Rousseauist principles, though she also took pains to point out that such foibles and shortcomings of character as might be found on the part of women were not, as Rousseau would have it, inherent in feminine nature but the consequences of a corrupt world and therefore capable of remedy.[43] The *Journal des Dames* likewise championed maternity as the vehicle for the regeneration of the nation under the editorship of the baronne de Princen, also known as Mme de Montanclos, who took over in 1774.[44] By 1789 the theme of 'Republican motherhood' had become a literary staple, popularised by novels such as Bernardin de Saint-Pierre's *Paul et Virginie* (1788), a moral tale which suggested how women could take the lead in the creation of a new and better world renewed by the love and devotion of mothers and natural feminine modesty.[45] Rousseau's message to women of empowerment through marriage and motherhood would long continue to reverberate through the nineteenth-century debates on the 'woman question'.

At its most liberating, the language of the Enlightenment offered women new possibilities for framing demands in pursuit of their rights. While the full implications of this language became evident only after the outbreak of the French Revolution in 1789, its potential was already apparent in the writings of a philosophe like Condorcet (1743–94).[46] A brilliant mathematician, elected to the prestigious Académie des Sciences at the age of 26, Condorcet also enjoyed a literary reputation as the biographer of two eminent fellow philosophes, Voltaire and Turgot, and was to become a political activist during the Revolution, being elected a deputy to the Constituent Assembly in 1790. Married to Sophie de Grouchy, a dazzling figure in the world of the Parisian salons, Condorcet was acutely sensitive to the injustices under which women laboured in the Old Order. In particular, he objected to their lack of educational opportunities, which he denounced in notes for a speech to the Academy in 1785. In 1787, he set out the case for women's political rights in his *Lettres d'un bourgeois de New Haven à un citoyen de Virginie*, arguing that men could not be trusted to enact laws which reflected the interests of women and that as tax-payers women should both vote and be entitled to stand for office. Women, he insisted, were rational, and should not be debarred from citizenship. Defective education was the true cause of differences between the sexes and that could and should be remedied.[47] In his *Essai sur la constitution et les fonctions des assemblées provinciales*, published in 1788 but written earlier, he again raised the question of women's direct participation in politics, arguing that property-owning women, like their male counterparts, should have the right to vote. At the same time he expressed a wider concern for women's social status, deploring the treatment of prostitutes and calling for a state-organised system of primary education for both girls and boys to raise the general standard of public morality.[48] For Condorcet, as we shall see, the French Revolution came as an opportunity to put his pre-Revolutionary theories into practice.

The legacy of the Enlightenment, then, was mixed. What is not in doubt, however, is that a vast amount of thought and discussion had gone into attempts to redefine the gender roles of men and women. An essentially new discourse had been elaborated, capable of appropriation by both feminists and antifeminists, as the nineteenth century would prove. At the end of the Old Regime, power remained unambiguously monarchical, personal and patriarchal. But, if women had no formal access to politics, they were not alone: most men were in exactly the same position and, as we have seen, at least some women managed both to exercise political influence and, perhaps more importantly, to shape the language of politics. Such, indeed, was their influence that it generated a good deal of male anxiety, evident not only in the political theory of a Rousseau but also in works of art such as the paintings of Jacques-Louis David. In powerful canvases like *The Oath of the Horatii*, *Brutus* and *The Tennis Court Oath*, David emphasised the contractual nature of the political culture of the future but he also represented political power as an exclusively masculine prerogative.[49] The French Revolution occurred at a moment when the precise relationship of women to the public sphere was in the process of being reformulated.[50] And, for revolutionaries like David, it was an article of faith that the 'rights of man' did not include the rights of woman.

Chapter 2

The rights of man and the rights of woman

Women and the French Revolution

The pre-1789 political culture of France was that of an absolute monarchy in which the person of the King was sacred and the royal will understood to be identical with the will of God. The monarch represented both the state and the nation, embodying national unity in his own person. The social order was explicitly hierarchical, divided into three estates (the clergy, the nobility and the commons, or Third Estate), and particularistic, numbering a host of corporate bodies which were entitled to send delegates to an Estates-General, a consultative assembly summoned by the King to proffer advice and to represent particular interests of the three estates. In practice, however, by the 1780s the Crown increasingly struggled to obtain the political decisions it wanted, confronted not only with the truculence of the Parlement of Paris (not a proto-parliament but a court of law which was supposed to dispense royal justice) but, more importantly, with the alienation of public opinion, moulded by a popular press and the outpourings of hack pamphleteers who diffused the thought of the philosophes to a wide audience. Hard-pressed financially by the late 1780s, the King and his ministers were forced to conclude that reform was imperative.

Thus when Louis XVI convoked the Estates-General which opened at Versailles on 5 May 1789, hopes were high that the situation could be resolved by wise counsel and good will. Most delegates anticipated that the shape of things to come would be the construction of a new political culture shaped by the doctrines of the Enlightenment and centred on a reformed monarchy. Others, however, were determined to fashion an entirely different social and political order. Royal efforts at reform foundered when on 17 June 1789 representatives of the Third Estate refused to meet as a separate order and declared themselves to be a 'National Assembly'. Overnight the principle of popular sovereignty was established and a constitutional revolution launched. Authority was no longer deemed to derive from God, nor was it vested in the King: it resided with the people and was entrusted to representatives of the nation. On 20 June 1789 the revolutionaries of the National Assembly swore their famous tennis-court oath not to dissolve the Assembly until it had given the country a new constitution. In August 1789 they issued their

'Declaration of the Rights of Man and the Citizen' which stated explicitly that 'all sovereignty emanates essentially from the nation' (Article 3) and that 'the law is the expression of the general will' (Article 6).

The 'patriots' of 1789 knew what they were doing. They were attempting to bring into being an entirely new political and social order. Their break with the past was quite conscious, and had in fact been decided upon in the debates on representation in 1788–89 occasioned by the decision to summon an Estates-General. As past precedent no longer seemed a serviceable guide to present action (the Estates-General had last met in 1614) it was necessary to begin afresh. The world was to be remade anew. True, it was not the initial intention to abolish the monarchy and establish a Republic, which happened only in 1792, but the radical thrust of the Revolution was evident from 1789. Contemptuously repudiating the pre-1789 order of things as the 'Ancien Régime', the revolutionaries worked for the demolition of the corporate society and its replacement by a social order based on the principles of individualism and equality before the law. The watchwords of the Revolution were proclaimed to be liberty, equality and fraternity. The key concept which would bind the nation together was citizenship.[1]

At no stage, however, did the revolutionaries think of including women within their definitions of citizenship. In the first constitution, drawn up in 1791, a distinction was made between active and passive citizens. Active citizens were males over the age of 25 who were both independent (domestic servants were excluded) and able to meet a minimum property requirement (payment by direct taxation of the value of three days' work). In 1792, under the Republic, so-called 'universal' suffrage was introduced, which in reality meant that citizenship was granted to all independent males over 21. Women, like domestic servants, were not considered autonomous human beings: they were nature's 'passive' citizens, irrespective of property considerations. Revolutionary legislators rendered women invisible in their constitutions: and all constitution-makers in France would do likewise for the following 150 years.

Women in search of citizenship

A number of dissentient voices protested against the Revolution's gender-specific definition of citizenship. The most eloquent was that of Condorcet, who in his *Essai sur l'admission des femmes au droit de cité* (*Essay on the admission of women to the rights of citizenship*) published in July 1790 argued the need to extend the sacred principles of the Declaration of the Rights of Man to include the rights of women to civil and political equality. Natural rights applied to all human beings, male and female, and in nature all persons were equal. Either no individual of the human race had genuine rights, Condorcet maintained, or else all had the same rights. Those who voted against the rights of others, no matter their religion, colour or sex, should forfeit their own rights. To deprive half the human race of the right to assist in the making of law was a violation of the principle of the equality of rights and an act of tyranny.

Nor, in Condorcet's view, could it be held that women were incapable of exercising the rights of citizenship. 'Pregnancy and passing indispositions' were no more a barrier to the exercise of rights on the part of women than were gout and the common cold on the part of men. Likewise it was absurd to exclude women from rights on the grounds of an allegedly – and entirely unproved – inferior intelligence, since application of the same principle to the male sex would disqualify huge numbers of dim-witted men. Dismissing, finally, the argument from 'general utility', that admission of women to citizenship would draw women away from the tasks which nature had allotted them, Condorcet contended that politics would always be the business of the few. To give women the vote would no more tear away the majority from their housekeeping than it would farmers from their fields or artisans from their workshops. In any case, in the upper classes, rich women were far from solely preoccupied with the affairs of the household: it would be better to engage their energies in serious occupations rather than have them dissipated, as at present, in the idle pursuits to which custom and bad education condemned them.[2]

Condorcet's plea for female citizenship is now celebrated as one of the founding texts of modern feminism. Less famous, but articulating the aspirations of women themselves, were the feminist demands which surfaced in at least some of the *cahiers de doléances*, the lists of grievances drawn up in the hope that they could be put to rights by the Estates-General. The authenticity of these cannot always be guaranteed: some were written by men and were merely lewd or trite. Others, however, were genuine, including the *Pétition des femmes du Thiers Etat au Roi* (1 January 1789) and the *Cahier des doléances et réclamations des femmes*, written by a Norman woman, Mme B.B. The former was addressed to the King, and identified better education as the most efficacious remedy for the present plight of women. It did not demand political rights, though it expressed a degree of hostility to the deputies who would deny such rights to women, and suggested that 'in this communal agitation' women should be able to make their voices heard.[3]

Madame B.B. was more forthright. Like Condorcet she used the argument that if rights were to be extended to blacks then they should also be extended to women. Describing women as 'the Third Estate of the Third Estate', Mme B.B. sought to turn the logic and the language of the Revolution to women's advantage. Women, she stated, payed taxes: and if it was the case that political rights were attached to property rather than persons, it was difficult to see how women could legitimately be denied their due. Moreover, just as commoners could not be represented by nobles, so men could not represent women: only women could represent women. Women's situation was deplorable: the surest remedy was to guarantee them a decent education: 'Do not raise us any more as if we were destined to furnish the pleasures of the seraglio'. At the same time, masculine privilege over women had to disappear, particularly the right of fathers to marry off their daughters to unsuitable husbands. In the context of the great reform movement of 1788/89, when new laws were to be made against oppression, Mme B.B. concluded that it was vital that the legislators remember the needs of women.[4] Her text struck chords with the sentiments of other women living in the French provinces. It was reproduced in its entirety under the title *Cahier des doléances et réclamations des femmes du département de la Charente* by a Mme Vuignerias from Angoulême and reprinted in the *Etrennes Nationales des Dames*, one of the feminist newspapers which emerged in the course of the Revolution.[5]

By far the strongest statement of the early feminists, however, was the *Déclaration des droits de la femme et de la citoyenne* drawn up by Olympe de Gouges in September 1791. The daughter of a Montauban butcher, de Gouges had been born humble Marie Gouze, and at the age of 16 married a much older man, Louis Yves Aubry, by whom she had a son. After the death of her husband, she determined never to remarry and, refusing to call herself by the conventional designation of Veuve Aubry, she fashioned a new persona for herself as 'Olympe de Gouges' (Olympe being her mother's name and the noble particule 'de' an addition which she later claimed was justifiable on the grounds that she was not the butcher's daughter but the illegitimate offspring of a liaison between her mother and a local *seigneur*). Under her exotic pseudonym, de Gouges embarked on a career as an actress and playwright in Paris, where she achieved a degree of success before 1789 (some of her plays, which were mainly dictated rather than written by herself, were performed at the Comédie Française). She was also known as an activist on behalf of women's rights. In her *Lettre au peuple, au projet d'une caisse patriotique*, a pamphlet published in 1788, she expressed the hope that women would play a key role in the forthcoming work of national regeneration and invited them to make financial sacrifices to help bring about a political reformation. From the outset of the Revolution, she sought to influence events, campaigning for causes as diverse as divorce, the rights of unmarried mothers and illegitimate children, the establishment of maternity hospitals and the end of slavery, as well as the establishment of a national theatre and clean streets. Always an ardent royalist, she dedicated her 'Declaration of the Rights of Women' to Marie-Antoinette, looking to the Queen to take the lead in defending the cause of women and restoring the morals of the nation – a courageous act at a time when Marie-Antoinette had come under the sustained attack not only of pornographers but also of newspapers like the *Véritable Ami de la Reine ou Journal des Dames*, for whom she was the personification of feminine intrigue at Court and the heart of a conspiracy to subvert the Revolution with the collusion of reactionary foreign powers.[6]

De Gouges opened her Declaration of the Rights of Women by accusing the revolutionaries of 1789 of appropriating all the benefits of the Revolution exclusively for the male sex and oppressing women:

Man alone has raised his exceptional circumstances to a principle. Bizarre, blind, bloated with science and degenerated – in a century of enlightenment and wisdom – into the crassest ignorance, he wants to command as a despot a sex which is in the full possession of its intellectual faculties; he pretends to enjoy the Revolution and to claim his rights to equality in order to say nothing more about it.

In a Postscript, she urged women themselves to wake up to the fact that they had been cheated by the Revolution, obtaining only greater scorn and disdain. In the past women had ruled only indirectly, through the shameful influence exercised in the boudoir. The time had arrived when women needed to repudiate these ways and demand their legitimate place in the conduct of public affairs in the name of reason and philosophy. What was good for men was good also for women, who had it in their power to free themselves, if only they wanted to. Women had to assert their rights, and in a direct adaptation of the language of the Declaration of the Rights of Man she applied the doctrine of natural rights to woman and defined the rights of women in seventeen articles. Article 4 stated that the only limit to the exercise of the natural rights of woman was 'perpetual male tyranny'. The principle of equality before the law meant that women must have full rights of citizenship and be able to participate fully in public life (Article 6). In the words of Article 10: 'Woman has the right to mount the scaffold; she must equally have the right to mount the rostrum'. Like men, women were entitled to freedom of thought and the free communication of opinion (Article 11) and also had a right to property (Article 17).[7]

Though intended primarily to be a statement of abstract principles, de Gouges's text was not free from special pleading for women *qua* women. When it suited her purpose, she was ready both to strike a personal note and to invoke feminine stereotypes as elements in her rhetorical strategy. In her Preamble, for instance, she refers to 'the sex that is as superior in beauty as it is in courage during the sufferings of maternity', and in Article 11, which affirmed the right to free speech, she makes the point that such a right is of particular concern to abandoned mothers seeking support from the fathers of their illegitimate children. Inequality in marriage was one of de Gouges's main preoccupations and to conclude the Postscript of her Declaration she appended a new 'Form for a Social Contract between Man and Woman', a model marriage contract which recognised the property due to children 'from whatever bed they come'. In her own acknowledgement of sexual difference, either implicit or explicit, de Gouges in a sense conceded what most revolutionary males maintained: that women *were* different, which was precisely why they refused to include them within the category of active citizens.[8]

Another feminist propagandist in the first phase of the Revolution was the Dutch woman, Etta Palm d'Aelders, a native of Gröningen. Born in 1743, she married the Frenchman Ferdinand Palm and, following his disappearance or death, came to live in Paris in 1774, where she moved in the progressive circles of the salon held by

Mme Condorcet. Welcoming the Revolution as an opportunity to promote the rights of women, she established herself as a public speaker in the revolutionary club movement, the organisations of factions and pressure groups which mushroomed to represent the divergent currents of political opinion inside and outside the National Assembly. A member notably of the Cercle social, a club founded in January 1790 by the abbé Fauchet, one of the few male revolutionaries to champion women's rights, and of the more populist Société fraternelle des patriotes de l'un et l'autre sexe, Défenseurs de la Constitution, Mme d'Aelders published a pamphlet entitled *Appel aux Françaises sur la régénération des moeurs et nécessité de l'influence des femmes dans un gouvernement libre*, which insisted on the need for women to organise themselves into an effective feminist lobby. Her notion was that women should form societies in each *département*, which would tackle problems such as wet-nursing, public education for women and social services generally, and thus help to spread Revolutionary ideals to the provinces.[9]

Likewise an enthusiastic supporter of women's involvement in the club movement was Théroigne de Méricourt, who, born Anne Tervagne and hailing from Liège, had made her way in the world as a singer and *demi-mondaine*. Founder of a club Les Amis de la Loi, she also cut a striking figure at the Club des Cordeliers, dressed either in red riding gear or in the white of a vestal virgin of antiquity. Aligned (as many of the early feminists seem to have been) with the Girondin faction, Théroigne won a degree of renown as an advocate of arming women and forming them into a legion of Amazons, or women warriors.[10] Still more radical was Pauline Léon, by profession a chocolate-maker, who was a member of the Société fraternelle and also a frequenter of the Cordeliers club. On 6 March 1791 she petitioned the National Assembly for the right to set up a female militia so that women could protect their homes from counter-revolutionary assaults.[11] Denying that her scheme meant the abandonment of the care of their families, she told the deputies: 'We wish only to defend ourselves the same as you; you cannot refuse us, and society cannot deny the right nature gives us, unless you pretend the Declaration of Rights does not apply to women, and that they should let their throats be cut like lambs, without the right to defend themselves'.[12]

For at least some French women, the Revolution stirred a new sense of feminist consciousness. In that sense, the Revolution, with the Enlightenment, gave birth to modern feminism, even if the Declaration of Rights never did get applied to women. In addition, the Revolution gave rise to new forms of feminine political action.

Women and revolutionary activism

Women were no strangers to political protest in the years before 1789. The presence of women of the popular classes in bread riots and in the politics of subsistence has been amply documented by historians of the seventeenth and eighteenth centuries.

In towns and cities, and notably in Paris, they were regularly the prime movers behind disturbances at the marketplace, some of which ended in the imposition of *taxation populaire*, the sale of commodities at a 'fair' price fixed by the rioters themselves. Fourteen women were among those arrested for their part in the 'flour war' in Paris in 1775, a classic case of protest against steep rises in the price of flour and bread. In an urban setting, too, women were involved in street politics as the champions of neighbourhood and community values, expressed in jeers and verbal abuse, lifting up their skirts, clapping, the beating of drums and the carnivalesque – in a word the politics of gesture, sanctioned by tradition and custom and by their status as mothers.[13]

On occasion, protest over subsistence mingled with political objectives, as in the winter of 1708–9, when women demanded both lower bread prices and an end to the war of the Spanish Succession. Though in France *émeute* (riot) was made a capital offence by a law of 1731, women rarely paid for riotous activity with their lives. On the contrary, both in Paris and the provinces the courts tended to extend leniency to women who, impelled by hunger and the need to feed their children, resorted to violence in their desperation. For this reason, women may well have been channels of wider community protest, selected for the role because of their ability to act with less risk to their persons than men. Female rioters also symbolised the shame of men and social arrangements which allowed the weakest elements in society to suffer: their action could serve as a spur to men who appeared to be lacking in courage and conviction.[14]

Many of these traditional features of female protest can be discerned in the participation of women in the uprisings or *journées* which punctuated the history of the Revolution. Only one woman is known to have taken part in the storming of the Bastille on 14 July 1789, but the event was celebrated and commemorated as much by the women as by the men of the Parisian *classes populaires* as a triumph for ordinary people against the forces of despotism.[15] In August and September 1789 they processed regularly to give thanks for their deliverance to Sainte Geneviève, the patron saint of Paris. In the October days of 1789, by contrast, the role of women was decisive. At a time when the constitutional revolution seemed stalled, and when, despite a good harvest, the price of bread remained high, anger and hunger fuelled their discontent. Early in the morning of 5 October a crowd of women, many of them armed with sticks, pikes and knives, gathered outside the Hôtel de Ville to demand that Lafayette, the hero of both the American and the French Revolutions, lead them to Versailles to oblige the King both to give them bread and to punish a royal officer known to have insulted the revolutionary cockade. Without waiting for the absent (and reluctant) Lafayette, however, the women, their ranks now swollen to about six thousand, set off for the royal palace, which they reached after a six-hour march in the rain. Several hundred invaded the National Assembly and left the deputies in no doubt as to their feelings about being the victims of a 'famine plot'. A small delegation was permitted to approach the King, who gave them reassurances that there would be no hold-ups of grain deliveries to the city.

This was not enough to satisfy the great majority, who refused to go home without some more tangible sign of success. Their resolution was reinforced by the arrival of the Parisian National Guard, bent on bringing the King back to Paris from Versailles. Louis XVI had already made up his mind to accede to the constitutional revolution but he balked at a return to the Louvre. It was Lafayette, not the women, who persuaded him that there was no alternative if the safety of the royal family was to be guaranteed. His words were speedily borne out by the deeds of unruly guardsmen, who forced their way into the palace, killing two of the royal bodyguards, in an attempt to murder Marie-Antoinette, 'the Austrian whore'. Prompt intervention by the National Guard company under the command of Lazare Hoche, soon to be one of the most celebrated of Revolutionary generals, saved the lives of the Queen and her children. Louis, however, now bowed to the inevitable, and returned to Paris along with the National Assembly. And so it was that an action initiated by women, but completed by men, brought back to the capital 'the baker, the baker's wife and the baker's little boy'.[16]

So far, so traditional, it might seem. But even at this early stage of the Revolution it was apparent that the political intervention of women of the popular classes had gone beyond previous experience. The very fact that the women turned to the National Guard and the National Assembly for assistance is indicative of their appreciation of the new political context and their identification with the Revolution. Denied the formal rights of active citizens, they learned to become *de facto* citizens as participants in the struggle to create a new political culture founded on the idea of popular sovereignty. From the outset, their aspirations for the rectification of particular grievances merged with the wider revolutionary goal of establishing a new political and social order. The *cahiers* of 1789 included not only the more abstract demands for rights of the kind penned by Mme B.B. but also requests from women of the labouring classes for royal protection against unfair competition from convents or from men who engaged in trades traditionally recognised as women's. Such, for instance, was the *Pétition des femmes du Thiers Etat au Roi* of 1789, which also asked the King to help women in their efforts to secure better education and training. Similarly, petitions written at the end of 1789 and the beginning of 1790 with a view to influencing the National Assembly in its work of national reconstruction identified particular areas where reform was necessary if women were also to benefit from the Revolution. The *Motions adressées à l'Assemblée Nationale en faveur du sexe*, for instance, specified job opportunities, while the *Vues législatives sur les femmes*, drawn up by a Mlle Jodin, put the case for divorce.[17]

The process of politicisation which produced the Jacobin Republic, the militancy of the sans-culottes and the Terror of 1793–94 had its impact on female as well as on male political consciousness. As already noted, the likes of Etta Palm d'Aelders helped to develop women's role in the club movement. The more radical clubs, like the Jacobins and the Cordeliers, though they did not admit women as members, allowed them to witness debates as spectators in the galleries. Women of the people were among the most assiduous attenders, and were thus exposed to the arguments in favour of the founding of a Republic of Virtue based on 'universal' suffrage. Not surprisingly, they were among the crowd who congregated on the Champ de Mars on 17 July 1791 to demonstrate their support for a popular referendum on the issue of the executive role of the monarchy, only to be dispersed by shots fired by the National Guard.[18]

Taxation populaire was imposed by the common women of Paris during the sugar crisis of early 1792, but significantly this followed their failure to receive redress of their grievances from the Legislative Assembly. Food shortages were now linked with the form of regime and after the abolition of the monarchy and the proclamation of the Republic, whose new legislature, the National Convention, was deemed by the revolutionaries to be the embodiment of the sovereign will of the people, sans-culotte women acquired a new aggressiveness. As ever, the principal focus of their discontent was subsistence: in February 1793 the people of Paris were hungry and their anger was expressed in demands for exemplary action to be taken against hoarders, speculators and all enemies of the Revolution both at home and abroad (after 1792 the revolutionary leadership had to contend with war against first the Habsburg Monarchy and Prussia, and then Britain from early 1793, as well as counter-revolutionary insurgency in the Vendée in the west of France). The Girondins, as supporters of a free market, were the particular *bête noire* of the sans-culotte women. The form taken by feminine revolutionary violence may have been traditional, but the context in which it took place made it an integral element of the bloody 'revolution from below' sought by the sans-culottes.[19]

In May 1793, as the power struggle between Girondins and Jacobins for control of the Convention was moving to its climax, some sans-culottes women formed what was to be the most significant of all the revolutionary women's clubs, the Society of Revolutionary Republican Women. Though never large – it had about 170 members at its foundation – the club was extremely militant. Its two leading lights, Pauline Léon and Claire Lacombe, had a track-record of revolutionary activism. Léon, whom we have already encountered, was born in 1758 and a sworn enemy of moderate revolutionaries like Lafayette. A veteran of the Champs de Mars demonstration of 1791, she was well known for her activity in her local Section and proud to acknowledge her extreme Republicanism and public advocacy of the death penalty for Louis XVI. Claire Lacombe was an actress from the provinces who arrived in Paris only in the summer of 1792. Since then, however, she had been a regular attender at the popular societies. Both had personal as well as political affiliations with the Enragés – the 'wild men' headed by the ex-priest Jacques Roux who articulated the most extreme views of the Parisian sans-culottes – since they shared a lover in Roux's collaborator Théophile Leclerc, whom Léon eventually married in November 1793, though by no means all of the Républicaines were committed to Roux's faction.[20]

Officially registered with the Commune of Paris on 10 May 1793 as a society whose objective was 'deliberation on the means of frustrating the projects of the Republic's enemies', the club met in the library of the Jacobin club on the rue Saint-Honoré. Instantly recognisable in their red pantaloons and red caps of liberty (for fashion, too, was now political), the Revolutionary Republican Women threw themselves into the struggle against the Girondins. A group of them attacked the prominent female Girondin Théroigne de Méricourt as she harangued the crowd, and, having stripped her, administered to her such a beating that she never recovered her sanity for the rest of her remaining twenty-three years.[21] The Society also collaborated closely with the Montagnards in their purge of the Girondin deputies in the Convention perpetrated between 31 May and 2 June 1793.

Over the summer, however, the Jacobin leadership fell far short of the revolutionary zeal expected of them by the Républicaines, who stepped up their campaign for a crackdown on hoarding and the enforcement of price controls as well as a reign of terror against enemies of the Revolution – causes supported also by the Enragés. A particular issue dear to the hearts of the Republican Women was that the law should oblige all women to sport the tricolour cockade to advertise their loyalty to the Republic, which was decreed by the Convention on 21 September. But this measure was greatly resented by the market-women, the *dames de la Halle*, who already resented the idea of price-fixing and objected equally to the presence of the Republican Women in their midst after they decided to transfer their headquarters to the nearby church of Saint-Eustache. A series of brawls between the market-women and the Républicaines gave the Jacobin government the excuse it needed to act against women who, from being useful allies, had become an embarrassment and a nuisance, since they tended to highlight shortcomings in government policy. On 30 October, in a measure to which we shall return, the Jacobin authorities banned the Society of Revolutionary Republican Women and all other women's political clubs and associations.

The outlawing of the women's clubs was not the end of the story of women's intervention in the popular revolution. In the year III of the Republic (1795), after the Jacobins themselves had been overthrown in their turn and replaced by the Thermidorians, whose sympathies were with the rich rather than the poor, food shortages again caused widespread distress, precipitating the last of the popular uprisings of the Revolution, the *journées* of germinal and prairial. On 12 germinal (1 April) women were to the fore in the revolutionary crowd which demonstrated outside the Convention, demanding 'Bread and the Constitution of 1793' (which had been put on ice on account of the war). Their pleas went unheeded, and as the famine deepened, women went on the rampage, sacking shops, seizing grain and kidnapping officials, before launching the essentially female uprising of 1 prairial (20 May). Once again, the sans-culotte women descended, unarmed, on the Convention, to plead for bread and democracy, only to be confronted with intransigence and violence. The sight of women being rifle-butted by troops galvanised their menfolk into action and in the ensuing days of streetfighting the sans-culottes made their last stand, before being crushed by superior force.[22]

The popular revolution may have gone down in defeat, but women's participation in it clearly went beyond the traditional forms which had characterised women's political action in the past. By identifying with the Rights of Man and the Constitution of 1793, and by publicly advertising their commitment to the Revolution by word, deed and even dress (Guillotine earrings were obviously an endorsement of the Terror as much as a fashion statement), women effectively made themselves into active citizens, whatever the law might say.[23] Though their intervention was prompted largely by the traditional motive of hunger and their collective action bore many of the features of the bread riot, sans-culotte women recognised that woman did not live by bread alone. Their concerns were also political and they appreciated the need for organisation. The days of germinal and prairial were not just spontaneous outbreaks against intolerable misery but manifestations of a well-orchestrated mass movement. Though the Républicaines went to the Convention unarmed, as eager spectators in the various assemblies, egging on the revolutionaries from the galleries, they readily identified with the political violence perpetrated in the name of the Revolution. In year III, their enemies spoke contemptuously of such women as *tricoteuses*, a term which in the course of the nineteenth century would acquire much more sinister overtones, evoking the 'unnatural' and bloodthirsty women who horrified readers of Charles Dickens's *A Tale of Two Cities*.[24] The typical member of the Society of Revolutionary Republican Women, according to the researches of Dominique Godineau, was an older, married woman with no small children. Feeding her family may have been less her concern than a desire to take forward the Revolution.

Women and counter-revolution

Of course, not all women of the popular classes wanted to take forward the Revolution. Peasant women saw few advantages in a new order which wanted to pay for their produce in a worthless, debased currency (the *assignats*). Nor were their material interests served by price-fixing: the gap between countryside and town was wide. The disruption to trade and industry caused by the Revolution and war had knock-on effects in rural areas, not least in the call-up of young men who were far from sharing the exalted idea of the *patrie* of their new political masters. The dismantling of the traditional forms of poor relief created problems throughout provincial France. Many rural women, especially those who lived in areas where attachment to the Catholic religion was strong, put up resistance to a Revolution which they regarded as an álien, urban, and especially Parisian imposition on their traditional way of life.[25]

The religious dimension of their protests was especially significant. Again, this was nothing new: peasant women had a long-standing history of resorting to riot to defend their religious faith.[26] Even before the outbreak of the Revolution there is evidence to suggest that the incidence of religious practice was higher among women than among men, and their greater religious commitment was translated into opposition to attempts to remove their village priests when they refused to swear an oath of loyalty to the new regime. By the Civil Constitution of the Clergy (voted on 12 July 1790 and subsequently condemned by the Pope in a brief of 10 March 1791) the Revolution had made priests into paid officials of the state, but in many places, such as Sommières, a small town near Nîmes in the south of France, women reacted violently to the mere rumour that their clergy should take the oath, even if they wanted to. Interestingly, in the Sommières case (30 January 1791) it was not the entire female community which opposed the constitutional clergy but a group of the most economically vulnerable and least educated, the wives, sisters and daughters of peasants and artisans.[27] The arrival of unwanted priests into local parishes generated conflicts in villages and small towns all over France, and ordinary working women were frequently the ringleaders of the opposition and the mainstays of the non-juring, or refractory, clergy who continued to say Mass and administer the sacraments.

Such women were even more opposed to the revolutionary cult of the Supreme Being and the programme of radical dechristianisation which the Jacobins attempted to implement in the provinces by the dispatch of *représantants en mission* and the *armées révolutionnaires* – the sans-culottes in arms. Fanatically anticlerical, the sans-culottes were driven by a hatred of priests which is difficult to comprehend but which undoubtedly owed something to sexual jealousy and a perception that priests exercised power over women, especially through the confessional, which allowed them to usurp the place which rightfully belonged to husbands.[28] Under the Terror, they demonised the refractory priest as the very epitome of counter-revolution, yet women risked their lives to shelter their clergy and attempted to maintain traditional religious practice by organising prayers in their homes and ensuring that their children learnt their catechism and stayed away from state schools.[29] Nothing less than the full restoration of Catholicism as a public religion was acceptable to them, however, and after 1795 they stepped up their protests by occupying churches, ringing bells, reclaiming religious objects confiscated by the authorities and even freeing refractory priests from prison. Their action was not in vain: as the researches of Olwen Hufton have shown, it paved the way for the successful religious settlement devised by the Napoleonic Concordat of 1801 which once again allowed Catholics to practise their religion freely and acknowledged that 'the Catholic, apostolic and Roman religion is the religion of the great majority of French citizens'.[30]

Women's identification with traditional religion and counter-revolution had a powerful impact on the minds of Republican revolutionaries, who acquired the conviction that women were the slaves of superstition and the natural enemies of enlightenment. In need of a scapegoat to explain why the Revolution had failed, the revolutionaries fastened the blame on counter-revolutionary women. Through the writings of the great Republican historian Michelet, this legend attained canonical status in the nineteenth century. In the words of one Republican commander, cited by Michelet, 'it is women who [are] the cause of our troubles; without women the Republic would already be established and we would be back home, happy'.[31] As we shall see, French Republicans would long affect to believe that the Revolution had been sabotaged by women in collusion with priests, and give this as their principal reason for their refusal to admit women to the ranks of full citizenship.

The public sphere redefined

It was not, however, the only reason. Most male revolutionaries, whether moderate or radical, objected not only to counter-revolutionary women but also to female revolutionary activists. As self-proclaimed heirs of the Enlightenment, and disciples, above all, of Rousseau, they believed fervently that a woman's place was in the home. Highly revealing are the debates on women's education which took place at various points during the Revolution. Talleyrand, the former bishop and liberal statesman, echoed Rousseau in a report commissioned in 1791: 'the happiness of everyone, and especially of women, demands that they do not aspire to exercise rights or public functions'. This was 'the will of nature'.[32] Mirabeau was of like mind. Nature had made men and women for different social roles: 'the delicate constitution of women, perfectly appropriate for their principal destination, that of perpetuating the species and of watching over with solicitude the perilous stages of infancy ... this constitution, I say, limits them to the timid chores of the household and the sedentary tastes which these tasks require ... to impose heavy tasks on these frail organs is to outrage nature with the most cowardly barbarity'.[33] The *conventionnel* Masuyer similarly affirmed that the education of a woman needed to be entirely domestic: a woman, he said, 'is only beautiful when she is sweet and modest: take away these charms and she has no other for the virtuous man. A woman-man [*une femme-homme*] is a monster politically and morally'.[34] Castigating the likes of Condorcet for supporting women's rights, the Jacobin polemicist Prudhomme condemned the activities of female political clubs as 'a plague to the mothers of good families' and enemies of 'good housekeeping'.[35]

A favourite argument against women's participation in politics was the familiar one that in the past it had brought only disaster. Prudhomme claimed that the Court at Versailles had long been corrupted by courtesans and made much of the allegedly ruinous influence of Marie-Antoinette.[36] The Queen's supposed extravagance, debauchery and treachery likewise loomed large in the pages of *Le Père Duchesne*, the favourite newspaper of the Parisian sans-culottes and the product of the pen of the violent Jacques-René Hébert. In Hébert's paper, Marie-Antoinette gradually ceased to be 'the Queen' and ended up as 'the Austrian wolf' who was devouring the Revolution, and who needed to be brought down by a blow from the axe of the good Père Duchesne. Debauchee, intriguer and counter-revolutionary, Marie-Antoinette was represented by Hébert as everything a good *citoyenne* ought not to be. At her trial, the main charge against her was that of high treason, but the prosecution also alluded to her 'intimate liaisons with infamous ministers, perfidious generals, unfaithful representatives of the people'. In short, the case against Marie-Antoinette was that she had been not only a bad queen but also a bad wife and mother. Such a person was an affront to the revolutionary ideal of constructing a 'Republic of Virtue'.[37]

Virtue, it has been suggested, was 'the most important word in the revolutionary vocabulary'.[38] Masculine virtue, however, was clearly distinguished from feminine, and was associated with the heroic dignity exemplified by the Stoics of antiquity who provided a model for a new kind of 'body politic', centred not on the body of the king but on the very human bodies of living males. But whereas men were offered new possibilities of self-realisation as active participants in the work of building a new political order worthy of the ancients (as depicted in the celebrated painting of Brutus by David), women were considered to be deficient in the moral and intellectual qualities which characterised male heroism. Female heroism was the product less of ideas than of devotion to duty. In the words of L.-M. Prudhomme:

> Women have never shown for civil and political independence that sustained and strongly pronounced taste, that ardour to which everything yields, which inspired in men so many great deeds, so many heroic actions: civil and political liberty is, so to speak, useless for women and in consequence ought to be foreign to them. Destined to spend all their lives enclosed under the paternal roof or in the marital abode: born for a perpetual dependency from the first moment of their existence until that of their decease, they have been endowed only with private virtues: the tumult of the camps, the thunderstorms of the public arena, the agitations of the tribunes in no way suit the second sex. To serve as company for her mother, to sweeten the cares of her husband, to feed and look after her children, these are the only occupations and the real duties of a woman. A woman is not right, is only in her place in her family and her household. Of all that goes on outside her home, she needs to know only what her parents or her husband judge proper to tell her.

As even Prudhomme admitted, however, women had a crucial role to play in the

28

creation of civic virtue. Though they should not themselves be active citizens, they were the mothers of future citizens. They had a duty to be patriot mothers, instilling in their children a love of country and rewarding their patriot husbands for their efforts in the struggle to build the new order. To cite Prudhomme once again:

> Returning to his hearth, it's from your hands that the patriot should receive the first prize for his patriotism; it is in your arms that the citizen should taste, sheltered from the laws which he has decreed in the senate, those chaste pleasures, those pure enjoyments that you will share with him, if he has been worthy of them.[39]

The ideal of the Republican mother or patriot mother was one to which even feminists, both in the late eighteenth century and after, were willing to subscribe. They recognised its possibilities as a language of empowerment, promising equality in difference – a theme to which we shall return. For most male revolutionaries, however, it was a language of subordination, intended to assign to women only an ancillary role in the great enterprise on which they were embarked. Its express purpose was to deny women access to the public sphere at a time when this itself was in the process of redefinition: and for this reason, the suppression of female political clubs by the Jacobins was much more than an opportunist act prompted by particular political circumstances.[40]

The immediate background to the closure of the clubs was the disorder generated between the sans-culotte women and the market-women over the issue of whether all women should be compelled to wear the liberty cap, the *bonnet rouge*, symbol of the freed slave. In addition, as already related, the Jacobin government resented the criticisms levelled at their policies by both the Revolutionary Republican Women and the Enragés, and wanted to be rid of two troublesome – and potentially united – sources of opposition. Moreover, in the wake of the assassination of Marat in July 1793 – significantly enough by a woman, Charlotte Corday – the Jacobins were increasingly hostile to women activists. In the short term, the decision to act against the club women was undoubtedly taken for reasons of practical politics.[41]

What needs to be stressed also, however, is the language in which women's political activism was condemned. André Amar, the Jacobin militant and member of the Committee of General Security which had responsibility for the censorship and surveillance operations of the Convention, reported on the disturbances involving women to the Convention on 9 brumaire 1793. Having warned against 'an exaggerated patriotism' which was in reality an excuse to foment disorder, he recommended that there should be no attempt to impose a code of dress by law and that popular societies of women be proscribed. Elaborating on the latter recommendation, Amar went on to state that his Committee had deliberated the question as to whether women should 'exercise political rights and meddle in affairs of government' and whether women should meet in political associations. In both cases, its answer was a resounding 'No'.

On the first point, Amar claimed that women lacked the attributes – knowledge, attentiveness, dedication and self-denial – required for participation in public life. On the second, he insisted that to devote themselves to the business of seeking out the enemies of the Revolution – the true goal of the popular societies – women would have to abandon 'the more important cares to which nature calls them'. In words which could have been penned by Rousseau he affirmed:

> The private functions for which women are destined by their very nature are related to the general order of society; this social order results from the differences between man and woman. Each sex is called to the kind of occupation which is fitting for it; its action is circumscribed within this circle which it cannot break through, because nature, which has imposed these limits on man, commands imperiously and receives no law.

Whereas man was fit for all the tasks of public life which demanded strength, intelligence and character, women had other functions to fulfil: 'To begin educating men, to prepare children's minds and hearts for public virtues, to direct them early in life towards the good, to elevate their souls, to educate them in the political cult of liberty: such are their functions, after household cares. Woman is naturally destined to make virtue loved'. There could be no clearer statement of what the Jacobins understood by feminine virtue and patriotic motherhood. According to Amar, to enter the hurly-burly of political life could only damage women's modesty: but to stay at home, nurturing the love of the *patrie* in their families, conferred power as well as dignity, since through peaceful discussions in the intimacy of the hearth men could be persuaded to take back women's useful ideas into the public arena.[42]

Protests by women to the Commune of Paris against the suppression of the Républicaines received short shrift from the Jacobin procurator of the Commune, Pierre Gaspard Chaumette. The Republican Women, he maintained, were viragos who had sullied the red cap of liberty: it was horrible and contrary to all the laws of nature for a woman to want to make herself into a man. In language comparable to Amar's, he posed the question:

> Since when is it permitted to give up one's sex? Since when is it decent to see women abandoning the pious cares of their households, the cribs of their children, to come to public places, to harangue in the galleries, at the bar of the senate? Is it to men that nature confided domestic cares? No, she has said to man: 'Be a man: hunting, farming, political concerns, toils of every kind, that is your appanage'. She has said to woman: 'Be a woman. The tender cares owing to infancy, the details of the household, the sweet

anxieties of maternity, these are your labours: but your attentive cares deserve a reward. Fine! You will have it, and you will be the divinity of the domestic sanctuary; you will reign over everything that surrounds you by the invincible charm of the graces and of virtue'.[43]

Between them, the Enlightenment and the French Revolution invented a new vocabulary of the rights of man, which at the end of the eighteenth century also became the language of feminism. Yet at the same time this was also the language which enunciated the doctrine of separate spheres, the ideological cornerstone of nineteenth-century antifeminism. It is important to appreciate that Republicanism, the principal vehicle for the development of French democracy over the course of the nineteenth century, was from the outset committed to a vision of democracy from which women had been excluded. The French Revolution was not a turning point in the history of French women in any positive sense but rather a defining moment where, in attempting to delineate the boundaries of both public and private life, the revolutionaries embarked upon a project in which women's contribution to society could be made only through the private sphere of the home. Far from making women into citizens, the Revolution gave a powerful boost to the ideology of domesticity which was soon to become the dominant discourse on women's place in the post-Revolutionary social order.

Chapter 3

Revolutionary aftermath

The reconstruction of the gender order

In denying political rights to women, the revolutionaries made no secret of their own preoccupation with the need to draw clearly delineated boundaries between the realm of the public and the realm of the private. On the other hand, they did not ignore the private sphere as one unworthy of the legislator's interest. On the contrary, hypersensitive to the ways in which private interests might clash with their own notions of the public good, they did not hesitate to enact legislation which affected areas of private life such as the family and the practice of religion.[1] In the process, however, they provoked widespread anxieties about the stability of the gender order: excesses in politics, epitomised by the bloodshed of the Terror, seemed to have their counterpart in revolutionary legislation such as the law on divorce, which threatened male authority in the family. To appreciate the eventual backlash against what were deemed to be dangerous experiments with the 'natural' order of gender relations, it is necessary first to review the extent to which the Revolution, drawing on those elements of Enlightenment thinking which stressed the importance of sentiment and emotional ties, broadened its agenda to include the pursuit of happiness in marriage and family life.

The French Revolution and the family

It was the aim of the Jacobins to effect not only a political but also a cultural revolution. The world was to be remade anew: even the Christian calendar was jettisoned in favour of a new, Revolutionary calendar, the *décadi*, which commenced with the inauguration of the Republic in September 1792.[2] The readiness of the Convention to legislate for the private as well as the public sphere was apparent from its stipulation in April 1793 that all French citizens, whether male or female, should be obliged to sport the tricolour cockade. Individuals were no longer free to dress as they pleased, even if a further decree of October 1793 conceded that the wearing of the red cap of liberty should not be made compulsory for women, as female sans-culottes would have preferred.[3] However much they might proclaim their attachment to the ideology of separate spheres and their devotion to the cult of domesticity, the Jacobins were prepared to obliterate the distinctions between the public and the private in the interests of a 'total' revolution.

Nothing signalled the resolve to prescribe for the private sphere more than Revolutionary legislation on the family.[4] The Constitution of 1791 recognised marriage 'only as a civil contract'. A subsequent law of 20 September 1792, the last day in the life of the Legislative Assembly, completed the process by which marriage was secularised: that is, it ceased to be a sacrament witnessed by a priest and became a civil act administered by the state in the person of the local mayor. Apart from the desire to remove marriage from the jurisdiction of the clergy, the revolutionaries were motivated by the belief that their reform would encourage the development of a more modern conception of marriage. Ideally, unions were to be formed by the exercise of free choice on the part of the spouses themselves, rather than result from coercive pressure brought to bear by the parents. A man and a woman aged 21 were allowed to marry without parental consent, whereas under the Ancien Régime the age of majority had been 30 for men and 25 for women.

The revolutionaries also sought to put relations between family members on a new footing. Having abolished the *lettre de cachet* as one of the most obvious and odious forms of the abuse of power under the Ancien Régime, they found themselves faced with the task of devising an alternative institution which would regulate the exercise of parental power over children. Their initial solution, embodied in a law of 16 August 1790, was to set up a *tribunal de famille*, or family court, which was intended to be a more democratic form of family organisation, giving more say to women and children while reducing the powers of the traditional *paterfamilias*. In line with Enlightenment thinking, the revolutionaries also wanted the court to take due account of feelings and emotions among family members. In consequence, married women gained near parity with their husbands as regards the supervision of children. The question of succession rights was also addressed in a series of acts, with the result that daughters gained the right to equal inheritance alongside their brothers. Moreover, the National Convention was responsible for even more controversial legislation (the statute of 12 brumaire, Year II, 2 November 1793) which gave illegitimate children the same rights of inheritance as legitimate children. New laws on adoption also allowed orphans and homeless children to be placed in families.

By far the most significant item of Revolutionary legislation on the family, however, was the introduction of divorce by a second law of 20 September 1792.[5] Disclaiming any desire to mount an attack upon marriage as an institution, the revolutionaries professed to want only to promote liberty and happiness within it. Divorce was necessary to terminate ill-assorted unions (often the consequence of ambitious parental strategies which made marriages of convenience without regard for the personal feelings of the husband and wife) and to eliminate the inconsistencies endemic in the system of judicial separation permitted by the Ancien Régime, which condemned the unhappy parties to either celibacy or illicit sexual relationships. The law permitted three types of divorce, in situations in which no reconciliation could be effected through the family court. The first was by mutual consent following a joint petition. The second recognised the right of a dissatisfied spouse to seek divorce on grounds of incompatibility of temperament, and required no proof, thus enabling the petitioner to file without having to divulge embarrassing or intimate details. The third form of divorce involved the recognition of matrimonial fault, and prescribed specific grounds on which divorce might be granted, namely mental illness, a prison sentence injurious to reputation, cruelty or serious injury, notoriously dissolute moral behaviour, desertion of at least two years, absence without news of at least five years and emigration. Divorced couples were free to remarry with the partners of their choice.

The divorce law of 1792 was not feminist in inspiration, but rather an element integral to the revolutionaries' vision of a new and regenerated secular society. Nevertheless, it was an extremely liberal measure and was made even more liberal by the law of 4 floréal, Year II, which permitted divorce to a husband or wife who could produce evidence of the absence of the other spouse over a period of six months. Many women seized the opportunity to rid themselves of unsatisfactory husbands. Some 30,000 divorces were granted between 1792 and 1803, the great majority of them affecting urban rather than rural couples (with Paris alone responsible for some 13,200 divorces, compared with 1049 in Lyon and 1046 in Rouen). Members of the artisan, merchant and professional classes tended to resort to divorce more readily than other social groups (in Rouen, for example, women workers in the city's textile industry were particularly prominent in the divorce statistics). Studies of Lyon and Rouen reveal also that women initiated more than two-thirds of the proceedings involving a matrimonial fault. Desertion was cited as the most common ground (as indeed it was also in the case of husbands seeking a divorce from their wives). Violence, on the other hand, was much more of a female than a male complaint. The Revolution may have had a negligible impact on the incidence of male violence towards women, but the divorce legislation, by providing an escape route for abused wives, was undoubtedly subversive of traditional patriarchal authority in the family.

It would, however, be wrong to exaggerate the incidence of marriage breakdown directly attributable to the Revolution. The statistics have to be read with caution. In the first two years following the introduction of the law, many of the petitions came from spouses who were already judicially separated: the failure of their marriages can hardly be attributed to the Revolution. Moreover, the wives of *émigrés* often resorted to divorce in order to protect both their own persons and the property of the family, which otherwise would have been confiscated by the state. Some would later remarry their former husbands. Divorce was also a short-cut for wives who feared that they had lost their husbands and who wished to obtain the right to remarry without having to allow the elapse of the five years necessary for a presumption of death. For all these reasons, the divorce rate in the years 1792–96 was bound to be abnormally high.[6] Nevertheless, after the fall of the Jacobins, a backlash against excessively easy divorce developed under the Thermidorians and continued under the Directory, the main target being the availability of divorce on the grounds of incompatibility of character, which was effectively a licence to repudiate a spouse. One man, an officer about to set off with the army of Italy, protested to the Directory that he was the victim of a wife who wished to abandon him 'on the frivolous pretext of incompatibility of temperament, but in reality to appropriate for herself part of his possessions'.[7]

The commander of the army of Italy, the youthful General Napoleon Bonaparte, would undoubtedly have sympathised with the sentiments expressed by his officer. At that time, he was madly in love with his new wife, Josephine de Beauharnais, whom he married just two days before his departure for Italy. His ardour would cool, however, when he later learned of her many infidelities. Josephine, a Creole-born aristocrat, was the widow of the executed revolutionary general Alexandre de Beauharnais, and a woman older and vastly more experienced sexually than her husband. An intimate friend of Thérésia Tallien, lover then wife of Jean-Lambert Tallien, the man who had dared to move against Robespierre in the *coup* of Thermidor, Josephine belonged to the circle of the 'Merveilleuses', a group of women who largely set the tone of Thermidorian society and were famed not only for their beauty but also for their flagrant hedonism and high living in the midst of general dearth and misery. Their dress was thought to be particularly scandalous, since it dispensed with corsets and undergarments in favour of tight-fitting and highly revealing tunics in the 'antique' or 'neo-classical' style promoted enthusiastically by the designer revolutionary and ex-terrorist Jacques-Louis David. Plunging necklines and split thighs enhanced the frankly sexual allure of the 'Merveilleuses'. In this world, presided over by Mme Tallien ('Notre Dame de Thermidor'), a new female elite had begun to reassert something of the influence which the *salonnières* had wielded in pre-Revolutionary society: only now their interest was less in ideas than in the unfettered pursuit of pleasure, partying and dancing.[8]

This was a world of excess, which both fascinated and repelled the young Napoleon. Impressed by the beauty of the women, he was disconcerted by their apparent power. In a letter to his brother he declared: 'Here alone of all the places on earth they appear to hold the reins of government, and the men make fools of themselves over them, think only of them, and live only for them'. In his view, women received too much consideration in France, whereas 'They should not be regarded as the equals of men. They are in fact mere machines for making children'.[9] Contact with some of the leading female lights of post-Thermidorian society may have reinforced rather than mitigated Napoleon's misogyny. Attracted in the first instance to the young and impossibly beautiful Mme Récamier, he never forgave her for rebuffing his advances. Nor did he warm to either the politics or the morals of the independent-spirited Germaine de Staël, daughter of former finance minister Necker and the wife of a Swedish diplomat. Madame de Staël kept a notable salon of her own for those who shared her liberal ideals and commitment to a moderate Republic, and made no secret of her many lovers, who included the writer and political theorist Benjamin Constant.[10] Josephine herself, before marrying Napoleon, had been the lover of a more famous revolutionary general, Lazare Hoche, and, virtually up to her wedding day, the mistress of the Director Paul Barras, Napoleon's political patron and one of the most powerful men in France. It may well be that when Josephine married Napoleon, she did so only reluctantly and out of a calculation that, should he be killed in action, she would inherit his pension.[11] If not, and if things still did not work out, like the wife of Napoleon's officer she could always file for a quick divorce.

By the end of the 1790s, the liberated lifestyle of the likes of Josephine de Beauharnais and her friends seemed to epitomise the Revolution's dangerous experimentation with the 'natural' order of gender relations. It was also the case that, after a decade of revolutionary upheaval, the desire for a return to stability was widespread, as no one understood better than Napoleon. Neither Josephine nor anyone else had any idea that in setting off for Italy the young general was launching himself on the path to military glory which would make him in rapid succession master of France, as First Consul, then Emperor. On coming to power, however, he was in no doubt that the restoration of order involved returning women to their proper 'place' – the home – and leaving the affairs of the outside world exclusively to the care of men: the boundaries between private and public were to be reaffirmed. In the Napoleonic order, women's place was made explicitly a subordinate one, their inferiority written into the law of the land.

Subordinating women: the Code and the double standard

For many of his admirers, the Civil Code of 1804 (renamed the Napoleonic Code in 1807) remains probably Napoleon's greatest and most enduring achievement. From a gender perspective, however, it assumes another guise, since it relegated all women, and particularly married women, to a position of inferiority and subordination in which they would remain for more than a century. Napoleon and his lawyers were motivated generally by the need to codify and systematise what had become an extremely confused legal situation because of the overlap between Revolutionary legislation and survivals of the customary law of the Ancien Régime, but there seems little reason to doubt that Napoleon's personal misogyny played some part in shaping the final text. Whereas the Revolutionary legislators had endeavoured to find ways to express Enlightenment notions of the sentimental and affective bonds which ideally bound families together, the Civil Code institutionalised the rather different strand in Enlightenment thought which held that man alone was the true social individual and that women were only 'relative creatures', to be defined by their relationship to men – fathers, husbands or other male relations. Marital and paternal authority were reinstated at the expense of individual freedom. In general, the Code marked the end of the Revolutionary experiment with a more 'modern' and egalitarian conception of marriage in which the happiness of the individual spouses was the paramount consideration. Instead, while reaffirming the right of the state to lay down the law in matters of private behaviour, it heralded the return to an overtly patriarchal model of family life and family relations.[12]

The legal situation of the single woman and the widow was considerably better than that of the married woman, but it could hardly be described as favourable. The Code preserved the Revolutionary legislation of 1791, which allowed unmarried women the same inheritance rights as men. On the other hand, until 1897, they, too, were denied the right to act as witnesses to legal documents (such as certificates of birth, marriage and death). Moreover, though widows had extensive parental rights over their children, it was possible for a dead husband to limit those rights, by leaving instructions for control over the children to be passed not to their mother but to a *conseil de famille*, or family council. If a widow remarried, it was for the family council to decide whether she was entitled to any further legal relationship with her children. Unmarried mothers, theoretically, enjoyed the same rights as the fathers, provided both parents legally recognised the child. In practice, however, the law attached more importance to the father, since Article 148 required his consent, not the mother's, to marry.

The injustices of the law, however, were even more apparent in the case of married women. True, the Code preserved marriage as a purely secular institution, and on the insistence of Napoleon himself (for reasons not unconnected with his personal experience of Josephine's unfaithfulness) it retained the right to divorce, though with a great many restrictions introduced by a new divorce law of 1803. Nevertheless, the specific grounds for divorce were reduced to just three: degrading criminal sentences, adultery and physical abuse. Divorce by mutual consent was still a possibility (Napoleon availed himself of it in 1809 in order to marry Marie Louise of Austria) but in practice it was hedged around by elaborate and expensive procedures. Divorce on grounds of incompatibility was abolished. The outcome of the new law was a steep decline in the divorce rate. In Rouen, where there had been sixty-seven divorces a year on average in the period 1795–1803, the number fell to just six a year under the Napoleonic legislation.[13]

The subordination of women written into the Civil Code was, in some regards, more complete than that prescribed by the Roman-inspired laws of the Ancien

Régime, which had, at least to some degree, acknowledged the existence of wives as legal persons in their own right. Under the Code, married women had the status of minors, placed, like children, under the protection of the head and master of the household. Husbands exercised both *puissance maritale* (marital authority) over their wives and *puissance paternelle* (paternal authority) over the children of the marriage. Article 213 of the Code obliged wives to obey their husbands: Napoleon was particularly keen that brides should be reminded of this stipulation on their wedding day, lest they 'forget their sense of inferiority' and so as 'to remind them frankly of the submission they owe to the man who is to become the arbiter of their fate'.[14] Married women were also required to reside where their husbands elected to live. The latter could compel them to return home by force: nineteenth-century jurisprudence furnishes ample evidence of the willingness of the courts to authorise the deployment of armed escorts to bring back absentee wives to the marital home.[15] Additionally, husbands were entitled to deny their wives the means of material support if they persisted in living away from home. The legal servitude of married women was further underlined by the Code's refusal to allow them to act autonomously. Thus, a husband's permission was required for women to take up employment and the earnings of a wife became by law the property of her husband. A husband even had the right to use violence against his wife in circumstances recognised as legitimate by nature and custom and where 'the legitimate end of marriage' would be served.

'The legitimate end of marriage' was, ultimately, the preservation of the family's property. Under the most common form of marriage settlement (deemed to apply when there was no formal marriage contract), the *communauté de biens* (community of property), the husband administered the joint assets of the couple. A wife's permission was required should a husband wish to dispose of the property which she had brought to the community, but it was possible for the husband to obtain a court order overruling her objections on the grounds that it was for him to decide how to act in the best interests of the family.[16] Under the *régime dotal* (dowry settlement) the wife made a one-off payment to her husband in the form of a dowry and he subsequently had no right to dispose of any property which remained to her in her own name. Nevertheless, the husband retained the right to administer her property and any income generated became his.[17] It was possible for a married woman to apply to the courts for a *séparation de biens* (separation of property) in order to protect her property, for the ultimate good of the family, but in reality few women did so.

In practice, it is true, the legal situation of women was not quite as dire as it might appear from the letter of the law.[18] In the first place, the theoretical powers of a husband over his wife were nothing like as extensive as they had been under the Ancien Régime, when he could – though not always easily – have her locked up for life in a convent by the expedient of a *lettre de cachet*. No longer could he chastise her with impunity: only a single case is recorded by nineteenth-century jurisprudence, and the accepted position was that the husband himself was liable to prosecution if, in beating his wife, he created a public disturbance. Likewise, his marital authority did not permit him to interfere with the practice of her religion, or stop her visiting relatives and friends. Often, the powers vested in husbands by the Code remained largely theoretical: few husbands seem to have been aware of their right to keep their wives' earnings, and fewer still seem to have exercised this right.[19] In any case, the legal incapacity of women was in good part overcome by the doctrine of the 'tacit consent', whereby a woman could act independently, taking decisions or perhaps buying goods on behalf of the family, on the assumption that all was done with her husband's unspoken authorisation. Some lawyers, indeed, feared that discretion under this convention became so great that the whole spirit, let alone the letter, of the Code was constantly subverted. An early twentieth-century case, decided by the Cour de Cassation on 8 November 1908, made a husband liable for his wife's operations on the Stock Exchange, despite their having lived apart for ten years. As one indignant commentator pointed out, it was hardly likely that the unfortunate husband had given his tacit consent, and such judgements therefore rendered the wife 'the absolute mistress of the conjugal partnership'.[20]

Such a claim exaggerated a good deal, though there were legal experts who came to consider that the abolition of the notorious Article 213 of the Civil Code was unnecessary, since no woman was likely to obey her husband all the time.[21] The fact is that the same article long continued to give rise to abuses, such as allowing a husband to open a wife's correspondence and to use in evidence against her any letters he may have come across by chance. Neither of these rights was permitted to wives. Even a simple social activity like a visit to the theatre could, in the eyes of the law, require the husband's authorisation, as did opening a bank account or obtaining medical treatment in hospital, or, when the opportunity came in the later nineteenth century, studying at university.[22] As legal non-persons, women were unable to participate in lawsuits, nor could they be called as witnesses in court or act as witnesses at civil acts. Nineteenth-century French feminists were not mistaken in identifying the law as one of the most powerful agents of discrimination against women, at once a source and a sign of their inferior status in society.

The law was all the more repressive because it was sustained, rather than undermined, by social custom and convention, especially in the realm of sexual morality. Integral to the bourgeois ethic – the dominant moral discourse in post-Revolutionary France – was a 'double standard', which prescribed fidelity for wives and chastity for daughters but tolerated sexual relations outside marriage on the part of men. (Balzac claimed that a man who was still a virgin at the age of, say, 28 would be a laughing stock in polite circles.)[23] In the double standard, the essential distinction was between the 'respectable' woman and the 'fallen' woman, which made the class dimension of the system plain to see. Given that bourgeois men were expected to acquire sexual experience while women of their class were required to retain their virginity until marriage, it followed that male debauchery could not take place in the beds of decent, well-brought-up young ladies. But if bourgeois men idealised the chastity of their own womenfolk, they regarded other, less fortunate, women as fair game. Prostitutes, recruited essentially from the ranks of the urban poor, were the necessary guardians of the bourgeois woman's virtue. There is a good deal of evidence to support the supposition that consorting with prostitutes and visiting brothels formed a normal part of the lives of bourgeois men in the nineteenth century.[24]

The double standard had deep economic and ideological roots, and was by no means a product of the Revolutionary era alone. Largely, it derived from the concept of marriage as a property arrangement, which some historians have connected with the rise of capitalism but which in fact had a much longer history, evident in the dynastic and familial considerations which characterised marriage transactions in both the Middle Ages and the Ancient World.[25] In the arranged marriage – which would remain common in the ranks of the nineteenth-century French bourgeoisie – it may well be that the virginity of the bride symbolised the inviolability of the 'property' being exchanged between the two families. That, at least, appears to be the message of the Code, which ensured that the double standard enjoyed the sanction of law, out of a concern to safeguard private property and the legitimate family in the face of the threat posed by the egalitarian laws of June and November 1793, which conferred equal inheritance rights on illegitimate children.

Sensitive to the fears of propertied families that they could be blackmailed by unscrupulous women who might claim to have been made pregnant by, say, a son of the family, Napoleon and his lawyers obligingly wrote into the Code (Article 340) that paternity suits were forbidden. Thus the mother of an illegitimate child was obliged to bring it up on her own, bereft of any help from the father. Moreover, under the Napoleonic divorce law of 1803, husbands could divorce their wives for simple adultery, whereas wives could only divorce their husbands for adultery when the offence took place in the marital home. Similarly, in the Penal Code the adultery of women was treated as a much more serious offence than the adultery of men, again on the grounds that a woman could infiltrate the child of an outsider into the *foyer*: a woman convicted of adultery could be imprisoned for up to two years, but a man faced no such punishment. If the husband discovered his wife and her lover *in flagrante delicto*, he had the right to kill them both on the spot.

Of course, the moralists who championed the double standard preferred not to dwell on either its sexism or its class bias. Rather, they expatiated on women's 'femininity', that is to say on those elements in their cultural conditioning which allegedly made them inherently more pure and more moral than men – a fairly new proposition, given that in the Christian West the daughters of Eve had long been regarded as 'the Sex', inherently more corrupt and more the slaves of their appetites than men. Sexual difference, so fundamental to Enlightened thought, was to be reflected in a different pattern of child-rearing and education for each sex, just as Rousseau had taught, though not necessarily in the precise manner which he had prescribed for Emile and Sophie. Nineteenth-century etiquette manuals agreed that young bourgeois girls were to receive a sheltered upbringing, and denied the freedom of movement and sexual opportunities which were often available to the daughters of the *classes populaires*. They could never go out unaccompanied, either by a maid or, on more formal visits, by their mothers, or an approved substitute. They were to be deliberately kept in ignorance of the world outside the home and treated as decorative ornaments who might on occasion help their mothers in the running of the household. As one nineteenth-century advice book for girls put it: 'in poor families the young girl makes deprivation seem less unbearable by the attention she gives to the household. In comfortably-off families she is an invaluable asset to her mother whom she helps out with supervising and giving orders. She embellishes the life of the interior by a thousand charming details: she is the poetry of the hearth'.[26] In this way, the double standard can be seen to merge with the ideology of domesticity, which, in the aftermath of the Revolution, was increasingly invoked as the key to women's destiny.

Revolutionary outcomes: separate spheres, the 'new domesticity' and the redefinition of womanhood

In general, the legacy of the Revolution to nineteenth-century France was one of division and disunity between *les deux France*, the France which identified with the revolutionary tradition and the France which viewed the Revolution as a disaster and an aberration in French history. Conflict became the chief characteristic of French political culture, readily apparent in the inability of successive regimes to establish themselves on a permanent basis: even the Third Republic, which was to last from 1870 until 1940, would never take its survival for granted.[27]

Women were to be found in both camps, which were the creation less of gender than of personal experience and collective memories specific to classes or regions. Charlotte Robespierre, the sister of Maximilien, sought to preserve the memory of her brother as the epitome of the *République pure et dure*, and it is certain that among sans-culotte women accounts of the heroic struggles for bread and the Jacobin Republic were passed on from mother to daughter, and helped form a new generation of militants who would themselves take part in fresh uprisings in 1830 and 1848.[28] The name of a Mme Roland or a Germaine de Staël, the adversary of Napoleonic authoritarianism, lived on among the liberal and republican women of the early Third Republic who would successfully create an organised feminist movement (though the name of an Olympe de Gouges or a Pauline Léon tended to cause

41

unease in such circles).[29] Counter-revolutionary women, the most numerous among female memorialists and authors of autobiography, remembered above all the crimes of the Revolution.[30] Mme de Fars Fausselandry, for example, who saw her mother executed for having corresponded with an *émigré* son, and who witnessed the murder of her uncle during the September massacres of 1792, wrote her memoirs as an act of revenge and a call for justice:

> Those who have seen only from a distance the bloody scenes of the revolutionary regime ... will not understand why the voice of revenge makes itself heard so imperiously in my heart; but those who grieve for their lost father, mother, their dearest relatives, for those who were sacrificed on the scaffold, shot down at Lyons, drowned at Nantes; who during months longer than years, have seen death hover over their heads, those people will understand the exultation of a soul for whom age has carried off only a tiny part of her energy. In memory of my uncle and my mother, my heart cries out once more.[31]

Similarly, the Marquise de la Rochejaquelein and other women of the Vendée remembered the sorrows and sufferings which accompanied the defeat of the uprising against the Revolution – defeat rendered all the more bitter because it was frequently accompanied by the loss of loved ones – fathers, husbands, brothers, sisters, even children.[32]

Nevertheless, across the ideological and political divide, there came to exist a remarkable degree of consensus among both women and men with regard to the new gender order of the post-Revolutionary period, which was to be based on the concept of 'separate spheres'. Man's destiny was to work and to participate in public affairs: woman's place was to organise the household and to raise children.[33] Of course, the concept of separate spheres was by no means new, and had flourished both in the Ancient World and in the Middle Ages. Medieval didactic treatises such as *The Goodman of Paris* (c.1393) exhorted women to cultivate the home as a shelter (for both men and women) from the turbulence and strife of the outside world.[34] In the seventeenth century, even a writer like Pierre Le Moyne, who recognised that women were the moral equals of men and had an equal aptitude for learning, nevertheless opposed any extension of women's public education on the grounds that 'I respect too much the boundaries that separate us'.[35] What was new in the nineteenth century was not the notion of separate spheres itself, but the unprecedented degree to which separate spheres ideology was propagated and diffused in post-Revolutionary society, in direct response to the Revolutionary experience.[36]

The stability of the social order was now seen to depend in no small measure on the maintenance of differences between the sexes and the avoidance of any confusion of sexual roles. Catholic and conservative writers, traumatised by the Revolution, were among the foremost advocates of domesticity. Joseph de Maistre, the Savoyard diplomat whose writings made him perhaps the most influential theorist of counter-revolution in early nineteenth-century Europe, paid homage to the work of Catholic women in forming what he called 'the moral man'. Through motherhood women could exercise an enormous and beneficial influence: in Maistre's view, any man not formed at his mother's knee lacked a proper moral upbringing.[37] The Viscount de Bonald, a prominent *émigré*, likewise insisted that women's education should be directed towards strictly domestic ends since they belonged to the family and not to political society. According to Bonald, one of the greatest evils perpetrated by the Revolution was the introduction of divorce, which overturned the notion of social hierarchy. In the political realm, it was for monarchs to command, for their minister (recruited from the nobility) to execute and for subjects to obey. Similarly, in the family it was for the husband to command, for wives and mothers to carry out orders and for children to obey. Divorce broke the chain of command and established a false equality between husband and wife.[38] It was to be largely through the efforts of Bonald that divorce was removed from the Civil Code under the restored Bourbons in 1816.

In the minds of many of its male apologists, at least, there seems little reason to doubt that the ideology of separate spheres was intended to circumscribe women's lives and to limit their freedom by confining them to an essentially domestic existence.[39] On the other hand, it needs to be stressed that the 'new domesticity' included women as well as men among its apologists, and that it cannot be regarded merely as a manifestation of post-Revolutionary misogyny. This was most obviously the case with the ideal of 'Republican motherhood', which we have already seen emerge from the Enlightenment and the French Revolution and which was espoused as much by women such as Mme de Genlis as by male novelists like Bernardin de Saint-Pierre. As women, Republican mothers were barred from the world of politics, which was reserved for men, but they had their own special mission to exercise influence over their husbands and sons, who were to be encouraged to be zealous in the defence of their rights and the observation of the law.[40]

But perhaps the most dramatic indicator of the emergence of a new gender order in the aftermath of the French Revolution was the adoption of domesticity by women of the former nobility, who came to repudiate the eighteenth-century aristocratic and Court-centred way of life as corrupt and consciously opted for a more sober and bourgeois mode of conduct. It has been argued – convincingly – that their new family-oriented strategy was driven primarily by political considerations, above all the desire to rehabilitate the upper classes as a whole in the eyes of early nineteenth-century contemporaries in the hope of keeping alive their aspirations to a return to power.[41] The enthusiasm for family life and the private sphere was accompanied also by a return to the ways of religion, sometimes genuine, sometimes merely expedient. As the Marquise de La Tour du Pin observed in her memoirs, whereas virtue in men and good conduct on the part of women were the object of ridicule among the Court-oriented nobility of the Ancien Régime, after the Revolution such licentious behaviour was considered to have been a prime cause of the catastrophe which had befallen the former ruling elite.[42] Another aristocratic woman expressed her delight in 'the hours consecrated to her children, to her husband, to her father, her mother-in-law, family evenings'.[43]

By 1814–15, womanhood had been truly redefined, and the domestic ideal had been established as the dominant model of femininity. Its diffusion, however, cannot be separated from a heightened sense of class awareness among all sections of French society in response to the social and economic changes associated with the progress of capitalism and the coming of an industrial civilisation. Nowhere was class consciousness more evident than among the 'triumphant bourgeois' of the nineteenth century, who sought to substitute their own middle-class values for the aristocratic codes which had governed conduct and social relations in the past. It is appropriate, therefore, to pursue the theme of domesticity by turning next to an examinination of its practical relevance to the lives of bourgeois women, for most of whom the ideal of woman as wife and mother represented not only a moral ideal but an important social reality.

Part II (1815–50)

Public man, private woman?

Chapter 4

'Angels of the hearth'?

Leisured ladies and the limits of domesticity

If the heyday of the bourgeoisie was to come after mid-century, its rise was an unmistakeable feature of the world which emerged from the Revolutionary upheaval. The downfall of Napoleon and the restoration of the Bourbon monarchy in 1814–15, far from leading to a return of the Ancien Régime, maintained the essential administrative and legal changes of the Revolution in place – much to the dismay of the most diehard reactionaries, the *ultras*, who felt betrayed by Louis XVIII and his ministers (though they took some crumbs of comfort from the abolition of divorce in 1816). The onward and upward march of the bourgeoisie proved unstoppable.[1]

In the bourgeois milieu, despite vast differences of wealth, status and interests which frequently divided the members of this large and variegated class, it is possible to distinguish a code of cultural values, a 'bourgeois ethic', adherence to which was a means of delineating the boundaries between the bourgeois world and that of other social groups.[2] True, many so-called 'bourgeois' ideals sprang originally from the values of the aristocracy, and were also shared by many members of the working classes. This, however, does not invalidate the point that the bourgeoisie had its own distinct sense of awareness and identity. Indeed, to the extent that bourgeois values were consciously or subconsciously embraced by other social groups, they may be thought of as constituting a hegemonic culture. Bourgeois values were explicitly set out in etiquette manuals which, in a deliberate break with the courtly rituals of the past, elaborated the rules and customs to be adopted in private life and social relations. Of course, this prescriptive literature cannot be taken as a sure guide to social realities, and, indeed, may express a degree of anxiety about the ability of the middle classes to obtain general adhesion to the values they espoused. Nevertheless, the literature (much of it written by women) offers unique insights into bourgeois ideals and aspirations: and a constantly recurring theme was the need to construct a new, and safer, model of femininity centred on the figure of *la femme au foyer* ('woman by the hearth').

The family was at the very heart of the bourgeois conception of the social order, and the model family was headed by its lord and master, the *paterfamilias*, husband,

47

father, and representative of patriarchal authority, upon whom wife and children alike depended. Women, if they followed their 'natural' destiny, fulfilled their social role above all as wives and mothers. They should also be ladies of leisure, far removed from the world of work, in order to underline the wealth and status of their husbands. This was particularly true in upper-class circles, the world of high society and the *Tout-Paris*, where fashionable ladies continued to entertain in their salons, setting an example of cultural refinement that was copied by women of more modest means among the petty and middling bourgeoisie.[3] At the same time, however, women had to know their place. Mme Celnart, author of one of the best known of the etiquette manuals which proliferated in the nineteenth century, warned that women must temper their behaviour to make themselves pleasing to men:

> But what is especially insufferable in a woman is a restless, bold, domineering manner, for this manner goes against nature ... No matter what her worth, no matter that she never forgets that she could be a man by virtue of her superiority of mind and the force of her will, on the outside she must be a woman! She must present herself as the creature made to please, to love, to seek support, that being who is inferior to man and who approaches the angels.[4]

In the cult of domesticity, the home was a sanctuary and refuge from the turbulent world outside: a woman's role was to be the guardian angel of the domestic shrine.[5] For the social historian, however, the interesting question is to discover the relevance of the rhetorical construction of the 'angel of the hearth' to the lives which middle-class and upper-class women actually lived in the first half of the nineteenth century: and here it may well be the case that, in practice, the limits of domesticity were less rigid and restrictive than the manuals would have us believe.

Wives and mothers

Marriage was the destiny of most of the population in nineteenth-century France. Only around 10% of men and 12% of women above the age of 50 never married, and over the course of the century the age of marriage dropped consistently, though there were significant regional variations.[6] In some regions – Normandy, Champagne, Lorraine, Burgundy, the Franche-Comté, the area around Orléans and the innermost parts of the west – the nuclear family predominated and both the age of marriage and the percentage of singles tended to fluctuate. In others – the south-west, the Nord and Provence – family structure was more elaborate but marriage was not necessarily under the strict control of families. In still other regions – Brittany, the Basque country, the southern Massif Central, Savoy and Alsace (also areas where religious practice remained high) – family structure was equally complex but marriage was tightly controlled by families. In these last areas, where a patriarchal and authoritarian family structure was the norm, women's age at marriage was higher than the national average and reflected the greater degree of control exercised by families over their daughters (and sons).[7]

Universally, however, it was the case that marriage formation in the ranks of the middle classes resulted not from romantic attachments but from family strategies designed to enhance material interests.[8] In this regard, bourgeois marriage had more in common with the aristocratic ideals of past centuries than with 'modern' notions of romantic love, defined by one historian as 'the capacity for spontaneity and empathy in an erotic relationship'.[9] In the sixteenth and seventeenth centuries, moralists had strongly warned against the dangers of marrying for love or of showing excessive emotion to one's partner within marriage. Montaigne, for example, counselled that one should marry not for one's personal happiness but for the good of one's family or line.[10] That such a view continued to represent aristocratic thinking on marriage may be seen from the *Livre de famille* of Antoine de Courtois (1762–1828), in which the author maintains that arranged marriages were best because parents had a better understanding of their children's real interests than they had themselves.[11] As for love, this was of less importance than mutual respect and trust. Marie de Flavigny, comtesse d'Agoult (1805–76), better known under the pseudonym Daniel Stern, recalled in her memoirs that Catholic confessors reassured well-born young girls that it was not necessary to love the man she married: love, as their mother also told them, came later.[12]

Like the aristocracy, the bourgeoisie of the nineteenth century attached little weight to the romantic inclinations of their daughters when choosing husbands for them. Among the rich textile families of the Nord, for example, what mattered was not the personal affections of a daughter but the prospects for conserving wealth within the region so as to finance the future expansion of industry and to strengthen inter-family alliances.[13] Some of the authors of etiquette manuals had misgivings about the excessively materialistic basis of marriage. Mme Romieu, for instance, complained that the wedding day was 'only too often the result of a calculation of interests and convenience, the first step along the road to unhappiness'.[14] On the other hand, the manuals generally stressed that, to be a success, marriage in the bourgeois ethic had to take place in accordance with very definite rules, which included careful attention to the financial aspects. The close consultations which took place between the families of the two partners (and their lawyers) suggest a hard-nosed approach to marriage which left little room for romantic attraction.[15]

The essentially mercenary character of bourgeois marriage is equally apparent in the notion of *mésalliance*, or an undesirable union between two persons of different social rank or fortune. A recurring theme in French literature is how such an imprudent match will ultimately lead to disaster.[16] It is true that marriage contracts declined in numbers as the nineteenth century progressed, but it would be wrong to interpret this trend as a sign of a decline in arranged marriages. These remained the norm throughout the century and gave rise to serious conflicts when the financial arrangements were breached. Families who reneged on dowry payments risked being taken to court by their newly acquired son-in-law. Nor did all husbands married under the *régime dotal* respect the separate nature of their wives' property.[17]

It is clear nevertheless that, even if a woman was obliged to marry in order to have any status at all, and even if she had a minimal say over the choice of her spouse, once she was married, she acquired a position of dignity and influence. In the eyes of most nineteenth-century contemporaries, both male and female, the domestic role was neither passive nor degrading and a far cry from the stereotype of the enslaved and oppressed housewife denounced by some late twentieth-century feminists in the Anglo-Saxon world. Indeed, a good case can be made in support of the view that, progressively, the status of wife and mother acquired a new importance over the course of the nineteenth century. Motherhood in particular was seen as the key, not the barrier, to progress for bourgeois women. By the end of the century, it had become a cliché to extol the virtues of motherhood in the most extravagant terms. As one author put it:

> The woman of high enough education, with a clear conscience, an enlightened mind and a generous heart, is the veritable master-key for the whole of society. It is she who, in the home, gives the children their earliest education, it is she who is the real moral bastion, often the consoler of father, brothers and husband; it is she who is the soul of the house and it is on her sense of order and on her worth that, very often, the happiness of the whole family depends.[18]

The extensive literature on domesticity is in itself evidence of a widespread desire to revalue and upgrade the status of women as wives and mothers. In France, the authors of etiquette manuals attached particular importance to the notions of the 'mother-teacher' and 'maternal education'. The latter term was used to denote three distinct functions. In the first place, mothers had primary responsibility for introducing their children to the moral and religious precepts which should serve as the guiding principles of their lives in adulthood. Secondly, they should take charge of their children's first steps in elementary schooling by teaching them to read, write and count. Finally, mothers should assume a special role in the upbringing of their daughters, not only ensuring that they acquire a thorough grounding in religion and morals but also inculcating a knowledge of how to run a household and supervising their academic education under private tutors recruited to teach them at home. For apologists of domesticity in France, the mother was the figure who loomed largest of all in the literature: there was no suggestion that any of the tasks involved in maternal education could be delegated to a nanny, as in England.[19]

The 'mother-educator' ideal was espoused by all sides of the ideological and political divide. The Catholic Church, which for the first three-quarters of the nineteenth century benefited from a remarkable religious revival, was naturally keen to stress the key role which women could play in preserving the faith against the inroads of unbelief. Modifying their former rhetoric on female vice and corruption among the daughters of Eve, the clergy increasingly spoke of women's piety and virtue. From around 1830 a veritable barrage of devotional manuals written by clerics began to reinforce the message from the pulpit that women no longer needed to be virgins to be ranked among the virtuous: married women, too, could be pious, their 'fallen' nature redeemed by their role as wives and mothers who practised good works and devotion to religion. In the words of the Archbishop of Bordeaux:

> O mothers! You are the living instruments, the visible heads of a power that is spiritual and redoutable. Your thought, in becoming the thought of each generation, is mingled with universal life, and so to speak with the very breathing of humanity. In order never to forget what your responsibility is, never forget what your power is: for, if men make the laws, women make the customs, which have still more influence than the laws on the destiny of the world.[20]

By the same token, the 'mother-educator' became the central figure in the discourse of 'Republican motherhood', a concept much in favour in liberal circles under the Restoration and in the July Monarchy period. Its appeal was attested by a work which became an international best-seller, running to at least ten French editions and appearing in English and Spanish translation. This was *De l'éducation des mères de famille, ou de la civilisation du genre humain par les femmes*, published in Paris in 1834 by Louis Aimé-Martin, a history professor at the Ecole Polytechnique. Committed to the secular state but concerned also to preserve spiritual values, Aimé-Martin was inspired by Rousseau, though he also acknowledged a debt to Catholic ideas on education to be found in the works of seventeenth-century writers such as Fénélon and Racine. His thesis was that women's power to influence men was vast. Not only were they the dominant moral influence within their own homes but precisely for that reason they inevitably prevailed in the world at large, since 'the thoughts which occupy the woman at home, are carried into public assemblies by the man'. In this way, according to Aimé-Martin, maternal influence shaped the development of civilisation and women had the potential to be the redeemers of the human race. On the other hand, the book recognised that if women were to maximise their potential, they themselves required a better education to give them 'more freedom and more enlightenment'. Peasant women in particular needed access to elementary education, since it was Aimé-Martin's hope and belief that renewal should come from below, from the women of the people, and not just from women of the middle classes.[21]

Another influential male exponent of the Republican motherhood ideal was the writer Ernest Legouvé, who in his *Histoire morale des femmes* (1848) insisted that it was only through marriage that feminine influence acquired 'a character of continuity and of purity'. Woman's highest virtue, he claimed, was devotion, which allowed her to draw on all of her feminine qualities. And, as the object of her devotion was her husband, she had no need of any other employment: 'Every wife who is truly a wife has for a career the career of her husband'.[22] But the 'Republican mother' was by no means a masculine model imposed by men on reluctant women. Female authors were among the most eloquent advocates of 'maternal education'. The Genevan Protestant Mme Necker de Saussure, a close friend and cousin by marriage of Germaine de Staël, published a study of education, *L'Education progressive*, between 1828 and 1838, which took issue with Rousseau's idea that women should be educated in order to meet the requirements of men. While accepting that marriage was the most likely destiny of the great majority of women and that women's role inevitably centred on the private sphere, Necker de Saussure saw the exercise of female influence within the family as 'a great and exalted object'.[23] In a subsequent volume, she produced a detailed plan of how mothers might oversee their daughters' education, with her recommendations as to how time should be apportioned between religious duties, cultivation of the intellect in literary and scientific studies, the fine arts and material tasks such as domestic care and female work.[24] Writing from a Catholic perspective, Mme de Rémusat also stated the case for improvements in girls' education as the best way of preparing them for their role as wives and mothers.[25] The deist Mme Guizot supported the idea that mothers should inculcate in their daughters a deep sense of morality, but was more insistent that girls should grow up with an understanding, and therefore acceptance, of the limitations on their freedom.[26]

Mme Guizot's preoccupation with morality was common to all exponents of the domestic ideal, which represented women as the guardian angels of the domestic sanctuary. Domesticity undoubtedly imposed limitations on women's freedom but the role of wife and mother was by no means confined to activities which centred on the family and which took place within the boundaries of home and hearth. The notion of women's superior moral worth, latent in the language of domesticity, encouraged the belief that feminine virtue could be harnessed to the project of moralising society as a whole and legitimated female attempts to expand their role from the private into the public sphere. Leisured ladies were by no means condemned to a life of idleness. Through charity, good works and involvement in organised religion, women of the bourgeoisie and upper classes had the opportunity to expand the boundaries of domesticity, sometimes to the point where they effectively subverted the original domestic ideal.

Expanding boundaries: charity, religion and female sociability

Through charitable work, women were able to embody feminine moral superiority in practical ways and to set an example for the rest of society. One study has found that by the end of the July Monarchy women can be identified as participants in some thirty-nine charitable enterprises, many of them devoted to maternity and infants, but others concerned with the sick, the old, the infirm, prisoners, home help and the provision of female apprenticeships.[27] Contemporary historians have been slow to write the history of such organisations, and, when they have done, it has sometimes been to present them in an unflattering light as lackeys of the capitalist system and as agencies of social control which attempted to moralise the working classes in order the better to keep them in their place. That, however, is a reductive and simplistic interpretation of what was a much more complicated story.[28]

The archetype of the female charitable organisation was the Société de charité maternelle, founded in Paris in 1788 by Mme Fougaret with the objective of providing help to legitimate children born of indigent parents and of encouraging the love of family among the poor. Having disappeared under the Revolution, the Society resurfaced towards the end of the Empire and, with consistent official backing which continued the tradition established by Marie-Antoinette, the Society's first patron, underwent expansion over the course of the nineteenth century. Some fifty sociétés maternelles existed by mid-century, most of them situated in the larger towns. By 1870, the figure had risen to eighty-two, and embraced many of the smaller urban centres. Dominated by the wives of local notables, it was sometimes the case, as in the textile city of Rouen, that the older social elites retained more prestige and influence on the committees than the newer elites of finance and industry.[29]

Women also joined societies originally founded by men, such as the Société pour la morale chrétienne, founded in 1821 by the duc de la Rochefoucault-Liancourt. By 1830 the Society included eighteen women as well as 371 men among its members and the women were able to carve out for themselves a special niche in areas concerning female orphans and prison work, which included funding legal aid for the defence of the indigent.[30] Prison work, in particular, received a good deal of attention in the 1830s and 1840s, thanks in part to the publicity given to the work of Elizabeth Fry in England by the likes of Alexis de Tocqueville. Sophie Ulliac, the author of numerous children's books and other works of moral edification, not only translated Fry but in 1837 was commissioned by the Minister of the Interior to draw up a report on a female prison at Clermont in the Oise. Following a visit to France by Fry in 1838, a Comité des Dames for prisons was set up under the presidency of the well-connected comtesse de Montalivet with a view to helping prisoners on their release as well as to improving conditions in prisons across the board, as regards hygiene, food, work and dormitory arrangements.[31]

In France, much of the female charitable work tended to be carried out in collaboration with the Catholic Church. In many urban centres women belonged to confraternities, voluntary associations whose members wished to promote the cause of religion through good works. In the first half of the nineteenth century, such organisations – which had a long history – were undergoing a period of renewal and expansion, as has been particularly well documented in the diocese of Besançon. Women – invariably members of the wealthier sections of society – joined groups such as the Dames de Charité and the Dames de Sainte Anne. Much of their work was devoted to poor relief, through the provision of soup kitchens and the distribution of food, but some groups concerned themselves more with the care of pregnant women who lacked the resources to pay for a midwife or to prepare a layette. Some groups tried to improve the employment prospects of young working-class girls by teaching them skills such as sewing, ironing or spinning, while others concerned themselves with the rehabilitation of 'fallen women' or the care of the elderly. In these different ways, such women contributed significantly to the provision of welfare services in their community and gained recognition and respect for their endeavours. In addition, they themselves developed their own talents for administration and organisation, along with new-found skills in negotiation, since the societies sometimes had to overcome resistance from both the secular and the ecclesiastical authorities.[32]

Seen in the light of these initiatives on the part of Catholic women, the Catholic religion more generally cannot be viewed exclusively as the constraining influence on women's experience which some historians, too ready to endorse the discourse of nineteenth-century anticlericals, have made it out to be.[33] It is certainly the case that the nineteenth century witnessed a 'feminisation' of Catholicism in France. Religious sociologists speak of a 'sexual dimorphism' of religious practice, evident in the figures for Mass attendance or the reception of communion at Easter and attributable to a clerical pastoral strategy which, in the light of the Revolutionary experience, targeted women through the encouragement of 'ultramontane' forms of piety which were emotional, sentimental and anti-intellectual.[34] Devotion to the Virgin Mary and the cult of the Sacred Heart of Jesus were the most obvious elements in the new strategy, which generally favoured a more festive and demonstrative approach to religion than the austere and Jansenist-influenced practices of the eighteenth century.[35] Almost two-thirds of the pilgrims who flocked to Ars, the most popular shrine in France in mid-century (60,000–80,000 visitors a year), were women.[36] A great deal of research remains to be done before the validity of the thesis which posits a paradigm shift from a 'God of fear' to a 'God of love' can be accepted as accurate, but what is not in doubt is that women became increasingly identified with participation in the rituals and worship of the Catholic religion over the course of the nineteenth century, and were the principal focus of the clergy's hopes for a rechristianisation of France.[37]

Perhaps the most striking manifestation of women's commitment to Catholicism was the remarkable rise in the numbers of female religious orders in the years after the Revolution.[38] Napoleon had rescinded the ban on the religious orders imposed by the Revolution, primarily for female congregations which engaged in teaching and nursing, but in 1815 there were still only 12,400 nuns in the country. By 1830 the figure had doubled and by 1851 they numbered 40,000. Thereafter expansion was even more rapid, numbers reaching 98,200 in 1861 and 128,000 in 1877. In addition, especially in areas such as the Massif Central, Brittany and Normandy where male emigration was common and female celibacy high, many young girls who lacked either the education or the means to enter an order took vows of celibacy and joined associations known as *tiers-ordres* which helped rural parish priests with the work of ministering to the sick. These *béates*, as they were called, did much to preserve the faith in scattered rural communities in the first half of the nineteenth century, though their numbers fell away after 1850 as women entered the regular orders in ever-increasing numbers.[39]

It needs to be appreciated that the vast majority of nineteenth-century nuns, unlike their medieval predecessors, were not confined to closed orders and convents, but carried out a wide range of jobs in schools and hospitals. At a time when professional opportunities, especially for middle-class women, were virtually non-existent, they were professionals providing services in education and health care. Far from retreating from the world, they engaged directly with it. Looking after the sick and the elderly, distributing alms, and educating generations of girls in their convent schools, they were a highly visible and generally popular presence, particularly in the more Catholic areas of the country such as Brittany. In Besançon, some 158 communities were at work between 1798 and 1850, with links to twenty-three different female orders, only two of which were contemplative.[40] In return for the sacrifice of marriage and family life and acceptance of the restrictions consequent upon their vows of poverty and obedience, such women led fulfilling and highly active lives. The founders of new congregations, in particular, enjoyed real status and power. It may be, too, that the attractions of the celibate life were not inconsiderable at a time when sexual activity still exposed women to the dangers of childbirth and all sorts of gynaecological problems, including veneral infections.[41]

The Catholic religion thus offered significant numbers of nineteenth-century French women opportunities to overcome at least some of the limitations on their freedom prescribed by the ideology of domesticity. The doctrine of separate spheres implied that women were restricted to the private sphere, but in practice, through the Church, whether as the *saintes soeurs* of the congregations or the *femmes fortes* of the confraternities and charitable organisations, many women gained access to the public sphere. Many effectively became career women, while others gained access to a recognised and respected space of female sociability. Whereas men could frequent bars and all-male clubs and *cercles*, women settled for the church and church-related activities. Such behaviour aroused the suspicions and the ire of nineteenth-century anticlericals, who accused priests of brainwashing their female charges, especially through the institution of the confessional. It is just as legitimate, however, to see the relationship between the clergy and women as a mutually supportive one. The clergy undoubtedly looked to women to help them in their work of evangelisation, but women might obtain a sense of their own worth through collaboration in the enterprise of pastoral care. Nor need the confessor–penitent relationship be seen in a sinister light: it may be that women welcomed the opportunity to gain a sympathetic ear for their worries and anxieties.[42] Religion brought comfort and consolation into women's lives as well as supplying meaning and inspiration to action. In a few cases, indeed, it could be the mainspring of a Christian feminism which sought to improve the social position of women generally through an emphasis on their moral mission in marriage and the family. The writer Hermance Lesguillon (1812–82) not only celebrated Catholic ideals of femininity in her poetry but also urged action on the 'social question' under the July Monarchy to assist the most vulnerable members of society and, following the February Revolution of 1848, initially entertained high hopes of both the Second Republic and the feminist group associated with the newspaper *La Voix des Femmes*.[43]

Protestants formed less than 2% of the French population, but it should be noted that Protestant women, too, found ways of negotiating and expanding the boundaries of domesticity. The wives of pastors were usually closely involved in the ministry of their husbands: receiving guests, visiting the faithful, instructing the young (and sometimes adults) in Bible classes, and caring for the sick and aged. Most importantly, they enjoyed a freedom of movement which allowed them to circulate in places which were normally out of bounds for respectable ladies, particularly when they were required to attend to the medical or nursing needs of female patients. The women in the entourage of the pastor – wives, daughters, but also maids – acted as role models for other Protestant women, setting an example of energy and activism that was at odds with the model of the idle or languorous woman who whiled away her day in idleness. A notable case in point was that of Mme Oberlin, wife of an Alsatian pastor, who with the assistance of her maid Louise Scheppler founded the first kindergartens in France. When Mme Oberlin died, Louise Scheppler continued to run the classes. As with the more numerous Catholic women, Protestant women were able to exploit the idea of women's moral superiority to fashion lives which were lived well beyond the confines of the home.[44] And, as we shall see, Protestant women were to become disproportionately involved in the French feminist movement over the course of the nineteenth century. In the period before 1850, Mme Necker de Saussure was undoubtedly an example of a Christian feminist, while the more radical Eugénie Niboyet became one of the leading lights of the feminist movement of the post-1830 generation.[45] Once again, it is apparent that, if religion formed one of the bastions of the ideology of domesticity, it also furnished one of the main escape routes from a purely domestic existence.

If religion and charitable work were important outlets for female sociability they were not the only ones. Just as aristocratic women had played a crucial social role as *salonnières* under the Ancien Régime, so in the nineteenth century upper-class women continued to animate this mixed social space which was revived under the Restoration and the July Monarchy as the meeting place of the fashionable *monde* of the *Tout-Paris* – the world of high society which no longer centred on the Court but on the haunts of the rich and which brought together the new elites of money, power and talent. As in the past, it was mainly women who organised the life of the salon, whether at the large evening receptions known as *soirées*, which might include a ball, or at the more serious and intimate gatherings held in the afternoon between four o'clock and six o'clock, known as *matinées*, where good conversation was the principal order of the day. As hostesses and mistresses of the household, women set the tone for their gatherings and gave each salon its distinctive character. Some women even acquired a reputation for being dictatorial: one memorialist, recalling the salon of Mme Broutin, a rich widow of a former colonial governor, mentioned how 'she exercised a sort of despotism over her guests and as soon as she had organised a concert or a game of proverbs she would be most reluctant to pardon you for having a cold or for refusing a role'. Elegance and refinement were the most highly prized accomplishments in this world and it is clear that a feminine contribution to these goals was indispensable. Emulated further down the social scale by the mistresses of middling or petty bourgeois households, the practices associated with receiving and entertaining formed a major element in the life of the middle-class woman and gave her a social and cultural role that it would be reductive to describe as purely domestic.[46]

In high society, the role of the salon and the hostess was also overtly political, with no attempt made to disguise political affiliations. Under the Restoration, certain salons were known as centres of ultra-royalism: those, for example, of the princesse de Trémoille, Mme de Rumford and Mme de la Briche. Others, such as those of Albertine de Staël, duchesse de Broglie, and of the comtesse de Rémusat, had a reputation for liberalism. The *ultra* salons were the most exclusive: those of the liberals were more open to talent. In each case, however, a common characteristic was that the salon was a vital meeting place and point of contact for political 'networking' as well as a school for the initiation of young men into the subtleties of politics. In the *ultra* salons women were expected to reinforce the notion of social hierarchy and respect for monarchy: in the liberal salons, they identified readily with parliament and constitutional government.[47] However much most upper-class women would have disowned the idea that women should have any part to play in political life, in practice many did not hesitate to urge the adoption of a particular policy or course of action. Albertine de Broglie, for instance, conducted an extensive correspondence with leading politicians such as Guizot, Molé and Barante and was free with her political advice. Céleste de Vaulchier, wife of a royalist prefect, seems to have been the 'political conscience' of her husband.[48] As under the Old Order, so under the Restoration and the July Monarchy, upper-class women exercised a real degree of influence on public life and they continued to do so under the Second Empire and the early Third Republic in the republican salons of the likes of Juliette Adam and Mme Kestner.[49] Some women were always part of the political 'establishment', with access to men of power on an informal basis which ran contrary to women's formal exclusion from politics and the tenets of the ideology of domesticity.

Beyond domesticity: education and work

Admittedly, for most bourgeois women, it was difficult to escape from domesticity altogether, particularly in the first half of the nineteenth century. It cannot be overemphasised that marriage was assumed to be the 'natural' goal of all women. Single women were the object of suspicion and scorn: in the post-Revolutionary definition of womanhood, it was an article of faith that a woman had to marry before she could enjoy either status or happiness. As one female author explained, the problems facing a woman who wanted to make her way independently in the world were so great that even a mediocre husband was preferable to none.[50] Mme Romieu, another of the self-appointed experts on manners and morals, suggested that in France the position of the single woman was even more difficult than in other countries: the term *vieille fille* was one of contempt and such unfortunates were obliged to cling to their families of origin and to feign ignorance of anything to do with love or marriage, no matter their age or experience of the world.[51] A woman unattached to the hearth was a social misfit. In the words of the historian Michelet: 'The woman who has neither home nor protection dies'.[52]

The prejudice which refused to envisage anything other than a domestic existence for women was buttressed by an educational system which took for granted that men and women had to be prepared for gender-specific roles in society. The nineteenth century inherited the eighteenth-century tradition that the daughters of the upper classes (and of the middle classes who aspired to 'live nobly') had no need of the classical education given to their brothers to prepare them for a life of service to the state. For girls, it was enough to pass their days at the convent school dabbling in fine arts and preparing for a life of domesticity.[53] In the liberal phase of the French Revolution, the likes of Condorcet and Talleyrand had put forward far-reaching plans to reform girls' education but these had come to nothing, not least because of the widespread belief that the proper place to educate girls was not the schoolroom but the family. The Constituent Assembly, indeed, closed convent schools partly out of a general antipathy to the religious orders but also because it wished to remove the religious dimension from girls' education. The Jacobins attempted to establish a universal system of elementary public education which was available to girls as well as boys, but the enterprise foundered for lack of adequate funding and the opposition of parents to the blatantly propagandistic nature of the education on offer.[54]

By the end of the Empire, the education of girls at both primary and secondary school level was largely back in the hands of the nuns, whose return was tolerated by Napoleon. Most institutions provided only a very modest continuation of primary school studies, in no way comparable to the programme available in the boys lycées and colleges. A number of girls went to the Legion of Honour schools which Napoleon had founded after the battle of Austerlitz 'for the free education of girls, sisters or nieces of members of the Legion of Honour', but all the plans to expand these schools collapsed with the Empire. Although reconstituted by a decree of 16 May 1816, they never became important centres for the dissemination of secondary education to girls.[55] There were also boarding schools run by lay mistresses. For the most part, however, the key institutions were the *pensionnats* run by the female religious orders, whose dramatic expansion under the Restoration and the July Monarchy was one of the principal traits of the religious renewal in France in the first half of the nineteenth century, as we have seen. In 1850, in response to the 'red menace', the notables who had gained control of the Second Republic passed the Falloux Law as a further massive boost to convent schools. Restrictions placed upon private education by the Napoleonic institution of the University were now removed. In particular, teachers were no longer required to obtain a certificate attesting their competence to teach, thus enabling nuns to open girls' schools which were more interested in recruiting pupils than in attaining high academic standards. Even if Republican historians of female education in nineteenth-century France can hardly be regarded as unbiased commentators, their strictures on the convent boarding schools doubtless contain a good deal of truth.[56]

The French state was slow to accept that it had any obligation to make provision for female elementary education. When the Guizot Law of 1833 stipulated that every commune must have its own primary school for boys, nothing was said about an elementary school for girls. Even after the Pellet Law of 1836 decreed that girls too should be provided for, no element of compulsion was added to ensure that the law was applied. Thus, at the end of the July Monarchy, some 40% of girls remained without formal education, a proportion which rose to over 80% in more backward areas, like Finistère. The situation improved considerably in the aftermath of the Falloux Law of 1850, which contained a clause requiring every commune with a population of more than 800 people to provide at least one girls' primary school, a figure reduced to 500 in 1867 by Victor Duruy, Napoleon III's radical Minister of Education. Duruy also tried to raise the status of the *institutrice* (woman primary teacher) but many posts continued to be occupied by incompetent teachers who took up jobs immediately upon leaving their convent schools. In 1870 there were only nineteen training schools (*écoles normales*) for women elementary teachers in the whole of France.[57] The curriculum in both state and religious schools left much to be desired. Commonly, more time was devoted to the teaching of religion and sewing than to reading, writing and arithmetic. According to influential pedagogic opinion of the time, the essential point of girls' education, irrespective of social class, was to turn out pupils who would be 'a good Christian, respectful child, virtuous woman, faithful spouse, tender but not weak mother, … [and] thrifty and prudent housewife'.[58]

Denied access to primary and secondary education, women had no possibility of going on to university and from there into a career in the liberal professions in the first half of the nineteenth century. In this period, however, it was still possible to find the wives of manufacturers working alongside their husbands. As long as production continued to be concentrated in the household, even bourgeois women participated actively in the direction of the family business. In northern France a remarkable number of businesswomen contributed significantly to the creation of the fortunes of the textile barons of the region, not only monitoring expenditure and keeping the accounts but also distributing raw materials to the workforce and inspecting the quality of the finished product. An intrepid few even travelled around on business trips, pursuing sales and concluding deals. Such women combined management of the family firm with management of the domestic economy and the duties of child-rearing, but they were quite prepared to put their infants out to a wet-nurse and to pack children off to boarding school. The businesswomen of the Nord of the first half of the nineteenth century were anything but the 'guardian angels' of their children and the hearth. The situation changed only when a shift occurred from mercantile to industrial manufacturing, and the factory overtook the household as the centre of production. The cult of domesticity established itself among the bourgeois women of the Nord only in the second half of the nineteenth century.[59]

If some middle-class and upper-class women succeeded in crossing the boundaries of the domestic sphere through industrial production, still more did so through cultural production. The expansion of print culture in the nineteenth century presented opportunities to a significant number of women – though, obviously, a minority – to make a career with their pens. Mme de Staël, George Sand and Daniel Stern were only the most famous of a cluster of female authors who acquired some sort of reputation as writers in the first half of the nineteenth century. Others included the now forgotten poets Hermance Lesguillon, Anaïs Ségalas and Amable Tastu as well as the dramatists Gabrielle Soumet d'Altenheym and the better-known Delphine Gay (Mme de Girardin).[60] Louise Colet, though perhaps remembered most for her eight-year affair with Flaubert, was a poet and novelist in her own right and a luminary of the life of the more literary salons.[61] Balzac himself had a younger sister, Laure Surville, who wrote, though she refused to publish until after her brother's death.[62] The sentimental novel with an increasingly social slant seems to have been a characteristically feminine production, from the publication of de Staël's *Delphine* and *Corinne* to Sand's *Indiana* and *Lélia*.[63] Women authors also specialised in works of non-fiction, such as etiquette books and works of moralisation, as well as in children's literature and translations. A case in point was the prolific Sophie Ulliac, daughter of a military engineer who had served in the *grande armée*, who was obliged to support herself and her sick parents through her earnings from writing (mainly children's stories).[64]

Many of these women also wrote for newspapers. The first half of the nineteenth century witnessed a huge upsurge in female journalism.[65] Apart from the newspapers associated with the radical women of the Saint-Simonian movement (who will be considered in a later chapter), organs such as Fanny Richehomme's *Le Journal des Femmes* found an audience among bourgeois women for their coverage of fashion and tips on good housekeeping. Eugénie Niboyet's *Le Conseiller des Femmes* and her *La Mosaïque Lyonnaise* likewise tapped into the burgeoning female market for articles on literature, art, fashion, theatre, science and industry, as well as for informed comment about current affairs.[66] The *Gazette des Femmes*, published between 1836 and 1838 by Charles Frédéric Herbinot de Mauchamps in collaboration with his partner Mme Poutret de Mauchamps, adopted an increasingly feminist and political slant which antagonised the censors of the July Monarchy and led not only to the journal's closure but also to the imprisonment of the audacious Herbinot and Mme Poutret.[67]

The arts generally provided an outlet for the talents of opera singers, ballet dancers and women painters. Under the Ancien Régime, a *prima donna* like Antoinette Saint-Hubérty (1756–1812) could become the queen of the Opéra, renowned especially for her performances in the operas of Gluck, before her career was cut short by the Revolution, which forced her into English exile (and ultimately violent death) alongside her lover and then husband, the Comte d'Antraigues. Another star of the pre-Revolutionary Opéra was Rosalie Levasseur (1749–1826), also highly esteemed by her teacher Gluck and the lover of the Austrian ambassador Mercy-Argenteau. In the subsequent age of Donizetti, Rossini and Bellini there was no lack of opportunity for coloratura sopranos to display their virtuosity. The famous mezzo Maria Malibran (1808–36) was adored by the Parisian public, as was her sister Pauline Viardot (1821–1910), greatly admired by the likes of Alfred de Musset and George Sand and a composer as well as a singer.[68] In painting, Elizabeth Vigée-Lebrun spent most of the Revolutionary and Napoleonic period in exile and seems to have ceased painting around 1810, though she would die only in 1842.[69] Her successor in terms of success was Rosa Bonheur (1822–99), who acquired enormous fame as a painter and sculptor skilled in the portrayal of animals. Trained by her father, she exhibited regularly at the Salon from 1841 on. An unconventional woman, she wore trousers, smoked and at one stage kept a lioness as a pet. In 1865 she was to become the first woman to receive the Grand Cross of the Legion of Honour.[70] Later still, Berthe Morisot

(1841–95) would likewise have an unusually successful career for a woman, painting Impressionist works which represented visually the bourgeois ideal of femininity.[71]

The fact remains, however, that success for women artists of the kind enjoyed by Bonheur and Morisot was entirely exceptional. Only as late as 1896 would the Ecole des Beaux-Arts in Paris open its doors to women art students. Until then, the only women to work there were the female models who became the objects of the male artist's gaze. Lack of formal training – exacerbated by the social conventions which barred women from the study of anatomy and forbade them to draw nudes – ensured that the world of high art was an overwhelmingly male preserve. Most women who sketched or painted watercolours did so for private pleasure rather than to make a living. In the first half of the nineteenth century, bourgeois women could subvert the constraints of domesticity, but they could rarely remove them altogether. For this reason, some middle-class women as well as working-class women would demand the 'right to work' in 1848, though their particular concern was to have access to 'respectable' employment which would allow them to enter the world of work without any compromise to their bourgeois status. In 1850, such a profound social change was still a long way in the future.

Chapter 5

Labouring women

Work, family and community
in the *classes populaires*

The plight of the working-class woman was perhaps the dimension of the 'woman question' which attracted most attention from nineteenth-century commentators. Women had always worked in European society, but it was only in the nineteenth century that women's work became an issue of public concern. The ostensible reason was that, in the eyes of many contemporary social critics, who ranged from Catholics with a social conscience to the likes of Marx and Engels, the working-class family had become the main casualty of the coming of a new industrial civilisation in which women were obliged to leave their homes to toil in appalling conditions in factories. Outraged by the findings of investigators such as Villermé, Buret and Blanqui, Michelet denounced the very term *ouvrière* as an 'impious and sordid word, which no language has ever, and no epoch could ever, have understood before this iron age'.[1] For Michelet as for the moderate republican politician Jules Simon, author of a widely read treatise on the condition of working women in mid-nineteenth-century France, work was a profanation of the ideal of femininity and incompatible with women's primary role of wife and mother. As Simon put it in a subsequent work, a woman who worked ceased to be a woman.[2]

The contemporary discourse on *l'ouvrière* is a matter which needs to be examined in its own right and at greater length, and we shall return to it in Chapter 8. The focus in the present chapter is rather on the social realities of the lives of women of the *classes populaires*, both rural and urban. It is common ground among economic historians that by the end of the eighteenth century early capitalism and Enlightened thought (especially the doctrines of the Physiocrats) had transformed not only working practices and social relations but also the very notion of what work itself involved. Such was the fear and resentment of workers that under the French Revolution their right to a corporate identity was swept away by the abolition of the guilds and the enactment of legislation like the Le Chapelier Law (14 June 1791), which banned association and attempted to set up a free labour market. The new, capitalistic, order was to be nothing if not individualistic.[3]

With regard to women, the question which has generated most historical controversy is the degree to which the lives of working women were transformed by industrialisation. The orthodox view is that industrialisation destroyed the family economy characteristic of 'proto-industrialisation' (the phase between the disintegration of the medieval peasant economy and the advent of fully fledged, mechanised, industrial production in place of the 'putting-out' system), redefining the relationship between home and work and creating a new and, for women, less advantageous, sexual division of labour. Under the family economy, so the argument runs, it was possible for a woman to combine three distinct functions: to earn a wage or to produce for the market, to manage her household, and to bear and rear children. With the coming of the factory system, by contrast, work came increasingly to signify waged labour which took place outside of the home, which for women generated a new dichotomy between home and work and obliged them to choose between one or the other. The flexibility to maintain a balance between women's domestic and productive roles was thus lost.[4] On the other hand, some historians have taken a more positive view of the effects of the advent of industrialisation on women's situation. Just as there were 'optimists' among nineteenth-century contemporaries who wrote about the benefits of industrial civilisation, so too a number of historians hold that the opportunity to earn a wage outside of the household allowed women to escape from the traditional constraints of community and to acquire a new-found independence that was both economic and sexual.[5]

Recent work (notably on British economic history) suggests that it is time to move the argument forward from this rather tedious debate between 'optimists' and 'pessimists'. What needs to be challenged is the premise shared by both protagonists in the debate, namely that the shift from a 'family' economy to an 'industrial' economy actually took place as the consequence of an 'industrial revolution'. The fact is that everywhere in western Europe, in France as well as in Britain, proletarianisation and urbanisation were already familiar features of the economic landscape in the so-called pre-industrial period. The great majority of people may have lived in a rural environment, but not all of them were engaged in agriculture.[6] Rural industry was widespread, and many workers worked for wages rather than in home-based domestic production. The young of both sexes, in particular, tended to work for wages outside the home, whether in agriculture or industry, notably as servants in the households of their employers. The arrival of a family wage economy did not have to await the coming of industrialisation. In most families, work would vary among family members, and involve elements of both household production and outside work. The type of work done would also depend on seasonal factors, the nature of the trades involved, and the particular stage one was at in the family life cycle.[7]

It is a mistake to assume that women had fewer opportunities to participate in economic activity in the nineteenth century than under 'proto-industrialisation'. Apart from the factory-based jobs which became available in regions such as the north and east of France, there was an actual expansion of domestic industry in certain sectors which allowed women to carry on doing the kinds of job which they had traditionally done.[8] Similarly, for the unskilled, and in regions where there were no other economic outlets, women would engage in the casual and makeshift labour which had been the lot of women of the poorer classes down the ages – hawking, peddling, cleaning, laundering, looking after children and the like – activities which may never have been recorded in any census of the 'active' population but which were vital to survival of poorer families.[9] Everything depended on personal and local needs and possibilities, but once again continuity rather than change is perhaps the theme which needs to be stressed. As we shall see, the pattern of female employment was diverse, and subject to cyclical developments rather than marked by a clearly perceptible linear progression from the 'traditional to the 'modern', or from the family economy to the industrial economy.

France and industrialisation

Historians now accept that France had a distinctive model of economic growth which was in sharp contrast to that of the first industrial nation, Britain. Nineteenth-century France remained overwhelmingly a rural country. It experienced no agricultural revolution, no mass exodus from the countryside, and only a modest degree of urbanisation and industrialisation. Whereas in Britain, manufacturing employed more labour than agriculture by 1840, in France this happened only after 1850. In 1850, only 14% of the French population lived in towns with more than 10,000 inhabitants, while in Britain the figure was 39%.[10] Stability was a striking feature of the French economy, as was a widely remarked upon 'Malthusianism' – slow demographic growth caused by deliberate decisions to restrict family size. Another noteworthy characteristic was the role played by state regulation: free trade was generally eschewed in favour of an interventionism designed to preserve economic and social stability.

Following the disruptions and dislocations occasioned by revolution and war between 1789 and 1815, the French economy underwent first a period of modest expansion between 1815 and 1840, and then a period of much more rapid growth between 1840 and 1860, the latter generated principally by the railway boom of those years. In the first half of the century, both agricultural output and the rural population increased significantly, peaking in the 1840s, when the agricultural sector employed some 20 million persons and accounted for 60% of the labour force.[11]

If the characteristic figure in the countryside was the small peasant farmer who cultivated his own plot and lacked the means to promote agricultural innovation, there was also a substantial population of landless labourers who worked not only in the fields but also in rural industry, sometimes an expanding sector in the period, since employers like the silk merchants of Lyon preferred to disperse their workforce in the countryside rather than permit the build-up of a concentrated and powerful urban proletariat. For the workers themselves, who might have their own plots of land on which they could grow food, the system also had advantages, since it meant that their low wages could be partly offset by a degree of self-sufficiency. Weaving was a case in point. In Britain, notoriously, handloom weaving declined precipitously in the first phase of industrialisation as mechanical looms supplanted handlooms, so that the male handloom weaver had all but vanished by the 1840s. In France, by contrast, handweaving expanded. As late as 1860, 70% of the 280,000 looms in France were still handlooms and weaving continued to be a predominantly male occupation.[12]

In short, much of French industry remained at the stage of 'proto-industrialisation', even in textiles, which in Britain had been revolutionised by the application of new technology. The split between home and work was something which French workers, male as much as female, resisted in the nineteenth century, principally because they valued the degree of independence and freedom from factory discipline which domestic production permitted. Thus in rural Lorraine women embroiderers resisted the attempts of manufacturers to make them adopt the frame technique of production in workshops, not only because they continued to be required for agricultural work first and foremost, but also because they preferred a work pattern which accorded best with the rhythms of rural sociability. For such women, embroidery was a trade which could be practised in the evening gatherings known as *veillées*, which afforded the pleasant opportunity to gossip with neighbours as well as to work.[13] In crafts where work and home could not easily be combined in the one location, workshops tended to be established in artisanal neighbourhoods where workers could easily return to their homes for their mid-day meal. Even under the factory system it was still possible to find the family as the basic unit of production, as was the case of the powerloom weavers in the linen industry, where the women and girls prepared the looms while the men and apprentices wove the cloth.[14]

On the other hand, because French industrialisation was not accompanied by the emergence of a huge factory-based proletariat, along with a massive rise in the urban population and the depopulation and de-industrialisation of the countryside, it would be entirely mistaken to assume that France was unaffected by the spread of industrial capitalism. Workers were subjected to unprecedented productivist pressures. Again, the case of weaving is exemplary. A study of Toulouse in mid-century has revealed that in both household and handicraft production important changes took place which subordinated master weavers in household production to exploitation at the hands of merchant capitalists, and master artisans in handicraft production to exploitation by a new breed of capitalist masters who employed workers in bigger workshops, increased the division of labour and slashed piece rates.[15]

There were, moreover, certain regions where something like an 'industrial revolution' did take place (though the term is one which even historians of British industrialisation use only with heavy qualifications). One was the Stéphanois basin of the Loire, a region of silk manufacture and heavy industry which witnessed the emergence of factory towns like Saint Chamond. Traditionally an area of ribbon-weaving and nail-making carried out through cottage industry, Saint Chamond experienced the elimination of domestic production and its replacement by factory work over the course of the nineteenth century, which also saw the town's population climb from 4000 to 14,000 inhabitants.[16] Textile towns like Mulhouse, the cotton city of Alsace, or Roubaix, the woollen centre of the north, heralded the arrival of mechanised and capitalist-based factory industry in France by 1830, while Lille, Rouen and Saint Quentin were other examples of industrial towns. Given the novel spectacle presented by life and work in these urban centres, it is hardly surprising that nineteenth-century social critics made them the object of their investigations, even if it needs to be remembered that they were not typical of France as a whole, which showed a marked dualism between the more industrially developed north and east and the more agriculturally oriented south and west. Generalisations about the sexual division of labour and about the conditions of women of the *classes populaires* can only be made against the background of uneven development which characterised the evolution of the French economy in the nineteenth century.

Home and work: the rural world

The great majority of the female population in France in the period before 1850 were born into rural families. In rural society, a woman had no status unless she was married and girls grew up in the expectation that marriage was their destiny. Single women effectively became the servants of their married brothers or sisters, whereas marriage was a rite of passage which denoted the attainment of adulthood and a position of responsibility in the local community. On the other hand, the concept of domestic life as a sphere separate from that of work had no meaning in the rural world. Women were the partners of their husbands in every sense – though not necessarily equal partners. The household was first and foremost an economic unit and it functioned on the basis of complementarity, even if the 'family interest' was defined predominantly from a male point of view.[17]

The precise division of labour varied from region to region. In the isolated Pays des Mauges to the south of the Loire Valley – the heartland of the Vendée uprising in 1793 – the peasant farmers of the *bocage* (a pattern of settlement characterised by the division of the land into small strips bounded by hedges and trees) worked their subsistence farms while their wives concentrated their economic activity less on farming tasks (though they were responsible, with the young and old of both sexes, for harvesting and threshing) and more on the spinning and sale of linen, which brought in extra cash for the household. The same female focus on the export trade in linen rather than on the farm economy was likewise characteristic of peasant households in Lower Normandy, the Mayenne and Southern Anjou.[18]

Certain activities, however, were always the province of women. Every morning they lit the fire under the cooking pot, having first gathered the necessary supply of wood. From ponds or wells, they fetched the water to be used for drinking, cooking and cleaning, often making several trips a day. They cooked, cleaned and did all the chores associated with housework (though this last was not a high priority and was fitted in around other more important tasks). They did the laundry, including a 'big wash' once or twice a year. As mothers, they saw to the upbringing and education of their children. As producers, they invariably took care of tasks such as making cloth, mending and knitting. They would look after the farmyard and the garden, since these areas were seen as extensions of the house, and take any surplus produce – eggs, poultry, vegetables – to sell at market. Earnings generated by these commercial activities provided the cash for everyday purchases, including beer and tobacco money for their husbands, and for annual payments of rent.

A number of tasks might be shared by both women and men. Women usually made bread for the household, but it was not unknown for men to heat up the oven or to mix the dough. Animals were not always the unique preoccupation of men, since women might also see to the cows and be responsible for milking and the making of dairy products (though it was men's responsibility to muck out the byres). Women might also work in the fields, helping men to plough by holding the team while the men held the plough. During haymaking, men alone would wield the big scythe but women might gather the sheaves with a sickle and help with making the ricks. To assume that women only did domestic tasks and looked after the yard while men worked in the fields would not be accurate.

It would be equally wrong to assume that 'home' corresponded to the bourgeois model of a haven of intimacy and privacy for the couple and the individual. The couple, effectively, did not exist in any meaningful sense in the peasant family, since it did not enjoy any privacy. The couple did not live a life separate from that of the family and the rest of the household. Living arrangements were communal, with one room serving as the space where all in the household lived, worked and slept together. It was even not unknown for animals to form part of this larger household, their body heat more than adequate compensation for any smells which they produced.

Subtle controls were also exercised over the family and the individual by the customs of the community. A wife known to have become slovenly in the execution of her allotted tasks – for example by neglecting her garden – would be subjected to a *charivari*, or ritual mockery, which in the north of France might take the form of the nocturnal erection of a straw man with a ladle in his hand in the garden. A household in which a wife was known to have beaten her husband likewise provoked a *charivari*, either at the time of the incident or at Carnival time, which in this instance would consist of the wretched husband being paraded around on a donkey, seated so that he faced backwards and held the animal's tail in his hands, in a ritual known as *asouade*. Such was the penalty for role inversion and the undermining of male authority, which created a 'world turned upside down'. On the other hand husbands who were wife-beaters might themselves be subjected to ritual humiliation, as in the ceremony in Brittany of parading them around in a wheelbarrow. Adulterers of both sexes – obvious threats to the community – were also shamed in public, sometimes by the scatttering of rotten vegetables outside their houses as a sign of contempt. In the traditional rural world, which had certainly not vanished in nineteenth-century France, there was no such thing as private life.

Whatever might be implied by misogynistic folklore and popular sayings, a peasant wife enjoyed a position of high standing, if not of *de facto* equality. Quite apart from the indispensable contribution she made to the economic viability of the household, she exercised a moral authority in the home which was not open to challenge. As part of her maternal duties, which gave her primary responsibility for the upbringing of her children, she would undertake any rituals or religious practices such as praying to local saints or making pilgrimages to protect them from harm or to restore them to good health. Whether good or evil befell a household was thought to depend largely upon the character and capacities of the woman of the house. Moreover, to quote Martine Segalen:

> Individual female power was reinforced by the collective power of the group of women. Nothing was more feared, nor felt to be more excluding, than a group of women gathered together at the wash-house or bake-house. The women spoke together, criticizing, denouncing, insulting, slandering, relating family histories, deepening rivalries, and through all this, supported that whole part of social relations which is expressed through a violent and slandering speech, of which they seemed to have a monopoly. To the woman alone, face-to-face with a man, corresponds the female society, face-to-face with male society, a society which feels threatened by its very existence because of the kind of remarks made within it.[19]

Women in peasant society were thus far from powerless. While an ideology of masculine supremacy was pervasive in the rural world it was shot through with apprehension and an awareness of female power. The wife who never sat down at the dinner table with her husband and the men of the household but waited on them like a servant was not engaging in an act of subservience or self-abasement, only following traditional custom which acknowledged the need to replenish the strength of the men who laboured in the fields and asserting her own role as provider of sustenance. Nor was women's exclusion from the world of male sociability in the tavern another indication of their subordination, since they had their own female forms of sociability, which allowed them to meet at places like the church and the wash-house. The separate spheres which undoubtedly existed in rural society should not be used as evidence to detract attention from the more significant reality of the importance of complementarity and partnership in the creation of a successful peasant marriage.

Home and work: urban women

As in the countryside, so in the towns: the women of the people participated in the world of work as a matter of course. Thus women's work as such was not an issue under the Ancien Régime or during the French Revolution, though the conditions of work, wage rates and the like in particular trades frequently gave rise to debate and complaints from women workers.[20]

In the artisanal economy, men were expected to provide for their families, but they were far from being the sole breadwinners, since often it was the family as a whole that formed the basic unit of labour. Moreover, the world of the eighteenth-century artisan trades was a highly unstable one. Far from inhabiting a fixed universe ruled by 'custom' and the statutes and regulations of the corporations, French artisans have been shown to be members of a 'bazaar economy' compelled to enter into short-term and makeshift arrangements with regard to both services rendered and remuneration. Many artisans experienced downward mobility, failing to progress from apprentice to journeyman let alone to master craftsman. Journeymen who remained with a single master for any length of time were the exception. Criss-crossing between trades was widespread, as was subcontracting across corporation boundaries.[21]

In these circumstances, the wives and daughters of artisans routinely contributed to the resources of the household: indeed, as in the rural world, in the poorest families of petty artisans and casual labourers, where the joint income of the spouses was insufficient to maintain the household at subsistence level, it was most often the wife who organised an 'economy of expedients' by resorting to begging, petty crime or prostitution in order to make ends meet.[22] On the other hand, the fact that a woman worked in no way signified that her family was in dire poverty. Young women who had a profession of their own did not give up their jobs on getting married to a husband who was capable of earning a good living. Nor were they to be found solely in traditional forms of female employment like washing and needlework. At the end of the eighteenth century the female labour force was characterised by both diversity and mobility. The same woman worker might at different times earn money by making buttons, street trading, or working under sweated conditions at home.

At the summit of the artisan world, certain women had their own businesses and directed workshops which might employ up to 200 *ouvrières*. Such women might own textile or clothing businesses, but they could also be inn-keepers, bar owners or manufacturers of goods such as soap or porcelain. Others were the true partners of their master artisan husbands, when necessary giving orders to the workers in the workshops, filling in for their husbands in their absence, and taking care of the accounting side of the business. Most commonly, women were themselves workers at artisan trades, working for manufacturers and merchant capitalists either at home on a 'putting-out' basis or in small workshops, usually in professions related to the clothing industry. The fashion and luxury goods sector situated in the centre of Paris was dominated by female labour in professions such as dressmaking, embroidery, artificial flowers, feathers, button-making, trimming, glove-making and so on.[23]

As already pointed out, industrialisation in France proceeded at a relatively slow pace, but in the textile industry certain regions of cotton manufacture did experience the impact of mechanisation. By the 1820s, rural proto-industry in the areas centring on Lille, Rouen and Mulhouse had entered a period of painful decline, as factory production began to replace domestic spinning (though not handloom weaving). The spread of industrialisation was most marked in Mulhouse, where the population grew by more than 118%, from 13,300 to 29,085 between the censuses of 1831 and 1846, mainly as a result of immigration from the surrounding countryside.[24] In such textile towns, employers were keen to hire both female and child labour, who were employed in low status and low paid jobs in the factories. Women and young girls were responsible for cleaning, carding and stretching, tasks carried out under the supervision of male foremen and male skilled workers, who alone were trained to work and service the machines. Right through the nineteenth century women made up around half of the labour force in the textile industry, whereas in areas of heavy industry they were a tiny proportion of the workforce.[25]

Sometimes industrialisation did indeed lead to the split between home and work which nineteenth-century 'pessimistic' commentators deplored so much. A case in point were the nail-makers of Saint Chamond and their families. As their traditional craft disappeared under the spread of mechanisation, these artisans abandoned their trade for other traditional sectors of the economy (building, carting, stone-cutting, cafe-ownership and the like) and watched their wives and daughters go off to work in the silk factories of the region. Family members accordingly came to live increasingly separated lives. Demographic evidence further reveals an increase in infant and maternal mortality, in effect confirming the verdicts of the 'pessimists'.[26] Much depended on local circumstances. In areas of heavy industry women constituted a tiny proportion of the workforce (around 5% in metals). In mining districts it was exceptional for women to work underground, though some were employed at the pithead as sorters of coal. Normally, however, in mining regions women worked at home, perhaps taking in lodgers or performing laundry work to raise extra resources for the family.[27]

Bourgeois observers of working-class life in the new textile towns had much to say about the harsh working conditions and even more squalid living conditions of factory workers in general and of women operatives in particular. What seems to have exercised them most, however, was the widespread practice of concubinage and the reluctance of proletarian couples to enter into married unions legalised by the state. Moral economists feared for the future of family life, and expressed concern about the numbers of illegitimate children who might become a burden on the public purse. Catholic commentators worried about couples 'living in sin' and deplored the creation of unions unsanctified by the blessing of mother church. So great, indeed, were these concerns that a special charity, the Société de Saint-François-Régis, was established to encourage the legalisation of their unions and the legitimation of their children. Established initially under the Empire as a charity to assist serving soldiers find wives during their absence from France, the Society assumed its new functions under the Restoration. According to its records, which date from 1826, it succeeded in legalising some 42,000 unions by the early 1850s – though its own estimate may well err on the low side.[28]

Some twentieth-century historians (notably Louis Chevalier) have identified concubinage as a distinctive feature of working-class culture, a way of life chosen deliberately to flout bourgeois conventions.[29] A number, indeed, go further, and represent such working-class behaviour as part of the proletariat's mission to be the vanguard of a 'sexual revolution' which would eventually work its way upwards to the bourgeoisie.[30] One historian declares the upward trend in illegitimacy statistics to be 'a clear indication of the new pleasure-seeking mentality' and suggests that many women 'bore their bastards gaily'.[31] Such verdicts, however, carry little conviction. For one thing, concubinage was by no means an exclusively working-class phenomenon: one study of cohabitation statistics for mid-nineteenth-century Paris reveals that a significant proportion of female concubines (at least 40%) were of non-working-class origin.[32] For another thing, concubinage was not necessarily a rejection of marriage. As the activists of the Société de Saint-François-Régis found, often the principal barriers to legitimising a proletarian union were bureaucratic and financial. Couples simply did not have the money to spend on notarial acts regarding vital documents such as birth certificates and the like, and they could therefore not afford to go through with the civil procedures which were the necessary prelude to a religious marriage. The Society's high success rate suggests that there was little objection in principle to the idea of legalised marriage.[33]

What is certainly true is that working-class couples had their own ideals of family life and did not subscribe to the bourgeois model of marriage as the norm to which they aspired. The female companion of the working man was formed in a different mould from that of the bourgeois housewife. As a young girl she enjoyed considerable freedom of movement and opportunities for sexual adventures. Sexual misbehaviour did not consist of entering into extra-marital relations but of selling sexual favours. Girls who became professional prostitutes were considered a scandal to their families and rarely allowed to return to the areas where they had been brought up. In the working-class code of values, vice was better represented by antisocial acts such as theft rather than making love. Thus, after a number of passing fancies, a girl would usually become attached to a young man whose intentions seemed serious, and, without bothering about the formalities of legal marriage, the couple would simply live together, perhaps after a simple family meal to consecrate the establishment of a new household.[34] And, as even disapproving bourgeois observers like Villermé and Jules Simon admitted, once settled, the working-class couple tended to stay together. Indeed, it might be suggested that the working classes were more genuinely committed to marriage than the bourgeoisie, since, able to earn their living at an earlier age and less concerned with the idea of marriage as a means of acquiring or transmitting property, they more readily entered into permanent relationships, whether matrimony or free union.

Perhaps nothing better illustrates the strong attachment to the family among proletarians than the fact that, even in the new textile towns, they often tried to work together as a unit. Mill owners recruited whole families to work for them, women and children as well as male mule spinners. The latter, who had responsibility for choosing their piecers, were keen to attract the extra income for their families, and therefore offered jobs to family members. The great majority of the women who went into the mills were unmarried, though instances can certainly be found in the 1830s in both Lille and Mulhouse of women who brought infant children to work and established a common fund to hire nurses to watch them. Mill hands were something of a breed of people apart, tending to follow different working and social rhythms to those of, say, skilled artisans. Families who worked in textiles tended to be self-perpetuating, the only 'outsiders' with no connection to the trade being perhaps young single women who had no alternative means of employment.[35]

To a considerable degree, the mills replicated ideas about the division of labour, rates of pay and work habits which derived from the traditional world of artisanal labour. Even in the large silk mills of Lyon, which employed young single women in considerable numbers, it was sometimes the case that the women in question were the daughters of peasants from the surrounding region who entered into contracts with local manufacturers who provided both for the bed and board of their daughters and for the remittance of their wages back to the family. Not infrequently, the dormitories in which the girls were lodged were entrusted to the supervision of nuns, who maintained a watchful eye over their conduct and personal morality. Single women who went off to work in factories did not automatically emancipate themselves from parental control.[36]

The family was thus a robust institution among urban proletarians, as much of an economic necessity for them as for traditional peasants and artisans. Yet it would be misleading to imagine that proletarian unions were mere marriages of convenience, held together only by the economic ties which bound family members together. Whatever distinguished twentieth-century historians might think about the incapacity of the lower orders to experience the refined sentiment of 'affective individualism' (aka love), working-class unions were most often cemented by strong bonds of affection between man and woman, as sympathetic nineteenth-century commentators well understood.[37] Only if the man were a callous brute or a hardened alcoholic did he forfeit his companion's trust. If on occasion he came home drunk or got himself into a fight, she might become angry and give him a good scolding. Such an incident, however, would in no way imply a permanent breakdown in relations, for she would soon forgive and forget. A woman might complain of her man to her neighbours, but she would be the first to spring to his defence if anyone else tried to run him down.[38] Love, it is safe to assume, neither was nor is a monopoly of the middle classes.

In proletarian families it was certainly the case that the unmarried mother was not a source of scandal in the community. It is unlikely, however, that such women would have regarded themselves as the harbingers of a sexual revolution. The unfortunates who found themselves forced on to the streets to supplement their earnings through casual prostitution were not so much extreme examples of the 'new pleasure-seeking mentality' as victims of a labour market which made it virtually impossible for a single woman to earn a living wage (female earnings were on average half that of male workers in textiles).[39] There is also evidence from Lyon which suggests that the rise in illegitimacy among the companions of journeymen weavers in the 1830s had its roots in the economic crisis which affected small workshop production in the silk industry. Young women who lived together with a worker in the expectation of eventual marriage increasingly found themselves abandoned and obliged to care for children born out of wedlock by themselves.[40] At Saint Chamond, by contrast, in the period 1815–48 ribbon-weavers and their wives attempted to limit the size of their families in an effort to maintain their standard of living in the face of the economic pressures to which they were subjected by industrialisation. For the very reason that the contribution of women to the viability of the family economy became even more crucial, mothers elected to have fewer children, to space them more deliberately and to send more of them out to wet-nurses. Unlike the nail-makers in their region, ribbon-weavers made the family the front line of defence against the consequences of industrialisation.[41]

The French working-class woman was thus by no means a passive or submissive creature, crushed by the demands of advancing industrialisation. On the contrary, women were in the forefront of working-class resistance to the new industrial order in the first half of the nineteenth century. It was women, for example, who as organisers of the family's housing arrangements, took the initiative in struggles against high rents and profiteering landlords. As housewives, they did not confine their activities to the home itself, since many household duties – taking the children for a walk, shopping, doing the laundry – took them into the outside world. With men at work, as Michelle Perrot has reminded us, the streets belonged to women. Meeting together in the marketplace or the *lavoir*, women exchanged gossip and grumbles, and perhaps above all gave one another support in times of need – when money was low, when a husband had run off with another woman, or when a daughter had an illegitimate child. In the working-class *quartiers* the women had a large role to play as defenders of community values: creating an appropriately festive atmosphere on feast days, assisting newly arrived provincials to adapt to the urban environment, and, not least, in their very language, maintaining a sense of the people's identity.[42]

Resistance and rebellion:
women and protest

As regards more overtly political protest, the point has already been made that women had a long history of involvement in collective action prompted by food shortages and other issues which affected the well-being of the family. Food riots by no means disappeared in the first half of the nineteenth century, erupting during the severe famine of 1817 and again during the grain shortages of 1846–47 and 1853–57. On each occasion women played a prominent part, notably in the north and west of France. After 1848, however, as a result of the coming of the railways, increased grain production and easier access to imported grain, food shortages, and with them the food riot, tended to die out. Subsistence issues increasingly arose in an urban rather than a rural context and assumed the form of protests against unemployment, high rents and starvation wages. In 1848 the Parisian housewives who organised *charivaris* against their grasping landlords by banging pots and saucepans in the streets outside their houses were acting out the rituals of a time-honoured form of female protest, but in a very different environment from the traditional village.[43]

Though feminine collective action along traditional lines survived in the period before 1848, of greater historical significance was the emergence of a new and heightened degree of political awareness which allowed them to identify with the goals of political radicalism, and especially with radical republicanism. As we have seen, in the 1790s militant sans-culotte women succeeded in linking traditional concerns with subsistence with political aspirations to found a *République pure et dure*, while feminists such as Olympe de Gouges articulated the demand for equal rights for women. Formally excluded from the political arena, urban working-class women developed their own gender-specific forms of political action based on the codes of female and male sociability adhered to by the *classes populaires*: raising the alarm, marching, demonstrating in the streets and rioting. By the time of the last substantial female uprising in 1795, a new tradition of female political protest had been invented. The French Revolution thus bequeathed to the nineteenth century a revolutionary tradition in which women of the *faubourgs*, or working-class suburbs, acting alongside their menfolk, had asserted their right to rebel in the name of the defence of their neighbourhoods and their aspirations for a more just social and political order. The memory of the revolutionary *journées* was kept alive by oral tradition, and would be invoked in the revolutionary situations of the nineteenth century, in 1830, 1848 and 1871.[44]

If anything, women's commitment to the politics of neighbourhood defence seems to have become stronger in the first half of the nineteenth century. The erection of the barricade as a form of revolutionary action, which first made its appearance in the course of the revolution of 1830, was a means of protest with which they readily identified, since it epitomised the struggle to defend the neighbourhood. Women took little part in the actual fighting, but they were happy to assist with the construction of the barricades, furnishing materials from their households and helping to uplift paving stones. They also kept the male fighters supplied with food and drink, tended the wounded and gathered up weapons and ammunition. When necessary, they made available their windows as look-out posts or vantage points for snipers. Isolated cases of female combatants can also be found, which was doubtless one reason why Delacroix commemorated the 'Three Glorious Days' of July 1830 in the shape of a woman in a Phrygian cap urging on male revolutionaries at the barricades in his famous painting *Liberty Guiding the People*.[45] The representation of Liberty by a female figure may have been symbolic and conventional, but it is striking nevertheless that the artist chose to make her recognisably a member of the female proletariat. The Salon was highly offended, disturbed by the image of a contemporary woman whose sexuality was threatening, and repelled by the picture's political implications, which suggested the irresistible rise of the proletariat.[46]

Though the 1848 Revolution was also to have an important feminist dimension, which will be explored in the next chapter, it is worth emphasising that women's participation in the February Revolution and in the June uprising of 1848 followed the pattern which had been laid down in 1830 and 1789. Thus in the highly charged political atmosphere of February 1848 women once again took to the streets. The dressmaker Adélaïde Bettette, for instance, raised the call to the barricades in her neighbourhood and helped to build them. She also searched for weapons for the male streetfighters and badly burned her face in the process of making gunpowder, which earned her the right to a state pension. As in 1830, only a few women took part in the actual fighting, though the dead corpses of women served among the insurgents as powerful symbols of the martyred common people.

In 1848, however, the most pressing problem was poverty, exacerbated by widespread unemployment and soaring rents, which led to the female-organised rent strikes in areas like La Villette and the Faubourg St Antoine to which reference has already been made. The inability of the Provisional Government of moderate republicans to remedy the situation intensified the distress. The Luxembourg Commission, set up under the presidency of the socialist Louis Blanc, recommended the creation of national workshops under workers' control to tackle the problem of unemployment, but this solution was rejected by the Provisional Government, which set up its own charity workshops aimed exclusively at dealing with male unemployment.

Only after mounting protest from unemployed women in March 1848 did the Paris municipal council agree to establish workshops for them too, inviting them to elect representatives to assist the authorities in allocating work contracts provided by the government. The feminist Desirée Gay was elected as a spokeswoman for the second *arrondissement*, but she soon recognised that the scheme was inadequate, since it applied only to the female unemployed of the garment industry and paid less than subsistence wage rates. In the feminist newspaper *La Voix des Femmes*, Gay drew attention to the desperate plight of women who, she claimed, were dying of hunger. The government's response to her demand for better pay and conditions for women workers was to sack her, since it had no intention of paying the price necessary to implement Louis Blanc's ideas on the organisation of labour. When it wound up the scheme altogether in June 1848, this action touched off a workers' revolt in Paris which was quelled only after six days of bloody streetfighting and the loss of some 1500 lives.

In the 'June Days', neighbourhood defence was once again women's principal motivation, allied to a strong sense of resentment of the rich, expressed in language redolent of that of the sans-culottes, which may well have been transmitted from mother to daughter. A survey of 292 insurgent women arrested in the aftermath of the June uprising (by no means the total number of female participants) reveals that the vast majority of these women came from either the small business or working class, with a particularly high proportion (more than 40%) coming from artisanal backgrounds, notably in the clothing industry. Around 20% came from service occupations such as charwomen, washerwomen and domestic servants. Some 11% were alleged to be prostitutes, but whether these were professional prostitutes or distressed workers engaged in casual prostitution is not clear.

A significant minority (40 out of 118 eventually found guilty and sentenced) took a leading role in activities such as building barricades, firing on troops and inciting rebellion. Some of these women had a history of militancy, none more so than the 76-year-old retired dressmaker, Veuve Anne-Marie Henry who was in the thick of the fighting in Belleville, or the unemployed furnisher-finisher, Elisa Parmentier, Femme Debeurgrave, who had led a rent strike the previous April and was arrested at the barricades dressed in the garb of a male worker and brandishing a red flag. As in the 1790s, women like Henry and Parmentier were particularly zealous in rounding up the men of their *quartiers* to fight, denouncing those who refused as cowards and shirkers. Other women played a lesser role, searching for arms and ammunition, carrying food supplies to the men on the barricades and hiding male rebels on the run. A number are known to have attended meetings of the political clubs which mushroomed in the era, or were the wives of known political militants. Politics as well as economic deprivation fuelled female insurgency.[47]

Public man, private woman?

The process of politicisation among women was not confined to Paris and other large urban centres. Despite repression at the hands of the forces of order, the radical republican and socialist Left (the *démoc-socs*) who aspired to the creation of a 'democratic and social republic' made considerable headway with their propaganda in the countryside, notably in the rural centre, the south-west and the south-east. In such areas, where the ties of community were strong, and in a situation where normal political activity was proscribed, political protest could be carried on by subterfuge, through the traditional rituals and festivities which punctuated the calendar. Women, the mainstays of such community activity, were well placed to participate in clandestine subversion, as the local police might discover. In the small Mediterranean fishing port of Collioure, for instance, two women were arrested for appearing dressed as Liberty in red costumes which had been designed by a local female *démoc-soc* agitator, Barbe Gerbal.[48] The extent of this politicisation became more fully apparent in the rebellion against the *coup d'état* perpetrated by Louis Napoleon in 1851 as a prelude to the overthrow of the Second Republic and the restoration of the Empire. In the department of the Var many women shared the attachment of their husbands to republicanism and anticlericalism and took part in the uprising. Similarly, some women were among the ringleaders of the rising in the Loiret, in central France.[49] No doubt it would be a mistake to exaggerate the role of women in these and the other revolutions of the nineteenth century, but the evidence suggests that female protest was no longer confined to matters of subsistence. Women could be mobilised behind a wider politics of community defence and the pursuit of abstract ideals of social and political justice. Whether they could be mobilised behind a politics of women's rights articulated by feminists was another matter.

Chapter 6

Femmes nouvelles

Feminists, socialists and republicans in the Romantic era

The France which emerged after the Revolutionary and Napoleonic wars was a constitutional state which sought to marry the principle of representative government with monarchical rule under the restored Bourbons. The latter, however, both under Louis XVIII (1814–24) and in particular under Charles X (1824–30), failed to bridge the chasm between *les deux France*, the France of the Revolution and the France of the monarchy. The liberal Orleanist regime of Louis Philippe (1830–48) fared little better. For French republicans, only the creation of a viable democratic Republic could embody the aspirations of the sovereign people: 'universal' suffrage was the principal demand of radical republicans who identified completely with the legacy of the Revolution, Terror and all.

Radicals further expressed their concern at 'the social question' – the plight of the poor in general and of the urban masses in particular – which exercised still more those reformers who called themselves socialists. Some were artisans, inspired by the traditions of the trade guilds of the Old Order and by memories of the great revolutionary *journées*, who avidly devoured the writings of social critics such as Louis Blanc and Pierre-Joseph Proudhon. Others were 'utopian' socialists – men like Henri Saint-Simon (1760–1825), Charles Fourier (1732–1837) and Etienne Cabet (1788–1856) who dreamed of society reorganised into new model communities. (Self-proclaimed 'scientific' socialists like the young Karl Marx had few adherents in this period, though they would be a force to be reckoned with in the future.) Ideological and political conflict, deriving from the legacy of the French Revolution and exacerbated by the impact of early industrialisation, was a distinctive feature of French political culture in the first half of the nineteenth century. In this general climate of contestation, there were women, too, who pursued their own agenda for change and reform, once again affirming their right to citizenship and to a decent standard of living. The period, in short, witnessed also the emergence of a second wave of feminism. The word may not have existed, but the thing did, conjured into being by a contemporary language which tended to speak of 'rights' and 'liberty' rather than 'equality'.[1]

One manifestation of the reawakened feminist consciousness was the recourse to petitions to the monarchy and to parliament. The petition was the one legal form of political action which remained open to women in the absence of any recognition of their right to be counted as full citizens. True, women were a distinct minority among the petitioners of the Restoration period, and those women who petitioned did so usually in order to obtain some personal favour, like a pension, rather than to seek political rights. But the situation changed noticeably under the July Monarchy, when a number of women submitted petitions calling for the reintroduction of divorce and criticising the legal disabilities from which women suffered under the Civil Code. Some, indeed, went further, and set out the case for the extension to women of the political rights conferred on men by the Charter of 1830.[2]

The latter campaign was largely the brainchild of the husband and common-law wife team who between 1836 and 1838 directed the newspaper *La Gazette des Femmes*, the most radical of the spate of journals which aimed to reach an audience of bourgeois women in the pre-1848 period. The paper's proprietor-director was given as Mme Poutret de Mauchamps, but its real editor was Charles Frédéric Herbinot de Mauchamps, who wrote many of the articles which appeared under his partner's signature, though there can be little doubt that Mme Poutret was a willing collaborator in the enterprise of seeking to raise the consciousness of middle-class women to the civil injustices from which they continued to suffer despite the advent of an ostensibly more liberal political regime in 1830. Thus the paper championed the right of *commerçantes* to have access to the Bourse and of female artists to take part in the prize competitions in painting, sculpture, architecture and music. Herbinot's real originality, however, was to highlight women's right to petition the legislature in pursuit of their civil and political rights. In its second number, the *Gazette* organised a petition to abolish Article 213 of the Civil Code, which obliged wives to obey their husbands, and argued instead for the introduction of sweeping legal reform, including the reintroduction of divorce and the decriminalisation of adultery. The paper also saw no reason why women should not have the right to vote and exercise a direct influence on the results of elections. Supported by former Saint-Simonian women such as Eugénie Niboyet and the writer Hortense Allart, the language of the *Gazette* became increasingly radical, particularly on the subject of women's right to sexual freedom and to control over their own bodies, which eventually provoked the censorship to close down the paper in 1838. Herbinot and Mme Poutret were put on trial on trumped-up charges of corrupting the nation's morals and given stiff prison sentences of ten years and eighteen months respectively.[3] So ended a short-lived but highly significant episode in the history of French feminism which demonstrated once again that to espouse the cause of women's rights in the early nineteenth century was to run the risk of victimisation at the hands of a repressive state.

Utopian socialism and feminism

In stimulating the feminist reawakening of the pre-1848 period no group of thinkers was more important than the utopian socialists, since they explicitly included a new deal for women in their blueprints for the ideal society. For the utopians, the 'social' took precedence over the 'individual': what mattered was how human beings related to one another in the life of society. Saint-Simon, for example, envisaged a new, classless, industrial social order ruled by 'producers' – scientists and businessmen – rather than 'idlers' – the nobility, the military, the clergy. He also dreamed of a 'new Christianity' which would be characterised by concern for the welfare of the poor. In this new religion of love, the figure of woman was identified as central to the search for peace and harmony. Barbarism and militarism would be replaced by the spiritual powers of women: pacifism was inseparable from feminism. The human race was thus to be regenerated on the basis of complete sex equality, which would itself be derived from the union of man and woman in the 'social couple', the fundamental unit of society.[4]

It should be understood that Saint-Simonian feminism did not spring from abstract notions of equal rights. On the contrary, in the Saint-Simonian vision of a new order of gender relations women were still held to be radically different from men. As much as for the philosophes of the Enlightenment, men were considered to be rational and representative of 'reflection', while women, by virtue of their nature, embodied 'sentiment' and emotion. Unlike the philosophes, however, who adhered to the universalist traditions of the Enlightenment, the Saint-Simonians were Romantics who shared Romanticism's predilection for the particular and for difference as well as its exaltation of the feminine. It was this positive re-evaluation of women's qualities and women's social role which made Saint-Simonianism so appealing in the eyes of its female adherents.[5]

The history of Saint-Simonianism falls into two stages. The first, 'the phase of the doctors', was male dominated, and centred on disputes among Saint-Simon's disciples on how to develop the master's doctrines after his death in 1825. Prosper Enfantin (1796–1864) emerged as the dominant figure. Preaching 'the rehabilitation of the flesh' and an end to the exclusive monogamy of the Christian tradition, he was a prophet of sexual liberation. He also believed in the existence of a female Messiah who would emancipate both women and humanity itself. A number of other leading Saint-Simonians refused to go along with Enfantin's promotion of 'free love' and the movement split in late 1831 to 1832. But the sect's preoccupation with gender relations continued to make it attractive to women, who shifted the movement into a second, feminist, phase, in which female activists articulated their own aspirations for a better world.[6]

Initially, the first women to join the Saint-Simonian sect were relatives or friends of the male leaders – among them Claire Bazard, Cécile Fournel and Aglaé Saint-

Hilaire. Others joined after exposure to Saint-Simonian propaganda – especially their public lectures, which according to Enfantin were regularly attended by some 200 women in Paris in 1830, amounting to up to 50% of the audience. In April 1832 a group of women decided to publish a newspaper exclusively written by women. Its first number (undated) was entitled *La Femme Libre* (*The Free Woman*), which provoked both scandal and ridicule. Subsequent changes of title – it became *The New Woman*, *The Apostolate of Women*, *The Emancipation of Woman* and finally, *The Women's Tribune* – remained suggestive of its programme.

Interestingly, the journalists wrote only under their first names, on the grounds that to use their husband's name was to perpetuate their condition of slavery. Regular contributors included Suzanne (Suzanne Voilquin, subsequently the author of a fascinating autobiography), Marie-Pauline (Pauline Roland), and Jeanne-Victoire (Jeanne Deroin). Both Roland and Deroin would later be prominent leaders of the women's movement during the French Revolution of 1848. Another notable feature of the Saint-Simonian female press was that its founders, the seamstresses Désirée Veret (Jeanne-Désirée) and Reine Guindorff (Marie-Reine), along with most of their collaborators, were women from a working-class background (unlike the male leaders of the sect, who were renegade bourgeois). For the first time, one can see an explicit link being forged between the struggle for women's rights and the cause of proletarians as a whole. As one *femme nouvelle* put it: 'Only by emancipating woman will we emancipate the worker'.[7]

The majority of these women reacted negatively both to Enfantin's authoritarian style of leadership and to his doctrine of sexual liberation, which, it was feared, might simply make women the objects of male licentiousness. Nevertheless, it cannot be denied that Saint-Simonianism was a route to feminist consciousness for a significant minority of women who were encouraged to express their grievances and aspirations in the language of the movement. Thus Claire Démar, boldest of the sexual radicals in the Saint-Simonian movement and the author of an *Appeal to the People on the Emancipation of Women* (1833), proclaimed that real freedom could be achieved only when the female half of the human race was set free from the many forms of exploitation to which it was subject.[8] In a second tract, also written in 1833 and published posthumously in 1834, she outlined her 'law of the future', in which she envisaged *'the emancipation of the proletariat, of the poorest and most numerous class'* to be accomplished 'only through *the emancipation of our sex*, through the association *of strength and beauty, harshness and gentleness, man and woman*' (italics in original). On the other hand, Démar recognised that the world was not yet ready for the triumph of the principles she espoused, since it was still poisoned by 'the pestilential atmosphere of a suffocating Christian moral law'.[9]

In terms of activism and organisation, the Saint-Simonian movement was a short-lived phase in the history of French feminism. Démar's death (she committed suicide along with her lover in 1833) was a serious blow, but the movement was riddled in any case with internal disputes as well as harassed by the authorities, who imprisoned Enfantin in 1832 on charges of immorality and subversion. By early 1834 the *Tribune des Femmes* had folded and most of the collectivist experiments had disintegrated. Members dispersed to other parts of France and abroad, Désirée Veret to London and Cécile Fournel and Clorinde Rogé to Egypt, where Enfantin on his release from prison had led an expedition to search for the female Messiah (also to disport himself with the native women and, more seriously, to explore the possibilities of linking the Red Sea and the Mediterranean by means of a canal: he was, after all, a product of the Ecole Polytechnique). Suzanne Voilquin joined them in 1834 and stayed for two years.[10]

Those who remained in Paris continued their activities as best they could. A number of Saint-Simonian women were attracted into the Fourierist movement, which was in some respects even more libertarian than Enfantin's community. In Fourier's ideal form of social organisation, the *phalanstère*, the family was to be abolished and women's right to sexual gratification outside marriage fully recognised (though, as in the case of of Saint-Simonianism, later disciples such as Victor Considérant were to tone down some of the more permissive teachings on sexual freedom). It may be, however, that whereas Enfantin was most interested in Fourier's theories of sexual liberation, Saint-Simonian women were more attracted by his economic and social theories. In his *Theory of the Four Movements* (1808), Fourier had insisted that social progress was to be measured in terms of the degree of liberty accorded to women in any given society, and in the phalansteries women had the same educational and employment opportunities as men: even dress was supposed to be the same for both sexes. (Women, however, still had collective responsibility for childcare and housework.)[11] Reine Guindorff for one recognised that Fourierism offered the prospect of reconciling women's obligations as wives and mothers with their need for a career path which would give them economic independence.[12] A few Fourierist communities were established in France but their best-known experiments took place in the United States, at Brook Farm, Massachussets (1841–46), and at Red Bank, New Jersey.[13]

Ex-Saint-Simonian women like Eugénie Niboyet (1800–83), a wealthy Protestant woman involved in charitable and literary activities in Lyon (she was a noted campaigner for prison reform and the translator of Dickens), tried to keep alive a female voice in the press. Having founded a newspaper *Le Conseiller des Femmes* in 1833 to spread the message of humanitarian socialism, in 1836 she and other socialist women supported the *Gazette des Femmes*, which, as we have seen, explicitly demanded 'political and civil rights for women' on its masthead and campaigned strongly for the reintroduction of divorce before succumbing to the censor. Niboyet for a time turned her energies to the cause of pacifism, founding a group around the newspaper *La Paix des Deux Mondes* in 1844, but she never abandoned her commitment to feminism. In 1848 she was to provide the capital and organisational skills for *La Voix des Femmes*, the principal feminist organ of the 1848 Revolution.[14]

The best remembered – though not necessarily the most influential – of all the French feminists of the pre-1848 era was, however, Flora Tristan (1803–44). Born in Paris the daughter of a Peruvian nobleman and a French *émigrée*, but denied her inheritance on the grounds that, in the eyes of French law, she was illegitimate since her parents' religious marriage had not been followed by a civil ceremony, she developed a sense of alienation which was exacerbated by marriage to a violent husband, whom she eventually left in 1826, after bearing him three children. Thereafter, she travelled extensively in Peru before coming to England, where she not only discovered the wretchedness of the working classes but also met Anna Wheeler and William Thompson, disciples of the British utopian socialist Robert Owen and heirs of the English feminist Mary Wollstonecraft. Back in France, she came under the spell of both Saint-Simonianism and Fourierism and in her book *The Workers' Union* (*L'union ouvrière*, 1843) she followed Démar and the other *femmes nouvelles* in propounding the theory that the emancipation of women was inextricably linked with the general question of the emancipation of the workers – an idea which would later be developed further by Marx.[15]

By any standards, Tristan was an exceptional woman: contemporaries commented on her striking appearance and her strong personality, and her published works have ensured her an enduring place in French literary history. (Both her autobiographical *Pérégrinations d'une paria* (*Peregrinations of a Pariah*) and her one novel, *Méphis*, were published in 1838 and sold well, while *Promenades dans Londres* appeared in 1840. The publication of posthumous works also testifies to the interest in her.) Tristan never became an entirely 'forgotten' figure, like Jeanne Deroin and most of the other women active in the pre-1848 feminist movement, who have been 'rediscovered' largely because of the rise of women's history as an academic discipline in the past generation. How far Tristan succeeded in getting her message across to working men (her target audience) is difficult to say, but in any case, she should not be seen as an isolated pioneer but rather very much as a product of her times, and in particular of a utopian socialism which made feminism integral to its doctrines. The workers' movement of the 1840s may have been unresponsive to calls from Tristan and others to take up the cause of women's rights, but the influence of utopian socialism was soon to make itself felt in feminist attempts to shape the political future of France in the course of the country's second experiment with a Republican form of government, established in the wake of the successful revolution of 1848, which replaced the July Monarchy with the Second Republic (1848–52).

Feminism and the 1848 Revolution

On 24 February 1848 a street revolution led to the proclamation of a second French Republic which introduced manhood suffrage. As in the 1790s feminists hoped that the democratic and social ideals of the new regime would lead to benefits for women.

To the fore were women who had been involved in Saint-Simonianism, such as the self-educated dressmaker Jeanne Deroin (1805–94) and the primary schoolteacher Pauline Roland (1805–52). Deroin, married since 1832 to a socialist comrade, Desroches, and the mother of three children, was a former member of the editorial team of *La Femme Libre* and its successors, and had subsequently obtained a teaching qualification which allowed her to run a neighbourhood school.[16] Roland, the daughter of a postmaster, grew up in comfort in Falaise in Normandy and had received a good education at home from private tutors. One of them, with whom she fell in love, introduced her to Saint-Simonian ideas, inspiring her to join the sect in Paris, where she immediately demonstrated her enthusiasm for Enfantin's theories on the 'rehabilitation of the flesh' by embarking on a series of love affairs. The mother of four children by two partners, she was a militant advocate of the rights of single parents, insisting upon her own responsibility for her children's upbringing. Aided by friends such as Pierre Leroux, another prominent ex-Saint-Simonian, she eked out a precarious existence by earnings from teaching and journalism in his community at Boussac.[17]

Along with other former Saint-Simoniennes such as Désirée Gay, Adèle Esquiros and Eugénie Niboyet, Deroin founded the Club de l'Emancipation des Femmes (Club for the Emancipation of Women), which in May 1848 changed its name to La Société de la Voix des Femmes (Society for Women's Voice) to emphasise the group's identity with its newspaper, *La Voix des Femmes*, established by Niboyet in March 1848. The first feminist daily newspaper in France, *La Voix des Femmes* proclaimed itself 'a socialist and political journal, the organ of the interests of all women'. Male collaborators were welcomed, and among the signatories of articles were prominent republicans such as Victor Hugo and Jean Macé. Feminists also joined mainstream democratic socialist clubs such as the Club des Amis Fraternels, the Club de la Montagne and the Club de l'Emancipation des Peuples, while the Fourierist newspaper *Démocratie Pacifique* opened its columns to feminist correspondents. A distinctive feminist voice could be heard in the French Revolution of 1848, even if feminist journals struggled to stay alive. *La Voix des Femmes* lasted only until 18 June 1848, though Jeanne Deroin succeeded in launching another paper, a weekly entitled *La Politique des Femmes* (*Women's Politics*), which came out between June and August 1848, followed by *L'Opinion des Femmes* (*Women's Opinion*), a monthly which she edited between January and August 1849.[18]

For the women of 1848 the 'social question' was an inescapable dimension of politics. In keeping with their socialist beliefs, they held that the problems of economic inequality and poverty (especially as manifested in the condition of the urban poor) could not be left to private philanthropy but required the intervention of the state. Democracy was not only about the right to vote but about the right to work. The political question and the social question were two sides of the same coin and the business of a democratic government was to establish universal suffrage and to guarantee jobs for all who needed to earn their livelihood. Deroin and Roland argued that women should be full citizens of the new Republic, which meant that they were entitled to both political rights and access to employment. In March 1848 Deroin headed a delegation of women which met with representatives of the Provisional Government to protest at a definition of 'universal' suffrage which excluded women, and the group maintained its pressure for political rights for women during the election campaigns of March and April 1848 for a Constituent Assembly. Deroin set out the feminist position in uncompromising language in a petition of 16 March:

> You say that our glorious revolution was made for everyone, well, as we are half of the human total, how could we not believe?
> You say that the sacred motto liberty, equality, fraternity, will be applied in all its aspects? Well, as our share should be proportionate to our needs, to our abilities, how could we not believe?
> You say that this sublime motto is one and indivisible; well, recognizing this like you, and recognizing furthermore that each of its terms is also indivisible, there cannot be two liberties, two equalities: that liberty, equality, fraternity of man are obviously those of woman – how could we not believe?[19]

The Voix des Femmes group also pressed for women's right to be recognised as electoral candidates. Deroin tried to persuade Roland to run for office, but she declined. Instead, Deroin declared the celebrated female novelist George Sand to be a candidate, without seeking her permission, and justified her choice on the grounds that Sand was precisely the kind of androgynous human being who combined both feminine and masculine virtues in conformity with the Saint-Simonian ideal. Sand, she wrote, was 'le type un et une, être male par la virilité, femme par l'intuition divine, la poésie' ('the type *un et une*, a man because of her virility, a woman because of her divine intuition, her poetry'). Sand was outraged, dismissing the suggestion as a bad joke and dissociating herself from the Voix des Femmes group in a letter fired off to the newspaper *La Réforme*. *La Voix des Femmes* reproduced the text in full and added its own rejoinder: 'No, we haven't wanted to shelter our cause under your glory, for our cause is good enough, just enough, to march with head held high, and to defend itself, because today one follows ideas, not men, principles, not the individual'.[20] Despite further protests, however, women were excluded from the elections of April 1848 both as candidates and as electors, and for feminists further disappointment lay in store once the election results were known. In a chamber of some 900 deputies, less than a third of the seats went to known republicans of the pre-February 1848 period. The majority were monarchists, even if during the election campaign they had prudently pledged their support for the new regime. The far Left of Jacobin democratic-republicans and socialists (the *démoc-socs*) – whom the feminists considered their closest allies – numbered only around fifty-five. The fight for feminism and for the 'social' Republic was going to be a hard battle.

This was confirmed by the outcome of the struggle for jobs. The Luxembourg Commission, set up under the presidency of the socialist Louis Blanc, recommended the creation of national workshops to tackle the problem of unemployment. Feminists were disappointed, however, when the Paris municipal council agreed to provide work only for unemployed men. In response to protests from unemployed women, the council agreed to establish workshops for them too, and invited them to elect representatives to assist the authorities in allocating work contracts provided by the government. Désirée Gay was elected as a spokeswoman for the second *arrondissement*, but, as we have already seen, her calls for improved pay and conditions for women workers fell on deaf ears.[21]

In participating actively in the political and social struggles emanating from the February Revolution, the feminists of 1848 rejected accusations that they were abandoning women's primary social role of wife and mother. On the contrary, having made their own the exalted discourse of the Romantics on motherhood, they insisted that it was precisely as wives and mothers that women met their obligations to society and that they were therefore entitled to corresponding rights of citizenship. Women, proclaimed Deroin, were the mothers of humanity and engaged in the most important work of all: reproduction. For this reason she continued to deplore the practice of naming children after their fathers rather than their mothers, since it devalued the status of motherhood and reinforced patriarchy by making children the property of fathers. She argued further that maternity deserved recognition from the state in the form of material support. On the other hand, to acknowledge gender differentiation was not to accept women's relegation to the private sphere. For Deroin, who continued to espouse the Saint-Simonian doctrine of the 'social couple', the true individual was androgynous, a mixture of both man and woman: the sexes were complementary. Her feminism was thus rooted in acceptance of sexual difference but was none the less radical for that.[22] Similarly, Pauline Roland, now converted to the virtues of monogamy, demanded 'the right to dedicate ourselves to the world', asking this 'in the name of the holy obligations of the family, in the name of the tender servitude of the mother'.[23]

Marriage, however, at least as constituted under the Napoleonic Code, was high on the feminists' agenda of reforms. Having witnessed at first hand the extent to which 'free love' as practised by Enfantin and his disciples could leave women struggling to bring up illegitimate children, Deroin had always favoured marital fidelity, but the existing marriage laws could not be allowed to endure without deep injury to women. Divorce became a feminist demand, though even Roland saw this as a last resort. Feminist hopes were raised when the Republic's Minister of Justice, Adolphe Crémieux, agreed to back a divorce law, but it never reached the statute book on account of opposition from the conservative deputies within the legislature.

Likewise a bill sponsored by Victor Considérant to give women the right to vote was defeated by the humiliating majority of 899 to 1.[24] The strength of the 'party of order' was much reinforced by the crushing of the workers' uprising in June 1848. In its aftermath, the police cracked down hard on the political clubs, and a law of 28 July 1848 explicitly banned women as members. Secret societies were likewise outlawed and press censorship reintroduced. In the face of this mounting political repression, some feminists such as Niboyet began to waver, but Deroin and Roland, in particular, refused to accept defeat, believing that women's best hope for reform still lay in an alliance with the democratic Left and its aspirations to construct a 'social' Republic.

After the surprising but emphatic electoral victory of Louis Napoleon Bonaparte in the elections for the presidency of the Republic held in December 1848, feminist and *démoc-soc* attention focused on the legislative elections of May 1849. Deroin decided to offer herself as a candidate, inviting the electors of the department of the Seine to see in her someone 'dedicated to establishing that great principle: civil and political equality for both sexes'. Appealing to 'the sovereign people', she explained to prospective voters that if they elected her, they would be establishing true republican principles: 'liberty, equality, fraternity, in their entirety, for all women as well as for all men'. Furthermore: 'A Legislative Assembly entirely composed of men is just as incompetent to pass laws to govern a society which includes men and women, as an assembly composed of the privileged would be to discuss the interests of workers, or an assembly of capitalists to uphold the honour of the country'. Deroin attended the electoral meetings held by other candidates of the democratic-socialist movement, and often received abuse when she tried to win audiences over to her own campaign. Echoing the sentiments of Flora Tristan and the utopian socialist activists of the 1830s, she affirmed that 'social reform cannot be carried out without the support of women, half of humanity. And in the same way that the political enfranchisement of the proletariat is the first step towards their physical, moral and intellectual enfranchisement, the political enfranchisement of women is the first step towards the complete emancipation of all the oppressed'. Women, according to Deroin, were 'the last of the pariahs' and without them 'the work of our social redemption cannot be accomplished'.[25] The *démoc-socs* were not persuaded. On the grounds that a vote for Deroin was a wasted vote, since the constitution did not permit women to run as candidates, they refused to endorse her candidacy, thus dealing feminism another heavy blow.

Undaunted, Deroin and Roland switched the focus of their feminist endeavours to education and to the formation of associations – in effect, trade unions – among groups of workers along lines already envisaged by Flora Tristan. Mutual aid and cooperation among workers loomed large in socialist thinking about the reorganisation of society in 1848 and the Voix des Femmes group readily involved itself in attempts to organise domestic servants and seamstresses. Suzanne Voilquin set up an association of midwives which demanded better training and a state salary in recognition of their work among poor women who were too poor to pay for their services. In February 1849 Deroin and Roland joined together with a number of male militants to found an Association of Socialist Primary School Teachers. By 1849 the association movement seemed to be making some progress: in August Deroin belonged to the council of a federation of some eighty-three associations and in October Roland, representing the teachers' union, joined the central commission of the Union of Fraternal Associations, the 'Association of Associations', which grouped some 104 associations.[26]

For Roland, education and work were inextricably linked: the right to both was fundamental to the building of genuine democracy and the emancipation of women. She envisaged equal education for all and the abolition of the division between primary and secondary schools, which served only to perpetuate class divisions. Moral education in the classroom was necessary to teach children the real meaning of the terms 'Liberty, Equality and Fraternity'. She was also a strong advocate of pre-school education and the establishment of crèches for children under the age of three, so that from the earliest age 'society should exercise over the child its inalienable rights and fulfil all its duties towards it'. At the same time, crèches would allow mothers the necessary space to work and to develop their own potential. Motherhood, she proclaimed, was woman's duty, 'a sacred duty, a religious one even; but at no time should it be considered her only duty'.[27]

But as the strength of the association movement grew (by May 1850 the Association of Associations united some 400 associations) so too did the power of political reaction. In a police swoop at a meeting held at Deroin's house on 29 May 1850, both she and Roland were arrested and, along with one other woman, Louise Nicaud of the Association of Launderesses, and twenty-seven male militants, they were put on trial for subversion. The women each received a prison sentence of six months. Though not tried for their feminist activities as such, these undoubtedly counted against them. According to the police, Roland was not only a fanatical socialist but a sworn enemy of marriage, a woman who refused to accept that married women should be subject to the control of their husbands – points which she cheerfully confirmed in court to the judge. Likewise Deroin's refusal to adopt the name of her husband (Desroches) was held against her, as was her protest in court that she refused to recognise the man-made laws by which she was to be judged. The only concession she made, with considerable reluctance and at the entreaty of her male colleagues, was to deny that she was the originator of the association idea, so as to receive a lighter sentence.[28]

The arrest and imprisonment of Deroin and Roland formed part of a wider crackdown on 'subversion' on the part of the authorities, fearful that the victory of *démoc-soc* deputies in by-elections held in Paris in the spring of 1850 portended a revival of the 'reds'.[29] Yet even in prison Deroin and Roland attempted to carry on their struggle. In February 1851 Deroin wrote to the Legislative Assembly to protest against the decision to remove one of women's few remaining political rights, that of petition. Roland maintained an extensive correspondence with fellow militants and devised courses of instruction for women prisoners. From her prison cell at Saint-Lazare (the prison-hospital whose normal inmates were prostitutes) she wrote a long letter in April 1851 to the eminent journalist, Emile de Girardin, editor of the *Bien-être Universel*, who had outraged Roland by repeating Proudhon's dictum that women's social role was to be either a housewife or a harlot. Affirming women's right to decide their own destiny, she declared that 'woman is a citizen by right, if not in fact, and as such she needs to become involved in life outside the home, in social life, which will not be a healthy one until the whole family is represented there'. Further: 'Woman is entitled to work as is Man, and to have productive, independent employment which will emancipate her from all dependence. She has the right to choose her work herself as well as a man and no one can legitimately confine her to the house if she feels she is called to live otherwise'.[30]

But the times were no longer propitious for feminists or democrats. On the night of 1–2 December Louis Napoleon Bonaparte, President of the Republic, staged a *coup d'état* against the regime to which he had sworn an oath of loyalty. Resistance was surprisingly widespread, especially in parts of southern France, but in vain. Massive proscriptions followed, along with the imposition of martial law. Among the 26,000 *démoc-socs* arrested was Pauline Roland, who was first imprisoned at Saint-Lazare and then, in June 1852, deported to Algeria, where her health rapidly deteriorated. Released after five months, as she made her way back to Paris and her children, she fell ill and died at Lyon. Deroin escaped immediate arrest and devoted herself to helping the families of political prisoners. Subject to police harassment, however, she increasingly feared for her own safety and in August 1852 sought political asylum in London, where she lived until her death in 1894. As under the First so under the Second Republic, feminists went down to defeat at the hands of a repressive state.

The antifeminist backlash

As we have seen, the conservatives and liberals who ruled France in the period of the Restoration and the July Monarchy were firmly attached to the doctrine of separate spheres. Feminists were right to expect little in the way of any improvement in women's lot to come from an established order determined to resist the introduction of democracy and mass politics. They expected more from opposition groups, however, and for that reason allied themselves with what they considered to be the most progressive forces of the age, namely republicanism and socialism. Here their disappointment was to be great. By and large, the feminist activists of the 1848 era received as little support or encouragement from the political radicals of the time as their predecessors had obtained from the revolutionaries of 1789. On the contrary, Jacobin antifeminism was perpetuated and brought up to date by some of the most prominent republican and socialist heirs of the revolutionary tradition.

No one was more devoted to the legacy of the Revolution and the revolutionary tradition than the historian and moralist Jules Michelet (1798–1874), author of a celebrated multi-volume *Histoire de France* which appeared between 1833 and 1867 and many other works. The son of a printer, Michelet was a brilliant student who rose through the academic system to become Professor of History at the Collège de France in 1838, a position which he combined with lecturing at the Sorbonne and another post at the Archives Nationales, where he had unique access to source material for his histories. For Michelet, all history was essentially the story of the struggle to affirm human freedom in the face of adversity and in a French context he equated this conflict with the struggle to establish a democratic Republic. Partly as a result of personal experiences which included the death of his first wife and that of his close friend Mme Dumesnil, in the 1840s he became increasingly hostile to Catholicism (though, like most fellow Romantics, not to religion as such). Identifying the Church as the main barrier to progress, he publicly attacked the Jesuits in a controversial lecture course at the Collège de France, for which he was suspended in January 1848. Having welcomed the Revolution of 1848 as the realisation of his dreams, Michelet was bitterly disappointed by the failures of the Second Republic, but, remaining true to his democratic beliefs, he refused to take an oath of loyalty to the Second Empire in 1852, and in consequence was sacked from his academic jobs.

Michelet, in short, was a democrat of conviction, imbued with a romantic and mystical faith in 'the people' and persuaded that the French Revolution of 1789 was the greatest event in world history. His vision of democracy, however, like his historical *oeuvre* as a whole, was profoundly gendered. According to Michelet, one of the lessons of history was that disaster soon followed whenever women forgot their true maternal role and meddled in the masculine sphere of government. Thus, whereas the fourteenth century in his view was an age of progress because royal authority was strong and patriarchal rule generally accepted, the fifteenth century was chaotic because of the influence of a woman like Catherine de Medici. Similarly, he held that the extent of female influence and intrigue at the Court of Versailles in the eighteenth century testified to both the feminisation and therefore the decadence of the monarchy. Like Rousseau, Michelet believed that in a Republic political power should be an exclusively masculine preserve.[31]

What Michelet feared most about women was their supposed susceptibility to clerical manipulation. In a celebrated tract entitled *Le prêtre, la femme et la famille* (*Priests, Women and the Family*), published in 1845 and reprinted numerous times in the nineteenth century, Michelet claimed that priests exercised power over women above all through the institution of the confessional. The result was division in the family, since men were usually non-believers and women pious, and the authority that rightfully belonged to husbands was therefore being usurped by priests. 'Our wives and daughters are raised, governed *by our enemies. Enemies of the modern spirit* of liberty and of the future', he wrote: '*our enemies*, I repeat, in a more direct sense, being naturally envious of marriage and family life'.[32] The suggestion that women were unfit to exercise the rights of citizenship on account of their subservience to the clergy was not new: as we have seen, it was made by the sans-culottes. Michelet, however, made it a staple of Republican discourse. Well into the twentieth century this remained the key argument of the French Left against the enfranchisement of women in France.

Sharing both Michelet's anticlericalism and his antipathy to women in public life was another influential left-wing intellectual, Pierre Joseph Proudhon (1809–65). A libertarian socialist who is generally regarded as the founder of the European anarchist movement, Proudhon was, like Michelet, the son of an artisan and grew up in poverty in the rural Jura region of eastern France. A printer and compositor to trade, he identified strongly with the world of the artisan and small peasant farmer. Having made his reputation in 1840 with the publication of his book *What is Property?* (where he affirmed that 'property is theft') he revealed himself to be much more conservative – not to say downright misogynous – on the subject of the 'woman question' in his *System of Economic Contradictions: or, The Philosophy of Poverty* (1846; English edition 1888), where, in an infamous phrase, he stated that women had only two possible roles in society: that of housewife (*ménagère*) or prostitute (*courtisane*).[33] Far from repudiating this dictum, many of Proudhon's heirs in the French labour movement continued to cite it as a definitive statement about women's position in French society.

Another prominent example from the era of 1848 was the artist and caricaturist Honoré Daumier (1808–79). Also from a modest background, he was an outspoken Republican who earned himself a jail sentence in 1832 for lampooning the July Monarchy, and he was later to be both an adversary of the Second Empire and a supporter of the Paris Commune. Happily married to a dressmaker, 'Didine', whom he revered as wife and woman of the people, Daumier was no woman-hater. For the *femmes nouvelles*, however, who dared to challenge the role which nature had intended for them, he had nothing but contempt. In a series of cartoons in the liberal satirical review *Le Charivari* and other periodicals, he heaped ridicule on feminists who advocated the reintroduction of divorce or the improvement of women's education. The *divorceuses* were represented by Daumier as man-hating harridans with no knowledge of the joys of family life: the *bas-bleus*, or 'bluestockings' were crazy, intellectual women who neglected their husbands and households in pursuit of their studies, a type already pilloried by the writer Frédéric Soulié whose *Physiologie du bas-bleu* (1841) was most probably the inspiration for Daumier's drawings.[34]

Daumier's prototypes were developed by other artists. Especially after the outbreak of the 1848 Revolution, female political activists like Jeanne Deroin and Pauline

Roland became the butt of much humour. Such women were unnatural, it was implied, and they left a trail of domestic chaos in their wake. They were represented as devoid of any talent for politics, staging political meetings which inevitably turned into a shambles. Some artists hinted that what the feminists wanted was sexual rather than political freedom, their real objective being to cuckold their husbands. In *Le Charivari*, Edouard de Beaumont devoted a series of cartoons to coquettish young warriors whom he called the Vésuviennes. There was indeed a contemporary women's society called the Vésuviennes, but it was a burlesque creation of the French police who drew up a constitution for it and provided it with prostitutes as members. For the state, ridicule and distortion were as much weapons of sexual harassment as repression and physical violence: and through de Beaumont's cartoons the police succeeded so well in their ploy that until recently historians regarded the Vésuvienne constitution as genuine.[35]

It would clearly be an exaggeration to claim that misogyny permeated the entire Republican tradition. Against a Proudhon, one can point to a Victor Considérant or a Pierre Leroux and in the future French feminists would benefit from the support of an Alfred Naquet, author of the divorce law of 1884, and a Léon Richer, co-founder with Maria Deraismes of the modern republican feminist movement. Nevertheless, by and large it is fair to say that republicans remained as staunchly wedded to the doctrine of separate spheres as political reactionaries. The case of Ernest Legouvé is a good illustration of the limits of republican support for feminism in the 1848 era. A professor at the Collège de France, Legouvé was encouraged to give a series of public lectures on the moral history of women by the Second Republic's first Minister of Education, the ex-Saint-Simonian Hippolyte Carnot. Legouvé himself had been influenced by Saint-Simonian ideas on the 'woman question' and in both the lectures given in April 1848 and the book of the lectures which appeared in 1849 he showed himself sympathetic to many feminist demands, notably those for reform of marriage and the law and for better education. Also a strong critic of the double standard of morality, Legouvé was recognised by the feminists of 1848 as a friend and ally.[36]

On the other hand, he in no way encouraged their more radical aspirations. Legouvé could not conceive of viable gender relations outside of the patriarchal family in which ultimate power resided with the husband and father. Women's essential mission remained that of wife and mother. While he envisaged that their talents could be mobilised in public life as administrators in hospitals, prisons and charities and that they should not be prevented from developing careers in the arts, literature, education and medicine, he explicitly ruled out any political role for women. Female suffrage violated the principle of sexual difference.[37] As in the 1790s, so in 1848 – and long afterwards – republicans rejected women's claims to the full rights of citizenship. Antifeminism was always a much more powerful current of opinion than feminism in the nineteeenth century.

Part III (1850–80)

Discourses on 'woman'

Chapter 7

Femininity

Constructions, consequences, control

We have already seen that, in what amounted to a veritable paradigm shift, the eighteenth century witnessed a transformation in beliefs concerning women's 'nature' and in representations of femininity. From the 'dangerous' sex of medieval and early modern times, 'woman' came to be represented as a 'spiritual' and morally superior being. By the high Victorian period, in France as in the United Kingdom, the new image had become one of the commonplace assumptions of the day. As a consequence, the discourse on 'woman' was invariably permeated by 'moral' considerations, whatever the precise subject at issue – be it women's work, women's civic and political rights, or, our immediate concern in this chapter, women's education and women's sexuality.

As Part 1 attempted to explain, the discourse on 'woman' elaborated in the course of the Enlightenment and the French Revolution was preoccupied not merely with how to define women as women but with how to define women's role in the wider society. Harmony in the gender order was deemed to be fundamental to harmony in the social order. The political instability which continued to be a feature of French political life for most of the nineteenth century and the problems created by the advent of a new industrial civilisation generated widespread anxieties about the future of France. Should France be a monarchy or a republic? An oligarchy or a democracy? A rural or an industrial civilisation? A country which valued tradition or modernity? Did the future belong to science rather than religion? These and other questions were hotly debated by the educated classes and furnished the raw material for a rich and animated political culture which was characterised more by conflict than by consensus. Integral to these national debates remained the question of women's place: politics and social relations, inescapably, had a gender dimension. Women, it was widely agreed, were 'different': but how different? Did the trend towards mass politics and a more industrialised society imply a new role for women and a new order of gender relations? Or was it the case that, in a changing world, gender should provide the one sure element of continuity and stability? By the middle years of the nineteenth century, debates on politics and what had come to be known as

97

the 'social question' inevitably involved the 'woman question' also. And, ultimately, what was at stake in these debates as far as women were concerned was the question of control. Who was to control women's minds? Who should control women's bodies?

Education

To take the question of minds first: as we have seen, it was widely accepted in the first half of the nineteenth century that the education of girls should be essentially moral and religious. Education manuals such as Lucille Sauvan's *Directions* were inspired by the educational ideals of writers such as Fénélon and Mme de Maintenon, whose prescriptions for the daughters of the seventeenth-century aristocracy were adapted for the needs of nineteenth-century girls of more humble origins: hence the emphasis on practical skills – sewing, above all – as well as on religion. According to Sauvan, what girls needed to learn were the virtues of 'sobriety, patience, love of work, resignation, moderation in desires, simplicity in tastes'.[1]

It is worth emphasising, however, that these ideals were inculcated in state schools as much as in the schools run by religious orders. Plans on the part of radical Republicans to abolish the teaching of religion in state schools in 1848 foundered in the aftermath of the June Days, which convinced the propertied classes of the continuing utility of the Church in the moralisation of the masses. By the Falloux Law of 1850 – effectively, an educational concordat signed between the Church and the *parti de l'ordre* – the privileged position of the religious orders in the educational system was recognised by their right to open schools staffed by unqualified teachers who lacked a teaching certificate, the *brevet*, and who required only a 'letter of obedience'. Article 51 of the Law recommended the establishment of separate schools for girls in all communes with a population of more than 800 and though it failed to make the provision of such schools compulsory, it gave a massive boost to the expansion of girls' elementary education, principally under the auspices of female religious congregations.[2] By 1866, in public and private schools combined, 55% of all girls were taught by nuns, who likewise were responsible for the running of the great majority of training schools (*écoles normales*) for female teachers. In 1870, of the seventy-four training schools in existence, two-thirds were directed by female religious orders.[3] Significantly, even Victor Duruy, Napoleon III's anticlerical Minister of Education, made no attempt to remove religion from the classroom in the 1860s, since he still subscribed to the view that religion was 'good for the people'.

Nevertheless, the rapid expansion of church schools, however beneficial it might have been to the cause of the spread of literacy, aroused consternation among Republican opponents of the Second Empire. Since the days of the Jacobins, it had been the dream of French Republicans to establish a viable democracy and a morally and socially united nation. The educational system had always loomed large in their projects, but following the demise of the Second Republic and the re-establishment of the Empire reform of education came to acquire still greater significance in the struggle to realise the Republican vision. Convinced that the Republic could be founded on a secure and permanent basis only if it won the battle against the Church for the minds of men – and more especially of women – Republicans launched a massive campaign on behalf of free, secular and compulsory schooling in the 1860s, spearheaded by the Education League of Jean Macé.[4] In the spring of 1870 Jules Ferry, one of the rising stars in a new generation of Republican leaders, made a strong plea for the adoption of equality in the education of the sexes, counselling the ladies in his audience to read John Stuart Mill's treatise on the subjection of women to discover how they had the same faculties for learning as men. For Ferry, as for Michelet, women would belong either to science or to the Church. Without an improvement in women's education, he affirmed, a barricade would divide husbands from their wives.[5] The humiliating defeat of France in the war with Prussia in 1870–71 served as an additional spur to action on the part of Republicans, since the Prussian victory was widely attributed to the superiority of the Prussian schoolmaster and reinforced the belief that the school system would ultimately determine the fate of the nation. Once Republicans had established a firm hold on the levers of power under the Third Republic, after seeing off threats to restore the monarchy in the 1870s, they would waste no time in implementing their educational programme in a series of 'laic laws'.[6]

The fact remains, however, that, across the political and ideological divide, there was a widespread consensus that education should both reflect and reinforce sexual difference. Readers such as Zulma Carraud's *Maurice ou le travail* and *La petite Jeanne ou le devoir*, in use in schools in some twenty departments in the 1850s, represented boys as dutiful sons and good workers, loyal to their future employers. Girls, on the other hand, were depicted as devoted daughters and dedicated mothers who knew how to run a clean, orderly household.[7] Under the Second Empire, girls continued to be expected to acquire quintessentially feminine virtues such as modesty, a pleasing disposition and, above all, a sense of order. In Marie Curo's *Etudes morales et religieuses ou éducation pratique des jeunes filles* (1860) the point is made by characterising the bad behaviour of one girl, Louise, with the exemplary conduct of another, Cécile, the role model, who is invariably pleasant, clean, sensible and charming. In Mme Paul Caillaud's *Résumé d'éducation pratique* (1873) the message was likewise conveyed to young girls that disorder and confusion were the enemies of domestic virtue, while order led to God.[8] The quarrel between Republicans and the Church over girls' education was largely about control, not content.

At the level of secondary education, the Falloux Law had served also to encourage the expansion of schools run by female religious orders. Initially viewed with a benevolent eye by the Imperial regime, which in its early days had developed a close rapport with the Church, this development was jeopardised by the rupture between

Catholics and the Empire as a result of Napoleon III's Italian policy, which threatened the future of the Pope as a territorial ruler, and provoked strong Catholic opposition, notably from the outspoken Catholic journalist Louis Veuillot, editor of the newspaper *L'Univers*. In addition to banning *L'Univers*, the Emperor was prepared to strike back at his Catholic critics in France by adopting a more anticlerical line in his educational policy, signalled by the appointment of Victor Duruy as Minister of Education. Duruy set out the case for reorganising the secondary education of girls, stressing that in part, at least, 'our present embarrassments stem from the fact that we have left this education in the hands of people who are neither of their time nor of their country'. In 1867 the Minister decided to establish secondary courses for girls to be given by male teachers from the Sorbonne and the male lycées. The idea was that girls should follow these courses for three or four years, six or seven months a year, progressing on the basis of examination results until eventually a diploma was obtained. But despite promising beginnings, the experiment ended in almost complete failure. By January 1870, the courses survived in only fourteen towns and by 1879, in only five, including Paris.[9]

In part, the Duruy experiment failed on account of clerical hostility, in particular because of the campaign conducted by Bishop Dupanloup of Orleans, who objected not only to the idea of more advanced studies for girls than was conventionally available, but also to the fact that in provincial towns the courses were usually held in the town hall, that is, a public place where all kinds of men would be in the vicinity, and worse still, 'evil-living women' (i.e. prostitutes).[10] In his *Second Letter* he accused Duruy of being motivated solely by a desire to detach women from the Church, and denounced him as one of the odious creatures (Darwinists) 'who saw man as a perfected orang-outang'.[11] Other members of the episcopate and clergy followed where Dupanloup led: for example in Besançon, Bordeaux, Périgueux and Agen clerical intimidation caused the withdrawal of pupils, though in a few places such as Rennes and Troyes the local bishops lent their support to the scheme.[12]

But it was not clerical hostility alone which wrecked the experiment. In most places – with the notable exception of Paris – the courses themselves were badly organised, in that each town was left to devise its own curriculum, which led to wide discrepancies in both the type and the quality of courses offered.[13] In addition, they catered almost exclusively for girls from the highest social circles, and these turned out to be somewhat dilettante pupils, reluctant to do any homework or any real classwork and attending 'the way one goes to a public lecture or a show'.[14] Finally, it is worth noting that even if the courses had turned out to be more successful, their effects would hardly have been revolutionary. Duruy's ideas on the actual content of girls' education were not all that different from Dupanloup's. Like the Bishop, he believed in the ideology of separate spheres and regarded domestic duties as women's essential preoccupation.[15] Developing their minds was a way of turning them into more interesting companions for their husbands and increasing their authority in the family and in society, but it was never the Minister's intention to create parity between girls and boys in the matter of secondary schooling.

Medical science and the female body

It would be difficult to contest the view that, generally speaking, nineteenth-century women – and mothers in particular – benefited from advances in medical science. Doctors devoted more attention to pre- and post-natal care. By the 1830s they could examine the uterus by means of the vaginal speculum, and could also use the stethoscope to listen to the foetal heartbeat. French doctors were also among the first to realise the importance of urine tests for pregnancy, and in France, unlike America, advances in the field of obstetrics led to the elevaton of the status of midwives as professionals rather than to their elimination. In the matter of after-care, French doctors were particularly sympathetic to the use of anaesthetics, though surprisingly, in view of the pioneering experiments of Pasteur, they neglected to institute the type of sanitary measures common in Britain and America by the beginning of the twentieth century, with the result that France continued to have a high rate of infant mortality.[16] The contribution of medicine to the development of a closer relationship between mother and child is not to be doubted, however, and medical progress also played a part in ending the practice of sending infants out to wet-nurses, while simultaneously encouraging maternal breast-feeding.[17] As far as the doctors were concerned, motherhood was women's supreme mission, and the thrust of much of their own action had the intended effect of raising the prestige of motherhood over the course of the nineteenth century.

In seeking to foster both the health and the general standing of women as mothers, however, doctors were also promoting a medical view of 'woman' which defined her primarily in terms of her child-bearing and child-rearing social role. Since the Enlightenment, the medical profession had sought to elevate the study of sexual difference to the status of a science. Alongside the new 'science of man', which studied the human species through close empirical observation and the application of deductive reason, there had developed a corresponding science of woman, or 'gynaecology', which studied and classified the properties peculiar to females and allegedly characteristic of a specifically feminine nature.[18] Building on the work of their eighteenth-century predecessors, nineteenth-century doctors affirmed with ever greater confidence that sexual difference was rooted in the facts of biology. In medical discourse, the sexualized female body thus became a site of multiple meanings which, in addition to defining 'woman', configured her place in the wider social order.

What fascinated doctors was the perception of woman as 'Other'. Whereas nineteenth-century artists, in thrall to 'the eternal feminine', invented an imaginary woman who often corresponded to the stereotype of 'muse' or 'madonna', doctors turned instead to female biology to unlock the mysteries of a specifically feminine nature. From the 1840s, they were convinced that the key lay in the function of the ovaries, and 'ovular theory', which rested on a (flawed) explanation of the workings of the menstrual cycle, rapidly became the scientific foundation of the biological understanding of femininity. As developed by doctors such as Achille Chéreau (1817–85), ovular theory held that the ovaries were the vital organs which over-determined women's entire existence as a sexual being and identified menstruation as the time when women both experienced maximum sexual desire and attained maximum fertility.[19] Among the most enthusiastic supporters of the theory was the historian Michelet, who undertook to popularise it in his work *L'Amour*, which contains pages which are a veritable hymn to the properties of menstrual blood, now demonstrated by medical science to be inextricably linked to women's glorious role as mother and reproducer of the race.[20]

Because women's physical and psychological characteristics were held to be the consequence of their reproductive functions, femininity was perceived to have its own pathology. Like the Jacobin Republic, the female body was deemed to be one and indivisible: female maladies were inseparable from female physiology. A notable case in point was that of female madness. Alienists were convinced that women's illnesses had moral rather than physical origins. Some believed that women were more susceptible to madness than men because they lacked men's natural capacity to cope with emotional turmoil and refused to acknowledge statistical evidence to the contrary. According to one specialist, such evidence was unreliable, since women were inveterate liars whose lies were the product of a residual modesty, designed to conceal their 'need for union between the sexes, all the stronger because it was repressed but encouraged by reading novels, or going to the theatre'.[21] Few alienists followed J.E.D. Esquirol in trying to engage sympathetically with the illusions of his insane patients. Most preferred to try to cure their charges by force, employing therapies which combined fear and torture, most horribly in the shape of 'hydrotherapy' which involved immersing patients up to their necks in bath tubs and then bombarding them for hours on end with jets of water, euphemistically described as 'showers' – a procedure which in a number of cases resulted in death. In the lunatic asylums of mid-nineteenth-century France, women patients were expected to be cured by pain and 'moral revulsion' at the enormity of their fantasies.[22]

The crudeness of their methods notwithstanding, in the period from roughly 1830 to 1880 alienists were remarkably successful in affirming their claims to speak with the authority of science, as was well illustrated by the fact that the criminal law increasingly turned to medical experts to make judgements about the motives of female criminals. Defence lawyers discovered that they could often best protect their clients by invoking mitigating circumstances, endorsed by medical opinion, which made the crimes explicable as moments of madness induced by biological impulses. In the new specialism of forensic medicine, deviant behaviour was frequently ascribed to mental illness, diagnosed as 'monomania', a temporary disorder which, in the case of women, could invariably be linked to the functioning of their reproductive cycle. Madness and neuroses were held to be the direct result of menstruation. Just as for the doctors woman was the female of the species, in thrall to her body, so for the law female crime could be explained away as irrational acts attributable to hormonal upsets. Theft, for example, was deemed to be an instance of *monomanie du vol*, which, according to the alienist Dr Brierre de Boismont, was most likely to manifest itself during menstruation: hence the willingness of the courts to acquit the accused when such arguments were produced.[23]

Sexuality and the double standard

The female crimes which most captivated public opinion, of course, were so-called crimes of passion. Though not officially recognised by the legal system, such crimes were regarded in French jurisprudence as belonging to a different order of deviant behaviour from routine crimes since they were directly related to the intimate lives of couples and their private quarrels and tensions. Spontaneity was held to be the hallmark of the *crime passionnel*, though in practice the courts accepted that they could be preceded by a degree of premeditation, indistinguishable from a compulsive obsession which the individual was unable to overcome. In the popular mentality, the *crime passionnel* was a normal, not a deviant, form of behaviour.[24] Outraged husbands had a right to vengeance against an adulterous wife – a right strongly reiterated by the playwright Alexandre Dumas *fils*, who in 1872 defended a man called Dubourg for murdering his adulterous wife.[25] Similarly, however, a wronged woman was deemed to have the moral if not the legal right to revenge herself against a man who had disgraced her. Woman, a creature who supposedly lived only for love, could not help herself when her love was betrayed.[26]

While the *de facto* recognition of the *crime passionnel* by the courts in effect contradicted the Code which had quite explicitly established the adultery of a wife as a much more serious offence than that of a husband, it would be wrong to view acquittals of women involved in crimes of passion as a serious blow against the double standard. The courts often reserved most of their sympathies for men of high social standing who found themselves in the glare of publicity following disclosure of their extra-marital affairs as a result of a *crime passionnel* committed by a lower-class woman. A case in point was that of the cabaret singer Maria Béraldi (real name Marie Bière) who tried to kill her lover M. Robert Gentien, a rich landowner from Bordeaux, after the break-up of their affair on her becoming pregnant. Gentien's parting advice to her had been to have an abortion, for he wanted nothing to do with the child. Having rejected this counsel, Béraldi was torn with grief when the baby died soon after birth. Her first thought had been to kill herself at Gentien's feet, but, having failed, she tried to kill Gentien instead. The jury, taking all the circumstances into account, acquitted her, instead of passing the death sentence as the law could have required. At the same time, however, the president of the court went out of his way to show sympathy for Gentien's position. As a man with important family commitments, he said, M. Gentien naturally wanted to keep his liaison secret to avoid all taint of scandal.[27] In other words, it was implied, the family name of an upper-class gentleman was not to be impugned on account of his passing infatuation with a mere *artiste*.

It might be noted also that, contrary to the vivid place which they occupied in the popular press and in the collective imagination, female perpetrators of *crimes passionnels* were far fewer in numbers than their male counterparts. Of the 824 crimes of passion committed in France between 1871 and 1880, 678 involved men (82%). In the department of the Seine, the proportion of women was only 10% (nine women to eighty men). The one crime where women outnumbered men was that of poisoning, which in the same period involved thirty-nine women and sixteen men. Nevertheless, the stereotyping of the *crime passionnel* as a female crime remains a contemporary fantasy, a discursive rather than a social reality. Additionally, the statistics reveal that such crimes were most commonly committed not by members of the bourgeoisie but by male members of the urban working classes – men mired in a subculture of unstable personal relations, job insecurity, poverty, drunkenness and domestic violence.[28]

In the nineteenth century the laws which discriminated between the sexual misdemeanours of women and those of men remained far from academic. Rather, they were sternly enforced in the courts. Thus in 1847 a poor woman called Mesnager admitted her adultery before the Police Correctionnelle, explaining how she had been forced to leave her brutal, drunken husband who never gave her enough to keep herself and her children. Their ex-lodger, a M. Soubret, had befriended her and taken her in permanently. The tribunal graciously admitted that there were 'very extenuating circumstances' in the case, but the president told Mme Mesnager that while her gratitude was understandable, she ought not to have shown it to the point where she forgot her familial duties: he then proceeded to sentence her and her companion to a week's imprisonment 'only'.[29]

Bad husbands continued to obtain the backing of the law right through the nineteenth century. Where adultery was concerned, wives were legally in the wrong and were made to face the consequences of their actions. In 1880, one Eugène-Julien Gentien, deported for life for his part in a murder, was later reprieved, and was outraged to find on his return home that his wife now lived with another man, and was pregnant by him. In vain the poor woman protested that she had never expected to see her husband again and considered herself a widow; likewise no attention was paid to the fact that he was 'a brute and a drunkard'. The verdict was six days' imprisonment for her and a fifty franc fine for her lover.[30] In another case, a M. Bourlier brought charges against his 33-year-old wife and M. André Rigaud, an elderly gentleman who was a distiller and a municipal counsellor at Levallois-Perret. Having seen the couple enter a hotel, Bourlier had sent for the police, who burst in to discover the lovers in a state of undress. At the trial, Rigaud admitted that they had had relations over the previous six years, but only at rare intervals, an allegation which the court admitted seemed very plausible in view of M. Rigaud's advanced years. Nevertheless, each was sentenced to three months' imprisonment.[31]

The double standard of morality thus remained firmly in place, now buttressed more by the findings of medical science than by the toleration supposedly characteristic of so-called 'Catholic' countries. In view of the growing prestige of medical science from the period of the July Monarchy onwards, it was the discourse of medicine which provided the most authoritative statements on women's sexuality in the nineteenth century, supplanting the primacy formerly enjoyed in this domain by spokesmen for organised religion. As apologists for science and a secular approach to the explanation of the world, doctors quite deliberately set out to undermine the claims of clerics to a monopoly on morality. Yet, if, in their own minds, medical men were the torchbearers of progressive ideas and the advance guard of civilisation, they frequently revealed themselves to be as restrictive in their attitude to women and to female sexuality as were contemporary churchmen.

Certainly, as Jean-Louis Flandrin has reminded us, from the sixteenth century onwards the Tridentine Catholic Church had embarked upon a large-scale exercise of sexual repression, with notable success in France.[32] By the nineteenth century, it was clear that this movement had been arrested among the popular classes, and in any case the severity of the Church's teaching on sexual morality had been tempered by the adoption in the seminaries of the more liberal moral theology of Alphonse Liguori (1687–1787).[33] Nevertheless, in so far as they remained pious daughters of the Catholic Church, nineteenth-century middle-class women were exposed to the doctrines of priests who insisted that sex should take place only within the confines of marriage and that the primary purpose of marriage was procreation.[34] Doubtless, in this way the Church may have contributed to sexual inhibitions on the part of some of the more religiously impressionable members of the female bourgeoisie. It was also the case, however, that some members of the medical profession were of the conviction that women's sexual urges were much less imperious than those of men. Dr Louis Fiaux, for instance, following the celebrated William Acton in England, attributed male recourse to prostitution and adultery in France to the relative sexual passivity of women.[35]

In general, however, doctors, like priests, subscribed to the view that it was better to marry than to burn. Auguste Debay, author of a hugely successful manual on marriage hygiene which was published in 1848 and reprinted 172 times by 1883, opined that 'marriage, in joining the two sexes the one to the other, prevents debauchery, moderates the sensual passions by the ease with which they may be satisfied, and becomes also the safeguard of good morals and the honour of families'.

Marriage both channelled the 'genital instinct' and subjected it to a moral purpose. Between the ages of 20 and 30, men should have sex two to four times a week; between 30 and 40 once a week. Once over 60 they should abstain. The rules for women – perforce, since Debay's prescriptions were for sex within marriage! – were the same, despite the fact that women were capable of more prolonged sexual activity than men. Restraint conserved women's charms, whereas excess caused them to wither. A 'reasonable woman' accepted her husband's performance without complaint. Nor did she attempt to take the sexual initiative:

> The horizontal position, that is to say the man lying on the woman, is the natural and instinctive position for the union of the sexes in the human race ... The peculiar fancy that some wives occasionally experience to take the husband's place disturbs the natural order.[36]

Doctors like Debay were thus unabashed, if more than a little anxious, apologists for male control of female sexuality. A colleague, Dr Villemont, similarly described women on top as 'an infamy, the worst of turpitudes, the man falling into the shame of allowing himself to submit to his wife'. For Villemont, the best position was the commonest one, which, he claimed, also happened to be the one which most favoured procreation. To make love within marriage, he affirmed, was always to have the hope of producing a child.[37] Clearly, for Villemont as much as for any churchman, procreation was the primary end of marriage. On the other hand, Villemont, Debay and most other doctors who wrote marriage and sex manuals in nineteenth-century France recognised women's right to sexual pleasure. Some even described in minute detail how to provide it, as in Jules Guyot's *Bréviaire de l'amour expérimental* (1882), which extolled stimulation of the clitoris.[38] In 1866 Gustave Droz, a journalist on the *Revue des Deux-Mondes*, wrote a book, *Monsieur, madame et bébé*, which advocated the practice of sexual love within marriage and recommended wives to show their husbands the same type of coquetry as they could expect from mistresses. The work became a best-seller and by 1884 had gone through 121 editions.[39]

It would be a mistake, however, to assume that doctors and liberal laymen were the only adepts of women's right to sexual pleasure. Picking up on a long theological tradition which distinguished pleasure from procreation in conjugal love-making – a tradition which had been partly suppressed by the prevalence of a Jansenistical tendency in French seminaries – some nineteenth-century authors of manuals for confessors found no fault with women who, after *coitus interruptus*, brought themselves to a sexual climax through masturbation.[40] Of course, for the Church, *coitus interruptus* was undoubtedly a sin – but for at least some theologians and priests it was a sin committed exclusively by the husband. Thus, in a situation in which this form of contraceptive practice was widespread throughout rural France, it was another reason – possibly the main one – for masculine hostility to religion, whereas the leniency shown to women further explains their greater propensity to remain within the Catholic fold. So great, indeed, was clerical concern about the extent of men's disenchantment with religion on the grounds of clerical interference in their sex lives that by the turn of the century some priests were prepared to give absolution to men who confessed to withdrawal – in vain, for it appears that, by then, irreparable damage had been done.

Reinforcing the double standard: the regulation of prostitution

The double standard was predicated on the belief that male sexual activity outside of marriage was legitimate whereas female sexual activity outside of marriage was illicit and immoral. Fundamental to the operation of such a system was the availability of a supply of prostitutes, which raised the question of regulation. The greatest apologist for regulation was Dr Alexandre-Jean-Baptiste Parent-Duchâtelet (1790–1835), author of a massive two-volume study of prostitution in the city of Paris which appeared posthumously and was widely read not only in France but in Europe as a whole. Parent defended prostitution on the grounds that it was endemic in society, on the one hand because of the permanent nature of the demand and on the other because of the existence of a morally defective class of women whose propensities for idleness, luxury and debauchery ensured a permanent supply of prostitutes. Prostitutes, in Parent-Duchâtelet's view, were born rather than made, their 'otherness' recognisable in physiological characteristics (such as height, physique, skin colour and the shape of their sexual organs) which identified them as members of a breed apart. At the same time, and in contradiction of his biologically determinist view, Parent was prepared to concede that prostitutes were most often hapless proletarian women driven to sell their bodies out of economic necessity and not necessarily committed to prostitution as a way of life or as a career. Either way, however, since prostitution could never be eliminated, it followed that the authorities had a duty to control it, in order to prevent the spread of disease and infection throughout society.[41]

Parent-Duchâtelet's study lent the weight of scientific opinion to the regulatory controls imposed on prostitution by the French state. In Paris, control was in the hands of the Prefect of Police, with whom all prostitutes were obliged to enrol: in the provinces, the municipal authorities carried on the necessary supervision. Women registered as prostitutes were subjected to periodic examinations and could be detained in prison for infringements of the regulations. When treatment for venereal disease was necessary, they should be assigned to special hospitals, such as the sinister prison-hospital of Saint-Lazare in Paris. Ideally, it was the intention of Parent and the regulationists to confine the practice of prostitution to a *milieu clos*, to prevent it from impinging upon the sensibilities of children and 'honest' women. Business should be transacted only in certain 'tolerated' houses (*maisons tolérées*), preferably in 'red light' areas, the better to facilitate surveillance. Prostitutes should be inmates of their brothels, allowed out only at extremely rare intervals. Even the compulsory medical inspection of prostitutes should take place at the brothel. In practice, it proved impossible for the state to devise a system which would ensure that all prostitutes were known to the police and subject to bureaucratic control – Parent himself discovered that many *insoumises* (unregistered prostitutes) were active in Paris – but in the interests of public hygiene it was Parent's aim and that of the French administration to make the system as comprehensive as was humanly possible.[42]

The system did not go unchallenged. Its most hostile critics advocated its entire abolition on account of its flagrant exploitation of women. The example of Josephine Butler's crusade against the Contagious Diseases Acts in England inspired kindred spirits in France to launch a similar campaign against state control of prostitution in the 1870s. Significantly, the most sympathetic French response to the Butler initiative was to be found among Protestants like the Monod family and the economist Frédéric Passy.[43] Additionally, however, and quite distinct from this moral assault on the double standard, another, more obviously politically motivated, attack on the *police des moeurs* (vice squad) was mounted in the mid-1870s by Parisian radicals and progressives, led by the liberal economist Yves Guyot. Acting in the name of the rights of the individual and of the common law, the Guyot lobby denounced the abuses of bureaucratic authority, all too evident in the conduct of the vice squad, with a view, first of all, to embarrassing the 'Moral Order' regime of Marshal MacMahon and his Prime Minister Dufaure, and secondly, in the longer term, to dismantling the powers of the Prefecture of Police and placing this body under the jurisdiction of the Paris municipal council. Under the stimulus of the Guyot lobby's propaganda and a second visit to Paris on the part of Mrs Butler, the Association française pour l'Abolition de la Prostitution officielle was founded in 1878. Meantime, on the municipal council itself, Guyot engineered the setting up of a commission to examine the workings of the regulatory system.[44] The latter campaign reached its climax between 1879 and 1881 in fierce criticism of Prefect of Police Andrieux, who vividly recalls the episode in his colourful memoirs.[45] But as Guyot himself was later forced to admit, this first wave of abolitionism in France soon fizzled out for lack of general support.

The greatest threat to the regulatory system thus came less from the abolitionist lobby than from the fact that, inevitably, large numbers of women managed to operate outside of the system, as *insoumises*. Estimated to number between 30,000 and 40,000 in Paris in 1878, these clandestine prostitutes increasingly loomed large in the popular imagination as the carriers of disease and a serious threat to society. Shaken by the social upheaval of the Paris Commune of 1871 and frightened by the prospect of further social and political change, the French bourgeoisie saw in syphilis yet another peril to the maintenance of social order. Writers such as Maxime du Camp painted a lurid picture of how indulgence in clandestine prostitution in France could transmit the dreaded disease of the 'dangerous classes' to solid middle-class homes, with appalling consequences for the birth rate and the future of the race itself.[46] Worse still, Zola's Nana, published in 1880, portrayed how a prostitute could be the instrument of class vengeance through her ability to ruin her upper-class lovers.[47] Doctors likewise sounded the alarm, and called for the strictest possible surveillance of clandestine prostitution. According to one study of insoumises in Paris in the years between 1878 and 1887, 2681 out of 6842 clandestines (31.2%) were domestic servants.[48] The dangers of infection in the midst of the bourgeois household were only too obvious.

By 1880, supporters of regulated prostitution were arguing for even tighter controls over women who posed a threat to the fabric of society. Nor did it escape their attention that these insoumises often passed themselves off as ordinary working women — seamstresses, dressmakers, laundresses and the like.[49] The connection with sexual danger was one reason — though by no means the only one — why the ouvrière was perceived to be perhaps the most controversial figure in the debate on the 'woman question', an affront to bourgeois morality and the very negation of the ideal of femininity.

Chapter 8

Representations of the *ouvrière*

The discourse on female labour

Women's work was not new in the nineteenth century. What was new was that over the course of the century women's work came to be regarded as a social problem and gave rise to an extensive debate on the role of women in the workplace. For bourgeois commentators, *l'ouvrière* was manifestly a woman who failed to correspond with the idealised image of the 'angel of the hearth': and to flout the gender order constructed around the ideology of domesticity and *la femme au foyer* was to challenge the social order itself. The discourse on female labour thus has to be regarded in its own right, not merely as a source of information about working-class conditions but more importantly as a reflection of the attitudes and outlook of the protagonists in the debate, who were preoccupied by larger questions of identity, power relations and social change.[1] The purpose of the present chapter is to examine representations of the working-class woman in nineteenth-century France for the light which they shed on cultural constructions of womanhood and contemporary notions of femininity and sexuality. These in turn reveal much about the ideological context in which real nineteenth-century French women lived their lives.

Discovering *l'ouvrière*

Among the earliest critics of the nascent industrial civilisation were Catholic conservatives with a social conscience such as Jean-Paul-Alban de Villeneuve-Bargemont, a former prefect of the Nord under the restored Bourbons and the author of a work on *Christian Political Economy*. Like many of his kind, Villeneuve-Bargemont was nostalgic for what was remembered as a traditional, rural, hierarchical and organic social order and a bitter critic of the industrial order pioneered by Britain and already discernible in the textile towns of northern France such as Lille, seat of Villeneuve-Bargemont's prefecture.[2]

At the opposite end of the ideological spectrum, spokesmen for the new liberal economic and political order such as Baron Charles Dupin, a pillar of the establishment under the July Monarchy, regarded industrial work as a huge opportunity for women. Describing them as one of the productive 'forces' which needed to be harnessed in the interests of economic expansion, he rejected the idea that industrial work was inimical to women's nature and argued that, on the contrary, machines offered women the possibility of circumventing some of the limitations which nature had placed upon them. Furthermore, he insisted, industrial work was infinitely preferable to the backbreaking work of the fields carried out by peasant women, who were brutalised in the process and ended up looking like 'Hottentots' or 'Tartares'. It was his belief that improved opportunities in industry would strengthen the bonds of marriage between women and men of the labouring classes, since they would enjoy enhanced resources and a greater sense of stability.[3] In its purest form, liberal political economy was optimistic, not to say complacent, about the prospects for women as well as men in the bright, industrial, future.

'Political economy', however, did not speak with a single voice on the question of women workers. It was not only conservatives like Villeneuve-Bargemont who expressed fears concerning the pernicious impact of industrialisation on women and the family. From the time of the July Monarchy, a succession of social investigators, many of them doctors and adepts of the new science of political economy, carried out extensive surveys of the social condition of the working classes in the industrial regions of France, paying particular attention to questions of sexual morality and the potential threat to the social order posed by behaviour which failed to conform to the bourgeois code of conduct. Though apologists for the new capitalist economy and champions of market forces, at least some of these men were also avowed Christians who declared themselves to be troubled by the presence of women in the new factory-based labour force, on the grounds that this was an encouragement to promiscuity and moral depravity.[4]

A case in point was Louis Villermé, a Christian economist and author of perhaps the most celebrated of the early studies of the new industrial order, published in two volumes in 1840.[5] In all of the textile centres which he visited in the course of his research, he never failed to note the prevailing state of morality among the workers. Thus, in his estimation the morals of the workers in manufacturing industry in Alsace were particularly bad, notably on account of the mixing of the sexes at the workplace, especially at night. The worst living conditions, by contrast, were to be found at Lille, where in the infamous rue des Etaques the poorest families lived in squalid single-room basements and attics, subject to horrors which Villermé's rhetoric invites his readers to imagine as incest. Yet elsewhere in his study Villermé paid tribute to the 'good qualities of the wives of working-men' and denied that they were spendthrifts, noting rather the excellent influence which they could exercise over husbands who might otherwise have abandoned themselves to drunkenness and debauchery. Whether or not any of Villermé's claims were in any sense accurate is not the point here, though it is worth recording that his findings have been criticised as contradictory, statistically flawed, and punctuated by flights of rhetorical fancy.[6]

The point at issue is rather the significance he attached to the matter of sexual behaviour, which for Villermé and his ilk was a crucial performance indicator of social disorder.

Villermé's survey was followed by other studies which explicitly acknowledged their debt to his model and attempted to update his information. Armand Audiganne, for instance, writing in the mid-1850s, was disappointed to observe that the working-class family at Rouen appeared to be 'very imperfectly constituted' on account of the widespread practice of concubinage. In consequence, 'the wife does not have the role which ought to belong to her: she is more often considered less as a companion than as a servant and treated roughly'. Furthermore: 'This subjection stems from the fact that factory work, by leading women away from their natural mission as wives and mothers, makes them a simple cog in the mechanism of industrial production. Still more does it come from the precocious demoralisation of girls, which extinguishes in advance the respect which the spouse ought to obtain'. At Louviers, likewise, young female factory hands were allegedly free from any sense of modesty: conduct which elsewhere would destroy for good a woman's reputation passed unnoticed. By contrast, according to Audiganne, the difference in morality between women who worked at home and women factory workers was startling. Citing the example of the lacemakers of Caen, he praised their excellent morals: 'A transgression brings for her who has committed it an idelible shame and often obliges her to leave her region. Women's habits visibly show the effect s of the delicate work to which they give themselves over.' Among such workers, to be found generally in the region of Caen and Bayeux, family life was pronounced healthy and religious attachment strong.[7]

Audiganne's survey reached a wide audience (it was re-issued in a new and enlarged edition in 1860) but still more influential was L'Ouvrière, a work published the same year by Jules Simon, academic philosopher, moralist, liberal politician and future Prime Minister of the Third Republic. Initially published as a series of articles in La Revue des Deux-Mondes, L'Ouvrière was already in its fourth edition by 1862 and its seventh by 1871.[8] Its author was an unabashed apologist for the doctrine of separate spheres, expounded forcefully in his work La femme au vingtième siècle.[9]

In L'Ouvrière, Simon expressed his disquiet at the degree to which individual progress allegedly undermined the ideal of wife and mother and ruined the working-class family. Even if women workers in factories earned higher wages than in other forms of female employment, the price to be paid was always the renunciation of femininity and the comforts of home and hearth.

According to Simon drunkenness and libertine behaviour were concomitants of factory life and he sketched a lurid picture of young female factory hands preyed upon by drunken and lascivious foremen, and unable to obtain protection from fathers who were themselves drunks, or mothers who were of dubious morals. Some heartless parents, indeed, even pushed their daughters into dangerous liaisons, hoping to profit by any financial benefits to the girls. Teenage pregnancies were said to be common in a city such as Reims, earlier identified by Villermé as a place where girls as young as 12 prostituted themselves and described by Simon as a notorious supplier of the brothels of Paris. A further undesirable consequence of women's work in factories was damage to their physical, as well as their moral, health. Perhaps most troubling of all, however, was the blow dealt to patriarchal authority within the family, since a married woman who worked became a worker rather than a wife. Furthermore, such a woman could never be a true mother to her children, who were destined to grow up in their miserable hovels bereft of any experience of maternal love.

On the other hand, as a man of progress and champion of modernity, Simon recognised the impossibility of arresting the march of industry. His book was written against the general background of the expansion of the French economy under the Second Empire and at the particular moment of the signing of a free trade treaty between France and Great Britain, which guaranteed further industrial development and the intensification of competition. The prospect was exciting for some, but worrying for others. Simon wanted to reassure his readers that economic progress need not be threatening or disruptive, provided it was accompanied by stability and order in the private sphere. At the same time, he was also aware that for many women waged labour was not an option but a necessity. His solution was to suggest that domestic industry – ideally located in the countryside – was the form of work best suited to women. Working in their own households, women could combine looking after their children with both household chores and productive work. The crucial point, in Simon's view, was to ensure that women returned to their *foyers*, because only in this way could they carry out their mission to moralise the family as a whole, starting with their husbands. For what was required in the interests of society at large was that working-class *men*, as much as working-class women, rediscover the joys of family life. *L'Ouvrière*, ostensibly a factually based survey of working-class women's lives, was in essence a homily on the virtues of domesticity.[10]

The writings of Villermé, Audiganne, Simon and others, though more critical of the impact of industrialisation on women than, say, a Baron Dupin, were significant contributions to the wider discourse of French 'political economy' in the mid-nineteenth century. As Joan Scott has shown, political economists constituted a significant lobby, organised into a society (La Société d'Economie Politique) and, from 1842, possessed of a journal (*Le Journal des Economistes*) as well as being well connected in the worlds of government, business and the academy. What added to their prestige was the aura of scientific accuracy which surrounded their use of statistics. Yet the economists' apparently 'objective' data have been deconstructed by Scott and demonstrated to have been deployed with the aim of reinforcing *a priori* ideological assumptions, among which was the axiom that women's paid work required to be remunerated at a rate lower than men's. According to Jean-Baptiste

Say, the founding father of French political economy, a man's wages were intended to support not only himself but also his wife and children, whereas those of a woman worker were meant only to be a supplement to the family income. A basic premise of all orthodox economist thought was that, married or not, a woman invariably lived as a member of a family, not as an isolated individual.[11]

Thus, the statistical reports compiled in the name of political economy did not so much record the existing social order as attempt to refashion it in conformity with a particular vision of social relations. Scott furnishes the example of the *Statistique de l'industrie à Paris*, commissioned by the Paris chamber of commerce and published in 1851, a text that was more political than scientific, inspired by the theories of the political economists and at pains to refute the idea that there were irreconcilable differences between bosses and their workers (both of whom were referred to as *industriels* in the report). The authors of the *Statistique* also attributed paramount importance to well-ordered family life. Good workers invariably led well-ordered lives based on family values: bad workers were immoral and unruly. Good conduct was to be learned first and foremost in the home and it was therefore the special mission of the married women of the working classes to moralise their husbands. By the same token, women living and working alone were represented in the *Statistique* as a malign and antisocial influence. Rightly unable to earn a subsistence wage because of the iron laws of the market, they were doomed to fall back on their sexuality, abandoning themselves to either prostitution or the support of a lover.[12] If the working woman became a 'problem' in the first half of the nineteenth century, it was in no small measure because of the image she assumed in the eyes of political economists frightened by deviations from bourgeois norms in the gender order.

Working men and women's work

Concern about the impact of industrialisation on women and the family was by no means confined to bourgeois circles. Working men, too, nurtured deep-seated anxieties, as was evident from an enquiry instigated in 1842 at the behest of *L'Atelier*, the newspaper of the Parisian artisan elite. The investigation concluded that women's work was a major cause of the demoralisation of society and identified women workers in the quintessentially feminine trade of the garment industry as the least well off of all Parisian workers, earning starvation wages and subject to long lay-offs. Nevertheless, the situation of women workers in the large manufacturing centres was deemed to be even worse.

But how was the problem to be resolved? At this point, for all its genuine sympathy with the plight of exploited women workers, the *Atelier* inquiry revealed itself to be shot through with contradictions, since its call for improvements in women's pay and conditions sat ill with its preferred option of removing women from the labour force altogether. Echoing Villermé, *L'Atelier* denounced the encouragement to moral laxity given by manufacturing industry through its promiscuous mixing of the sexes in the workshops. The report also deplored the situation of women day labourers, 'obliged to abandon their households and the care of their children to indifferent neighbours'. Acccording to *L'Atelier* the real problem was that men's wages were insufficient to allow the upkeep of their entire family. In an ideal world, women would remain at home, perhaps working a little to supplement the family income, but primarily devoted to the tasks of child-rearing and household duties.[13]

L'Atelier had only 1000 subscribers but it spoke for the working-class elite among the skilled artisans of Paris – the vanguard of the most politically conscious and articulate workers in the 1840s.[14] By the 1850s and 1860s, this stratum of the working classes was at the forefront of attempts to give working men a voice through an organised labour movement, publishing a political declaration, the *Manifesto of the Sixty*, in 1864 and furnishing delegates for the French Section of the International Working Men's Association, or First International. At this juncture, however, organised labour in France was steeped in the doctrines of Pierre-Joseph Proudhon, the prophet of mutualist and cooperative socialism but also, as we have seen, a misogynist of the deepest dye. Like Proudhon, most of the artisan elite had little sympathy for the burgeoning industrial working class in general and for women workers in particular. The *Manifesto of the Sixty* pledged its opposition to a situation in which 'women readily abandon the home for excessive work, contrary to their nature and destroying the family'.[15] In 1866, at the first congress of the International, the French delegation submitted that: 'From a physical, moral, and social viewpoint, women's work outside the home should be energetically condemned as a cause of the degeneration of the race and as one of the agents of demoralization used by the capitalist class'.[16]

True, two of the French delegates (Varlin and Boudon) objected to this formulation, and pointed rather to exploitation and lack of education as the real causes of physical and moral decline – causes which could be eliminated by effective organisation of work and the practice of mutualism. Work, they maintained, was a necessity, not an option, for women, and labour militants should strive to ameliorate their conditions rather than suppress their livelihoods. These words, however, fell on deaf ears and the congress as a whole voted to adopt the resolution put forward by the French majority.[17] Similarly, in the poems and songs of Eugène Pottier, the author of the workers' anthem *L'Internationale*, women's activism was to be confined to pacifism and the search for peace, in which cause they were exhorted if necessary to follow the example of Lysistrata in withholding their sexual favours:

A bas la guerre! en grève! en grève!
La femme doit briser le glaive,
Nargue à l'époux, nargue à l'amant!
Jusqu'au désarmement:
Les femmes sont en grève.

S'il faut recruter vos milices
Fécondez tigre ou guenon
Nous ne sommes plus vos complices,
Pour fournir la chair à canon.

('Down with war! Strike! Strike! Woman must break the blade, flout the husband, flout the lover until disarmament: women are on strike. If you must recruit your militias, fecundate the tiger or the she-monkey. We are no longer your accomplices in furnishing cannon-fodder.')[18]

The defeat of the Paris Commune and the repression which followed drastically curtailed the development of the French labour movement and it was the mid-1870s before signs of life began to be visible in the shape of 'workers' congresses'. The first of these national gatherings of militants was held in Paris in 1876 and delegates devoted an entire day to debating the topic of women's work. Male delegates continued to entertain grave reservations about the presence of women in the factory-based labour force, though reluctantly they conceded that on account of the inadequacy of male wages women might be compelled to engage in domestic work to supplement the family income. Women's work likewise featured prominently on the agenda of the next congress, held at Lyon in February 1878. On this occasion male militants put forward the formula of 'equal pay for equal work' as a none-too-subtle stratagem to remove women from the workplace altogether (since they believed that there could never be any equality between the work performed by men and that done by women). The congress also reaffirmed the primacy of a woman's role as wife and mother and characterised female labour as a necessary evil tolerable only till such time as men's wages were sufficiently high to permit women to commit themselves to the ideal of *la femme au foyer*.[19]

The third workers' congress, however, held at Marseille in October 1879, appeared to mark a decisive shift in attitude on the part of French organised labour. For once only a minority of the delegates spoke against women's rights, while the majority rallied behind the notion of complete civil and political equality, ardently defended at the congress by the young feminist firebrand, Hubertine Auclert, a collaborator on the newspaper *Le Prolétaire* and the delegate of the feminist society Le Droit des Femmes. In a gesture designed to attract women to the cause of collectivism, the Marseille conference voted in favour of a resolution which emphatically endorsed the right of women to a place of equality within the working-class movement. Abandoning the idea that men alone should work and provide for their families, the resolution of the congress called for an equitable division between men and women, so that work which involved skill should be given to 'the weaker persons, men or women' as appropriate, and that work involving muscular effort be given to the strong. Women, proclaimed the resolution, had not only the right but the duty to work and they should take their place alongside men in leading humanity to a brighter future:

Men and women ... will govern this society together and will share in the exercise of the same rights, in public life as in private ... in all circumstances, women will have their freedom of action like men. The congress, considering that a role must depend on the choice of the individual who fills it, if it is to be filled, assigns no special role to women, they will take the roles and the places in society to which their vocations call them.[20]

It seemed that, at long last, women themselves were beginning to have a crucial say in debates on the 'woman question'.

Women's voices

Women's voices, in truth, had never been absent from the debate on the social consequences of industrialisation, but they had certainly struggled to make themselves heard. As has been seen, in the 1830s and 1840s, working-class women, many of them fired by the doctrines of Saint-Simonianism, acquired a heightened sense of political consciousness and threw themselves into the struggle to improve women's lot. In 1848 they identified with the struggle to create a democratic and social Republic, which would confer on women full rights of citizenship and recognise their 'right to work'. The demise of the Second Republic and the establishment of the Second Empire may have ended the prospect of obtaining change by means of collective action, but it did not eliminate female voices from the controversies surrounding women's work.

Jeanne Deroin, in her English exile, prepared several editions of an *Almanach des femmes*, which, in addition to pressing the case for political emancipation, reaffirmed women's rights as the basis for the organisation of labour and looked forward to a day 'when work for all will guarantee to each member of the human family, without distinction of sex or race, the complete development and free use of their moral, intellectual and physical faculties'. True to her utopian socialist formation, she continued to link the destiny of women with that of the proletariat – a theme underscored by her inclusion of a moving tribute to her martyred friend and comrade, Pauline Roland, whose example 'will fortify the apostle of the new faith and add new recruits to their ranks'.[21]

In exile, Deroin necessarily remained a marginal figure, unable to make much of an impact on the debate on female labour as it unfolded under the Second Empire. More weighty was the contribution of Julie Daubié (1824–74), a native of the Vosges and the woman destined to become the first of her sex to take the *baccalauréat*, in 1862. Fired by a determination to become educated, she mastered Latin with the help of her brother, a priest, and earned her own living as a governess. In 1859 she submitted a prize-winning essay to the Academy of Lyon on the subject of female poverty, a study subsequently published in 1866 as *La femme pauvre au xixe siècle*.[22]

Daubié's work was intended to be – and indeed was recognised as – a serious treatise on political economy, though her viewpoint was informed by a feminist perspective and a sympathy for poor women which made her a critic of both classical economic theory and the moralising of the likes of Villermé. Nor did she share Jules Simon's vision of an economic order in which women were no longer compelled to work for wages but could devote themselves fully to the role of wife and mother. Far from wishing to see women excluded from the labour force, Daubié lamented that industrialisation had brought about a reduction in the jobs available to women, since many of their traditional occupations had been mechanised and taken over by men. Dressmaking was an obvious example, dominated by wealthy capitalists whom she ridiculed as 'bearded *couturières*'. Poverty, in Daubié's estimation, was caused by low wages, and low wages were the result of relegating women to so-called 'feminine' jobs. Whether in industry, the arts, letters or science, women were the victims of discrimination.

The solution for Daubié was twofold. As far as single women were concerned, what was required was the introduction of measures which would ameliorate women's working conditions. Fundamental was co-education, along with technical education and training, to ensure that young women had the same job opportunities as young men. Equal wages should also be paid for equal work. As regards married women, Daubié's concern was to ensure that husbands should be made to face up to their family responsibilities: hence the need for legal reform to give women equal rights within marriage, and political reform, to give women a say in the legislative process. Paternity suits should be permitted and absentee husbands made to contribute to the upkeep of the families which they had abandoned.[23]

It may be that, as Joan Scott maintains, Daubié was naive in seeking to differentiate so sharply between single women and married women – in effect, like the political economists generally – taking for granted a rigid separation of spheres between work and family and a strict compartmentalisation between the categories of 'economy' and 'morality', but by the standards of the mid-nineteenth century her position was an advanced feminist one.[24] Consistent with the views which she expressed in *La femme pauvre*, she became an activist in the campaign to abolish legalised prostitution and participated in the feminist movement of the late 1860s and early 1870s, founding her own society called the Association pour l'Emancipation de la Femme.[25]

The interest aroused by works such as that of Daubié and Jules Simon was evident in the debates on women's work organised under the auspices of republicans, socialists and trade unionists in the late 1860s, which provided a platform for feminists such as Paule Minck and André Léo to articulate their disagreement with Proudhonist male militants who persisted in prescribing only a domestic role for working-class women. At a public meeting in July 1868, Minck poured scorn on this ideal and suggested that what needed to be addressed was not ideals but practicalities – in particular the practical matter of female exploitation in the workplace. That this took place was not in doubt, but the appropriate conclusion to be drawn was not that women should be banned from working: rather, they should be paid a living wage. It was not excessive work on the part of women which threatened 'the bastardization of the race', but rather 'the faulty distribution of women's salaries, which leads so fatally to debauchery, and all the evils it engenders'. Work in itself was a good and enriching thing, for women as much as for men. Rounding on the Proudhonists, Minck accused them of degrading woman and putting her under man's yoke:

> By ceasing to make her a worker, you deprive her of her liberty, and thereby, of her responsibility (and this is why I insist so much on this issue), so that she no longer will be a free and intelligent creature but will merely be a reflection, a small part of her husband.

In any case, she continued, not all women were wives and mothers. Daughters, widows, wives maltreated or abandoned by their husbands also had their rights and needs. Such women required to earn their own living, but it certainly did not follow that women's work would therefore force down men's wages. True justice was to be sought in the formula 'equal pay for equal work'.[26]

Though a champion of women's economic (and political) rights, Minck should not be considered an exponent of the view that gender should have no part to play in the allocation of social roles. Subscribing to Ernest Legouvé's notion of 'equality in difference', she regarded women and men as having been equipped by nature to perform different gender-based activities in the world of work. Men would take on the heavier tasks; women those which demanded dexterity and skill. Other feminists of the 1860s such as André Léo rejected any such putative complementarity and argued rather for complete sex equality.[27]

It would be untrue, however, to suppose that Proudhonism numbered no disciples among women. When trade unionism began to revive after the disaster of the Paris Commune, female delegates were among those who attended the workers' congresses of the 1870s. In 1876, the obscure Valentine Raoult accepted that 'it would be more natural for men to provide a living for their wives and daughters' and advocated the setting up of 'cooperative workshops' from finance provided by 'people's banks', to be administered by the menfolk of the women who worked in them.[28] More commonly, however, women affirmed their opposition to any attempts to exclude them from the labour force. At the Lyon congress of 1878, one woman delegate, Marie Finet, reiterated the argument of Paule Minck that work was beneficial in itself. Women should always work, she declared, even if they were not obliged to do so for reasons of economic necessity. Work made them free and independent and was the means to obtain equality with men.[29] As we have seen, a growing number of working men seemed to be susceptible to such arguments and at the Marseille congress of 1879, thanks in part to the persuasive powers of the feminist Hubertine Auclert, the delegates passed their wide-ranging resolution on female equality.

Subsequently, both trade unionists and collectivist socialists would reveal themselves to be incapable of living up to the principle of gender equality so comprehensively stated in 1879. By this date, however, some women at least had grounds to hope that the alliance between feminism and socialism, forged initially in the days of the July Monarchy but tested to breaking point by the experience of the Second Republic and the rise of Proudhonist antifeminism, might be renewed and extended at a juncture when newer forms of socialism – Marxism in particular – seemed poised to relaunch collectivism as a serious political and ideological force in French society.

Chapter 9

Reformulating the 'woman question'

From literary polemics to organised feminism

After the *coup d'état* of 1851 and the resuscitation of the Empire in 1852 the outlook for feminism in France was not promising. Napoleon III liked to think of himself as a man of progress but his modernising ideas did not include the advancement of women's rights. Above all a *politique* and political manipulator, Napoleon III's main preoccupation was maintaining himself in power and perpetuating his dynasty. Though not the despot that his many enemies on both Left and Right made him out to be, he had more than enough problems without seeking to add to them through embroilment in the 'woman question'. His interest in women remained personal and sexual, as a long stream of mistresses attested.[1]

Feminist aspirations were therefore centred on opponents of the Empire, and above all on its most committed opponents, the Republicans. In the 1850s, the republican movement still suffered from the damage inflicted by the repression which had followed in the wake of the *coup d'état* and which deprived it of leaders who were either in prison or in exile. Effective opposition was also impossible on account of laws which banned free assembly and a free press. Even so, a clandestine republican movement continued to operate underground, especially in the larger cities like Paris and Lyon, where its members included workers, disaffected members of the bourgeoisie (frequently lawyers and doctors), intellectuals and students. Though divided internally and in no way able to mount a serious challenge to Napoleon III's regime, the Republicans reminded the Emperor that he faced a hard core of opposition which would not rest until he had been removed. By 1858, and in spite of all the pressures brought to bear on the electorate to support only 'official' candidates, they even had five deputies in the Legislative Body.

In the 1860s, as the Empire underwent progressive 'liberalisation', republicanism expanded rapidly, taking full advantage of the restoration of freedom of the press in 1868. Though many old-timers from 1848 were still involved in the struggle, what was striking about the republican revival was the emergence of a new generation of leaders who had pondered the lessons of failure in the past. While committed to democracy, they now appreciated that there was more to establishing the Republic than introducing universal suffrage. It was, after all, manhood suffrage that had brought Louis Napoleon to power in the first place in December 1848, while both plebiscites and the ballot box continued to confer on Napoleon III's rule an element of legitimacy which testified to the counter-revolutionary potential of the principle of popular sovereignty. Republicans now believed that the electorate had to be thoroughly educated in republican principles if the Republic were to be founded on a truly lasting basis. It was not enough to capture power: to hold on to it, minds and hearts had to be won over, which is why Republicans came to attach paramount importance to controlling the educational system, and adopted an implacable anticlericalism in the face of the determination of the Church, abetted by reactionaries, to resist the progressive secularisation of the state and of society.[2]

It was understandable, therefore, that feminists should wish to align themselves with what appeared to be the most progressive force in France in the mid-nineteenth century. As we shall see, however, it was their misfortune to do so at a time when the new leadership of the republican movement harboured deep fears about the viability of democracy and would show itself highly resistant to experimenting further with the franchise by extending it to women. The alliance between feminism, republicanism and anticlericalism, which was to succeed in bringing an organised feminist movement into being, was not one which, in the long run, would work necessarily to women's advantage.

Literary feminism

In the 1850s, at a time when American feminists were laying the foundation of a mass movement and British feminists, inspired by the American example and grouped in the Langham Place circle, established a platform in the *English Woman's Journal*, French feminists could do little more than offer individual literary responses to the demeaning discourse on women to be found in the works of writers such as Proudhon and Michelet.

That the antifeminist backlash of the 1840s had not abated was apparent from Proudhon's *De la justice dans la Révolution et dans l'Eglise* (*On Justice in the Revolution and in the Church*), published in 1858. A defence of atheism, materialism and the scientific outlook against what Proudhon dismissed as the obscurantist claims of religion, *De la justice* devoted two chapters to the themes of women and the family which furnish further evidence of his misogyny, which became even more explicit in a later work, *La Pornocratie ou les femmes dans les temps modernes* (*Pornocracy, or Women in Modern Times*), published posthumously in 1875. *De la justice* sought to demonstrate the inferiority of women from every point of view – physical, intellectual and moral – and, in a grotesque parody of the positivism of the age, even tried to express this as a mathematical formula. Attributing women's physical inferiority to the more aggressive sexual drives of the male, Proudhon affirmed that man alone was the complete human being. Woman, by contrast, was 'a diminutive of man, and lacks an organ necessary to become anything other than a potential adult'. Nature had bequeathed to man the gift of semen, which made him strong, whereas nature had made woman a 'passive being, a receptacle for the seed that man alone produces, a place of incubation – like the earth for the grain of wheat'. By Proudhon's calculations, this physical superiority of men over women worked out in the proportion of three to two. Its logical consequence was that man was the master and that woman should obey.

Nor, according to Proudhon, did women make up for their physical inferiority by superior intellectual or moral qualities. On the contrary, their intellectual inferiority he held to be yet another of nature's iron laws, impervious, even, to the remedy of better education. Genius, for Proudhon, was an attribute of masculinity, a 'virility of the mind'. Women, like children and eunuchs, lacked the capacity for abstract thought, generalisation, invention and conceptualisation. Once again a mathematical formula allowed men's intellectual superiority to be represented as three is to two. The same ratio applied to women's moral inferiority, which was manifest to Proudhon not only in prostitution and feminine vanity but also in women's supposed indifference to the principles of justice and equality and their alleged preference for privilege and flattery. Altogether, in Proudhon's crazed arithmetic, men were superior to women in the proportion of 27 ($3 \times 3 \times 3$) to 8 ($2 \times 2 \times 2$).[3]

To deflect the charge of misogyny, Proudhon explained that he had ventured to write about the social function of women only with some reluctance. His quarrel was not with women themselves but rather with those who demanded rights on their behalf (Ernest Legouvé was a prime target). Having 'proved' – at least to his own satisfaction – that woman was demonstrably inferior to man, he drew the conclusion that her subordination was inevitable, the work both of nature and of justice. So-called emancipation would bring not happiness but only misery and servitude to women. Their one hope of salvation lay in marriage, an institution of which Proudhon strongly approved. True to his peasant origins, however, he envisaged a patriarchal arrangement in which the head of the household reigned supreme. Wives would perform household chores, raise the children, and perhaps engage in good works, but would have no truck with the outside world: politics and public life were the equivalent of war and as such should be left to men. On one point at least Proudhon agreed with the Church, which he otherwise reviled: the essential purpose of marriage was procreation. Disdaining to pretend, like the Romantics, that women were merely different but still equal, Proudhon made no secret of his view that subordination was required of women. In a letter to a friend written in 1851, he explained that he himself had taken the decision to marry at the age of 41 so as to become the father of a family, and had chosen a simple working woman who was neither a *bas-bleu* (bluestocking) or *cordon bleu* (expert cook). Love, in Proudhon's view, had no part to play in marriage formation, since 'a marriage born only of love is so close to shame that a father who gives it his consent deserves reproach'.[4]

The full extent of Proudhon's misogyny was revealed in the posthumous *La Pornocratie*, a work he was preparing at his death in order to hit back at his feminist critics. It included a defence of the double standard of morality, denying a wronged wife the right to resort to the law against an errant husband but championing a husband's right to justice against a wife who had wronged him, even to the point where he should have the right to kill her in a wide variety of cases, including adultery, immorality, treason, drunkenness, debauchery, financial wastefulness, theft, or 'obstinate insubordination' ('*insoumission obstinée*'). He also declared his opposition to birth control, denouncing the widespread contemporary practice of *coitus interruptus*.[5] Proudhon's hatred of women verged on the pathological.

Proudhon found his audience mainly among skilled workers and professional revolutionaries. Jules Michelet reached a much wider reading public with his works *L'Amour* (1858) and *La Femme* (1859), which he consciously conceived of as popular books designed to fulfil the educative role that Republicans now regarded as fundamental to their project. For Michelet the woman question was inextricably bound up with the idea of the Revolution and the establishment of the Republic, because it was his belief that women were largely to blame for the failure of the attempts to found the Republic in 1792 and 1848. With proper education, however, they could play a vital role in the creation of a viable republican regime. For Michelet, the matter was of great urgency. As he attempted to show in his history of women during the Revolution, published in 1854, women remained implacable enemies of progress and the slaves of superstition. Working hand in hand with the priests, women had been the heart and souls of resistance to the Revolution in the Vendée, where 'in each family, in each house, the counter-revolution had an ardent, zealous, tireless preacher, in no way suspect, sincere, passionately naive, who wept and suffered, and did not say a single word which wasn't – or didn't seem to be – the bursting of a broken heart. An immense force, truly invincible'. In the words of one republican commander cited by Michelet, 'it is women who are the cause of our troubles; without women, the Republic would already be established, and we would be back home, happy'.[6]

At the same time, women, in Michelet's view, were to blame for many of the ills of the contemporary world: they were frivolous and spendthrift in the upper classes, given over to the celibate life and to prostitution in the poorer classes. These faults, however, were not innate, but the product of misguided education and a failure of comprehension. Other social critics, like the utopian socialists, had rightly seen the connection between politics and morality, but they had proposed the wrong solutions. The destruction of the family and female emancipation were not the answer: rather, it was necessary to understand woman in the light of the laws of biology. Michelet therefore approached the woman question from a standpoint that reflected his familiarity with contemporary scientific and medical treatises as well as his own moral and political views. His disquisitions on women were essentially a discourse on the female body, based on the premise that woman was a permanent invalid, the slave of nature and her menstrual cycle.[7] The latter was also decisive in determining her intellectual qualities. Whereas man was a brain, because his sexual energy was transformed into cerebral energy, woman for Michelet was a womb, the organ which was 'the principal seat of their affections, their caprices, their passions'.[8]

Women's debility meant that their proper place was in the home, not the workplace. It was man's privilege to be the breadwinner: a wife fulfilled her marital obligations by taking care of her husband, lavishing on him her love and tenderness and refreshing his heart. A woman should marry at the age of 18, choosing a husband who was at least ten years older. They should live in splendid isolation in the countryside, far removed from the corrupting influences of the city, though they might employ a live-in rustic maid who would have no share in the couple's intimate *têtes-à-têtes*. In this way, the husband would be the sole educator of his wife and she would be removed from the interfering presence of relatives (and of course priests).[9]

The views of Michelet and Proudhon caused deep offence to feminists and provoked two significant counter-blasts. The first came from the pen of Juliette Lamber (1836–1936), later more famous as the celebrated political hostess Mme Edmond Adam.[10] Encouraged to develop an independence of mind by her father, a republican medical practitioner from Picardy, she married young and gave birth to a child before separating from her husband, Alexis La Messine, a civil servant. In Paris, she made contact with the Saint-Simonian circle which published the review *La Revue Philosophique* and it was these radicals who encouraged her to vent her outrage against Proudhon in print. Published under the name of Lamber, a variant on her real maiden name of Lambert, in a vain attempt to prevent her husband profiting from her royalties, *Idées anti-proudhoniennes sur l'amour, la femme et le mariage* appeared just months after *De la justice* in August 1858 and assailed Proudhon's proposition that women had been subordinated to men by nature. Lamber well understood that what Proudon had effectively done was to legitimise the principle that might is right – an unpardonable crime in the eyes of women who were conscious of their own moral worth and their capacity for autonomous action. Quite apart from the fact that women had their own kind of physical strength – the ability to endure childbirth, for instance, which was beyond even a Hercules – Proudhon was also mistaken in regarding physical force as the basis of the social order. The strongest men were by no means those with the most power, since brains always held sway over brawn.

Faithful to the Saint-Simonian creed, Lamber ridiculed Proudhon's assertion that love was related only to procreation and affirmed her personal conviction that society was founded on two principles, the masculine and the feminine. Each was indispensable for true social harmony and the progress of humanity, which meant that there was a *de facto* equality between the sexes. Each sex had duties proper to it and a sexual division of labour was also appropriate in the labour force. Men should do jobs which required muscle power, women those which required taste, tact and dexterity. Thus men would be masons, carpenters, joiners, locksmiths and the like; women would be seamstresses, retailers, milliners, florists and so on. Like the women of 1848 Lamber had no doubts about women's right to work and to form part of the productive forces in society, and argued that they should receive training and vocational education. According to Lamber, it was work which had emancipated men and it would be work which emancipated women.

Denying that she was in any way the enemy of the family, Lamber claimed that she shared Proudhon's desire to see women become good wives and mothers. Where she parted company with him, however, was over his attempt to reduce the whole of women's experience to family life. Not every woman was cut out for the role of mother hen. Many did not marry, and even within the household there were those who legitimately wanted to work, for the obvious reason that two wages were better than one. Prostitution and poverty were not the consequence of female labour but of inadequate earning power. Work, provided it was not excessive (in which case it was brutalising), was always a force for good. Careers for women would lead to the closure of the brothels – a prospect some men would doubtless view with dismay. In her conclusion, in language which still has a modern ring to it, Lamber pleaded for women to be considered not merely as playthings of men or as baby machines but as autonomous individuals, free to develop their own values and their own laws. In what was obviously an extrapolation from her own experience, she set out the case for divorce in the event of irretrievable marriage breakdown.[11]

A second riposte to Proudhon and Michelet came from Jenny d'Héricourt (1807–75) in the form of a two-volume work entitled *La femme affranchie* published in 1860 and in an English version which appeared in New York in 1864. D'Héricourt, in fact, had already crossed swords with Proudhon in private correspondence and in the pages of *La Revue Philosophique* in December 1856 and February 1857, and Lamber had initially expected her to lead the attack against *De la justice*, only entering the fray herself when the older woman declined to do so. Hailing from the Franche-Comté, d'Héricourt seems to have attempted to study medicine in Paris in the late 1840s and eventually practised as a midwife. Self-consciously an intellectual, she nevertheless disapproved of the irregular lives of women writers like George Sand and Daniel Stern, but refused to accept Proudhon's derogatory remarks about her sex. Rejecting his suggestion that she herself might be an exception to the general run of feminine humanity, she declared her solidarity with all women and informed him that, if she herself had acquired any honour, that redounded to the honour of the female sex as a whole.[12]

In 1860, however, it was not Proudhon but Michelet who was her main target, on the grounds that a false friend was more dangerous than a declared enemy. The honeyed words of the poet were seductive, whereas those of the polemicist had the bitterness of absinthe, yet in d'Héricourt's view intelligent women had much to object to in Michelet's pronouncements. First and foremost, they were outraged by Michelet's claim that woman was 'a perpetual invalid, who should be shut up in a gynoceum in company with a dairy maid, as fit company only for chickens and turkeys'. Michelet's biology was defective, since it violated the simple biological law that no physiological condition could be a morbid condition: a woman's period was not a disease, but something normal. It was also outrageous of Michelet to claim that woman was created for man. Women, like men, were human beings possessed of intellect and free will, with the right to develop their faculties and to act freely. To maintain women in subjection, as proposed by Michelet, was a violation of human rights and 'an odious abuse of force'.

As for the charge that women were counter-revolutionary by nature, d'Héricourt turned Michelet's argument on its head. Women's rights had the same foundation as men's rights: to deny the former was to endanger the latter. Women had played a prominent part in the Revolution of 1789 precisely because they, too, wanted civil and political rights. It was not they who had rejected the Revolution but the Revolution which had rejected them. The same thing had happened in 1848. Women were essential to the success of the revolutionary enterprise: if they were not included, all the struggles would be in vain. The real enemies of progress and the Revolution were those who opposed liberty for women, and in a stern warning to Michelet and other Republicans d'Héricourt predicted that if 'the friends of progress and of the Revolution' would not emancipate women, women in search of their rights might turn to their adversaries.[13] Here d'Héricourt touched a raw nerve of the burgeoning republican movement. By daring to suggest that Republicans were not as progressive as they liked to make themselves out to be, she courted unpopularity and disavowal. Lamber did not go so far out on a limb: indeed, when later she had to choose between feminism and republicanism she plumped for the latter and became a pillar of the republican establishment after 1870. The prescient d'Héricourt, on the other hand, remained a more marginal and isolated figure.

The beginnings of organisation

In replying to Michelet, d'Héricourt recognised that rhetoric alone was not enough to effect change: women needed to act and to organise. She therefore called on them to establish a journal, to propagandise among the people, and to found a Polytechnic Institute for women. Working-class women should be encouraged to form trade unions, and assistance should be provided for the redemption of 'fallen women'. In these ways there would emerge an 'Apostleship of Women' based on the principle that unity is strength. On the question of women's suffrage, d'Héricourt agreed that there was a case for postponing the extension of the franchise to uneducated women. It was true that uneducated men had the vote, but the consequences had been disastrous. In the first instance, it was better that women should concentrate on obtaining civil rights and better education rather than demanding immediate political equality.[14] With these counsels, d'Héricourt anticipated the strategy which would be that of the bourgeois liberal feminist movement which came into being in the last years of the Second Empire and took off under the Third Republic.

The potential for such a movement began to be apparent in the 1860s, when other women added their own voices to the protests of Lamber and d'Héricourt. One of the more strident was that of Olympe Audouard (1830–90), a native of Marseille who was the victim of an unhappy marriage and travelled extensively after she separated from her husband, earning income from travel books which she wrote about her observations of the Ottoman Empire, Russia and the United States.[15] In 1862, aided by a number of friends who included Alexandre Dumas *père*, she started a literary journal *Le Papillon*, but her plans to found a political review *La Revue Cosmopolite* incurred the opposition of the Imperial censors, who objected not only to her anticlericalism and her radicalism but also to her sex. Furious at being told that, as a woman, she was banned from political journalism, Audouard riposted in 1866 with a tract entitled *Guerre aux hommes* (*War on Men*), which gave full reign to her feminist rage by dividing men into fifteen categories of villain, which included the 'toad' and the 'chameleon' as well as the 'sphynx' and the 'skilled seducer'.[16] Audouard also petitioned the Imperial parliament in 1867 to make women citizens by granting them civil and political equality. A well-known public lecturer, Audouard was strongly in favour of the re-enactment of a divorce law. On one occasion, in a debate between conservatives and socialists on the subject of marriage, separation and divorce held in February 1870, she denounced conventional marriage as 'based on the despotic tyranny of man and on the subjugation, the total annihilation, of the will of woman', which impelled the police to stop the proceedings.[17]

Other feminists of the Second Empire era included the novelist André Léo (1832–1900). *Née* Léodile Bréa, she was the widow of the Saint-Simonian and forty-eighter Grégoire Champseix exiled to Switzerland after the *coup d'état* and was the author of a number of fictional works which explored the contemporary plight of women: *Un mariage scandaleux* (1862); *Une vieille fille* (1864); and *Un divorce* (1866).[18] Virginie Griess-Traut (1814–98), who subsidised a Fourierist school run by Victor Considérant from her considerable personal fortune, was another veteran of the utopian socialist cause, while the *Revue Philosophique* group to which Lamber and d'Héricourt were attached testified to the lingering importance of Saint-Simonianism as a source of feminist inspiration.[19] Similarly, it was the ex-Saint-Simonian, François Barthélemy Arlès-Dufour (1797–1872) who helped Julie Daubié become the first woman to be allowed to sit the *baccalauréat* examinations, in 1862.[20]

Among the more radical militants, who, in the tradition of Jeanne Deroin and Pauline Roland, continued to identify the cause of women with that of proletarian revolution were the future *communardes* Paule Minck and Louise Michel. Minck

(1839–1901) was the daughter of an exiled Polish nobleman and made an independent career for herself as a dressmaker and language teacher in Paris following the breakdown of her marriage to a fellow Pole, gaining a reputation as an orator in radical circles in the later 1860s (she joined the International in 1869).[21] Michel (1830–1905), soon to pass into legend as the 'Red Virgin' of the Paris Commune, was the daughter of an illicit liaison between a nobleman and a servant, and grew up in the château at Vroncourt (Haute-Marne) where her mother worked. Having qualified as a primary schoolteacher, she refused to teach in a state school so as not to have to swear an oath of loyalty to the Empire and came to Paris in the hope of making a literary career and promoting the Revolution. Passionately keen on education, she was an assiduous attender at the night school classes run by prominent republican leaders like Jules Favre, Jules Simon and Eugène Pelletan.[22]

The feminist revival was thus nourished by different sources. Individuals were crucial, but they themselves formed part of wider currents of opinion such as utopian socialism and reform movements of various kinds. Campaigners for causes as diverse as dress reform, divorce, anti-vivisection, vegetarianism and spiritualism (the last included Olympe Audouard) might serve to stimulate a degree of feminist consciousness. Pacifism was another cause which attracted women such as Eugénie Potonié-Pierre, wife of the prominent pacifist campaigner Edmond Potonié-Pierre and later a prominent feminist leader in the 1890s.[23] Educational reform, and notably the demand for free secular and compulsory elementary schooling, promoted energetically by the influential Education League of Jean Macé and his fellow Freemasons and free thinkers, inevitably fuelled the debate concerning women's education after 1866, as did the secondary courses for girls set up by Victor Duruy in his spell at the Ministry of Education.[24] Equally important was the revival of trade union activity and the founding of the First International in 1864, which led to further polemics on the subject of women's work.

From June 1868 public meetings were organised on this issue under the auspices of republicans, socialists and trade unionists and it soon became clear that, in the light of the social investigations carried out by the likes of Jules Simon and Julie Daubié, the question had become even more controversial than it had been back in 1848. Indeed, the attitude of many male trade unionists, who were largely Proudhonist in outlook, had hardened against the notion of anything but a domestic role for working-class women. At the public meetings of 1868, feminists like Minck and André Léo took the lead in expressing their dissent and in defending women's right to work, though their positions on the matter were far from identical. Minck, though a champion of women's economic and political rights, subscribed to Ernest Legouvé's formula of 'equality in difference', and viewed women and men as equipped to perform different gender-based activities in the labour force: men would do the heavier work, women those tasks which required dexterity and skill. Léo on the other hand rejected the notion of complementarity and insisted on complete equality.

In July 1868 she and her supporters issued a manifesto which called for the establishment of a socialist-feminist league of women to defend women's rights.[25]

What more than anything brought coherence and a measure of solidarity to the nascent feminist movement of the 1860s, however, was its close identification with the cause of a new, dynamic and anticlerical republicanism which had as its prime objective the overthrow of the Empire. And nowhere was the alliance between republicanism, anticlericalism and feminism more apparent than in the careers of Maria Deraismes and Léon Richer, the two individuals who, more than others, deserve the credit for launching feminism as an organised movement at the end of the Second Empire and who can rightly be regarded as the joint founders of liberal feminism in France.

Maria Deraismes (1828–94) was born into a freethinking and republican family of the *grande bourgeoisie* and grew up in Pontoise. After receiving an excellent classical education of the kind conventionally prescribed for sons, she was left a wealthy woman by the death of her parents and never married, probably so as not to compromise her much prized independence or to be obliged to submit to marriage laws which she despised. Keen to establish a literary reputation, she was the author of a number of plays and by 1865 was also addressing herself to aspects of the woman question in pamphlets and journalism which called for better education for women and for recognition of their right to participate in the wider world of the economy, politics and the arts. She made her debut as an orator in 1866, when a vicious series of articles on the subject of 'bluestockings' (that is, literary women) by another misogynist writer, Barbey d'Aurevilly, prompted her into a public response. Stung in particular by Barbey's remarks about the aged Eugénie Niboyet, she accepted an invitation from sympathetic friends among the Freemasons to lecture at their hall, the Grand Orient, where she enjoyed a notable success.[26] Sex inequality, she told her audience, was not something natural but 'a social fiction, a human invention'.[27]

Following on from the lecture series, Deraismes agreed to participate in a feminist group called the Société pour la Revendication du Droit des Femmes, which met for the first time in 1866 at the house of André Léo. A heterogeneous collection of women, the group included Paule Minck and Louise Michel as well as the utopian socialist Eliska Vincent, the anarchist Elie Reclus and his wife Néomie, Mme Jules Simon, the wife of the moderate Republican politician and future Prime Minister, and Caroline de Barrau, whose prime concern was with the rehabilitation of prostitutes. Because of the range of political opinion represented in the Society, it was decided to settle on a minimum programme on which all could agree, and its main objective was therefore defined as being to work for the improvement of girls' education.[28]

Deraismes found her closest collaborator, however, not with other women but with a man, Léon Richer (1824–1911). A former notary clerk turned journalist, a

Freemason and a republican activist of pronounced anticlerical bent, Richer was best known in republican circles for the column entitled 'Letters of a free thinker to a village priest' which he wrote for the newspaper *L'Opinion Nationale*. A married man, he had a son and enjoyed the support of his wife in his commitment to feminism, which he embraced primarily out of the conviction that the legal subordination of women prescribed by the law was unjust. In 1869, putting his legal knowledge and journalistic experience at the service of the burgeoning feminist movement, he founded a weekly newspaper *Le Droit des Femmes*, the main purpose of which was to campaign for reform of the legal situation of women.[29] The first number contained articles by, among others, Ernest Legouvé and Maria Deraismes. The former stated that the paper would promote two desirable goals: equality between spouses and the establishment of a family council through which women could obtain redress against abusive husbands or fathers. Deraismes, in an article headed 'What Women Want', maintained that women wanted 'their fair share of rights and freedom' and the opportunity to develop their potential to the maximum degree. For this to happen, they wanted men to treat them as human beings rather than as figments of their fantasies, and to recognise that they, as much as men, possessed the faculty of reason and were not the slaves of their emotions. In terms of concrete proposals, *Le Droit des Femmes* demanded better education for girls; higher wages for women workers as an antidote to prostitution; revision of the Civil Code; the implementation of a single standard of morality; the opening up of the liberal professions to qualified women; equal wages for equal work; and women's control over their own wealth and property.[30] Notably absent from this list of demands was any mention of political rights, which Richer claimed to support in principle but to which he would always show himself implacably opposed on grounds of expediency.

The political orientation of *Le Droit des Femmes* was clear enough, however. Unswervingly republican, it called for the further democratisation of the Empire and the return to parliament of deputies who opposed militarism and conscription and were in favour of the separation of Church and state along with the introduction of free, compulsory and universal primary education. Richer's hope was that he could sell feminism to the wider republican movement and to this end he had recourse to the banquet campaigns which had been a feature of opposition tactics in the late 1840s. One such event was staged on 11 July 1869, but the occasion was notable both for the indifference on the part of the democratic politicians who attended and for hints of the unease experienced by many of the women in the group at Richer's determination to keep editorial control firmly in his own hands.[31] More successfully, in April 1870 Richer and Deraismes took the next obvious step of founding a feminist society which could have the newspaper as its principal platform. Entitled the Association pour le Droit des Femmes, the new organisation produced a mission statement which recapitulated the aims and objectives already set out in the journal. Having noted the progress being made by women's movements in other parts of the world (notably in the United States and in Britain), it declared that France, too, must play its part in the work of women's emancipation, above all through acceptance of the principle of sex equality before the law.[32] The Society expanded rapidly to a membership of around one hundred – well short of Richer's ambition to be the head of a mass movement but encouraging nevertheless. At this juncture, however, both the Association and the country at large were overtaken by events which were fraught with significance for the future.

Revolutionary interlude: the Paris Commune and after

In the early summer of 1870 the liberalisation of the Second Empire appeared to have given the Imperial regime a new lease of life. A plebiscite held on 8 May 1870 overwhelmingly approved of the reforms by 7.35 million votes to 1.5 million, though there were some 1.9 million abstentions. What no one foresaw was that in July 1870 France would be at war with Prussia and, still less, that the war would end in catastrophic defeat. On 2 September 1870 at the battle of Sedan Napoleon III was obliged to surrender and became a captive of the Prussians. On 4 September, in response to the anger and outrage of the Parisian crowd, the Republican opposition leaders proclaimed a new, Third, Republic at the Hôtel de Ville in the conviction that the Republic would succeed where the Empire had failed with regard to the prosecution of the war against the Prussians. Instead, after a long and cruel siege of the French capital which lasted from September of 1870 until the end of January 1871, the new Government of National Defence in its turn capitulated to Prussia. Adolphe Thiers, who became the chief of the executive power following the elections to a new National Assembly which met at Bordeaux on 13 February, received parliamentary approval for the humiliating terms imposed on France by Bismarck, which included the Prussian right to a victory parade down the Champs-Elysées as well as the loss of Alsace-Lorraine.

The Commune was, in the first instance, a patriotic reaction on the part of the ordinary people of Paris to humiliating defeat, but it rapidly became another experiment in revolutionary government and the latest incarnation of the French revolutionary tradition.[33] The social explosion was touched off on 18 March 1871 when the Parisian crowd, which included women and children as well as men, frustrated an attempt by the army to recover weapons seized by the National Guard, brutally murdering two officers in the process. Thiers, the government and the army withdrew to Versailles, leaving the Parisians to establish self-government in the form of a Commune, which in the aftermath of hastily organised elections, was under the direction of the extreme Left whose allegiances were, for the most part, with either radical republicanism or Proudhonist socialism, though there was also the odd disciple of Karl Marx. As Marx recognised, the most revolutionary thing

132

about the Commune was its very existence, since it proved that power need not necessarily be exercised exclusively by the social elite.[34] In practice, it lacked the opportunity to carry through far-reaching social reforms, and spent most of its short life struggling to survive in the face of an onslaught from Versailles masterminded by Thiers. Once again the city endured a state of siege and held out for some five weeks. On 21 May, however, the Versaillais broke through, and the dénouement was the appalling slaughter of the *semaine sanglante*, or 'bloody week', which saw the worst scenes of streetfighting and civil disturbance to trouble France since the 1790s as the Commune went down to crushing defeat.

It cannot be claimed that women's rights were at the top of the Commune's priorities.[35] Indeed, in the newspaper *La Sociale* André Léo complained that women who wanted to serve the Commune might find themselves rebuffed by male militants whose inherited antifeminist prejudices were rooted in a tradition which, as we have seen, stretched back from Proudhon to the Jacobins. Nevertheless, many women wholeheartedly identified with the revolutionary cause and sought to serve the Commune as best they could. Elisabeth Dmitrieff, a member of the First International and one of the few followers of Marx in France, established the Union des Femmes pour la Défense de Paris et les Soins aux blessés, which deployed women from all the proletarian *quartiers* of Paris as auxiliaries to care for the wounded and to provide support at the barricades. The Union also campaigned for equality of pay and conditions for working women, however, which upset Louise Michel, who feared that Dmitrieff's organisation might appear to prize women's rights ahead of the Revolution.

Michel and some of her associates nevertheless took full advantage of the opportunities afforded for political activism by the reappearance of a host of popular political clubs on the model of the Great Revolution and of 1848. Michel herself was the leading light at the Club de la Révolution, which met in the church of St Bernard de la Chapelle, while certain clubs, such as the Club de la Délivrance, were notable for having a largely female membership. Through the club movement, women could make themselves into *de facto* citizens, and they did not refrain from raising grievances which had a feminist dimension, such as calls for the legal recognition of *union libre* and for the reintroduction of divorce. Nor was the Commune indifferent to the women's voices. Its leadership addressed the question of girls' education in some earnest, creating new primary schools and secularising church schools. Paule Minck, for instance, opened a school for girls in the chapel of St Pierre de Montmartre, while Marcelle Tinayre, the first woman school inspector in France and a woman with a career as a novelist ahead of her, took charge of the secularisation process in the twelfth *arrondissement*. Vocational education was also encouraged, and a commission, one of whose members was André Léo, was set up to direct the entire female school sector. A decree of 21 May provided for parity of salaries between male and female teachers.[36]

Legend even has it that women fought shoulder-to-shoulder with their male comrades in defence of the Commune against the army of Versailles. Louise Michel and her friend Victorine Louvet may have served in the 61st battalion of the National Guard under General Eudes, Louvet's lover. A number of all-women battalions reputedly fought under female commanders such as Colonel Adelaide Valentin and Captain Louise Neckbecker, the latter a widow and lacemaker known for her political activism in the clubs of the seventeenth *arrondissement*. In the final week of the struggle, it was often women, who, clad in uniform, undertook to organise the barricades in their *quartiers*. The story goes that Michel, Dmitrieff and her colleague Nathalie Lemel were among the women who put up heroic resistance at the Place Blanche against regular troops, and that there were similar stands at the Boulevard Magenta and the Place du Château d'Eau, where female combatants fought to the last woman.[37] Hard evidence for these episodes is lacking, however, and it is by no means established that any battalion of women was ever formed. As with so much of the Commune's history, history and myth are frequently conflated.

Participation in military combat would in any case have amounted to a highly exceptional form of female insurgency in 1871. Women were more often content to turn over their premises to *communard* sharpshooters, while others sewed sandbags for the barricades, or made military uniforms, or brought meals to the front-line fighters. In rallying to the Commune, working-class women were engaged in the kind of defence of their communities with which women of the *classes populaires* had traditionally been associated, whether under the Ancien Régime or the Revolution. A number assumed the more sinister traditional role of rooting out shirkers and denouncing as cowards men who tried to avoid involvement in the fighting. The correspondent of *The Times* in Paris reported the scathing comments of a young woman member of a club on the Boulevard d'Italie about the cowardice of the National Guard: 'they called themselves the masters of creation and are a set of dolts. They complain of being made to fight, and are always grumbling over their woes. Let them go and join the craven band at Versailles and we will defend the city ourselves'.[38] The most fanatical *communardes* arrested innocent passers-by in the streets and incited the rebels to murder their hostages (one of the most prominent to be shot being the Archbishop of Paris). So extensive was women's involvement in the Commune that, for hostile witnesses especially, the rebellion became the very symbol of the havoc wreaked by the 'unruly woman', whose unnatural presence in political revolution was in itself sufficient explanation for the crimes committed by the insurgents. So was born the legend of the *pétroleuse*.

The Commune gave rise to many myths and legends, but none was more enduring or of more significance for the future development of feminism in France than that of the *pétroleuse*. The shelling of the Versaillais troops was responsible for setting off a number of fires, notably at the Ministry of Finance, but what horrified contemporary observers were the incendiary blazes deliberately started by the retreating *communards,* who set alight some of the most famous buildings in Paris – the Palais Royal, the library of the Louvre, and the Tuileries Palace, which was razed to the ground. Most of these fires were the work of men, but the myth developed rapidly in conservative circles that they were largely the work of a special breed of woman – the *pétroleuse,* a harpy who had 'forgotten her sex' and was everything a woman ought not to be: cruel, lascivious, depraved and insane. In the words of the Paris correspondent of the *Pall Mall Gazette,* such women were 'hideous viragoes – furies intoxicated with the fumes of wine and blood'. Despite the fact that, out of the 1051 women arrested in the immediate *semaine sanglante,* only five were convicted of incendiarism at the show trials held under military jurisdiction which began in August 1871, the word *pétroleuse* was used by conservatives as a synonym for any female supporter of the Commune and expressed not only revulsion at the revolution itself but also at the part in it played by women who had abandoned the normal codes of respectable feminine behaviour to such an unprecedented degree.[39]

For feminists like Deraismes and Richer, the Commune could never be a source of inspiration. Rather, it was a nightmare to be forgotten. Just as moderate republicans strove to obliterate the connotations of republicanism with the violence and disorder of the Commune, along with the bloodshed of the June Days and the Terror, so too feminists endeavoured to dispel memories of any links between feminism and political and sexual radicalism. Intent on living down the past, republicans and feminists alike were concerned above all to establish their respectability. And, given the relationship between the two movements in the early years of the Third Republic, it was perhaps to be expected that Deraismes and Richer would opt for a course of prudence, moderation and gradualism which even to some contemporary eyes came to look very much like timidity.

The progress of liberal feminism

The legend of the *pétroleuse* did not facilitate the work of Richer, Deraismes and the *Droit des Femmes* group. In September 1871 Richer thought it prudent to change the title of his newspaper to the more neutral *L'Avenir des Femmes* (*Women's Future*). The work of propaganda continued, however, with the emphasis placed firmly on women's civil rights rather than their political rights. In their *politique de la brèche* (strategy of the breach) Richer and Deraismes advocated gradual piecemeal reforms and the postponement of political emancipation, which both deemed to be too risky in a situation in which the Republic was still struggling to establish itself against the forces of reaction (monarchists retained a majority in the Chamber of Deputies until 1777 and in the Senate until 1879, and the 'Moral Order' regime installed under President MacMahon in 1873 was much feared as the prelude to a restoration).[40] As Deraismes explained in her pamphlet *France et progrès,* progress was inseparable from the establishment of the Republic and nothing should be allowed to jeopardise this greater good.[41]

The objectives of liberal feminism were spelled out by Richer in a series of books which he published between 1872 and 1883. In *La femme libre* (1877) he identified education as the crucial battleground for women. Girls had to be emancipated from the religious schooling which they traditionally received and which not only produced division in the family, as Michelet had argued, but kept alive anti-republican sentiment. The Republic, he affirmed, would never take root if women continued to oppose it. He denied, however, that his intention was to make women less womanly. To develop women's intelligence was not to encourage them to renounce their sex. Women should have an equal, but not identical, education with men. Similarly, the legal reforms which he envisaged were meant to improve rather than to undermine women's position in the family. Equality under the law for married women would reinforce their authority in the home, while equality of the sexes would promote a single standard of morality, applicable to both sexes: hence his advocacy of a law against seduction and a law permitting *recherche de la paternité*. Divorce was similarly a desideratum and the proposed law which he outlined in 1873 served as the starting point for the bill drawn up by Alfred Naquet which was eventually to reach the statute book (after much modification) in 1884.[42]

Deraismes was even more outspoken. Outraged by two works written by Alexandre Dumas *fils* which defended the right of a duped husband to kill an adulterous wife, she published *Eve contre Monsieur Dumas fils* (1872), rubbishing the writer as a pale imitation of his more famous father and castigating the value-system which sanctioned such acts of barbarity. Change in Deraismes's view would come only with the spread of democracy and the adoption of a new morality propagated by the Republic.[43] Deraismes's republican sympathies made her *persona non grata* with the 'Moral Order' regime, which banned her Amelioration Society. Undaunted, she renewed her commitment to the cause of the Republic, notably in her country retreat in the Seine-et-Oise, where she orchestrated the campaign which secured the election of a republican deputy in the hard-fought elections of 1877. In 1881 she also became the director of the local republican newspaper, *Le Républicain de Seine-et Oise*. As regards the 'woman question', she agreed with Richer on the need to prioritise women's education and reform of the law.

In 1878, to coincide with the International Exposition held in Paris, Deraismes and Richer collaborated in the organisation of an international congress on women's rights, which brought together women from eleven countries and sixteen feminist organisations. Some 219 'official' delegates attended, though another 400 or so visitors turned up for part of the three days of speeches and debates. Political rights did not feature on the programme, which was presented under four headings: education, the economy, morality and legislation. In a series of resolutions, the congress made its top priority revision of the Civil Code 'in the direction of the most absolute and complete equality between the sexes'. It also called for the reintroduction of divorce and an end to the distinction made by the Penal Code between the adultery of a wife and the adultery of a husband. The delegates also voted in favour of the criminalisation of seduction, the introduction of paternity suits and the suppression of the morals police.[44]

At the end of the 1870s feminists had grounds for believing that their alliance with the republican movement had been well judged. The future lay clearly with the Republicans, who by the end of the decade had won their battle to control the Republic, and Deraismes and Richer anticipated that their conference resolutions would soon become the law of the land. In the wake of the congress, the Amelioration Society recovered its legal status and Richer felt confident enough to change the name of his journal back to the original title of *Le Droit des Femmes*. But the expectations of the leaders of the French liberal feminist movement were to be fulfilled only in part. With the exception of reform of the secondary schooling of girls and the reintroduction of divorce – both prompted by adhesion more to anticlericalism than to feminism – the male political establishment ignored feminist demands. Furthermore, the *politique de la brèche*, which kept women's political rights off the feminist agenda, had already begun to provoke resentment among some militants like the young Hubertine Auclert, who had clashed with Richer over the decision to exclude the issue from the programme of the 1878 congress. In a pamphlet entitled *Le droit politique des femmes*, she reiterated her objections and resuscitated the arguments first advanced by Condorcet and Olympe de Gouges in favour of full citizenship for women.[45]

Auclert belonged to a new generation of feminist militants. Born in 1848 in the village of Tilly in the Allier department, she was the fifth of seven children and grew up in a prosperous family of local notables who gave her a traditional, convent education. At the age of 16, she contemplated becoming a nun, but the Sisters of Charity had the good sense and the foresight to reject her as unsuitable. Having tragically lost both of her parents, she was traumatised by the decision of her eldest brother to place her in an orphanage run by nuns until she reached her age of majority. When she left the orphanage in 1866 she was already a republican and anticlerical. Attracted by the feminist stirrings at the end of the Second Empire, she came to Paris and collaborated with Deraismes and Richer, but increasingly found herself at odds with their *politique de la brèche* as the 1870s wore on. Turning instead to the labour movement, which had begun to revive after the disaster of the Commune, she spoke at the socialist workers' conference held at Marseille in 1879. Linking sex oppression to class oppression in the tradition of the utopian socialists, she succeeded in persuading the delegates to adopt a resolution in favour of sex equality. The time was ripe, according to Auclert, to adopt a new strategy of *l'assaut*, or assault.[46] Much to the consternation of the founders of French liberal feminism, she was ready to become the first suffragette of the Third Republic and to shift the struggle for sex equality into a new, suffragist, phase.

Part IV (1880–1914)

Gender relations in crisis?

Chapter 10

A new Eve?

Bourgeois women in the *belle époque*

In the years before 1880 and 1914, the debate on the 'woman question' both intensified and diversified. Under the impact of the rise of socialism and the emergence of an organised labour movement, governing circles began to show appreciably more concern with the 'social question', which in turn, when focused on the plight of female workers, generated further debate on the 'woman question'.[1] The simultaneous rise of feminism, set alongside legal changes such as the reintroduction of divorce in 1884 and the opening up of secondary and higher education to women, convinced many contemporaries that they were witnesses to the advent of a 'new woman' – one who was ready to turn her back on the traditional domestic ideal in favour of a career and the pursuit of individual self-fulfilment.

In France, such perceptions were charged with added significance on account of widespread preoccupation with the spectre of *dénatalité*, or depopulation. In 1871 France had a population of 36.1 million: by 1914 it numbered 39.6 million, an increase of only 9.7%, whereas the German Empire had grown by 57.8% from 41.1 million to 64.9 million in the same period. By 1911 France had the smallest proportion of young people (under 21) in Europe (34.9%, compared with 43.7% in Germany). France also had the highest percentage of old people (over 59): 12.6%, against 7.9% in Germany. From 1901 to 1911 the annual rate of population increase was a mere 0.2% and in several years between 1890 and 1914 the number of deaths exceeded that of live births.[2] In this context, women's emancipation was easily represented not only as an abdication of women's natural role but as a threat to the security of the state itself.[3]

On the basis of the alarmist note sounded in contemporary literature and polemical discourse, some historians have suggested that the *belle époque* was not only a period of significant advances in the social status of French women but also an era characterised by a heightening of tensions in relations between the sexes: new Eve aroused fear, not to say panic, in the breast of old Adam. Perhaps most troubling of all to the male sense of sexual identity was the image of a masculinised woman – one who smoked, dressed as a man, cut her hair short, rode a bicycle and, horror of horrors, possibly had a sexual preference for other women. Masculinity, it seemed, could be threatened with redundancy. The resulting crisis in gender relations, it has been argued, was to be resolved only by the First World War and its aftermath.[4]

Such an interpretation, however, is open to question. Certainly, contemporary cultural perceptions form part of the wider social reality but, in the *belle époque*, as in any other period, they should not be equated with actual female experience. The vision of a gender order turned upside down may well have been a distinctive cultural feature of the French – and indeed the European – *fin-de-siècle*, but whether the pre-1914 world of bourgeois women is best viewed from the perspective of a coterie of frightened male intellectuals is another matter. Their fantasies need to be distinguished from social realities. As the present chapter aims to make clear, the conditions under which the great majority of middle-class women lived their lives bore little resemblance to the emancipated existence imagined by troubled male minds. A process of evolution there certainly was, but to describe it as a social revolution which precipitated a 'crisis in gender relations' is to exaggerate a great deal.

Progress and prospects

New images

The belief in the emergence of a 'new woman' owed much of its currency to contemporary literature, though the debate was also stimulated by the posthumous publication of the journal of Marie Bashkirtseff, a Russian *émigrée* in Paris and an aspiring artist with unconventional views who died tragically young.[5] The literary prototype, of course, was Ibsen's Nora who, in *A Doll's House*, shocked the bourgeois play-going public of Europe by walking out on her husband and three children in order to escape from a suffocating marriage and to take control of her own destiny.[6] In France, Ibsen was followed by the novelist Jules Bois, who enthused about the arrival of a 'new Eve'.[7] Most commentators, however, dwelled rather on the dangers posed by the new woman to the future of the bourgeois family. One moralist complained about how 'turn-of-the-century girls' were taking liberties which could 'compromise their futures'.[8] The novelist Marcel Prévost alerted his readers to the appearance of a female type which he classified as *demi-vierges*, young women in fashionable Parisian society who reputedly flouted all the genteel conventions to which modest, well-brought-up young girls were expected to adhere.[9] Even more alarming was the literary unmasking of the lesbian, allegedly often formed in single sex schools and the new institutions of higher education developed by the Republic if one were to believe her fictional representation in works by the likes of Prévost, Colette and Colette Yver.[10] For many sections of the press of the so-called *belle époque*, the new woman was most commonly represented as a dangerous creature,

A new Eve?

masculinised but man-hating, emancipated politically and sexually, a perversion of the natural order of things and a threat to morality and civilisation itself.[11]

For both her enemies and her friends, the new woman was the product not just of a new morality but of new technology. The fact that she was almost invariably shown riding a bicycle, whether in antifeminist cartoons or in poster art, was the most obvious evidence of the connection between female emancipation and technological progress. Adepts of the new woman delighted in the bicycle not simply as a means of transport which offered an exhilarating new freedom of movement but also as an excuse to cast off the layers of clothing in which the Victorian woman had been forced to encase her body. Petticoats and corsets were incompatible with cycling, and new garments – knickerbockers, bloomers and skirts – were adopted to free women's lower bodies and legs for the business of pedalling their bicycles. More alarmed commentators – usually male – saw technological change as the harbinger of a world in which sexual difference would be eliminated. At the popular level of science fiction, Alfred Robida, author of the widely read *Le XXe siècle: la vie électrique*, conjured up images of a new race of superwomen who, dressed as men and technologically expert, gained control of the universe. In the more rarefied pages of the *Revue des Deux-Mondes*, George Valbert communicated the fears inspired in him by the celebrated Paris Exhibition of 1889. In an article entitled 'L'Age des machines', he expressed dismay at what he considered to be the dehumanising features of technology when contrasted with the individual genius of the creative artist and forecast a future in which technology would generate a world of uniformity in which the differences between the sexes could no longer be discerned. Women would become *hommesses*, a kind of cross-breed who were neither male nor female and who lacked all traditional femininity and charm.[12]

Such reactions were hardly original, and evoke echoes of the 1848 era, which also witnessed an antifeminist backlash against the 'new women' of the day. Arguably, however, the satirists of the *fin-de-siècle* were even more virulently misogynist than their predecessors back in 1848. In journals such as *Le Grelot* and *L'Assiette au Beurre*, a leading anticlerical and left-leaning illustrated organ of the pre-war period, feminists and 'new women' were ridiculed as eccentrics and sexual misfits. Grandjouan, one of the principal artists for *L'Assiette au Beurre*, specialised in antifeminist caricatures which portrayed women's emancipation as a recipe for havoc in both the private and public spheres. One of his cartoons showed a suffragist rehearsing her electoral manifesto oblivious to the smell of burning emanating from her kitchen. Another depicts feminism as the ideology of 'old maids' frustrated by their inability to attract a husband and shows a suffragist proclaiming that when women get the vote marriage will be not only secular and civil but obligatory.[13] The theme of sexual inversion was also pursued in journals such as *Gil Blas Illustré*, where 'new women' were invariably depicted as adepts of 'free love' and sexual immorality. One cartoon of 1893 suggested that the old 'double standard' of morality no longer applied since, in a seduction scene with a difference, it is the woman who is shown to have picked up the man and to have paid him for sexual favours.[14] Similarly, in another cartoon in *Le Rire*, a couple of newly weds are seen conversing on their wedding night. The bride remarks to her husband how similar he appears to a man she once loved very much. Asked by her husband whether this was a long time ago, she replies: 'No – last night'.[15]

If the new woman as conceived by the most virulent of her opponents was essentially a nasty male fantasy, the fact remains, however, that she was more than a literary or artistic creation. Contemporaries who spoke of a new woman could claim to have seen her with their own eyes. As a result of changes in fashion, women undoubtedly looked different. Gone were the crinolines and tight-laced corsets of the high Victorian period in favour of looser-fitting gowns and skirts. As already explained, the new look owed much to the invention of the bicycle, which required the adoption of simpler clothes. Indeed, sport more generally – tennis, swimming, walking – contributed to the generalisation of the perception that women were no longer what they had been.[16]

So too did another new and preponderantly feminine pastime: shopping. New women graced the essentially new urban space represented by the department store. *Grands magasins* such as the Bon Marché, Printemps and the Samaritaine dated back to the time of the Second Empire but it was in the late nineteenth century that they developed into both the motors and the symbols of a consumer revolution which was driven by female spending power. Designed to impress and delight, the stores provided a legitimate social space in which women could move. On the one hand, they furnished an endless variety of merchandise which women could buy in their role as domestic provider. On the other hand, they offered a point of contact with the 'outside world', opening up possibilities for meetings and encounters in a luxurious environment far removed from the everyday domestic routine. From the 1890s, aggressive advertising and marketing techniques directed at women attempted to persuade them to make their homes 'modern' in the sense of replete with the goods which money could now buy and which the department store was only too willing to supply.[17] Domesticity itself, it seemed, had moved with the times.

Education

Whatever else she was, the 'new woman' was an educated woman, and female education was a field in which women undoubtedly secured a genuine new deal in the 1880s. After the disaster of the Franco-Prussian war, the outcome of which was widely attributed to the superiority of the Prussian school system, followed by the experience of the 'Moral Order' and the monarchist threats to the security of the regime in the 1870s, Republican leaders became more convinced than ever of the need to establish a secular and national educational system. Reform of girls' primary education was an integral part of their strategy. Jules Ferry, the principal architect of the law of 9 August 1879, was concerned to ensure that teaching in girls' primary schools was carried on only by trained, qualified teachers, and his legislation stipulated that every department now had to have at least one training school (*école normale*) for women primary teachers. The lecturers in the training schools had themselves to be of very high quality, graduates of the new Ecole Normale Supérieure at Fontenay-aux-Roses. Another law, of 16 June 1881, provided for free and secular education for all children, girls as well as boys. Compulsory attendance between the ages of six and thirteen was required by the law of 26 March 1882.

The massive expansion of educational opportunities which followed the enactment of the school laws was regarded by Republicans as one of their greatest achievements. On the whole, historians have been right to endorse this claim, although we should bear in mind Theodore Zeldin's point that the consequences of the laws were not always those envisaged by their authors.[18] In the case of girls' primary education, one should also remember that the law requiring obligatory attendance proved difficult to enforce. One inspector noted in 1903 that 'almost everywhere' young girls left school at 11 or 12, or even earlier. Absences were particularly high in the west (where more than 50% of the pupils were affected) and in the Bourbonnais, the Allier and Lorraine. Thus, among poorer families, the expectation that girls would continue to make some kind of contribution to the family budget frustrated the hopes of the legislators of the early 1880s.[19]

At the secondary level, anticlericalism provided the overriding impetus to reform. Introducing a bill to set up state secondary schools for girls, Camille Sée made no attempt to conceal his objective of replacing clerical control with state control. So long as women's education ended in the primary school, he said, it would be impossible to overcome the old prejudices, superstitions and routine. In his view, priestly power over women was already so great that through them the Church enjoyed political mastery, for, although women could not vote themselves, they could influence the votes of their husbands, in keeping with the directives which they received from their confessors. The Sée Law of 21 December 1880, which created lycées and colleges for girls, was inspired not by feminism but rather by the anticlerical project of secularising the state and consolidating the republican regime.

Hence it was no part of the original republican plan to put girls on an equal educational footing with boys. The curriculum of the new colleges and lycées prepared girls not for the *baccalauréat*, the passport to higher education and the professions, but for a largely ornamental diploma of secondary studies. Camille Sée's intention was to reinforce the ideal of domesticity, not to destroy it. The aim of girls' secondary education as established by the law of 1880 was merely to broaden the cultural horizons of girls in order to make them less susceptible to 'superstition' and more capable of taking an intelligent interest in the intellectual preoccupations of their husbands. As Sée put it, if girls learned about science it was to make them aware of matters such as the influence of the atmosphere on health, the best types of food and clothing for children and how to treat ailments until a doctor could be fetched. Nothing was further from his mind than the creation of female lawyers, doctors or politicians.[20]

Nor did the Sée Law become effective overnight. Much indifference, if not actual hostility, towards girls' secondary education had to be overcome, particularly in the provinces. The law, after all, had been passed not in response to public opinion but in order to bring the popular mentality into alignment with the enlightened views of the new elite. In 1885 the Rector of the Academy of Aix had to report that Digne was the only town in his department to have consented to the sacrifices involved in establishing secondary schooling for girls. He envisaged no improvement in the immediate future as the population was too sparse and too poor to allow courses to be established with any chance of success.[21] Clerical opposition was still creating difficulties in a number of places at the turn of the century, as at Le Mans in 1900, where the mayor told the municipal council that girls' education was almost completely under the control of the clergy, with the result that good republican families had of necessity to send their daughters to religious establishments.[22] Such schools as did exist had to cope with immense material problems, not the least being the lack of a proper school building because municipalities would not contribute towards construction costs. Thus at Castres courses continued to take place in a building owned by a private individual who would not carry out necessary repairs,[23] while at Carpentras the only improvement was that the lavatories were no longer 'veritable homes of infection'.[24] At Calais, the building was also badly in need of repair and there was an acute lack of teaching materials, especially science equipment, while no books apart from the personal library of the headmistress were available for teaching literature.[25]

The root of the problem was that the central government was excessively tight with money: it wanted to establish secondary education for girls on the cheap. Every minute item of expenditure had to be accounted for to the Minister of Education, who personally checked every last detail. In the early days the elite at Sèvres (the training school established to educate future teachers in the new lycées and colleges) were allowed to take a bath only once every three weeks, though in a moment of generosity the Minister consented to the installation of showers in 1888. An enquiry was ordered to see that there was no unnecessary usage of heating and lighting, as when the students were not in their rooms. A request for an increase in the school's hospital budget was turned down.[26] With such a cheese-paring outlook typical of most French governments of the period, they can hardly be said to have done everything in their power to promote secondary education for girls in the years before the First World War.

In the end, however, the secondary education of French girls was to develop in directions which the legislators of 1880 had not anticipated. Intended largely for the daughters of the upper middle classes, the schools came to recruit their pupils mainly among lower middle class girls: almost one-third were the daughters of teachers or civil servants while another third were the daughters of self-employed businessmen. Although in Paris the pupils tended to come from a higher social bracket (parents were frequently top civil servants or fairly wealthy bosses), in the provinces most girls – particularly in the colleges – came from the ranks of the petty bourgeoisie. Thus the girls often came from backgrounds where parents were less interested in the acquisition of the diploma than in obtaining a primary certificate which would qualify their daughters for some kind of employment. In this way, many establishments came to provide what was in effect a higher primary education with a distinctly vocational bias.[27]

In certain other schools another very different development also served to undermine the original dilettante ideal. This was the clandestine introduction of Latin classes, which allowed girls to prepare for the *baccalauréat* and therefore for university entrance. Here, private educational establishments took the initiative, with the Collège Sévigné, a private secular school founded in 1880, leading the way, and a number of Catholic schools following suit. It would be wrong to attribute the Catholic initiative to a sudden conversion to feminism. Rather, it was prompted by the vigorous anticlerical measures which were enacted in the aftermath of the Dreyfus Affair and which culminated in the law separating Church and state in 1905. By way of retaliation against these attacks and in order to refute republican allegations about the inferior standards in Catholic schools, Catholic headmistresses seem to have decided to upstage their rivals by making provision for the teaching of Latin in their schools.[28] Faced with such a challenge from the private sector, some heads of state establishments in Paris and other large towns saw no alternative but to allow their own pupils to study Latin and to sit the *bac*. In the Academy of Poitiers Latin teaching began in 1902, the courses being given by a male teacher from a boys' lycée. In 1910 five candidates were successful in the *baccalauréat* examinations. By 1913 there had been twenty-nine passes altogether.[29] Though still small, these figures were a sign of the times: female secondary education was now set on a course towards identification with the male programme, much to the dismay of Camille Sée, who continued to argue the case for a distinctive syllabus for girls, even if the diploma were to be replaced by a special female *baccalauréat*.[30]

The number of girls who succeeded in going on to higher education remained comparatively small. In 1880 only the Medical Faculty in Paris expressly allowed women students to take its courses: even so, there were only thirty-two females registered there in 1879. By 1914 this figure had risen to 578. In practice, if not in theory, women had established their right to a university education from the 1860s, but it was only in 1890 that Julie Chauvin became the first woman to graduate in Law, and later in the same decade that institutions like the Ecole des Chartes and the Ecole des Beaux-Arts opened their doors to women students. By 1900 there were 624 native French girl students in the French higher educational system. As more and more girls took the *baccalauréat*, numbers reached 1148 in 1905 and 2547 in 1914. One should note, however, that in the French faculties the proportion of French women students exceeded that of foreigners for the first time only in 1912–13.[31] Moreover, many girls, even those who had worked furiously to obtain a place, failed to complete their course, opting out as soon as they met a suitable husband.[32] Bourgeois parents often showed little or no interest in the academic attainments of their daughters. As the journalist and feminist Louise Weiss would recall, her father was unimpressed by her scholarly success at school: far from encouraging her to go on to university, he wanted to send her to a college of domestic science.[33] Progress in the field of women's education over the period 1870–1914 was undoubtedly real, but it was also slow and undynamic.

Career women

According to the contemporary stereotype, the new woman was not only an educated woman but also a career woman, prepared to reject a life of domesticity for a profession and engagement in the world of work. In the first half of the nineteenth century, professional opportunities for respectable middle-class women had been virtually non-existent. By the end of the century the expansion of female education had created new possibilities for a select band of women to become doctors, lawyers and academics. Though few in numbers, such women were widely thought to symbolise the future. Marie Curie, twice winner of the Nobel Prize, was a living refutation of misogynist arguments about the unsuitability of women for an intellectual career.[34]

Career prospects for bourgeois women were perhaps brightest in teaching. The reforms of the 1880s resulted not only in the secularisation of the schools but also in the feminisation of the teaching personnel, at least at the primary level. In 1906, there were some 57,000 *institutrices* – almost 50% of the profession.[35] At the same time, in the period 1876–1906, the number of nuns working in state primary schools fell from 20,000 to below 1000, though at the turn of the century some 237,000 girls in public schools still received their primary education at the hands of the female religious orders.[36] A similar and less well-known process went on in the hospitals, where nuns were also replaced by civilian nurses at the behest of administrators in the Assistance Publique who shared the commitment of their political masters to the realisation of the *idée laïque*. The drive to make nursing a respectable profession was marked by the opening of a number of nursing training schools in the last third of the nineteenth century and culminated in the establishment of the Ecole de la Salpêtrière in 1908, which was open to young, single women aged between 18 and 25 of good health and good morality who had met the necessary educational entrance requirements (which included the hospital's own entrance examination). Recruits seem to have come mainly from the daughters of the petty and middling bourgeoisie.[37]

It was young women from the same social background who participated in what was perhaps the most striking change in the pattern of women's employment by the early twentieth century, namely the female invasion of the 'tertiary' sector of the economy, a process frequently described by contemporaries as the 'feminisation of office work'.[38] By 1914, some 30% of the female workforce worked in the tertiary sector, constituting two-fifths of the employees in either offices or department stores. Technological change, such as the invention of the telephone and the typewriter, combined with the ever-growing complexity of the industrial economy and the widening spheres of government interest, brought women into the workplace as clerks, shorthand typists, secretaries, cashiers, post-office workers, telephonists, shop assistants in the luxury stores such as the Louvre, Bon Marché and Printemps, and as employees in banks, credit houses, government departments, railway companies and the like. Some of these young women were of proletarian extraction, but more were the daughters of lower middle-class families who, in the first half of the nineteenth century, would have considered it unthinkable for a bourgeois woman to work.[39]

The Post Office (PTT) provides a good illustration of what was going on. The postal services had employed women under the Ancien Régime but they had been deprived of their positions in the course of the French Revolution. The few provincial postmistresses who retained their jobs were subjected to repeated attacks in the nineteenth century, as in the insulting series of articles published in *La France Administrative* between 1841 and 1846. It was only in 1877 that women were once again employed in Paris, initially at the Central Télégraphique, then in the Postal Savings Bank opened in 1881, and finally in the telephone company after it had become a state monopoly. The *Journal des Postes, Télégraphes et Téléphones* kept up the barrage of criticism of female employees in the 1890s, but their numbers continued to grow until they reached 21,457 in 1906 (22% of the labour force).[40]

It would be a mistake, however, to exaggerate the extent to which bourgeois women became career professionals in the years before 1914. Women constituted only a tiny fraction of the legal profession – 0.29%. In medicine, they may have made up 49% of the profession as a whole, but this impressive figure reflects their presence in the almost exclusively feminine professions of midwife (100%) and nurse (96%) as well as the majority (68%) of hospital personnel. Those who were actually doctors numbered only 573 in 1906 – 3% of the profession.[41] Moreover, in both the law and medicine, women were advised by careers guides that their best chances of success were to specialise exclusively in cases involving women or children.[42] Women did furnish a higher proportion of French dentists (8%) even if their numbers were lower than the doctors (280). The 659 pharmacists added up to only 3% of the profession. A mere 2.6% of French chemists and engineers were women.[43] It was still impossible for a woman to become a senior civil servant as a law of 31 August 1908 permitted only males to take the appropriate examinations.[44]

The ambiguous status of women teachers confirms the impression of only a limited advance in the sphere of employment. At the primary level, the *institutrice* was very often an isolated figure, misunderstood by a public which saw her as the agent of Ferry's anticlerical revolution, even when she herself remained loyal to her religious upbringing and was only vaguely aware of the 'laic ideal'.[45] This of course was most true in areas where clerical influence was strongest. The reactionary newspaper *Autorité* took great delight in informing its readers that in the commune of Le Montiel in Savoy, the two secular women teachers could only attract one solitary pupil to their new school, since the local parish priest had raised money to keep the old school, run by nuns, in existence.[46] Material hardship was also common. Mademoiselle N. of Selles-Saint-Denis in the Loir-et-Cher department complained bitterly that her school was housed in the filthiest building in the commune and that she herself had inadequate living space, having no kitchen – or rather a kitchen which also served as a classroom. Consequently, she had begun to take her meals out, at the village hotel, but this in turn gave rise to gossip and scandal, and she was obliged to eat at home again. A strained relationship with her male colleague did not make life easier: and even her one pleasure, going for solitary walks in the woods, set the tongues wagging anew.[47]

Mademoiselle N. may have been an atypical case and she may even have been given to exaggeration, but it seems abundantly clear nevertheless that the private life of a village *institutrice* could be intolerably difficult. Others, too, stressed that loneliness was the greatest problem which they had to face, a problem exacerbated by the difficulty of finding a suitable marriage partner. Many, particularly those of bourgeois origin, driven into the career by a reversal of family fortunes, could not bear the idea of living with a peasant or worker of lower culture. In any case, in the early days of the Third Republic, a married *institutrice* gave scandal, even when married to a fellow school teacher. One young mistress told the feminist newspaper *La Fronde* that a jealous inspector had prevented her from marrying a colleague in a neighbouring *canton* on the grounds that she would be 'compromised in the eyes of the population'.[48] It is true that at the beginning of the twentieth century official policy on this matter underwent a dramatic about-turn, so that marriages between male and female primary teachers were actually encouraged.[49] But the *institutrice* still had plenty of other difficulties to contend with. The question of dress could prove vexatious (with male colleagues among the harshest critics) in that she was expected to dress elegantly enough to be distinguishable from the peasant woman, but yet not so fashionably as to attract too much admiration. Monsieur Bédorez, Director of Primary Education in the Seine, laid down that his *institutrices* could cycle only on Sundays and in the countryside: they were forbidden to arrive at school on their bicycles on the grounds that if an accident occurred in front of the pupils the teacher's authority over them would be diminished.[50] Finally, to complement these moral sufferings, the salary of a woman teacher was equal to that of a man only at the bottom of the scale: in the higher grades they were paid less.[51]

If anything, the position of *femmes professeurs* in the new secondary schools was even worse. They too fared badly by comparison with their male colleagues. They worked longer hours for lower salaries. If they had passed the *agrégation* they did not receive the annual bonus of 500 francs given to men. Absence for illness (and pregnancy was deemed to fall within this category) led to deductions from salary, though this was never the case with male teachers. Women *agrégées* were not allowed to present a thesis for the *doctorat d'état* and women did not have the right to vote in elections to the Conseil supérieur d'Instruction publique. For society at large, the woman secondary teacher was a dangerous creature, threatening the natural order of male supremacy, the kind of person who ought to be seen only rarely in public. Ideally, she should be 'moderate in her opinions, neutral in her dress, nil in her personality and ugly for preference'. Living under a constant regime of 'liberty under surveillance', many succumbed to nervous depression. As was pointed out in the *Revue Universitaire*, this took a particular toll on the health of unmarried women, who formed the majority of the profession: they failed to eat properly and suffered from the continual intellectual strain, exacerbated by solitude and the pressure from prejudiced public opinion.[52] Thus only exceptionally did these women see themselves as agents of profound social change or as militants on behalf of the rights of women. Rather, they seem to have conceived their role as being that of secular missionaries whose essential task was to see to the moral education of their pupils. Here it is interesting to note the significant number of Protestant women who entered the profession, including the first Directress of Sèvres, Mme Favre.[53] The fate of the *femme professeur*, alongside that of the *institutrice*, hardly supports the view that the *belle époque* was characterised by the bourgeois woman's abandonment of domesticity and her emergence as a career professional.

The authors of careers guides for bourgeois girls contemplating entry into the world of work confirm that, though the workplace offered new opportunities, it was still a problematic sphere for the daughters of the middle classes. Mme Georges Regnal, while insisting on the obligation of mothers to prepare their daughters for a life of work, noted nevertheless that they would have the greatest difficulty in living exclusively by the fruits of their labour, since conventionally women were obliged to work for low pay.[54] Some authors, indeed, were of the view that only girls from families which had suffered a reverse of fortunes should work for wages, though they conceded that women unlucky enough to be married to men with incomes insufficient to support them in the style to which they were accustomed might have to take a job to supplement the family income. Under normal circumstances, however, the proper place for a woman remained the home. As one author put it:

> The best, the healthiest, the most noble of situations is that of the woman as wife and mother, conscious of her duties towards her husband and children.[55]

Economic and cultural change had by no means eroded the ideological assumptions which governed the gender order in the years before 1914, even if the law itself was obliged to register at least some signs of cultural change.

The legal situation of women

The years after 1880 saw a limited improvement in the legal position of French women, notably in the area of their rights over their own property and earnings. In 1881 women for the first time obtained the right to open a bank savings account without the assistance of their husbands, while a law of 1886 extended this right to make the husband's consent unnecessary. A major step forward came for single or separated women in 1893 when they were granted full legal capacity. In 1897, all women became eligible to be witnesses in a civil action. Another law, of 13 July 1907, allowed married women to dispose freely of their own earnings, and also to obtain part of their husband's earnings if they did not contribute enough of their income to the upkeep of the household – an improvement on a situation where previously the lord and master could squander his wife's income with impunity. In 1909, women were granted the right to initiate an action concerned with family property and to be consulted before the alienation of family property by their husbands. Inroads on the omnipotence of the *paterfamilias* were also made by legislation on compulsory schooling and the law of 1889 on delinquent children, which for the first time challenged a father's exclusive right to discipline his offspring. Another law, of 1912, carried this process a stage further by instituting a regime of 'liberty under surveillance' for delinquents who would duly be handed back to their families if they proved cooperative.[56]

By far the most significant legal change affecting the position of women in French society in this period, however, was the law of 27 July 1884 which reintroduced divorce. It took Alfred Naquet, the main sponsor of the 1884 law, eight years to get his bill through parliament (in a greatly amended form).[57] Naquet, a former professor of chemistry and a socialist, was a sworn enemy of the bourgeois family who had served a prison sentence for the views expressed in a book which he published in 1869. Entitled *Religion, Property and the Family*, it urged the abolition of marriage as a weapon in the war to destroy bourgeois society.[58] As a deputy, Naquet originally aimed to revive the far-reaching legislation on divorce of 1792, but attempts to steer bills on these lines through parliament foundered in 1876 and 1878. Recognising the need for compromise, he fell back on the more limited divorce legislation enacted under the Empire, and it was a bill along Napoleonic lines which obtained the backing of the Chamber of Deputies in 1882. Even this, however, was too much for the Senate, to which Naquet had been elected in 1883, and only further concessions – notably agreement to drop the provision for divorce by mutual consent – finally secured majority support in the second chamber in 1884. Under the terms of the

152

new law, four grounds for divorce were envisaged: adultery; *excès et sévices* (physical violence inflicted by one spouse on the other); *injures graves* (a very flexible category which amounted to virtually any kind of moral cruelty); and finally *condemnation afflictive et infamante*, which would apply in the case of, say, a spouse sentenced to life imprisonment. The actual procedure by which one obtained a divorce was deliberately made as complicated as possible, though it was simplified slightly by a law of 18 April 1886.[59]

It should be stressed that the Republican legislators who passed the divorce law did so, for the most part, reluctantly. Advocates of easy divorce were few, though further liberalisation of the law did take place in 1904, when the partner guilty of adultery was allowed to marry his or her accomplice.[60] From the constant rise in the number of divorces, it would appear that the law met a real need: shortly after the passage of the divorce law, the annual number of divorces rose to more than 7000, which was double the annual number of separations immediately prior to the enactment of the law.[61] Moreover, just as women had been the main beneficiaries of the original divorce legislation of the Revolution, so, too, women outnumbered men in submitting divorce petitions under the terms of the 1884 act. (According to one study, six out of ten divorces were demanded by women.)[62] It may well be true, however, that the law sometimes made it harder for a wife than for a husband to obtain a divorce, especially on the grounds of adultery, where it was first of all more difficult for her to establish the guilt of her husband, and when, secondly, the prevailing climate of opinion continued to support a double standard of morality. Thus a decision of the Cour de Cassation in February 1914 rejected one woman's plea for divorce on the grounds that the bad conduct of a wife mitigated the offence of her husband.[63] Yet if the husband's culpability was notorious, a wife could certainly have her divorce – as was well illustrated by perhaps the most celebrated divorce case of the *belle époque*, that of Anna Gould, daughter of American tycoon, Jay Gould, who eventually tired of seeing her fortune squandered by her husband, the spendthrift, playboy aristocrat, Boni de Castellane.[64]

In any event, the mere existence of a divorce law served to undermine the absolute authority of the husband in the household. Many instances can be found in jurisprudence which show that the law was often well disposed to the many and various actions brought by women under the heading of *injures graves*. An offence against public decency was sufficient, for example, as was the seizure of property for no good reason.[65] Equally, the law prevented unworthy husbands from ridding themselves of their wives when they became inconvenient. A wife's obligation to live with her husband was not absolute; one man who deliberately moved to a place where his wife would be unable to follow him in order to file a divorce suit had his plea rejected.[66] Another husband who brought his wife from Algeria and abandoned her in Paris was unable to obtain a divorce on the grounds that his wife would not return to the conjugal home.[67]

Continuities

Domestic ideology and marriage

The availability of divorce notwithstanding, the ideology of separate spheres remained as pervasive at the beginning of the twentieth century as it had been at any point in the nineteenth century. A gender order based on sexual difference rather than on sex equality was still widely considered to be fundamental to the well-being of society. Catholic apologists, of course, continued to be among its most prominent champions. More aware than ever that it was women rather than men who turned to the consolations of religion in an increasingly 'dechristianised' society, churchmen looked to women to transmit Catholic ideals to subsequent generations through the process of the socialisation of children, in which mothers, indubitably, had the dominant role. As one priest put it in a series of sermons on 'The Duties of Men Towards Women':

> Man and woman will be to each other as the head and the heart. To man intelligence, reason, reflection, wisdom, majesty, strength, energy, resolution, authority. To woman delicacy, sensibility, grace, sweetness, goodness, tenderness, discreet attention, devotion, enthusiasm, communicative warmth.[68]

Most Catholic women had no difficulty in identifying with such sentiments. Anatole de Ségur, drawing up a plan for the education of a Christian mother, described her role thus: 'My mission with regard to my children is that of a visible Angel, whom God has placed in their midst to help them traverse life. I am the auxiliary of their Guardian Angel, preparing their souls to receive and understand the good thoughts he suggests to them, imprinting these on their fickle imaginations, and helping them to put these into practice. The goal of my mission is to help them reach Heaven'.[69]

But it was by no means only Catholics and conservatives who cherished the image of the 'angel of the hearth' and who preached the delights of domesticity. In the late nineteenth century, as earlier, the doctrine of separate spheres was embraced with enthusiasm by adepts of the Republican tradition. While it is true that Republicans were responsible for measures such as the development of a free and compulsory state school system and the establishment of state secondary schools for girls, as well as for the reintroduction of divorce in 1884, as we have seen the primary objective of such legislation was not to promote women's rights but to attack the position of the Catholic Church in public life and to secularise the state. Jules Ferry, principal author of these 'laic laws', subscribed to Michelet's view that the Church's hold over girls' education had to be broken in order to break down the barriers between rational and progressive-minded husbands and superstitious, backward-looking wives but he had no wish to use educational reform as the means by which to move forward to a new era of sex equality.[70] Positivism, the creed to which most of the regime's rulers subscribed in its formative years, taught that women were made for the home, where their role was first and foremost to exercise a moral influence over the rest of the family.[71] As the moderate republican politician Jules Simon put it in the late nineteenth century:

> What is man's vocation? It is to be a good citizen. And woman's? To be a good wife and a good mother. One is in some way called to the outside world: the other is retained for the interior.[72]

Marriage thus continued to be depicted as women's 'natural' goal. Baronne Staffe, author of a phenomenally best-selling etiquette book, *Usages du monde* (1887), warned women against the perils of attempting to abandon their separate sphere.[73] In 1900 the female novelist Daniel Lesueur reminded her readers that respectable ladies did not work, affirming that 'women's work declasses her'.[74] A bourgeois woman had to be a lady, and by definition a lady did not work. Her exclusive devotion to the hearth was a touchstone of her respectability, and an important symbol of the family's bourgeois status. By the same token, prejudice against unmarried women remained strong. In 1912 a savage issue of *L'Assiette au Beurre* represented them as shrivelled, sterile, emotionally barren and obnoxious creatures who spied on their neighbours, spread malicious gossip, hypocritically pretended to be pious and who, with no human companion to turn to, focused their limited affections on some pet – a cat, a dog, or a parrot.[75]

As far as marriage formation is concerned, very little evidence can be adduced to support the view of one historian who contends that 'increasingly marriages were founded on that elusive emotional tie which we call love'.[76] As in the first half of the nineteenth century, the arranged marriage remained the norm. Under the Second Empire, if the contemporary stage can be regarded as any guide to social values, marriage amounted to little more than a financial transaction for the middle classes.[77] As one commentator noted, marriage was the most important financial decision a bourgeois would make in his life.[78] Maria Deraismes, one of the founders of the modern French feminist movement, complained that marriage lacked any special esteem because it was thought of primarily as a lucrative investment (significantly, she herself chose to remain unmarried).[79] Such laments were to continue right up to the First World War, with the satirical journal, *L'Assiette au Beurre*, flaying the venal side of bourgeois marriage in a series of merciless caricatures.[80] In 1898 Mme George Renard objected that girls still had too little say in the choice of their marriage partners, and suggested that they ought to have the right to take the initiative in proposing – an idea shocking to the bourgeoisie of the *belle époque*.[81]

What may be true is that, over the period from roughly 1860 to 1914, a slow but perceptible shift in sensibility took place in the relations between married couples in a process which Alain Corbin has labelled 'the eroticisation of marriage'.[82] As already seen, a significant number of doctors and moralists advocated the idea of marriage as a concomitant relationship in which sexual pleasure should have a central place in the life of the couple. Works such as the manual by Dr Dartigues *On Experimental Love, or The Causes of Adultery in Women in the Nineteenth Century* (1878) championed the married woman's right to orgasm, recommending it as the best remedy against the temptation of adultery.[83] The youthful Léon Blum, later to be France's first socialist Prime Minister, believed that women, like men, should engage in sexual adventures prior to marriage in order to eliminate the gap between male and female sexual experience which existed under the double standard.[84] The 'neo-Malthusian' League for Human Regeneration, founded in 1896 by Paul Robin and Eugène Humbert, constituted an active birth-control lobby which called on women to stage a *grève des ventres* (strike of the womb) – a phrase that was taken up by one of France's most outspoken 'new women', the feminist activist and orator Nelly Roussel, who gave lecture tours throughout the country preaching the need for women to separate the pleasures of love from their natural consequence of procreation.[85] Another sign of the new times, the emergence of the discipline of sexology, may have been more advanced in Germany than in France, and likewise the full impact of Freud's ideas may not have been until after the First World War, but in doctors such as Auguste Forel France, too, had serious students of sexual practices who sought to classify and categorise sexual acts from an exclusively scientific, rather than a moral, point of view.[86] In this changing climate of opinion, which for the first time uncovered the homosexual and the lesbian as distinctive types, new rules concerning the 'conventional' sexual behaviour of 'normal' heterosexual married couples may have begun to establish themselves in the bedrooms of the bourgeoisie.

The 'eroticisation of marriage' was a project undertaken by middle and upper-class rather than proletarian couples and one of its manifestations was the widespread adoption of the practice of birth control. By the turn of the century, the average bourgeois marriage produced only two children. Couples resorted to a variety of contraceptive devices in order to limit family size, but even if the most common methods (withdrawal and the condom – later improved by the vulcanisation of rubber) left the initiative to the male, it seems safe to assume that women were willing to cooperate in the general strategy of frustrating pregnancy. Significantly, by the late nineteenth century, devices such as sponges, douches, pessaries and diaphragms were increasingly available to women who wished to control their own fertility.[87] Though bourgeois marriage may have begun as a financial transaction, over the years of life together it may well have developed into an intimate union in which both partners could be regarded as emotional equals. In that sense, marriage, too, 'modernised'.

In 1914, however, French society was still a long way away from the sexual revolution of the late twentieth century. As Corbin himself admits, whereas sexuality is central to the modern conception of marriage, in the late nineteenth century it remained 'merely a backdrop to married life'.[88] Property, rather than sex, was the foundation of bourgeois marriage. The *belle époque* was essentially a pre-Freudian world where sexual behaviour did not carry post-Freudian meanings. Bourgeois couples may have been prepared to limit the size of their families, but few right-thinking and respectable people were prepared to be identified with the open advocacy of birth control. On the contrary, the neo-Malthusians were vilified by the nationalist press and branded as dangerous subversives by the state, which classified their birth-control propaganda in the National Archives as obscene literature.[89] The pro-natality lobby, by contrast, enjoyed official approval. In any case, the concomitant relationship within marriage, where it existed, did not in itself eradicate acceptance of masculine and feminine roles, which were defined in accordance with the doctrine of separate spheres. It may have tempered, but it did not transform, the fundamentally patriarchal structures of society.

The double standard and prostitution

Continuity rather than change was apparent also in the matter of sexual morality. The views of a Léon Blum or a Nelly Roussel elicited outrage rather than approval in bourgeois circles, however fashionable they may have been in Bohemia. In the *belle époque*, most young girls of good family continued to receive a sheltered upbringing with the aim of making them into virginal brides rather than emancipated 'new women'. They were never allowed out unaccompanied and their conduct was scrutinised at dances and other social gatherings by their mothers or chaperones. Their reading material was likewise the object of strict surveillance. Marcel Prévost, even though a successful novelist himself, warned against the perils of allowing girls to read novels, since in his view they were likely to wound their delicate sensibility.[90] Another advice book addressed to the 'model' girl of the early twentieth century claimed that reading novels led only to an overworked imagination, a distaste for duty and a preoccupation with the frivolous.[91] Both these would-be moral experts advocated only safe, traditional writings for female youth – the tales of Mme de Genlis, the proverbs of Mme de Maintenon, the moralising stories of the comtesse de Ségur. The *Journal des Demoiselles*, also standard reading for the bourgeois girl, never tired of making the point that marriage was the proper goal of a woman's existence, and that even young ladies of no fortune could hope to be rewarded in the end by a happy match, provided they remained virtuous.[92]

In short, the double standard remained firmly in place, sanctioned not just by social mores but by the law. True, in the years before 1914 the courts appear to have softened their line towards women found guilty of adultery. The penalty imposed on them became purely nominal, as in the case of a Mme Martinelli, who was fined sixteen francs for receiving regularly a lover in the absence of her husband.[93] Nevertheless, the usages associated with the *crime passionnel* still allowed husbands to kill their adulterous wives with impunity, even when the crime was premeditated. Henri Fougère, seeing his wife become intimate with his supposed friend Rivet, rented a room opposite Rivet's place to watch them: at the same time he bought a revolver and started to put in some target practice. One day, having pretended to go to work, he observed that Rivet came round to spend the morning with his wife. When they came out, Fougère followed them and shot Rivet dead as he tried to run away. The court acquitted him of murder.[94] Another husband, abandoned by his wife after seven years of marriage, pleaded with her to come back when he met her in the street. She refused. He shot her, and was duly acquitted by the court.[95]

The concept of two moralities did not go completely unchallenged in the period before 1914. If the classic regulated system of prostitution came under fire from doctors, politicians and moralists on the grounds of its inefficiency, other more hostile critics advocated its entire abolition. As we have seen the abolitionist campaign of the 1870s had produced no concrete results but Mrs Butler's final triumph in England in 1884–86 breathed new life into the cause of abolitionism in France. For the nascent feminist movement in particular abolitionism became a primary objective, and, making good use of the arguments already formulated by Yves Guyot and his friends, the feminists concentrated their propaganda on the excesses committed by the vice squad and on the appalling conditions of women prisoners detained at Saint-Lazare.[96] In time, press coverage of arbitrary and high-minded behaviour on the part of the *police des moeurs* (especially after a number of unsavoury incidents, the most serious of which involved the wrongful arrest of two respectable women for soliciting) led to the creation of an extra-parliamentary commission on morality in 1903. Among its seventy-seven members it numbered the first woman ever to be appointed to such a body in the person of the feminist leader Mme Avril de Sainte-Croix, who as a journalist writing under the pseudonym 'Savioz' had been one of the most outspoken critics of the state regulation of prostitution. Deliberating over a period of three years, the commission encouraged abolitionists to believe that the end of the regulated system was in sight, especially when its recommendations were incorporated into a parliamentary bill tabled by the deputy Paul Meunier in June 1907.[97]

Unfortunately for the abolitionists, however, their hopes were speedily dashed by effective lobbying on the part of the Société de Prophylaxie and the Medical Academy, which prevented Meunier's bill from making any headway in the Chamber. In the end, its only provisions to reach the statute book were those relating to minors, covered by a law of April 1908. Indeed, by focusing attention on the question of the prostitution of minors, Senator Béranger and his fellow neo-regulationists strengthened their case for greater and more effective regulatory controls. Deliberately exaggerating the perils of the 'white slave trade' (by which they meant the international traffic in under-age virgins) they successfully headed off abolitionist attacks on the *maisons tolérées*. Instead, with powerful backing in the press, they set out to persuade public opinion that young girls stood in need of protection against the ever-present menace of sexual assault and that ultimately such protection depended on their own vigilance over their chastity.[98] The state, of course, would do its utmost to see to the rigorous supervision of all extra-marital sexual activity. As in Augustinian theology, so in the code of bourgeois morality in the France of the *belle époque*, the brothel justified its existence to the extent that it preserved the virtue of respectable young ladies. The fact that it degraded and marginalised the prostitutes themselves seems to have mattered little.

The so-called 'crisis in gender relations' which supposedly provoked angst amid the bourgeoisie of the *belle époque* can thus be seen to have been, at best, the affair of a minority. Even the image of the lesbian was by no means as threatening as some historians have claimed, since there is evidence that contemporaries viewed them with indifference or even thought of them as 'charming'. Lesbianism was not proscribed by French law, which reserved its sanctions for sex acts committed in public, molestation and transvestism. Provided lesbians were obviously women from a wealthy and cultured background, indulging their sexual preference in the privacy of their own homes, they had little to fear. Admittedly, the same could not be said for lesbians from the ranks of the popular classes, who were ridiculed, reviled and harassed.[99] What this suggests, however, was that class was a more serious issue than gender at the turn of the century, and it is to the condition of the working-class woman of the period that we turn next.

Chapter 11

Gender at work

Women workers and the sexual division of labour

In the period after 1850, the French economy continued to exhibit many of the traits which had characterised it in the first half of the nineteenth century. Population growth was sluggish; agriculture retained many of its archaic features; and industrial development was extremely uneven. In 1891, 17.5 million people (46% of the population) still derived their livelihoods from the agricultural sector. Nevertheless, the second half of the nineteenth century was a crucial period of economic change. Agriculture itself underwent a dramatic break with the past, transformed by the new technologies and the application of fertilisers with a resultant increase in productivity. At the same time, the transport revolution opened up new markets and paved the way for the commercialisation of the sector. Subsistence crises became a thing of the past. Industrial growth, having slackened off in the 1870s and 1880s after the impressive progress made under the Second Empire, began to expand once more in the mid-1890s, and especially after 1905, with the most dynamic growth evident in new industries such as chemicals, electricity and car manufacture and in related older industries such as iron and steel. The rapid development of the tertiary sector was further evidence of economic modernisation.[1] All of these changes impacted on the lives of working women in both town and countryside in ways which are not susceptible to facile generalisation.

Work and family: change and continuity in female employment patterns

Despite the unreliability of official statistics (and in particular their tendency to under-represent casual female labour in 'hidden' employment such as street-vending and taking in lodgers), it is clear that the female labour force expanded considerably in the second half of the nineteenth century (Table 1).

While the apparent dramatic leap in the agricultural labour force may be discounted because of the fact that it was only in 1906 that for the first time the statisticians

Table 1   Women in the active population (in millions)

Year	Active population			Non-agricultural active population		
	Total	Men	Women	Total	Men	Women
1866	15.143	10.500	4.643	8.181	5.413	2.768
1881	16.491	11.129	5.362	8.635	5.665	2.970
1896	18.994	12.575	6.419	10.493	6.842	3.651
1901	19.715	12.911	6.804	11.471	7.329	4.142
1906	20.721	13.028	7.693	11.891	7.535	4.356
1911	20.931	13.212	7.719	12.414	7.943	4.471

Source: J. Daric, L'Activité professionnelle des femmes en France (INED, Cahier no. 5, Paris, PUF, 1947), p. 15

included the wives of peasant farmers in their own right (which makes any previous comparisons invalid) the non-agricultural female labour force grew by 1.6 million, or 37%. In terms of levels of activity relative to the 19.745 million women in the total population in 1906, the overall percentage of working women was 38.9% and the percentage of women in the non-agricultural labour force was 22%.[2]

The composition of the female labour force was as shown in Table 2.
As regards the non-agricultural female labour force, it should be noted that more than half a million women were classified as heads of substantial enterprises (chefs d'établissement) while another million and a half were either small employers (petites patronnes) or women working at home (travailleuses isolées). Women working as waged labourers in industry (ouvrières) accounted for just over a million, of whom the vast majority (around 700,000) were evenly divided between textiles and the clothing industry.[3] A breakdown in percentage terms is given in Table 3.

Thus, even at the beginning of the twentieth century and at a time when many sectors of the economy were undergoing rapid expansion, the statistics show that the female factory worker had by no means become the most representative figure of the female labour force in France. True, in the Nord, the female labour force in

Table 2   Professional occupations of women (in millions)

Profession	1901	1906	1911
Agriculture, forestry and fisheries	2.668	3.330	3.241
Industry	2.360	2.519	2.535
Commerce	0.698	0.779	0.835
Liberal profession and public service	0.295	0.293	0.337
Domestic service	0.784	0.773	0.771
Total active population	6.805	7.694	7.719
Active non-agricultural population	4.137	4.364	4.478

Source: J. Daric, L'Activité professionnelle des femmes en France (INED, Cahier no. 5, Paris, PUF, 1947), p. 30

Table 3 Percentage of women in different professions of the female non-agricultural labour force in 1906

Profession	Percentage
Heads of enterprise	12.2
Self-employed	35.9
Salaried employees	7.9
Workers	25.1
Domestic service	17.4
Unemployed	1.5

Source: J. Daric, *L'Activité professionnelle des femmes en France* (INED, Cahier no. 5, Paris, PUF, 1947), p. 44

the textiles factories increased significantly. In the urban conurbation of Lille-Roubaix-Tourcoing, textile factories which in 1882 employed 16,500 women over the age of 18 alongside 30,000 adult men by 1914 employed around 70,000 women in a total workforce of about 241,000 men and women. But it was only in textiles that women entered large-scale industry in any significant numbers (in 1906 they constituted 55.2% of the total labour force in this sector). In metal work, by contrast, the comparable figure was only 5.8%, however much this represented a substantial increase on the position in the 1860s.[4] Textiles, moreover, accounted for only 14% of the total female non-agricultural labour force in 1896, whereas domestic service provided 19% and the clothing industry 26%.[5] It is worth underlining, further, that within the female factory proletariat, the typical worker was not a mature married woman but a young single woman. Whereas youths under the age of 20 comprised only 19.33% of the male labour force in factories, girls under 20 accounted for 39.13% of female workers.[6] Male factory workers were most numerous in the age group 25–29, while women were most heavily represented in the category of those under 20.[7]

On the other hand, it would be wrong to imply that in France married women did not form a significant proportion of the non-agricultural labour force. At around 20% of the total, they provided twice the percentage to be found in Britain.[8] The proportion of French married women in manufacturing industry was particularly high (about 32%).[9] Such statistics, however, are not at odds with the suggestion made in an earlier chapter that, on the whole, working-class women in France derived their identity more from the family than from work. As we have seen, much of women's work was sporadic, varying according to the needs of the family. The relationship between work, family and household was, and continued to be, a distinguishing feature of women's work and underscored its gendered nature. Women's wage-earning capacity was often a 'reserve resource', to be called upon when the family found itself in straightened circumstances. As in pre-industrial times, this contribution to the family budget should not be underestimated, since it was vital to the family's economic survival. An invaluable study carried out by the Board of Trade into the conditions of working-class life in the early twentieth century discovered that women contributed 8.6–14.5% of total family income.[10] The wage-labour of married French women was not so much a rejection of bourgeois notions of domesticity as a sign of their commitment to providing for the most basic needs of their families.

One reason why France had a large proportion of married women among the non-agricultural labour force was demographic. Thus France had a higher proportion of married women in the population than, say, Britain. In 1901 some 42% of French women aged between 20 and 24 were married, whereas in Britain the figure was only 25%.[11] Moreover, the decline in the French birth rate was more marked than in other countries, with a fall from 25 per 1000 in 1851–55 to 20.7 in 1901–05.[12] Among the working classes, it is true, the decline was less steep than the national average, but it was perceptible nevertheless. In the mining town of Anzin, the figure for 1861 was 37.2; in 1906 it was 26.5. Similarly in Roubaix, one of the principal centres of the textile industry, the equivalent figures were 42.8 and 27.[13] Like middle-class women, but for different reasons, working-class women sought to control their own fertility. Their techniques may have been crude, and certainly included abortion as a 'back-up' method.[14] The point remains that, however hostile many socialist leaders were to the campaigns of the neo-Malthusians, working women welcomed advice about birth control, largely so that they could continue to bring in an additional wage to the family.[15]

The demographic circumstances which rendered married working-class women in France more available for work than in a country like Britain were complemented by economic factors which had the same effect. As Scott and Tilly point out, married women tended to find paid employment in the least industrialised sectors of the labour force, that is 'in those areas where the least separation existed between home and workplace and where women could control the rhythm of their own work'.[16] While the type of labour they engaged in depended largely on the occupational structure of a particular town, on the whole they did unskilled and casual jobs (as laundresses, charwomen, street-hawkers, bread-carriers and so on). Alternatively, where the opportunity was open to them, they continued to work for wages at home as domestic workers, an option available to many women in late nineteenth-century France because of the uneven spread of the industrialisation, notably in the clothing industry, which was often still organised on a 'putting-out' basis.[17]

Indeed, some of the economic developments of the mid- to late nineteenth century stimulated still more demand for domestic labour. The expansion of the large department stores created the possibility of mass sales to an urban market.[18] The invention of the sewing machine likewise acted as another stimulus to domestic manufacture, as too did the passing of protective legislation on behalf of women factory workers in the 1890s, which encouraged many employers to resort to domestic workers who were unaffected by the new laws.[19] Sometimes artisan families, desperate to maintain their traditions of independent household production in the face of ferocious pressures to cut the price of their products, made conscious decisions to preserve the craft in the male line and to push daughters into 'sweated' labour at home. Such, for example, was the practice of weavers in the Pays des Mauges.[20] For these various reasons domestic industry was very far from extinct in France at the turn of the century: on the contrary, in some sectors numbers expanded and overall it is reckoned that there were some 250,000 workers in the Paris region and another 750,000 in the provinces.[21] Most of these women were married with families. A survey of Parisian seamstresses carried out by the Office du Travail discovered that 50% of the sample consisted of married women while another 33% were either widows or divorcees.[22] A similar study of artificial flower makers showed that 52% were married and 22% either widowed or divorced.[23] As in pre-industrial times and in the early nineteenth century, the economic activity of married women in the *belle époque* testifies not to the breakdown of the working-class family but rather to the crucial and continuing importance of the family in working-class culture.

Perhaps the most striking change in the pattern of women's employment by the early twentieth century was one which has already been mentioned, namely the rise in 'white blouse' jobs in the tertiary sector of the economy. In the new jobs as in the old, however, women's work continued to be gendered at two levels: in the first place, through being channelled into occupations which were increasingly defined as 'feminine'; and secondly, through their perceived inferiority to work carried out by men in the same general sphere. Usually, the commercial and administrative jobs held by women were those involving little initiative and no authority. In government departments, women were recruited mainly as shorthand typists, and on the grounds that they could be paid lower wages than men.[24] Until at least the turn of the century, many of the new office jobs were restricted to the female relatives of male employees. In the railway companies, for instance, preference was given to the wives, daughters and sisters of men already on their staff, though some others did get taken on. The same was true in banks like the Comptoir National d'Escompte, the Crédit Lyonnais and the Bank of France. Not surprisingly, there were more applicants for office jobs than there were places available.[25]

Underlying this situation was the lack of establishments to provide girls with an adequate technical training for a career in commerce or industry. The earliest attempts to meet this deficiency were made by Elisa Lemonnier, who founded a Society for the Professional Education of Women and established the first of her vocational schools in 1862. After her death Mme Julie Toussaint carried on her work, but the state remained slow to follow their example. Eventually, on the initiative of MM Gréard and Buisson at the Ministry of Education, a law of 11 December 1880 created a number of manual apprenticeship schools, which was followed by further legislation establishing practical schools of commerce and industry. But despite the encouragement which all of these schools received from various governments before 1914, the type of training they provided was intended only to prepare girls for the lower reaches of business life – as typists, as secretaries and so on. Managerial positions remained almost exclusively in the hands of men.[26]

Lives of labour: women's experience of work

As in the period before 1850, so in the *belle époque*, agriculture continued to be the single largest sector of the economy in which women were employed. This, however, is not to say that the rhythms of rural life went on in some timeless manner. In the second half of the nineteenth century, under the impact of agricultural change which was already under way in the 1830s and 1840s, some regions such as the Pays des Mauges in western France were transformed from areas of subsistence farming into thriving centres of commercial livestock farming. In such cases, whereas women had formerly been engaged in spinning and petty commerce rather than in farm work, they increasingly found themselves obliged to take on the less skilled and the more tedious of the agricultural tasks. Their previous involvement in the latter had been with harvesting and threshing: now new technology in the shape of reaping hooks and long-handled scythes made these activities into man's work. In the countryside as in the cities, superior skill was a masculine preserve: women were left with the drudgery of cultivating the vegetables used as winter fodder for the animals. As the countryside became more rural and de-industrialised with the decline of rural industry, peasant women experienced a process which could not unfairly be described as proletarianisation.[27]

Still more dramatic was the transformation in the lives of at least some sections of the urban working classes, as families found themselves having to adapt to a situation in which work was removed from the home and reorganised on a non-familial basis in large, mechanised factories. The case of Saint Chamond was exemplary. Whereas the ribbon-weavers and their wives, unlike the nail-makers, had fought hard to maintain the family economy in the face of industrialisation in the period before 1850, after the modernisation of the textile industry carried out by manufacturers in the wake of the free trade agreement between France and Britain signed in 1860 they were obliged to give up the struggle. In consequence, large numbers of women – many of whom were married – entered the new braid factories where, in spite of the claims made by apologists for the factory regime, conditions were wretched. The women worked twelve-hour shifts in humid conditions and, if young and single, were housed in freezing dormitories. Such work was a necessity for hard-pressed families in a situation where even skilled male workers, whether in textiles or in metals, found it almost impossible to support a family on the strength of their own wage alone. The only alternative to the contributions of a working wife was recourse to charity – a strategy which not a few families in Saint Chamond adopted in a community dominated by a Catholic *patronat* with a social conscience. The reduction of family size also became a proletarian imperative even for the workers in the metal industry who, in the first half of the nineteenth century, had disdained the practice of birth control, as workers sought to find ways of resisting the harshness of everyday life and working conditions.[28]

For the working women of the textile industry, whether at Saint Chamond or elsewhere, long hours, low wages and bad conditions remained the rule well into the twentieth century. Working life started young. Jeanne Bouvier, the daughter of a cooper and small farmer in the Isère, relates in a rare example of female working-class autobiography how she became an *ouvrière* at the age of 11 in 1876. Starting work at 5 a.m. and finishing at 8 p.m., with rest breaks of two hours for meals, she was paid 50 centimes for a working day of thirteen hours. To supplement this meagre pittance, she spent her evenings at crochet work, sometimes working through the entire night so that the house might have bread:

> I recall that one time among others I went almost two days without eating. In the evening, on coming home from the factory, I got down to work. My mother spent the night with me to give me a shake when in spite of myself I fell asleep. She said: 'Don't go to sleep, you know that you mustn't sleep. Tomorrow we won't have any bread'. I made superhuman efforts to stay awake. It was very cold. The snow hammered against the windows. Despite all these tortures, I kept working until 4.30 a.m., the time at which I got ready to return to the factory.[29]

In the textile mills of the Nord, women routinely worked the same hours as men, putting in a twelve- to fourteen-hour day in the 1880s. During breaks, workers were effectively obliged to stay by their machines, to clean or service them (work for which they received no pay) and they virtually never closed down the machines for fear of losing wages, which were paid on a piece-rate.[30] Factory work, moreover, was often dangerous as well as physically draining. It is true that, by the 1890s, conditions had ameliorated since the time of Villermé's investigations, when girls in textile factories doing the work of beating by hand often contracted 'cotton pneumonia', and when silk workers died young from tuberculosis. But dangers were still much in evidence. Women weavers at work on Jacquart looms had to be wary of the toxic poisons given off by the counter-weights of lead when they rubbed together.[31] In linen mills, the heavy, hot, humid atmosphere was a constant threat to the workers' health, while in the silk factories defective machines for conducting steam away meant that factory hands had to work enveloped in clouds which prevented them from seeing their neighbours and which soaked their light garments, so that the slightest drop in temperature could bring on chills capable of developing rapidly into pneumonia.[32] Also, quite often young silk workers continued the practice of sleeping on site in dormitories, returning to their families only at weekends. Factory inspectors discovered that their sleeping arrangements could be atrocious. One inspector reported that the dormitory was an attic where air and light never penetrated; in other places, no wash basins were to be found, and beds consisted of piles of straw over which were strewn filthy sheets and blankets. A further report of 1901 noted a few changes for the better, but deplored the fact that girls still generally slept two to a bed.[33]

Sexual harassment was another feature of factory life in the textile mills. In the Lille area, local newspapers regularly carried stories of harassment, and women workers themselves gave evidence to a parliamentary enquiry of 1904. Forms of harassment varied from physical violence to touching up and verbal abuse. Sometimes older women who tried to intervene on behalf of younger women harassed by foremen and managers were fined or even fired. Workers who tried to resist or to protest earned a reputation for being 'difficult' and might be punished by being given impossible tasks or subjected to regular fines for breaches of factory discipline.[34]

Wages were invariably low. Women were paid 'women's' wages, that is they were paid not as workers but as women who sought to supplement the family income with meagre extra earnings – what the French called a *salaire d'appoint*, or 'pin money'. Kaethe Schirmacher, author of an exhaustive statistical survey on the situation of the *ouvrière* at the turn of the century, calculated that the maximum wage of a woman in industry did not reach even 50% of the maximum obtained by a male worker.[35] There were a few exceptions to the general rule: for instance, the matchmakers, whose wages rose by 76% in the years between 1890 and 1904, and the tobacco makers, whose pay went up 21% between 1894 and 1904. Women typographers, too, earned well above the average wage for women, but their 5–6 francs a day still left them well below the 7–8 francs earned by their male workmates.[36] Nevertheless, it remains true that in the early 1890s the average pay taken home by a woman in a large to middling firm in the department of the Seine was 3 francs to a man's 6fr.15, with the corresponding figures in the provinces being 2fr.10 and 3fr.90.[37] From the statistics released by the Ministry of Labour in 1914, no significant diminution in the gap can be discerned in the years just before the Great War.

If in certain sectors it is clear that industrialisation did disrupt older modes of domestic production and propelled women into waged labour in factories, it remains the case that in other sectors continuities with the past were retained. The clothing industry was the most obvious case in point. Throughout the nineteenth century the garment trade employed women in massive numbers (1,380,000 in 1906, as compared with 594,000 in 1866) and became progressively feminised (women comprised 89% of the total labour force in 1906 as opposed to 78% in 1866).

Production took place in either small workshops or, most commonly, in the homes of a dispersed female workforce. As we have seen, the invention of the sewing machine had further feminised the sector and by the end of the century the sewing machine had replaced the needle as a symbol of femininity. But whether she worked in one of the many small workshops in central Paris or at home, the woman worker in the clothing industry was as exploited as any factory worker in the textile industry – indeed, often more so, as investigators into 'sweated' labour revealed.[38]

The Parisian dressmaker was often represented as the quintessential woman worker, renowned for her coquetry and good humour and said to be an incurable romantic, addicted to popular love stories and fond of trips to places like Suresnes, Meudon or Robinson in the company of her boyfriend, as if a character out of an Impressionist painting of a Sunday afternoon by the Seine.[39] If the representation has any basis in social reality – and it does seem that the dressmakers had a genuine relish for life – their *joie de vivre* owed nothing to their working conditions. Work was irregular and seasonal, because of the variations in demand for their products. In busy times – before a big society occasion like a ball, a Grand Prix or a funeral – long hours of frantic toil were the rule, as the young women put in astonishing overtime hours known as *veillées* in order to finish the garments on time. One labour inspector reported that when Czar Alexander III died in 1894, all the great Russian ladies placed orders with the Parisian fashion houses, who then required their dressmakers to slave day and night to meet the deadline.[40] Jeanne Bouvier has recalled how, having become a garment worker, she often put in long *veillées* till 2 a.m., in most cases without stopping for dinner and sustained only by a roll and a bar of chocolate taken at 4 p.m. Strict discipline in the workshop, including the imposition of absolute silence, made life even less bearable. Finishing at 2 a.m., she then faced a walk of some three-quarters of an hour before she reached her lodgings – a daunting prospect on an empty stomach in freezing winter. On reaching home, more often than not, she was not up to preparing a meal: it is hardly surprising that after such a season she needed hospital care. On one occasion, she worked a shift from 8 a.m. to 5 a.m. the following morning.[41]

In the 'dead season', by contrast, garment workers went without work. Between January and March, and again between July and September, there were periods when consumer demand for clothes and goods such as household linens dropped dramatically, with the result that garment industry workers were laid off. A dressmaker had to reckon with the fact that she would be unemployed for long stretches during the year: top hands could count on earning a full wage on only 260–300 days, while a second would be lucky to have full employment on 200–215 days.[42] The irregular and seasonal nature of employment in the clothing industry therefore exacerbated the problem of pitifully low pay, which barely improved in the period before 1914. Dressmakers were paid by the day rather than by the hour. Between 1893 and 1900 wages remained much the same. Small increases came only in 1908, and again after

1910, though these pay rises served only to keep pace with the cost of living which rose by 5% between 1900 and 1914. Workers were probably best off in small and middling workshops. Apprentices who in 1893 lived *au pair* with their employers and received no wage at all were paid 50 centimes a day in 1914; small hands who got between 1 and 1fr.50 in 1893 received between 1fr.78 and 2fr.25; while first hands got at least 4 francs a day instead of 3 francs. In the bigger houses improvements were even less marked – insignificant in the case of apprentices and second hands and perhaps attaining about 0.50 francs in the case of first hands who could count on earning 5–6fr.50 a day in 1914.[43]

Because of unemployment, however, even in the few cases where daily wages were relatively high, annual income remained low. One worker, who earned 4fr.75 a day in 1895, told the social investigator Charles Benoist that she would rather be paid only 3fr.50 a day if she could be guaranteed 300 days of full employment in the year.[44] At the time of Benoist's enquiry, women workers in the clothing industry were not being paid a living wage, as he showed by drawing up a list of specimen annual budgets.[45] Similar studies show that there were still many women in a comparable situation in 1913, earning barely subsistence wages. With an abundance of skilled labour available on the market, the law of supply and demand worked very much to the advantage of the employer. The author of a report in the *Bulletin* of the Ministry of Labour concluded that even in 1914 'the level of the daily wage barely provides for the indispensable means of subsistence: it does not even permit independence, nor the least saving, or leisure or pastime which promotes intellectual or physical development'.[46]

For young women living at home, this 'pin money' may have been acceptable as their contribution to the family income; but for women living alone and trying to earn their own living, the material difficulties presented by these pittances could usually be overcome only by cohabitation with a male worker. The alternatives were prostitution or suicide. Among Jeanne Bouvier's neighbours on the seventh floor of her apartment building were women even poorer than she was. The most wretched was a young seamstress who worked for a big fashion house on the rue de la Paix: despite the high quality of her work, she could afford only 0.15 francs a day for food (bread and milk). Unable to pay her rent, she had to move to another place nearby where she survived miserably until, overcome by the strains and pressures involved in merely staying alive, she jumped out of her top floor window.[47]

A great many of the women who worked in the clothing industry (particularly if they were married) did so not in factories or even small workshops but at home. Of all working women these were, generally speaking, the most exploited, though it should be said that for many home work was a conscious choice, based on the desire to maintain the traditional balancing act between family commitments and contributing to the upkeep of the household. An analysis of 510 such *ouvrières* in an enquiry carried out by the Musée Social in 1908 found that, out of 217 who gave their wage by the hour, 109 (60%) got less than 3 sous, and 186 (83%) got less than 5 sous.[48] Some unfortunates, forced to work under the so-called 'truck' system, might see hardly any money wages at all but receive only some token in kind.[49] No limitation (beyond the strength of the worker) existed on the duration of the working day: the official enquiry into the state of domestic work in needlework in Paris found that 43% of the women workers laboured between ten and twelve hours a day, while 13% did more than twelve hours.[50] Even children were cruelly exploited: as one contemporary observer pointed out, it was complete nonsense to argue that small industry and domestic industry preserved the family better, for reality showed 'the little girl of ten kept from going to school and made to do housework and look after the smaller children, while the mother sews at her machine'.[51] Few of these women could afford to eat properly or to live in decent lodgings: 'Those who have 95 centimes or 1 franc a day for food constitute the aristocracy. Others don't have more than 50 or 75 centimes'.[52]

The various enquiries initiated by the Office du Travail confirm this picture of generalised misery. Occasionally, an extremely skilful woman capable of prodigiously hard work could make more than enough to survive on. Such was Mlle B., aged 30 and a former dressmaker who claimed to have earned 1200 francs in 1904 by putting in sixteen hours daily for ten months and managing some irregular work in the other two. She declared that she had got used to long hours of work with her *veillées* and did not mind them much now that she was able to remain at home.[53] But in sharp contrast, and much more typical of the average Parisian domestic work in sewing, was Mme I., at 28 the widow of a policeman with no family to help her out. Although able to sew, she lacked the skill of a professional and earned only 10 centimes an hour, working an eleven-hour day. Out of an income of about 30 francs a month, she had to pay 12 francs towards the cost of her machine which left her with only about 1 franc a day for food, whereas she reckoned that she needed to spend at least 1fr.50 if she were to maintain a proper diet. Usually her meals consisted of milk and sugar in the morning, cutlet or beefsteak at 30 centimes and a vegetable for lunch, with three pounds of bread to last her two days. She took no evening meal. The rest of her resources went on washing, heating and lighting, though fortunately she had her rent paid by her widow's pension. For the previous fifteen months she had been able to get by only because of her savings: she had no idea how she could cope once these ran out.[54]

For a single parent the situation was even more desperate. One woman, aged 26, and abandoned by her husband at the birth of their second child, was able to earn only about 600 francs in 1904. She now lived with her mother in a filthy hotel room near the Panthéon and told the interviewer that no one had eaten since the previous day. Her female employer exploited her situation to pay her less than other women workers, humiliating her because of her irregular marital situation. When she tried to get help from another woman she found herself even more cruelly exploited, receiving only 2fr.50 for a week's work in which she worked three days and three nights: that is, she was paid less than 5 centimes an hour.[55] A single woman could survive only if she had someone else in her family to help her out. Mme H., a 43-year-old widow living in Plaisance who said she made only 2fr.25 a day (though the enquirer thought she possibly made more) was able to live quite comfortably because two of her remaining three children were gainfully employed, so that the annual resources of the household totalled 1779fr.50.[56]

Overall, the Parisian survey of domestic seamstresses discovered that a sizeable proportion (17%) were over 60 years of age. Out of 540 interviewed, some eighty were suffering from ill-health and probably a lot more refused to reveal the real state of their health. Around 25% seem to have experienced a deterioration in their eyesight. Half (50%) were married, while 33% were either widowed or, very rarely, divorced. A total of 16% were single women, of whom ten out of eighty-three said they had children. The majority (60%) earned less than 400 francs a year, 24% got between 400 and 600 francs, while 15% made more than 600 francs. Accommodation was usually poor: 135 lived in a single room and twenty-four of these were occupied by households with three or more persons. The average rent was 150–300 francs a year. Some 68% of the residences could be considered satisfactory from the point of view of hygiene, but 32% were extremely bad.[57]

The picture was equally depressing in the provinces. In the Cher, domestic seamstresses averaged a maximum of 0.10 francs an hour (59%); a mere handful (1%) earned more than 0.21 francs.[58] In the Loir-et-Cher 52% of the women workers earned a maximum of 200 francs a year.[59] Fairly representative was Mme C. (department of the Indre), aged 35, married with four children. Her husband earned about 100 francs a month working in a chemical laboratory. For the previous sixteen years, she had made all kinds of articles for an entrepreneur specialising in military equipment – shirts, flannel belts, jackets, etc. – working fourteen hours a day and receiving a little help from her mother, who also helped the children with some of the housework. Her daily wage usually came out to be about 0.80 francs net.[60]

As ever, the hardest lot was reserved for the single woman fending for herself: a widowed shirtmaker from Rouen said that only a very good worker could hope to make 1fr.25 a day, and only then by doing with a minimal amount of sleep. She herself had made 127 shirts in a week, sleeping only two hours a night, but for this her net gain had been a mere 10 francs. She was one of the many who had to buy thread from her *Maison* at an inflated price or else be refused work. The interviewer summed up:

> This worker, who is forty-seven, looks as if she is sixty. Her food is made up of little more than little balls of minced pork, salted herrings and the cheapest of vegetables. She says that she gets no help from anyone and that life for her is an unalleviated burden.[61]

The same pattern is to be found in other domestic industries. An investigation of the wages and budgets of domestic workers in the Lyon area conducted by Léon Bonnevay in 1896 confirmed the reality of low pay.[62] All sections of opinion, from the Catholic social reformer Albert de Mun on the Right through to the Socialists on the Left, were agreed that it was a matter of deliberate policy on the part of employers not to pay women a living wage.[63] Only in the case of artificial flowers were wages generally somewhat higher. Even so, the median daily wage for a woman working alone was 2 francs – and an income of at least 3 francs a day was required for subsistence. Just over a quarter (27%) earned that amount.[64]

Essentially a Parisian trade, the artificial flower industry was designed to complement the products of the great fashion houses and underwent considerable expansion in the late nineteenth and early twentieth centuries. A skilled specialist could do very well. Mme N., who specialised in natural flowers, was able to make a gross income of 631fr.25 working a six-hour day in 1907–8. Her husband, a mechanic with a bus company, earned a good wage and her daughter brought in 90 francs a month. The family lived comfortably in the Clignancourt area and the wife felt that she would be able to stop working altogether in a year or so. Another of these better-off women workers was Mme V., whose income in 1907–8 amounted to 1088fr.50 for an average eleven-hour day. Her husband, an electrician, earned 1127 francs a year and they lived comfortably with their two children in the Combat *quartier*.

But by no means all the women working in the artificial flower industry were as fortunate. Mme S., a widow of 30 with five young children, one of whom had recently died and of whom two others were seriously ill, was unable to continue working for a large department store because she had to live in Ménilmontant, on the outskirts of the city, where the family occupied a single room. The woman herself was tubercular, and her work was often interrupted by illness; the physical effort involved in her work of making artificial chrysanthemums periodically caused her to vomit blood. Another poor woman was Mlle C., aged 48, who suffered from a liver complaint and lived in a squalid furnished room. For meals she ate only a sou's worth of horse meat with a sou's worth of bread. Working irregularly, she had made in the region of 456 francs the previous year. Likewise 31-year-old Mme G., whose pale, ravaged face bore the marks of excessive effort and a life of deprivation, struggled to earn enough to bring up her family by making violets 10–12 hours a day, without ever receiving more than 1 franc for her labours. Her husband, a casual labourer, was of no great help since he was often out of work. In general, for Paris and its suburbs, 81% of the women engaged in making artificial flowers at home had worked at some previous stage in a workshop, and had therefore obtained some kind of training and skills. Fifty-two per cent were married, 22% were widowed or divorced and 21% were single. Most worked at home for family reasons and were prepared to put in long hours – more than 40% did between eleven and eighteen hours a day.[65]

Perhaps the most glamorous female profession for a working-class girl in the *belle époque* was that of *demoiselle de magasin*, or shop assistant in one of the luxury stores.[66] But, while they may have enjoyed a superior social status to that of their brothers in the working-class suburbs of Pantin, Saint-Denis and La Chapelle, from where they commuted into the stores in central Paris, shop assistants remained poorly paid and, perhaps worse, were constantly made to feel inferior by the hierarchical structure of power in the store. Liable to instant dismissal, denied the right to answer complaints by a customer, the shop assistants worked on average a thirteen-hour day, having to arrive before opening time at 8 a.m. and not being able to go home after closing time at 8 p.m. until all goods had been rearranged. Apprentices were kept busy all day long with the most menial tasks – sweeping up and running errands. Other girls had to sell the shop's wares on the street pavement, where they could freeze in winter and stew in summer. But perhaps the most distressing aspect of their situation was the isolation and ferocious rivalry which existed among them as a result of the *guelte* system of payment (a bonus system based on the quantity of sales). Assistants regarded one another as competitors and made few friends with their colleagues. The customers, too, were rivals, for the sales girls depended on them for their livelihood. While they envied their wealthy and well-dressed customers, they themselves were the objects of the bitter resentments of their petty bourgeois clients, who took pleasure in ordering them around in the most humiliating fashion before making purchases worth a few pence. In front of the counters, as Zola observed in his novel *Au bonheur des dames*, it was a case of woman eating woman.[67]

With the exception of food stores, in general the bigger the shop the worse were the conditions: shop workers were continually overworked in a confined and unhealthy atmosphere. According to Dr Paul Berthod, tuberculosis was a not uncommon consequence.[68] Some were lodged by the shop in a *mansarde*, a small, cramped, extremely uncomfortable attic with no washing facilities and where they were forbidden to have visitors. Placed under the strict surveillance of a *concierge*, they had to return to their miserable dwellings by an 11 p.m. curfew, which left them little time for relaxing on their own or for meeting a lover. The smiling, elegant *demoiselle* of the daytime store belied the lonely, miserable girl of the *mansarde*.

No survey of women's working conditions would be complete without an examination of the profession which, in the non-agricultural labour force, was actually the single largest employer of female labour: domestic service. For the prosperous middle classes, at least one domestic servant in the household was a necessary status symbol. In 1906, there were 206,000 servants in Paris, some 11% of the population.[69] Before the French Revolution the profession had numbered as many men as women, but in the course of the nineteenth century it, too, was 'feminised'. In 1851 in Paris there were still thirty-one men for every sixty-nine women: by 1872 men constituted only 29% and in 1911 only 17% of the total servant population.[70] Though heavily concentrated in Paris, most domestics were provincial in origin (in 1831, 60% of the servants who died in Paris had been born elsewhere).[71] One study suggests that domestic service should be seen as an important avenue by which women from a rural background came to join the modern, urban way of life; while this may be true, it was also the case that many domestics entered service in the hope that eventually they would be able to save enough money to allow themselves to retire or establish themselves back in their native region.[72]

Domestics were far from forming a homogeneous body; on the contrary the structure of the profession was extremely hierarchical. At the top of the female hierarchy came the chambermaid, generally aged between 17 and 25. Her tasks included dressing her mistress, some darning and occasionally some ironing. A well-informed observer, Octave Uzanne, claimed that chambermaids were given to snooping and searching in drawers and were avid readers of other people's letters. A main objective, according to him, was to squeeze as many old dresses and hats out of their mistresses as they could. In Uzanne's view they were usually ugly as well as opinionated, and paraded their prudishness by frequent visits to church. In family quarrels they would be on the side of Madame against Monsieur. Earning between 40 and 75 francs a month, at around the age of 35 they were generally in a position to return to their native village, where they would marry and perhaps open a small shop. The great rival for pre-eminence with the chambermaid in the household was the cook, who was commonly acknowledged as a pilferer of the household's food. Her earnings worked out at about 50–75 francs a month.

Next in the hierarchy came the children's maid, who might be a foreigner (English or German). In Uzanne's stereotypes, she was aged 20–25, often pretty, and bent on wringing more clothes out of Madame than the chambermaid. Frequently, she was bored by the children, paying attention to them only when out on a walk or in the park in order to attract the attention of men. In her free time she supposedly read romantic fiction, fantasised about the possibilities of marvellous adventures, and haunted the *brasseries* of the Latin Quarter, where, unlike most domestics, she habitually squandered her 35–50 francs a month.

The hardest-worked servant was the maid-of-all-work, very often a sturdy country girl who had to be ready to do any kind of job. Rising early and going to bed late, she was depicted by Uzanne as spending her day in a constant battle to avoid breakages and scoldings – and to ward off the sexual advances of the master, his sons, and any man-servants in the household. She saved her 20–40 francs a month and often ended up marrying a farmer back in the country, where she would sweat blood to make the farm pay – 'a beast of work and a beast of pleasure', in Uzanne's estimation. Finally, at the bottom of the hierarchy, there was the poor cleaning woman, who would leave her village with her children and husband (typically a coachman or a factory worker, or perhaps a porter at the Bon Marché) to come to look after a bachelor. Rarely did she end her days back in her native parts, dying worn out after a life of hardship, having suffered beatings from her husband and undergone frequent pregnancies, yet remaining to the end honest, tender and devoted – all for 20 sous a day. For Uzanne, she was 'the real woman of the people'.[73]

Despite all these gradations in the ranks of domestic service, it is important to emphasise what servants had in common rather than what might appear to keep them apart. One feature they shared was the necessity of working long and hard: usually their day began at 7 a.m. and did not finish before 10 p.m. or even 11 p.m., with only one hour off to attend to personal matters – hence their habitual lack of cleanliness. Only a few managed to have one afternoon a week free – certainly general maids never did – while others counted themselves lucky to be off every Sunday, or perhaps once a fortnight. A holiday was possible only when the family was away. This lack of any time to oneself explains why servants were continually dodging and trying to steal time in desperate attempts to have some freedom and privacy.[74] Jeanne Bouvier, who in her varied career as a working woman spent some time in service, furnishes ample evidence of the incessant demands placed upon a young maid by an exacting mistress. Obliged to look after two spoiled and insolent children – though their mother would never hear a word against them – she had in addition to do all the shopping and housework, which included the particularly heavy task of the laundry. When the family entertained lots of friends before the holiday of 14 July, this washing load was made almost intolerable as she struggled down stairs with two large buckets of water which weighed more than herself. The last straw came when the old clothes line broke and she was both insulted and punished by her mistress.[75]

It was this kind of reaction which produced in the servant class as a whole another common trait: a bitter class hatred of their masters, intensified by an ever- increasing awareness of themselves as a distinct social group, almost a caste. Most of the literature on servants has of course been written from the point of view of the masters, but it is interesting and instructive to note the virtual unanimity on several points: the lack of any kind of sentimental bond which some claimed had existed formerly in a 'feudal' relationship between masters and their *anciens serviteurs*, and on top of this, exclusive emphasis by domestics on the cash nexus, as well as a certain truculence and barely concealed resentment against their betters. As early as 1837 one author wrote: 'Everyone complains about domestic servants! If you train them yourself they leave you, it is said, as soon as they can find a place elsewhere with higher pay'.[76] Mme Romieu, the self-styled expert on bourgeois etiquette, likewise lamented the readiness with which Parisian servants quit their positions and concluded that the most powerful force at work between masters and servants was mutual hatred.[77] Other commentators said much the same thing, one even bemoaning the abolition of the *livret*, in which he saw the 'only real security for the masters'.[78]

From such remarks, it seems reasonable to deduce that bourgeois masters and mistresses felt themselves to be confronted by a discontented servant class, and sound reasons for their discontent are not hard to find. Even if the legendary devoted *ancien serviteur* was largely a myth – Ernest Legouvé described the chambermaids in the plays of Molière and elsewhere as 'the confidantes of young girls, the messengers of amorous correspondence, the born enemies of husbands and fathers'[79] – it was true none the less that servants had once been more fully integrated into family life. A major development in the nineteenth century, mainly associated with the large-scale building of blocks of luxury flats under the Second Empire, was the separation of the maid from the rest of the family by having her live in a tiny room at the top of the building (*la chambre de bonne*): this inevitably made masters and mistresses more indifferent to the fate of their servants and in turn encouraged the latter to feel more independent and even less loyal. In these garrets it was not always possible to find somewhere to stand up straight. The windows were often too small to admit sufficient light or air, making for excessive heat in the summer and perishing cold in the winter. The only furniture would consist of a small iron bed, a wash basin, a table, a chair and a waterpot. Outside would be a filthy toilet. A domestic servant lacked not only the time for, but also the means of, keeping herself clean. At a congress on tuberculosis held in Geneva in 1906, one delegate claimed that the designer of these rooms, the engineer Mansart, had done more than any other single person to promote the spread of the disease.[80]

To compound these material sufferings, domestics were continually demoralised by their superiors' assertion of rank. Jeanne Bouvier has a very revealing story of how she lost another domestic job by getting on a bus before the two children whom she was paid to look after, and then sitting down on the only seat available. Madame, who witnessed the whole incident, was outraged: 'I was told I was ill-bred and bad-mannered – I could only have served with louts who did not know how to behave'.[81] Of course, critics pointed out that often servants wanted only to emulate their betters: one author was scandalised by their desire to eat the same food as their masters and their aping the manners and dress of their mistresses.[82] But servants, like the fictional Célestine created by Octave Mirbeau, who knew all her mistress's foibles and all the family secrets, mingled contempt with their envy.[83] Domestics were acutely conscious of their lowly status, and though their wages rose continually throughout the nineteenth century, they were all too aware that they lacked prestige in the eyes of the public. Evidence of a desire to improve their standing can be seen in their insistence on being called *gens de maison* rather than *domestiques*, and in their attempts to form trade unions and mutual aid societies. While it was usually male servants who were responsible for these initiatives, there are indications that their efforts met with a favourable response among female servants also.[84]

One reform, solicited particularly by the Catholic trade union Le Ménage, was of prime relevance to women – namely the suppression of the *bureaux de placement*. These, often fictitious, employment agencies were responsible for luring many innocent peasant girls to non-existent jobs in the towns, while others were simply fronts for brothels. A law was passed in 1904 establishing free placing, with remuneration for the agents to come entirely from the employers. But, as with a previous decree of 25 March 1852, the law was not rigorously enforced and abuses continued. *Placeurs* were still able to obtain large sums from prospective employees as a result of wide advertising campaigns in the provinces. If domestic service was a route to 'modernisation', it was one fraught with danger. One legal improvement from which servants did benefit, however, was the law of 3 July 1890 which obliged a master to give his servant a certificate at the end of the term of service, stating only factual information about the date of entry to employment, the date of departure, and the nature of the work done: no derogatory comment was allowed.[85]

Finally, it is right to remember that not all women's waged labour was captured and categorised in official employment statistics. Women (and they were often married women) can be found doing all sorts of odd jobs, working as bread-carrriers, fruit-sellers, fish-sellers, toy-sellers, news-vendors, and the like. There were also women who worked in small shops, selling bread, cheese, jam and all sorts of other specialities such as herbs (herbalists were also said to be frequent practitioners of back-street abortions).[86] There was also that most characteristic of women workers, the laundry woman. In the mid-nineteenth century a soaping woman would work a laborious fourteen-hour day for 2fr.50 and an ironing woman, more skilled and having served a longer apprenticeship, would get only 2fr.75 for a twelve-hour shift.[87] According to Octave Uzanne, a close and sympathetic observer of working women, the least fortunate of all was the washerwoman, who was set apart from other laundry women. Arriving by the Seine at 6 a.m. to start work, they rarely finished before 7 p.m. Exposed to the wind in winter and sweltered by the heat in summer, they easily became bronchial or rheumatic: and 75% suffered from hernia as a result of carrying their heavy loads of washing. The only highlight in their backbreaking day was around 3.30 p.m. when their *patronne* traditionally brought over coffee or a glass of wine. They were also well known for their strong language and willingness to exchange insults as they fought each other for the best washing places.[88] For them, as for virtually all French women workers of the *belle époque*, the experience of work was hard in the extreme.

Protecting women workers? Social reform and state intervention

The preoccupation with the condition of working women which had given rise to extensive debate and comment over the course of the nineteeenth century climaxed in the 1880s and 1890s, when a substantial body of influential opinion – which included economists, sociologists and trade unionists as well as politicians from the entire spectrum of political opinion – became convinced of the necessity of social reforms to 'protect' the *ouvrière*. After the passage of the child labour law of 1874, the prime target became a ban on women's work at night, which was effected by a law of 2 November 1892. The same legislation stipulated a maximum working day of eleven hours for women and provided for a weekly day of rest. A subsequent law of 1900 further shortened the working day to ten hours (to take effect by 1904). Other reforms included the extension of health and safety standards to female employees in shops and offices, though it was only after the outbreak of the First World War, by a law of 10 July 1915, that a minimum wage was introduced for domestic workers.[89]

It seems clear enough that the driving force behind protective legislation was supplied by middle-class reformers, not by women workers themselves. A study of the prime movers behind the 1892 act has highlighted the role played by the obscure deputy Richard Waddington (brother of the better-known William Waddington, Prime Minister in 1879 and later ambassador to London). As well as being a politician, Waddington was a prominent industrialist in Rouen, descended from a Protestant English family and motivated less by humanitarian concerns for women than by 'pronatalist, patriotic and familistic rationales'. Like his colleague the physician-legislator Gustave Dron, Waddington was much exercised by the spectre of depopulation and believed also that industrialisation was destroying the family: his fear was that, as a result, the military capacity of France could be impaired, the future of the country as a Great Power compromised and the French state weakened. On the other hand, republican legislators such as Strauss and Dron were realistic enough to appreciate that women could not be expelled from the labour force altogether. Their objective was to create a situation in which women's productive work would not interfere with their reproductive work. Their aim was to protect maternity, but not to prevent women from undertaking waged labour.[90]

Feminists, however, objected to legislation which discriminated against women workers on account of their gender. In the feminist daily newspaper *La Fronde*, Maria Pognon, president of the Ligue Française pour le Droit des Femmes, delivered a stinging attack on the ban on night work and the limitation of women's working hours. Her protest was all the more vehement because the 1892 law directly affected the newspaper's own all-woman team of workers, which included female compositors and typesetters who had to work at night. The law, Pognon maintained, had not been made in the interests of women, but was the work of antifeminists who wanted to reserve all the best-paid jobs for male workers. Hence the exceptions permitted for women workers engaged in certain kinds of so-called 'women's work' – seamstresses, hatmakers and the like – but the ban on work which men were willing to do. Pognon called for complete equality in the workplace. Protective legislation was only acceptable if it applied to both sexes. In her view, the way forward was not to deprive women of their jobs but to encourage them to join trade unions.[91]

Whether Pognon spoke for working women as well as for bourgeois feminists on the subject of protective legislation is a moot point. At Saint Chamond, they drew up a petition in protest at the ban on night work, affirming that many married women preferred the night shift so as to be free to look after their families during the day and in particular to be able to prepare the noon-day meal. On the other hand, they were put up to this ploy by their employers, who objected to the law because they feared it would hurt production and therefore profits.[92] In the Nord, the act was routinely subverted by textile manufacturers, perforce with the connivance of their women workers, though whether the latter complied willingly or not it is difficult to say, since refusal would have led to dismissal and blacklisting. Stratagems included compelling women to take work home to finish (for no pay) and speeding up the work process.[93] Another way round the law was the adoption of shift work in teams (the *système des relais*) which often kept women workers on the premises for longer than eleven hours a day in cases where they lived too far away from home to go back at mid-day.[94] Employers also warned one another of impending visits from the labour inspectorate, which allowed them time to conceal illegal workers or violations of safety and hygiene regulations.[95]

In any case, the administrative machinery to enforce the 1892 legislation was woefully deficient. The fines for violations of the law were derisory and hardly a deterrent to employers (Article 26 of the law of 1892 provided for a fine of between 5 and 15 francs). A decree of 26 July 1893 permitted many specified exemptions to the 1892 act, with regard to both the length of the working day and night work: hence the need for further legislation in 1900, though this, too, continued to be flouted.[96] The labour inspector Caroline Milhaud was well aware that in some factories in Roubaix and Tourcoing in 1906 women workers were still working shifts of up to nineteen hours, but she despaired of being able to catch the employers *in flagrante*. It appears that the average day in weaving in the years before 1914 continued to be ten hours, and eleven-hour days were not unknown in the silk factories of the Rhône as well as the cotton factories of the Nord.[97]

In the clothing industry, the legislation of 1892 and 1900 led to no serious diminution in the practice of *veillées*: before a Grand Prix race in 1900, the inspectorate unearthed a case where work was continuous over thirty hours.[98] As in textile mills, women were given work to finish off at home and to be brought back completed first thing in the morning. They also sent workers home when the inspectorate appeared, with instructions to come back once the coast was clear. Legal technicalities were also effectively exploited to get round the law: thus, inspectors had a legal right to enter factories only if they could show that they had good grounds for thinking that they would discover a breach of the law, and this was not always the case. But even when they gained right of access, they might encounter employers who had packed their workers off to work in their own apartments, which the inspectors could not search without violating domestic privacy. Such a situation came to light in 1906 in the horrible case of a young woman who died of suffocation in the wardrobe of a prominent couturier, who, after the inspector's departure, had forgotten to let her out.[99]

In the clothing industry, *veillées* were finally eliminated by a decree of 17 February 1910, which restricted female labour between the hours of 9 and 11 p.m. to the fabrication of articles required for funerals by women and children, and more especially by the law of 22 November 1911 which brought France into line with the resolutions of an International Convention on women's work held in Berne in 1906, and fixed the minimum duration of night rest for women at eleven hours, with 10 p.m. as the extreme limit of the working day.[100] Obligatory weekly rest became more widespread after the law of 13 July 1906, the terms of which applied not just to industrial workers but also to employees in the commercial sector.[101] Of course, some bosses continued to break the rules. A woman inspector, Mme Maître, discovered excessive work at the Maison Alexandre in Paris. Arriving at 7.40 a.m., she found that work had already begun, though she had previously been told that starting time was 9 a.m. No notice was displayed giving the hours of the working day, nor was any register kept.[102] By 1914, however, *veillées* had become exceptional. Yet it should be remembered that in season these *ouvrières* still worked a twelve-hour day, returning home only about 9.30–10.00 p.m.; and since most of them had to travel back to working-class suburbs like Clichy, Batignolles and Levallois, they were often too exhausted to eat, and consequently failed to look after their health properly.[103]

Nevertheless, over time, and thanks largely to the vigilance of the labour inspectorate, protective legislation began to make some difference to the working conditions of women workers. A law of 1894 brought some action on the problem of the temperature in textile factories, while better provision was made for conducting the dust from the carding rooms.[104] The law of 9 April 1898, penalising employers who were responsible for industrial accidents occasioned by their machinery, led to a tightening up of security in factories by measures such as fencing off machines and providing female employees with protective clothing.[105] In 1913 the Ministry of Labour was able to say in reply to a parliamentary question that the factory inspectorate was vigilant in enforcing the regulation that women should not clean out powerlooms in textile factories.[106]

The one area where the state balked at 'protection' was that of wages. Despite widespread denunciation of 'sweating', particularly of domestic workers in the clothing industry, no pre-war government was prepared to legislate on the question of a minimum wage. Bills to enact such a measure were initiated in parliament by politicians representing different shades of political opinion, such as the social Catholic Albert de Mun and the ex-socialist René Viviani, but they were invariably defeated. In 1911, however, a more restrictive bill confined to women workers in the clothing industry was introduced and it eventually secured a majority in the Chamber in 1913. It had not yet become law, however, when war broke out in 1914, and though it did provide the basis for the law of 10 July 1915 which established a carefully controlled minimum wage of between 0.40 and 1.25 francs an hour, the measure has to be seen as a product of the war-time situation, passed in the teeth of powerful and intransigent opposition from employers.[107]

Women workers and collective action: syndical organisation and industrial militancy

As has been seen in earlier chapters, working-class women were in the forefront of resistance to the new industrial order in the first three-quarters of the nineteenth century, playing a leading role in struggles against high rents and profiteering landlords as well as in defence of community values, most notably during the Paris Commune. After 1880, however, it has been suggested that such traditional forces of popular resistance declined, as protest 'modernised', and characteristically assumed the form of strikes staged by an organised labour movement in which women were of only marginal significance.[108] By and large, this interpretation is correct, but it requires qualification. For, while it may be true that French women workers did not join trade unions in massive numbers, it would be a mistake to ascribe their behaviour to any innate 'docility' or propensity towards conservatism. Rather, what needs underscoring is the extent to which they encountered obstacles to participation in the life of the trade union movement on the same basis as male colleagues, whose attitude to women's work was often far from benevolent.

Older forms of protest did not die out completely – which is hardly surprising, given the pivotal place women continued to occupy in the families of the popular classes in both town and country. Thus in 1907 peasant women sporting their traditional costumes were among the 280,000 protesters who demonstrated in Nîmes against restrictions imposed by the government on the wine-growers of the Languedoc. In 1911, women were well to the fore in violent food riots which broke out in parts of the industrial north. Earlier, in March 1906, following the pit disaster at Courrières in the Pas-de-Calais in which over a thousand miners lost their lives, miners' wives swelled the ranks of the angry crowds which demonstrated against inadequate safety measures in the mines, and they continued to support their husbands during the general strike in the coalfields which followed. In such incidents, women can still be seen as acting as the guardians of their households and communities, rather than as women workers acting in pursuit of their own professional interests.[109]

Even so, protest of this kind did not entirely replicate the models of collective action of the late eighteenth and early nineteenth centuries. The wine-growers' protest was no *jacquerie*, and took the form of an urban street demonstration complete with banners, placards, slogans and speechifying. The women of the Nord who protested against hunger in 1911 likewise resembled workers on strike more than the rioters of the earlier era and their grievances focused not exclusively on bread and grain prices but on the high price of food generally, particularly staples such as butter, meat and eggs. If the miners' wives resorted to practices which recalled the *charivaris* of old – attacking blacklegs by banging pots outside their doors and spanking their bare behinds in public – they were also demonstrating their class solidarity with their menfolk, joining in renderings of the *Internationale* and hurling abuse at the forces of order.[110] Similarly, the angry women textile workers of the rural Isère who stripped and humiliated a male strike-breaker were not so much re-enacting a traditional form of protest as resorting to the characteristically modern weapon of strike action – proof that, with the spread of the silk industry from Lyon into the hinterland of the Isère countryside, these peasant women had acquired the mentality of workers, and militant workers at that. By 1914, to the considerable embarrassment of the leadership of the CGT (Confédération Générale du Travail), the women workers of the Isère were more effectively unionised than the men of the region.[111]

From the 1880s, women staged strikes of their own, which after 1890 were recorded by the Office du Travail (though it is very likely that many strikes of short duration did not feature in the official statistics). General trends are clear, however. The proportion of women who went on strike varied enormously over time and place, but was invariably a much smaller percentage than the percentage of women in the active population. There was no evidence of any growing trend towards militancy. On the other hand, in periods where there were more generalised strike movements, as in 1905/6, the number of women strikers rose accordingly, and the number of women-only strikes was relatively large.

Women-only strikes differed from those launched by male workers in a number of respects. On the one hand, they were less often about such issues as pay rises, reducing the working day without loss of pay and the suppression of piece work, and on the other hand, they were more often concerned with attempts by employers to reduce wages, to impose fines, and to have workers or foremen sacked for sexual harassment. Whereas men's strikes tended to arise more from a systematic campaign for better pay and conditions, women's strikes were usually spontaneous and defensive reactions against exploitation on the part of particularly vulnerable workers who were susceptible to particular pressures on account of their gendered experience of work.

Less skilled, more numerous and therefore more easily replaced, women workers were also more subject to victimisation as a result of strike action. Some employers made union membership itself a cause for dismissal, and in certain areas they had the support of clerics who refused to administer the sacraments to women on strike, as in the case of the extremely Catholic *sardinières* of Douarnenez in 1905. Women workers might also encounter opposition from within their families. Fathers who feared to lose the wages of a striking daughter – or, worse, to lose their own jobs – might counsel against strike action, and in other cases striking women incurred the wrath of their husbands. The fact that women were less unionised than men meant that they received less material support in the course of a strike, and were therefore unable to hold out for long periods for want of resources. The competition between male and female workers in certain sectors sometimes produced a notable lack of class solidarity and a gendered response to industrial disputes. Between 1890 and 1908, at least fifty-six cases can be found of strikes staged by male workers for the dismissal of women who were accused of being responsible for a reduction in wages, the majority of these disputes being found in printing, textiles, leathers and skins and the metal industry. Male workers were also resentful of women workers who refused to back industrial action initiated by men.[112]

On the other hand, the militancy of women workers should not be underestimated. However exceptional, the tobacco workers were a case in point. Numbering around 18,000 at the turn of the century, these women, who were more skilled and better paid than the average *ouvrière*, had already begun to develop a high commitment to unionisation and were led by vociferous champions of their interests such as Marie Jay, who did not hesitate to put forward their demands either at trade union congresses or in negotiations with their employer (tobacco was a state monopoly). Thus, in the years before the First World War, they campaigned strongly for maternity leave and for the provision of uniforms to be worn at work. In every respect, the tobacco workers acted out of a consciousness of themselves as workers rather than women, and sought, like male comrades, to obtain better pay and working conditions through their union.[113]

Other women workers, while remaining more traditional than the tobacco workers, showed that they too could be extremely militant when the occasion warranted. The *sardinières* of Douarnenez found devotion to the Virgin a help rather than a hindrance in pursuit of their demands to be paid by the hour rather than on piece-rates, and pooled their meagre resources to light a huge candle to Our Lady of Lourdes during their strike of 1905. Similarly the *'cabanières'* of Rocquefort offered a Mass of thanksgiving after successful industrial action in 1907. The pious women wool workers of Mazamet took to the streets in 1909 and sang the *Magnificat* as well as the *Internationale*. Soup kitchens (*'les soupes communistes'*) organised by women were often a feature of protracted strikes involving mainly male workers, as at Fougères in 1907, and they demonstrated that class loyalties were by no means always vitiated by gender loyalties. In general, the strikes by women workers had a distinctive feminine flavour, as the women laughed, sang, presented the police with bouquets of flowers, or, in some cases, taunted them by raising their skirts.[114] Physical violence, of the kind graphically represented by Zola in *Germinal*, was practically non-existent.[115]

It remains true, however, that women workers showed a marked reluctance to join trade unions. In 1900 there were 30,975 women registered as trade union members (5.26% of total union membership). By 1911 the corresponding figures were 101,049 and 9.81%.[116] Women, receptive to the doctrines of class reconciliation preached by social Catholics in the 1890s, were also much more likely than men to join the 'yellow' unions organised by either employers or the Catholic Church rather than the 'red' unions which affiliated to the CGT, which espoused the doctrines of revolutionary syndicalism and overt class warfare.[117] A high proportion of women workers in a particular sector was in itself no guarantee of a high incidence of union membership. Textiles was a classic case: though half the workforce was made up of women, women workers were only a tiny proportion of the membership of the textile unions and only rarely can women delegates be found at their congresses. Even in an industry as feminised as the clothing industry, women were likewise a rare presence at union congresses.[118] The reasons for women's low incidence of unionisation were the same as those which generated a different pattern of strike activity from that of men, and were rooted in their gender-specific experience of work rather than in any innate 'docility'.[119] Nevertheless, it was a regular grumble of male militants that women only came to the *syndicat* when they needed help and quickly abandoned the labour movement once a strike was over.[120]

What the great majority of male trade unionists failed to appreciate, however, was that their own attitude to women's work acted as a strong disincentive to union activity among women workers. As we have seen, the doctrine of 'woman by the hearth' was fervently championed in the 1860s and 1870s by union leaders whose outlook reflected the misogynist ideas of Proudhon. In the years following the Marseille congress of 1879, male syndicalists remained slow to evolve new ideas about the proper role of women in society. Disciples of Proudhon kept alive the master's ideas. Commemorating the centenary of Proudhon's birth in 1909, the militant Edmond Berth insisted that Proudhon's views on the woman question were of continuing relevance and denied that women had any valid role outside of the household.[121] At the fourth congress of the CGT, held at Rennes in 1898, a motion was carried that 'man must provide for woman'. In the unfortunate case of a widow or single woman, obliged to look after her own needs, the formula of equal pay for equal work was to be applied. Men should be prevented from taking up jobs which by rights belonged to women.[122] It was likewise in the name of domestic bliss that the CGT, from 1912 onwards, began to mount a vociferous campaign for *la semaine anglaise* (Saturday afternoon and Sunday free). Central to its propaganda was the view that the working-class woman, as much as her bourgeois counterpart, required the free time in order to devote herself to the needs of her family and household. Defenders of women's right to work in the labour movement like the theoretician of revolutionary syndicalism Alfred Rosmer were driven almost to despair by the reactionary views of so many male militants in the syndicalist movement with regard to the question of women's work.[123]

A good deal of the syndical opposition to female labour was based on narrow corporatist considerations as much as attachment to a 'natural' gender order. In the minds of many male trade unionists, women were dangerous rivals in the labour market and, because of their willingness to accept lower wages than men, a threat to the living standards of the working-class family. The printing unions were among the most hostile to women's work. The first conflicts dated back to the early 1860s, when on several occasions male workers went on strike and were consequently arrested (at a time when strikes were still illegal) because employers had brought in women workers prepared to work at below the going rate. Inability to stop the spread of female labour in the printing works (by 1901 women accounted for 26% of the labour force) served only to increase the bitterness of the male workers. At their congress in Lyon in 1905 the printers even rejected the concept of 'equal pay for equal work' – a slogan to which a number of unions happily adhered confident in the belief that in practice employers would never wish to hire women at 'men's' rates.[124] Moreover, after the Fédération du Livre officially adopted the 'equal pay for equal work' strategy at their congress in Bordeaux in 1910, many rank and file members remained attached to the old policy, most notably in the local branch at Lyon. There, in 1912, the *syndicat* not only rejected the membership application of a woman printer called Emma Couriau who was paid full union rates, but also expelled her husband Louis because he refused to use his marital authority to make her give up her job. Worse still, the Central Committee of the Federation upheld the local decision against the Couriau's appeal.

The case caused consternation throughout the labour movement and generated immense debate on the question of women, work and the unionisation of women workers. What further complicated the issue was that, in the first instance, the most vigorous defence of the Couriaus was undertaken not by fellow trade unionists but by the bourgeois feminists of the Feminist Federation of the South-East.[125] At first ignored as an irrelevance by militant syndicalists, feminism had gradually come to be seen by perceptive union leaders as having a potentially disruptive impact on the working-class movement. Evidence of this existed from the turn of the century and the affair of *La Fronde*, the feminist daily newspaper founded by Marguerite Durand. In keeping with her all-woman policy for the production of the paper, Durand had organised a printers' union, which the Fédération du Livre refused to recognise. In 1901, during a strike of printers at Nancy, Durand agreed to send twelve of her women workers to take the place of men on strike. It is clear from her correspondence that she was willing to repeat this service for the same employer and in the eyes of male printers she and her union represented blackleg labour.[126]

In 1907 Durand again antagonised syndicalist militants by organising a conference in an attempt to put pressure on the Ministry of Public Works to fulfil its promise to establish a special department to deal with the problems of female labour. Her interference was deeply resented by militant trade unionists, female as well as male – one militant woman who attended Durand's conference was expelled for branding the delegates 'lackeys of capital'.[127] The feminist defence of the Couriaus made feminism impossible to ignore, and syndicalist leaders such as Pierre Monatte made no secret of their antagonism, arguing that working-class women needed no help from women of the bourgeoisie, however sincere their motivation.[128] On the other hand, the Couriau affair did produce a change in attitude on the part of some male militants. The most prominent figures of the new generation of syndicalists – men such as Rosmer and George Dumoulin – all sided with the Couriaus against the Lyon printers. Rosmer, in particular, was contemptuous of the printers' union, denouncing their 'antediluvian mentality' in a series of articles in *La Bataille Syndicaliste*.[129] Nevertheless, even after the massive participation of women in war work between 1914 and 1918, little evolution in union attitudes can be discerned, especially among the rank and file.[130] There were few stauncher champions of the sexual division of labour than the French trade union movement.

Socialists were only marginally more enlightened than syndicalists and in general failed to appreciate the potential of harnassing the mass of women workers to their cause. In classic Marxist theory, as we have seen, the emancipation of the working class as a whole took precedence over the emancipation of women, and Marxism was the basis on which French socialists formed a united party (the SFIO) in 1905. Nevertheless, the attitude of French Marxists to the question of women's work was complex, and not simply a matter of dogma. The Parti Ouvrier Francais (POF), the party of Jules Guesde, was the principal vehicle for the diffusion of Marxist socialism in France before unification and its base in the northern textile towns of Lille and Roubaix meant that it could hardly ignore the women workers who constituted such a high percentage of the factory-based labour force in the region. Indeed, it was Guesde's view that the progressive feminisation of the labour force was an inevitable consequence of capitalism as machines eliminated the need for male brawn and created a demand for cheaper female (and child) labour.

The Guesdist dilemma was how to respond to this new situation. Unlike many of the syndicalist leaders, French Marxists never seriously entertained the option of seeking to ban women from the workforce. On the other hand, they were unsure whether to regard women workers primarily as women or as workers, at times representing them as wives and mothers and on other occasions identifying them as committed revolutionary proletarians. Hence the contradictions which characterised French Marxist discourse around the turn of the century. Sometimes the Guesdists called for paternalistic social reform; sometimes they repudiated reformism as a pointless attempt to arrest the tide of historical progress towards the inevitable proletarian Revolution. At the core of the Guesdist failure to reach out to women workers was the party's essentially 'productivist' vision and its focus on the factory as the characteristic locus of work. The great majority of working women – who were not to be found in factories – were thereby ignored.[131] In effect, Marxist socialists acquiesced in the existing sexual division of labour, as was apparent from their iconography. Man came to be represented as 'the worker' – the brawny, muscular proletarian who had to undertake heavy physical labour to earn his daily bread.

Woman, on the other hand, was typically depicted as man's companion, the epitome of the suffering proletarian and the most exploited victim of the capitalist system.[132]

While accepting the inevitability of a sexual division of labour, French socialists sought to turn it to their advantage through propaganda. Whether revolutionary or reformist, they all believed in the reality of the class struggle and were ready to seize every opportunity to highlight the iniquities of the existing social order, which they rightly claimed was biased in favour of the peasantry and the bourgeoisie. The image of the hapless proletarian woman had much to offer in propaganda terms. For example, it could be alleged that it was 'bourgeois justice' which allowed the rich to seduce working-class girls with impunity (before the introduction of affiliation suits in 1912). Bourgeois vice and corruption could be poignantly expressed in the image of the seduced and abandoned female and a contrast established with the love and devotion which bound the faithful working man to his companion. The moral superiority of the working class over the bourgeoisie was thus affirmed.[133] Not only did such images refute bourgeois accusations that working men were uncouth, even bestial, in their relations with women, but in addition they gave the lie to that equation of the labouring classes and the 'dangerous classes' which had been a feature of anti-socialist propaganda since the days of the July Monarchy.[134]

It was likewise to assert the moral superiority of the working class over the 'Malthusian' bourgeoisie that socialists, on the whole, were strong opponents of birth control. The 'population question', it was argued, served only to divert attention from the class struggle and, worse, made a virtue of a highly individualistic and antisocial act which interfered with nature and made sexual pleasure the fundamental criterion of human happiness.[135] In the language of class struggle, French socialists expressed their own adherence to the doctrine of separate spheres and helped to perpetuate traditional gender divisions in the workplace. Similarly, as we shall see next, they proved to be less than reliable allies of feminists who were seeking to create the female citizen in the *belle époque*.

Chapter 12

In search of citizenship

Feminists and women's suffrage

In the 1870s the feminist agenda had been set by Maria Deraismes and Léon Richer, whose *politique de la brèche* deliberately excluded the issue of women's suffrage as too controversial. As we have seen, however, even before the decade closed the 'breach' strategy had come under fire from a younger generation of militants headed by Hubertine Auclert. In the 1880s, virtually singlehanded, Auclert launched a debate on the female franchise which was aimed at making women full citizens of the Republic. It was her profound conviction that political rights were 'the keystone [*clef de voûte*] which will give them all other rights' and her strategy was one of frontal assault on the bastions of male power.[1]

Storming the citadel: Hubertine Auclert's campaign, 1880–88

Auclert's campaign began in February 1880 with an attempt to register herself as a voter on her local electoral list in the tenth *arrondissement* of Paris. Arguing that the Republican constitution had proclaimed rights for '*tous les Français*' and spoke of the 'universality' of French citizens, she and other members of her group attempted to add their names to the annual roll kept at the town hall. Having been refused, she then sought to publicise the scandal of the exclusion of women from the rights of full citizenship by announcing her intention to withhold payment of her taxes, on the grounds that 'in a country where women don't have any rights neither can women have any obligations'. The government remained implacable, however. The Prefect of the Seine ruled that, as far as the vote was concerned, 'Français ne signifie pas Française' and the bailiffs were sent into Auclert's home to seize furniture and personal effects. Nevertheless, Auclert's tax boycott, which she publicised through a series of lectures, attracted the attention of the national press. Even right-wing newspapers like *Le Gaulois* were forced to concede that she had logic on her side. Her defiance served also to inspire other women to join the feminist movement, one case in point being Jeanne Oddo-Deflou, founder of the Groupe Français d'Etudes Féministes. In the short term, Auclert had at least succeeded in raising the suffrage issue before French public opinion.[2]

Nor did she let up. Another tactic, which even self-consciously advanced sections of opinion found shocking, was to attend civil marriage ceremonies at town halls and then harangue brides on the iniquities of the marriage laws – a course of action repudiated even by the Free Thought society and eventually banned by administrative fiat of the Prefect of the Seine. Auclert was also prepared to take her campaign on to the streets. Seizing the opportunity provided by the first Bastille Day celebrations of 14 July 1881, she and a number of her supporters from the Droit des Femmes group paraded their banner decked in the black crêpe of mourning to the Bastille monument, where Auclert roundly denounced the contemporary Bastille which continued to imprison women – the Napoleonic Code. She next tried to persuade Maria Deraismes to emulate the example of Jeanne Deroin in 1849 by running as a candidate in the parliamentary elections of May 1881. Deraismes – a republican first and foremost – refused, invoking the – by now traditional – excuse that she would not be party to a manoeuvre which could only benefit the clerical enemies of the Republic, who would have no difficulty in manipulating a female electorate. In the radical press, Auclert attacked Deraismes for lack of feminist conviction, while Deraismes chided Auclert with ignorance of political realities and adventurism.[3]

Auclert's contribution to the cause of women's suffrage was always that of a propagandist rather than an organiser. From February 1881 until 1891, her principal platform was *La Citoyenne*, her weekly, then monthly, newspaper, the very title of which – *The Citizeness* – was intended to underline the point that women were not, in fact, citizens. At the same time, it evoked memories of the Revolution of 1789 and affirmed her personal affiliation with the socialists of the 1880s. With important financial backing from a former deputy, Joseph de Gasté, and assistance from three other male friends (the lawyers Antonin Lévrier, whom she was to marry in 1888, Léon Giraud, and a Dr Verrier), Auclert made *La Citoyenne* the voice of French suffragism in the 1880s. Her constant theme was that women's suffrage was a question of justice: in a Republic which officially owed justice to all, women were entitled to equal rights, and should not be treated as exceptions. To deprive women of the rights of citizenship violated the principle of the sovereignty of the people and left the work of constructing the Republic incomplete. An all-male electorate effectively made men into 'the feudal noblemen of the nineteenth century', responsible for electing '557 monarchs' as deputies. This was a masculine 'royalty of sex', which, if perpetuated, would give rise to a new revolution. For Auclert, the cause of women's suffrage was essentially about the genuine democratisation of French society.[4]

It was also a matter of logic. The new masters of the Third Republic, as positivists and self-conscious heirs of the Enlightenment, liked to affirm their faith in reason and progress as well as their commitment to science and the construction of a secular order. Auclert attempted to convince them of the merits of women's suffrage by arguing her case in their own language of logic and rationalism. Thus she argued that to refuse women the right to vote because their primary role was that of wife and mother was as illogical as depriving bakers of the right to vote because they had to bake bread, or cobblers because they had to make shoes, or lawyers, because they had to plead in court: the right to vote was not something which depended on a person's sex or skills. Just as men could learn to cook, so women could learn to legislate. Maternity, she admitted, made women different. But in Auclert's view women no more deserved to be excluded from citizenship because of the fact that they gave birth to children than men deserved to be excluded from citizenship on the grounds that they could not give birth to children.[5]

Auclert by no means confined herself, however, to abstract arguments based on the notions of equal rights and natural justice but pressed her case also with arguments from expediency. Her main line of attack was to suggest that the marginalisation of women was bad for the political process as a whole: the specific interests of women happened to coincide with the larger interests of society. Thus she refuted the classic anticlerical case against votes for women by accusing the politicians in power of not being anticlerical enough. Whereas Auclert favoured the expulsion of the Jesuits from France, Opportunist republican leaders continued to maintain the Concordat between Church and state as well as diplomatic relations with the Pope. They similarly connived with clericalism by allowing priests both to vote and to run as candidates in elections. Why, then, Auclert wanted to know, should women be denied voting rights because many went to Mass? It was precisely the exercise of the female suffrage itself, in Auclert's view, which would act as the strongest barrier to clericalism. Once women extended their horizons beyond the demands of domesticity and assumed an active role in public life, they would have little time for religion or prayer.[6]

Whether advocating women's suffrage on grounds of rights or of expediency, the thrust of Auclert's propaganda efforts in *La Citoyenne* was to present herself as a model female citizen who met all the criteria necessary for full participation in the public life of the Republic. She realised, however, that propaganda was not enough: organisation was also required and, impressed by the growth of women's movements in the United States and Britain, she attempted to build a national suffrage league. Encouraged by a visit to Europe of Susan B. Anthony in 1883, she relaunched Droit des Femmes as Suffrage des Femmes. Far from becoming the mass movement of her dreams, however, the society never had a membership of more than 100 and remained little more than a discussion group. Auclert's activism therefore consisted largely of tactics which she could pursue alone, such as writing to deputies and presenting petitions to parliament. Between 1881 and 1885 she drew up some sixteen petitions, the largest of which had 2000 signatures. Nevertheless, because parliamentarians were obliged by law to act upon petitions, Auclert succeeded at least in obliging the Chamber of Deputies to recognise that the enfranchisement of women was a political issue which merited consideration, however cursory. The first debate on women's suffrage in the Chamber of Deputies took place in 1885.[7]

In retrospect, 1885 can be seen as the year when Auclert's activism reached its high point. Building on previous experience in the municipal elections of 1881 and 1884, when women headed by Léonie Rouzade had stood as candidates, Auclert and a number of like-minded women mounted another shadow electoral campaign to coincide with the legislative elections of that year. Though not a candidate herself, she was the galvanising influence behind the campaign, despite the fact that rival suffragists rejected her idea of running a single symbolic candidate – ideally Maria Deraismes – in favour of a number of candidates. These included Rouzade and Louise Barberousse (1836–1900), a schoolteacher, former *communarde* and ally of the eccentric socialist lawyer and fellow *communard* Jules Allix, while Deraismes caused a stir by agreeing to allow her name to go forward, though she also made it clear that she would not campaign actively for votes. In all, six women stood as candidates. Their share of the poll is unknown, since the government ordered that no count be taken, but the campaign revealed that, however small and fragmented it might be, a movement for women's suffrage was now a permanent feature of the French political scene.[8]

Yet in the France of the 1880s Auclert's militancy obtained no concrete results. Even when she adopted a more gradualist stance in 1887 by petitioning for votes for only single women (including widows and divorcees) she was unable to persuade more than a handful of deputies to espouse her cause. For all her assertiveness in public, privately she had to cope with doubts and disappointment. To her diary she confided her sense of isolation and loneliness, describing herself in the word once favoured by Flora Tristan as a 'pariah'. The ridicule and abuse heaped upon her for daring to challenge the established order of gender relations wounded her deeply.[9] According to a police report of 1880 she suffered 'from madness or hysterics which made her think of men as equals' and this was a common accusation from opponents of women's suffrage.[10] Another was that she was a libertine who supported 'free love' and sexual freedom for women – a charge which she indignantly repudiated. While she supported divorce and reform of the marriage laws, she did not condone *union libre*, which in her view only enhanced men's opportunities to exploit women sexually.[11] In 1882 Auclert had refused Lévrier's offer of marriage in order to devote herself full-time to the cause, but in 1888 she relented and following their marriage the couple left Paris for Algeria, where Lévrier had been appointed a justice of the peace. Auclert's colleague Maria Martin took over as director of *La Citoyenne* and despite occasional contributions from Algeria, she was effectively sidelined. When Lévrier died in 1892 Auclert returned to Paris but by then *La Citoyenne* had folded and she herself thereafter remained on the fringes of the French feminist movement, her work as a pioneer already behind her.

Feminism *fin-de-siècle*: the spectrum of activism, 1889–1900

Despite Auclert's headline-grabbing activities in the 1880s, throughout the decade it was her rivals Richer and Deraismes who continued to set the distinctive tone of the French feminist movement. Holding fast to their own strategy of *la brèche* and condemning Auclert's strategy of *l'assaut*, they insisted that nothing should take priority over the goal of establishing a viable, secular Republic, even if this meant that for the time being women could not be admitted to full membership of the political nation.[12] Deraismes, it is true, did have second thoughts about women's suffrage, but as we have seen, disapproved of Auclert's combative style. Richer, on the other hand, never wavered in his opposition to votes for women, which he claimed to support in principle but always dismissed as inopportune. The Boulangist crisis of the late 1880s further reinforced his conviction that the time was not yet ripe to entrust women with the franchise. As he put it in 1888:

> I believe that at the present time it would be dangerous – in France – to give women the political ballot. They are in great majority reactionaries and clericals. If they voted today, the Republic would not last six months.[13]

In 1882, confronted with the challenge from Auclert and preoccupied by Deraismes's apparent change of heart regarding the suffrage question, Richer launched a new French League for Women's Rights, the LFDF (Ligue Française pour le Droit des Femmes) to regain the initiative for his programme of moderate legal reform. Modelled on the highly effective Education League founded in 1866 by fellow Freemason Jean Macé to campaign for free, secular and obligatory education, Richer initially entertained hopes of building up a mass movement. Instead, he had to be content with a membership of around 200, half of whom were men. Richer believed that male support was vital if the cause of women's rights was to make any headway within the all-male political class: hence he turned to sympathetic men to run his feminist organisation. Of the ninety-eight women members, some two-thirds were married or widowed: independent single women were a tiny minority in the society. During the 1880s, numbers actually dwindled to around 100 and the LFDF was reduced to the role of a mere pressure group. Its one gesture to the politics of the street was when it joined the thousands who flocked to follow the funeral cortege of Victor Hugo, the League's honorary president, in 1885.[14]

The centenary celebrations of the French Revolution of 1789 served to effect a rapprochement between the LFDF and Deraismes's Amelioration Society. As part of the official programme of events, the government had agreed to sponsor a congress on 'feminine works and institutions', which was organised largely by women with links to the world of French Protestant philanthropy, such as Mme Emile de Morsier and Mme Isabelle Bogelot. Held in July 1889, this explicitly prohibited discussion of women's suffrage or other controversial matters.[15] Both Richer and Deraismes were keen to stage a more overtly feminist congress, and, after some tough negotiations, renewed the collaboration which had made possible the feminist congress of 1878. Their grandiosely entitled Second French International Congress for Women's Rights was convened in advance of the official congress, opening in June 1889 in the presence of an audience of 200, overwhelmingly drawn from the ranks of the bourgeoisie. Though numbers were down on 1878 (largely because of the absence of foreign delegates) it was encouraging that the proportion of female participants had increased significantly to 70%, signalling a trend which would be evident in the aftermath of the congress within the LFDF itself, with a female takeover of all the top positions in the organisation.[16]

The congress, having studied aspects of the woman question in sections devoted to history, economics, morality and legislation, reaffirmed the strategy of *la brèche* in a set of resolutions which called for immediate and practical legal reforms: legislation to give women control over their own income, the removal of barriers to women's entry into the professions, the introduction of paternity suits and the demolition of the prison-hospital of Saint-Lazare. Richer stifled an attempt by Jules Allix to raise the suffrage issue from the floor and suppressed a report on this issue sent to him by Auclert from Algeria. The congress also established an International Federation for the Demand of Women's Rights (Fédération internationale pour la Revendication des Droits de la Femme) which adopted the LFDF's journal *Le Droit des Femmes* as its official organ.[17]

The 1889 congress undoubtedly gave a boost to the moderate feminism advocated by the feminists of the mainstream Republican centre. The oldest and wealthiest – though not the largest – group remained the Amelioration Society. Following Deraismes's death in 1894, the presidency passed to her sister Mme Anna Féresse-Deraismes (1822–1911), though the everyday running of the Society was left to Mme de Montaut, a leading light of the Red Cross and a woman more interested in charities than in women's rights. In 1894 the Society adopted a new constitution which prioritised reform of the Code and rejected militancy. It further underscored its moderation by electing as vice-president the deputy Charles Beauquier, a man sympathetic to reform of the law, but known to be hostile to women's suffrage.[18] The LFDF, on the other hand, evolved in a more radical direction after Richer's retirement in 1891. Under the new leadership of Maria Pognon (1824–1925) as president and Marie Bonnevial (1841–1918) as secretary-general, the Society increased its membership from 95 in 1892 to around 150 in 1900. Pognon, who had only recently left her native Normandy to settle in Paris, found her feminist vocation at the 1889 congress and became one of the principal activists of the 1890s, before leaving France to live abroad with her husband. Bonnevial, unusually, came from a working-class background, having been born into poverty and brought up by an uncle who was an artisan in the environs of Lyon. Having qualified as a primary schoolteacher, she participated in the republican struggle to secularise the educational system and was barred from teaching by the 'Moral Order' regime of the 1870s. Forced into exile as a result, she was reinstated as a teacher on her return and became a militant in the teachers' union and a frequent delegate at the congresses of the labour movement. Increasingly attracted to feminism in the mid-1890s, with Pognon she steered the LFDF towards a suffragist position, so that by 1900 some moderate feminists were ready to include votes for women along with their other demands.[19]

Centrist feminism could also claim other new adherents in the 1890s. The Polish émigrée and writer Marya Chéliga-Loevy (1853–1927), having initially collaborated with Deraismes, founded her own Universal Union of Women (Union universelle des Femmes) in 1889 in the hope that it would serve as the basis for a large feminist party but soon found that her society could no more fulfil this role than could the LFDF or Amelioration. Presided by the distinguished Mme Clémence Royer, the translator of Darwin, the Union folded in 1892, though Chéliga-Loevy continued to be active in the movement, founding a feminist theatre in 1900 and publishing an Almanach féministe.[20]

More influential were two other moderate groups. The first, the Avant-Courrière, was founded in 1893 by the Englishwoman Jeanne Schmahl (1846–1915), the daughter of an English father and a French mother. A friend of Sophia Jex-Blake and in touch with the English feminist movement, she had discovered at first hand the iniquities of the French Civil Code with regard to married women as a medical student in Paris. Convinced of the need for a French equivalent of the English Married Women's Property Act of 1882 after learning about a female patient who was forced to surrender her wages to a violent and abusive husband, Schmahl made reform of the law her top priority and committed the Avant-Courrière to just two objectives: the right for married women to dispose freely of their own earnings and the right of women to be civil witnesses. Schmahl's society grew to a membership of around 200 and attracted support from a wide spectrum of female opinion, ranging from the royalist Duchesse d'Uzès to the republican Juliette Adam and the Parisian journalist Jane Misme, soon to become one of the key figures in the mainstream feminist movement. The law on civil witnesses was enacted in 1897, but the earnings bill took longer to reach the statute book. Passed by the Chamber of Deputies in 1896, it was delayed by the Senate until 1907 and until its enactment Schmahl refused to be diverted from her single-issue approach and thus refused to participate in the growing suffrage campaign of the 1890s.[21]

The other newcomer to the ranks of moderate feminism was the Groupe français d'Etudes féministes, founded in 1898 by Jeanne Oddo-Deflou, the wife of Henri Oddo, a librarian at the French Chamber of Deputies. Deflou was an admirer of Auclert and supported votes for women in principle, but like Schmahl agreed that reform of the law had to come first. Unlike Schmahl, however, she wanted wholesale rather than piecemeal legal reform. A republican and Freemason herself, she hoped nevertheless that her group could be the basis for a non-partisan approach to the woman question and cultivated Catholic as well as Protestant and republican women. Unsympathetic to feminist radicals who preached either pacifism or free love, she preferred to concentrate on the issue of *recherche de la paternité* and her society did more than any other pressure group to achieve the law which was eventually enacted in 1912.[22]

If the tradition of *la brèche* found new recruits in the 1890s, so too did that of the suffragism associated with Auclert, albeit in less militant form. Egalité, established by Mme Eliska Vincent, one of the feminist pioneers of the 1860s, was intended to be a continuation of the work of Le Suffrage des Femmes after Auclert's departure to Algeria. Having supported the Commune and been lucky to escape execution, Vincent maintained her involvement with the workers' movement and regularly attended syndicalist gatherings, though she herself was a widow of substantial means. A feature of her feminism was her demand for the restoration of rights allegedly lost since the Middle Ages. Egalité had fewer than a hundred members, but Vincent was a pivotal figure because of her ability to reach out to the moderates in a way that Auclert had been unable or unwilling to do.[23] Likewise Solidarité des Femmes, the creation of Mme Eugénie Potonié-Pierre, was intended to fill the gap left by Auclert. Potonié-Pierre (1844–98) was an *institutrice* of utopian socialist leanings married to a well-known pacifist, Edmond Potonié-Pierre, whose convictions she shared. Formerly a collaborator on Richer's journal *Le Droit des Femmes*, she hoped that her group would help to bring together the women's movement and the workers' movement and serve as the basis for a united feminist movement.[24] After Potonié-Pierre's premature death, the leadership of Solidarité passed to the more militant Caroline Kauffmann (1851–1926), who placed the suffrage issue at the top of her agenda and showed herself markedly more hostile to the male sex, a trait which is at least in part explained by her experience of an unhappy marriage.[25]

Militant suffragism also had a monthly newspaper, *Le Journal des Femmes*, directed by Maria Martin. Another Englishwoman, she had married the Frenchman Jules Martin and had come to live in Paris in 1872. An active Freemason, she was originally Auclert's closest collaborator at *La Citoyenne*, assuming the direction of the paper when Auclert left for Algeria in 1888. By 1891, however, relations had become strained to breaking point by Auclert's constant interference and criticism and Martin decided to allow *La Citoyenne* to fold – a decision which earned her Auclert's undying hatred. *Le Journal des Femmes* was its successor, campaigning for women's suffrage until 1910, albeit in a less strident tone, since Martin was prepared to open her columns to the different currents of feminist opinion and, despite her own personal political predilections, preferred to avoid controversial and divisive issues such as the Dreyfus Affair.[26] Auclert herself returned to Paris after the death of her husband in 1892 but remained on the margins of the militant movement. At first she was so grief-stricken that she even contemplated suicide. When she eventually recovered her will to re-enter the struggle she lacked the platform which *La Citoyenne* had afforded her and in her desperation turned to the unlikely outlet of *La Libre Parole*, the organ of Edouard Drumont, author of *La France juive* (1886) which had claimed that France was being overrun by Jews. A xenophobe as well as an antisemite, Drumont was no advocate of women's rights but for six months in 1894 he gave Auclert space to propagate her ideas before she found a job as a columnist with the more personally congenial *Le Radical*, though it, too, was no friend to the suffrage cause.[27]

To the left of the mainstream feminist groups of the Republican centre (whether moderates or radicals, *brèchistes* or *assautistes*) were socialist feminists of various sorts. The older generation of *communardes*, such as Louise Michel, though strongly in favour of rights for ordinary working women, tended to remain convinced anarchists alienated from the parliamentary system. Thus Michel, having returned to France from deportation in New Caledonia after the amnesty granted to supporters of the Commune in 1880, founded a Women's League (Ligue des Femmes) to put an end to war and prostitution, but showed no interest in participating in Auclert's suffrage crusade. At the time of the latter's shadow campaign of 1885, she ridiculed the idea that filling the Chamber of Deputies with women would achieve anything for the female proletariat and her refusal to renounce violence in pursuit of her revolutionary goals earned her three further spells of imprisonment in the 1880s.[28] Similarly, the young socialist journalist Caroline Rémy (1855–1929), better known under the pseudonym Séverine, concentrated her efforts on the 'social struggle' in her capacity as director of the newspaper *Le Cri du Peuple* founded by her *maître à penser* (and lover) Jules Vallès. By temperament a loner, she also worried about the potential damage to the ideal of femininity caused by the activities of bourgeois feminists. The veteran Paule Minck likewise had little faith in political rights but looked rather for a general transformation of society to bring about women's emancipation.[29]

On the other hand, a small band of women did seek to unite socialism and feminism. The embroiderer Léonie Rouzade (1839–1916), born Louise-Léonie Camusat, the daughter of a Parisian watchmaker and grand-daughter of a delegate to the Estates-General in 1789, turned to socialism after discovering the doctrines of Fourier and Cabet. With the encouragement of her husband Auguste Rouzade, she expressed her ideas in the form of novels and attempted to continue the work of Flora Tristan by linking the cause of women with that of the working class. Present at the feminist congress of 1878, she initially joined forces with Auclert in Le Droit des Femmes before founding a group called the Women's Union (L'Union des Femmes) in 1880 in collaboration with Eugénie Pierre and the Protestant schoolteacher, novelist and fellow utopian socialist Marcelle Tinayre, who had been exiled for her part in the Commune and whose husband had been shot during its repression. Rouzade's Union at first had close ties with the Guesdist (Marxist) wing of the French socialist movement but she gravitated towards the reformist faction dominated by Paul Brousse after the socialist party decided to support her candidature for a seat on the Paris municipal council. In the event she received fifty-seven votes – a not insignificant result, as Auclert noted in *La Citoyenne*, since despite her ineligibility she had polled considerably more votes than previous socialist candidates. For a time Rouzade remained close to the reformists Brousse and Malon, and in 1885 participated in Auclert's shadow electoral campaign, but this bruising experience resulted in her complete disenchantment with and withdrawal from political activity.[30]

Another abortive attempt to fuse socialism and feminism was made by Aline Valette, the party secretary of the Guesdist POF. Born Aline Goudeman in 1850, she was initially a teacher and a militant alongside Marie Bonnevial in the schoolteachers' union, but gave up her job on marrying a wealthy lawyer. The author of a best-selling domestic manual which instructed housewives on how best to fulfil their household duties, she was widowed young and threw herself into a range of charitable activities, which included the moral reform of prostitutes. Through her work as a volunteer labour inspector, she came to discover the plight of the working-classes, and was drawn to socialism for its commitment to the eradication of the problems caused by the advent of industrial society. At the same time, she was attracted to the burgeoning feminist movement, and assisted Eugénie Potonié-Pierre with the organisation of the feminist congress of 1892. Sharing Potonié-Pierre's ideal of uniting feminism with the cause of the workers, she launched a short-lived newspaper *L'Harmonie sociale* which affirmed on its masthead that 'the emancipation of women is in emancipated labour'.[31]

Never a true Marxist, Valette developed her own theories about how the emancipation of women was to be accomplished. In collaboration with Dr Pierre Bonnier, she claimed to reconcile socialism with feminism in a doctrine which they labelled 'sexualism', the fundamental premise of which was that the productive work of workers and the reproductive role of women were equivalents. In the long run, Valette looked forward to a new era in which women would liberate themselves from the degradation inflicted on the feminine condition by rediscovering the joys of motherhood. In the shorter term, she called for immediate reforms to promote the legal, economic and political emancipation of women.[32] Valette's ideas found little support among other feminists, and were denounced notably by Potonié-Pierre as retrograde nonsense, calculated to keep women in a position of inferiority. Valette's exceptional position in the Guesdist party derived less from her feminist theories than from the male leadership's desire to have a high profile, but essentially token, woman to broaden its appeal to working-class communities in the north of France. As party secretary Valette committed herself loyally to the party line that paramount importance ought to be attached to the proletarian revolution and that women's rights should be subsumed within overall party strategy. This was a position which French socialist women would continue to hold long after Valette's premature death (from tuberculosis) in 1899.[33]

At the opposite end of the political spectrum from socialist feminism was what could be called the feminist Right, consisting of groups which often drew their feminist commitment from a religious inspiration. Such were the Protestant women of the Conférence de Versailles, headed by Sarah Monod.[34] A newcomer to the scene was the Catholic group founded by Marie Maugeret in 1897 to promote 'Christian feminism' (Le Féminisme chrétien) and explicitly intended as an alternative to the anticlerical, republican and socialist varieties of feminism. Maugeret (1844– 1928) was the daughter of a doctor and grew up in comfortable circumstances in the Sarthe. Having inherited a substantial fortune, she was free to indulge her passions for literature and journalism, publishing a literary review and a number of novels. An intransigent ultramontane Catholic who exulted at the doctrine of papal infallibility proclaimed by the first Vatican Council of 1870, Maugeret was also a diehard political reactionary who identified with the nationalism and antisemitism preached by the French extreme Right. According to her the Dreyfus case revealed the country to be in the hands of the Jews, since revision was obtained only 'by intrigues and by gold'. The Jews were, in her appalling phrase, 'the people whom God has vomited from his mouth' and 'those beings without altars and without a homeland, those cosmopolitans forever and everywhere condemned to be foreigners'. Even the Freemasons – her other bête noire – in her view were in thrall to the Jews and her mission was to preserve France from 'the jackals of judaeo-masonry'.

Given this general political orientation, it may come as a surprise to discover that Maugeret regarded herself as a feminist. Whereas many Catholic women balked at the term, she willingly embraced it. Refusing to allow feminism to be monopolised by women who came from a background in republicanism and free thought, she launched a crusade in her journal Le Féminisme chrétien to establish that feminism was not incompatible with adherence to the Catholic religion. While reaffirming that women's primary role in society was that of wife and mother (though she herself never married) she wanted women to be able to improve their lot. They should have the right to work and access to careers as well as control over their own finances – the Civil Code she denounced as a 'Code of slavery'. Moreover, from the outset political rights featured on her programme. At a time when many of the centrist republican feminists had doubts about women's suffrage, Maugeret and her associates were adamant that women should have the right to vote.[35] As the Countess Marie de Villermont explained, the logic of 'universal' suffrage was that the vote be given to both sexes, and not just to men: to deprive women of the vote 'placed the most intelligent woman below the lowest manual labourer, the most imbecile coal-man and the most sottish drunk'.[36] In the 1890s, few Catholic women followed where Maugeret led as regards women's suffrage but in time Catholic women's organisations would grow into the biggest of all the suffrage societies.[37]

By the 1890s, therefore, it was clear that the French women's movement was growing, even if numbers were small and factionalism all too evident. The three distinct tendencies in the movement essentially replicated the ideological and political divisions of French national politics. In the mainstream centre were the bourgeois republicans, who like the Republican movement itself were divided between moderates and radicals. Only the latter were prepared to agitate seriously for women's suffrage: the moderates, following Deraismes and Richer, concentrated on legal reform and the campaign against the double standard of morality. On the feminist Right the Protestant women of the Conférence de Versailles reinforced the tendency to moderation in the centre, while Maugeret's Christian Feminism was beyond the Republican pale. On the feminist Left, the group of socialist women around Louise Saumoneau set its face against collaboration with bourgeois feminism. Fragmentation and disunity were prominent features of the movement in the 1890s.[38]

Yet expansion took place, encouraged both by a series of feminist congresses which gave the movement some momentum and by the appearance of a feminist daily newspaper, La Fronde, in 1897. The congress was a useful vehicle for setting out the feminist stall and for recruiting future leaders, as well as being a potential force for unity. Eugénie Potonié-Pierre, who harboured the idea of creating a French Federation of Feminist Societies, organised another congress in 1892, out of which emerged a central committee charged with drawing up a list of women's grievances which could be presented to parliament. The list, the work primarily of Aline Valette, called for the civic, economic and political emancipation of women and was sent to each of the mayors of the twenty arrondissements of Paris on 1 May 1893.[39]

A subsequent congress of 1896, in which Potonié-Pierre and her Solidarité group were again the prime movers alongside Maria Pognon and the leadership of the LFDF, operated on a larger scale and brought together women of the different feminist tendencies from the socialists through to Maugeret. The delegates discussed a wide range of issues including abortion and free love as well as political rights for women, though in the end the resolutions they passed were less controversial ones involving reform of the law.[40] The 1896 congress received substantial press coverage from the big Parisian dailies such as Le Temps and Le Figaro – almost all of it hostile – but Pognon's strong advocacy of suffrage made at least one notable convert, the veteran radical journalist Henri Rochefort, who affirmed his support in his newspaper L'Intransigeant in April 1896.[41] The most notable conversion at the congress of 1896, however, was that of Marguerite Durand, at the time a journalist on the conservative Le Figaro who had been sent along to scoff at the participants. Instead, she left determined to make her own distinctive mark on the movement.

By launching La Fronde in 1897, Durand (1864–1936) put feminism on the map as never before. The illegitimate daughter of a general, she was brought up by her grandparents and received a conventional education, but broke with her milieu to become an actress at the Comédie Française, where she achieved star status. In

1886 she married the rising young Radical deputy Georges Laguerre, an ally of Clemenceau and an early supporter of General Boulanger. It was on Laguerre's newspaper *La Presse* that Durand learnt the trade of journalism and her salon achieved notoriety as a hotbed of Boulangist intrigue. Having split from Laguerre, she carried on her journalistic career at *Le Figaro*, where she was also the lover of its director Périvier, by whom she had a child. As director of *La Fronde*, Durand sought to create a quality feminist newspaper which would have a real impact on public opinion and be recognised as the heavy-weight feminist equivalent of *Le Temps* – '*Le Temps* in skirts'. Not only did she edit the first ever feminist daily newspaper, but one which was entirely produced by women.[42]

La Fronde won for French feminism a new prestige and authority, and did much to change its dowdy image: the elegant and beautiful Durand was not an easy target for misogynists, though her colourful love life provided plenty of gossip for detractors even within the movement itself, and her lovers undoubtedly contributed to the financing of her newspaper. As she was wont to say, 'feminism owes much to my blonde hair'.[43] Having gathered around her a team of talented writers, she ensured that the paper was launched with *éclat*: the first issue was preceded by extensive poster advertising in Paris and was given a print run of 200,000. The feminist themes which it concentrated upon tended to be women's work and female education: in its pages the *institutrice* was represented as the militant pioneer who would bring feminism to the French provinces. Nor did *La Fronde* confine itself exclusively to women's issues, but tackled also the big stories of the day, including the Dreyfus Affair, which was covered by Séverine as court correspondent at the retrial of Dreyfus at Rennes in 1899. Durand nailed the colours of *La Fronde* firmly to the Dreyfusard mast: some, indeed, whispered that it received subventions from the pro-Dreyfus lobby, which Durand denied. Among its backers, however, was Gustave de Rothschild. In general, the paper's leftist tone reflected Durand's own radical republican leanings. The same ideological orientation, of course, largely explains why in the first instance *La Fronde* refused to throw its weight behind the campaign for women's suffrage, though suffragists like Pognon and Auclert were given space to argue their point of view.[44]

Thanks to *La Fronde* and the feminist congresses of the 1890s, by 1900 feminism was no longer the novelty for French public opinion which it had been in the later 1870s. The impending arrival of the new century encouraged feminists to believe that better times lay ahead and in 1900 they could point to three separate congresses which appeared to mark the new century as the dawn of a new age of opportunity. The first to meet was the Congrès catholique des Oeuvres de Femmes – not properly-speaking a feminist congress at all, but a gathering of upper-class and aristocratic ladies under the patronage of Cardinal Richard, the Archbishop of Paris, intended to enlist female support in the fight against anticlericalism. The resourceful Marie Maugeret, however, seized the opportunity afforded by the congress to raise her own feminist concerns, and both denounced the Napoleonic Code and called for the introduction of women's suffrage. Extensive discussion also took place on the subject of women's work, female education and moral questions like *recherche de la paternité*.[45] In these ways, therefore, Catholic women were exposed to the kinds of issues which preoccupied the feminists of the mainstream centre.

The second congress of 1900, the Congrès des Oeuvres et Institutions féminines, also had a religious as much as a feminist flavour. Organised by the Protestant women of the Conférence de Versailles, it was presided by Sarah Monod and focused essentially on the philanthropic activities of women, notably the fight against alcoholism and other 'social scourges' such as prostitution. The Protestant work ethic was much in evidence: in all some 230 reports were presented to the delegates. Nevertheless, the congress reached the important conclusion that charity alone was not enough to solve all the problems raised by the 'woman question'. Though unwilling to address the issue of political rights for women, the congress, having received an impressive report on the shortcomings of the Code from the woman barrister Jeanne Chauvin, endorsed the struggle for civil rights and no longer shrank from identifying with the label 'feminist'.[46] Explicitly feminist was the Congrès international de la Condition et des Droits des Femmes organised by the LFDF. Attended by some 500 delegates, the congress ranged over the whole spectrum of feminist concerns, some of which, such as women's work, gave rise to sharp exchanges between socialist women and bourgeois women opposed to any notion of 'protective' legislation. The congress passed some seventy-two resolutions, calling for such reforms as 'equal pay for equal work', the eight-hour day, wages for housewives, co-education, an end to the double standard, equal civil rights and divorce by mutual consent. Following a powerful speech from the independent socialist deputy (and lover of Marguerite Durand) René Viviani, there was also a call for votes for women: Viviani himself promised to introduce a suffrage bill in the next session of parliament.[47] French feminism had come a long way since the lonely suffrage campaigns of Hubertine Auclert in the 1880s.

Suffragism on hold: the CNFF and the consolidation of the centre, 1900–5

La Fronde and the congresses of 1900 served to stimulate the appearance of new moderate feminist groups. The Union fraternelle des Femmes (UFF), founded in 1901, was the creation of Mme Marbel, a teacher, who conceived of her society essentially as a study group. Most of its members, whose political leanings inclined towards the Radical-Socialist party and anticlericalism, nurtured literary or journalistic ambitions. Hellé (Marguerite Dreyfus, 1870–1966) wrote for *La Fronde*; Parrhisia (Blanche Cremnitz, 1848–1918) likewise; Héra Mirtel (Louise Jacques, 1868–1931) wrote poetry; Harlor (Jeanne Perrot, 1871–1970), the daughter of

Amélie Hammer of the LFDF and later the librarian of the feminist library founded by Marguerite Durand, wrote novels. Yet another society, the Union de Pensée féminine, started in 1910 by Lydie Martial (Anna Carnaud, 1861–1929), a member of Amelioration, reiterated the message that the goals of feminism could only be attained progressively, through moderate reform.[48] The same theme was amplified by *La Française*, the feminist newspaper founded in October 1906 to take the place of *La Fronde* after its demise in 1905. Quickly recognised as the mouthpiece of the mainstream movement, it was edited by Jane Misme (1865–1935), who had been the drama critic of *La Fronde* and was a close collaborator of Jeanne Schmahl in Avant-Courrière. Throughout her career she strove for feminist unity.[49]

After 1900 a growing number of feminist militants were similarly predisposed and increasingly accepted that the way forward was to build a strong and united mass movement on the American model. Already the International Council of Women (ICW), created after the Washington congress of 1888, attempted to promote unity world-wide, and as the ICW was an organisation dominated by Protestant women prominent in the world of philanthropy it was hardly surprising that in the French context it should eventually turn to its counterparts in the Conférence de Versailles to develop the initiative in France. Isabelle Bogelot, who had attended the founding congress in Washington, was a vital link between the Conférence and the ICW, whose president May Wright Sewell on a visit to France actively promoted the establishment of a French section in the aftermath of the congresses of 1900. Whereas Maugeret and her Catholic feminist group predictably rejected any alliance with a foreign and predominantly Protestant body, leading figures from the Conférence and the organising committee of the LFDF congress came together to establish a French section of the ICW, the Conseil national des Femmes françaises (CNFF) in 1901. The objective of the CNFF was to unite in a single large-scale association all the groups, whether feminist or feminine charities, which concerned themselves with the condition of women and children: its ultimate aim was to act as a 'women's party' which would ensure that women exercised an influential role on public life.[50]

Although most of the adhering societies (which included philanthropic organisations, temperance groups and pacifists, along with female trade unionists and representatives of women's professional associations) were more feminine than feminist in their inspiration, the appearance of the CNFF immediately transformed French feminism into a mass movement which could boast a membership of 28,000. At a stroke, the profile of moderate, mainstream feminism in France was raised and its status enhanced. The leadership – almost all eminently respectable bourgeois matrons with unimpeachable republican credentials – could not easily be dismissed as cranks or misfits. What was striking was the extent to which they construed their feminism as an extension of their long involvement in philanthropic activity – philanthropic activity which was often Protestant in inspiration. The first president of the CNFF was Sarah Monod, whose career in charitable works dated back to

1870. Vice-president, and subsequently president in succession to Monod, was Mme Julie Siegfried (1848–1922), *née* Puaux and likewise a daughter of a Protestant clergyman, with a brother also in the ministry. Married to the cotton magnate and deputy Jules Siegfried, she shared with her husband a lifelong devotion to good causes, notably temperance.[51]

Mme Avril de Sainte-Croix (1855–1939), in effect the CNFF's administrator in the post of secretary-general, had a similar career pattern, arriving at feminism after a long-standing involvement in the fight against the state regulation of prostitution and the double standard of morality, issues which she pursued also as a journalist on *La Fronde*, writing under the pseudonym 'Savioz'. In 1904 she became the first woman to be appointed to an extra-parliamentary commission when an enquiry was set up to investigate the functioning of the vice-squad *(police des moeurs)*.[52] Isabelle Bogelot was the first honorary president of the CNFF, while another leading light from the world of Protestant philanthropy was Marguerite de Witt-Schlumberger (1856–1924), daughter of the conservative deputy Conrad de Witt and grand-daughter of the Protestant statesman Guizot. Married to a rich businessman from Alsace, by whom she had six children, she made a name for herself in charitable work concerned with the rehabilitation of prostitutes. On the International Council of Women she was a vehement advocate of the abolition of regulated prostitution, and she also presided over the International Commission for a Single Standard of Morality and against the White Slave Trade. After prostitution, the vice which she was most determined to stamp out was alcohol abuse (she suggested that one should never take drink oneself, nor even offer it to guests). She was honorary president of the Union of French Women against Alcohol and also a member of the National League against Alcoholism.[53] For all of these women, who are perhaps best described as 'social feminists', feminism was a means rather than an end, the real goal being the reform and moral regeneration of French society.[54]

The creation of the CNFF powerfully reinforced the feminist centre and the bias which already existed towards what might be described as 'extreme moderation'. Its committee did include representatives from the more explicitly feminist groups (notably Maria Pognon and Marie Bonnevial) but the tone and general orientation of the organisation reflected the influence of the philanthropic feminists. Thus, while the CNFF divided its work into 'sections' such as education, philanthropy, the law and women's work, with a hygiene section added in 1902, initially it set its face against a suffrage section, which was added only in 1906. Discussion of sexual freedom for women was also off-limits, nor did the leadership encourage criticism of the men in power who showed so little sense of urgency in the face of their demands.[55] It was the hope of the CNFF moderates that feminism could be developed as a non-sectarian movement which would attract support from French women irrespective of creed or class. They soon discovered, however, that neither Catholic women nor socialist women were likely to heed their appeals for unity.

Marie Maugeret and her Catholic feminist group would have nothing to do with a body which they perceived to be predominantly Protestant and susceptible to foreign influences. Maugeret's action was conceived essentially as a contribution to the work of a Catholic reconquest of French society, in line with the social Catholicism inspired by Pope Leo XIII's encyclical *Rerum Novarum* (1891), a disquisition on how Catholics should confront the problems attendant on the advent of industrial society and the development of the liberal capitalist state.[56] Groups of social Catholic women were formed such as *Action sociale de la Femme*, a study circle founded by Jeanne Chenu in 1900 with a mission 'to inform women about their role in society, to make them understand better how their action can be influential in the family, in education, in the professions, in the city, and to assist them to defend the principles on which our French way of life has always rested'.[57] Potentially, at least, such women were possible recruits for Christian feminism and Maugeret's organisation could also count on the backing of a growing number of clerics like the well-known *abbé démocrate*, abbé Naudet, and the celebrated Dominican preacher Père Sertillanges, as well as prominent laymen like Charles Turgeon, a professor of political economy at the University of Rennes, who expressed the view that the woman question was too important to be left to non-Catholic women.[58] According to Turgeon, who supported women's suffrage but drew the line at women deputies, Christian feminism was 'a reasonable feminism which deserves the encouragement of the laity and even of the clergy' since it was 'above all a conservative force which aimed at defending marriage and society against the audacity of the revolutionaries'. Touching a raw Radical nerve, he added that, if women were allowed to vote, it was unlikely that they would vote for Freemasons and free thinkers.[59]

Maugeret sought to rally all Catholic women beneath the banner of Joan of Arc rather than of Marianne. In the late nineteenth century Churchmen were increasingly keen to reclaim Joan from republicans as the symbol of a specifically Catholic idea of the nation and the campaign to have her adopted as a Catholic saint and martyr was enthusiastically supported by the Catholic women of groups such as the Ligue des Femmes françaises (LFF), founded at Lyon in 1901, and the Ligue patriotique des Françaises (LPF), founded in 1902. Maugeret therefore launched a Fédération Jeanne d'Arc with the aim of staging an annual conference dedicated to Joan, the first of which was held in 1904. Discussion centred mainly on religious, philanthropic and social matters but Maugeret seized the opportunity to raise the question of women's political rights also. In 1906 at the third Congrès Jeanne d'Arc she went further, devoting the last day of the proceedings to 'women and politics' and even bringing in as a speaker the veteran suffragist and former *communarde* Eliska Vincent to argue the case for votes for women. Having waited until most delegates had gone off, Maugeret forced through a motion which endorsed the introduction of the female franchise. Her triumph was short-lived, since suffrage was repudiated by the delegates to the congress of 1910, but in 1906 Maugeret's coup caused quite a stir, outside of Catholic circles as well as within them.[60]

Socialist women objected to the CNFF from a different ideological perspective. A new attempt to combine socialism and feminism was launched in 1899 by the two founders of the Feminist Socialist Group (Groupe Féministe Socialiste, GFS), Elisabeth Renaud and Louise Saumoneau. Renaud (1846–1932) came from a working-class background and worked abroad as a governess in St Petersburg before her marriage to a printer, after whose death she supported herself and her two children by running a boarding house and giving private lessons. Well known in socialist circles, by 1898 she identified more readily with the Independent Socialist Party of Jean Jaurès than with the Marxist hardliners of Jules Guesde's French Workers' Party (POF). Saumoneau (1875–1950), a seamstress from Poitiers, lived by her own toil and knew poverty and deprivation at first hand. Whereas Renaud's instincts were conciliatory and her inclination was to seek accommodation both with the radical wing of the republican movement and with bourgeois feminism, Saumoneau was a natural class warrior whose antipathy to bourgeois feminists was visceral and whose loyalties within the socialist movement lay with the Guesdists. For her, class allegiance always took precedence over gender allegiance and in the turmoil over the Millerand affair of 1899 (when the independent socialist Alexandre Millerand split the socialist movement by accepting a post in the government of René Waldeck-Rousseau) Saumoneau had no hesitation in siding with Guesde's denunciation of class collaboration.[61]

From the beginning there were tensions between the two leading lights of socialist feminism and by 1902 they were no longer on speaking terms. Renaud abandoned the group and its 100 or so members to Saumoneau. Their application to join the United Socialist Party (SFIO) created in 1905 was turned down on the grounds that women should, like men, join only on an individual basis, and not as a group, as in the German Socialist Party, the SPD. In consequence, socialist feminism in France always lacked the mass base which it attained through the organisational skills of a woman like Clara Zetkin of the SPD and the cause of women's suffrage could never be identified with proletarian women to the extent that it was in Germany.[62]

The moderation of the CNFF was also resented by the more radical elements in the mainstream republican feminist movement, who considered that suffrage should be the top priority and were ready to resort to greater militancy to obtain it. Their spirits had been raised by the return to the fray of Hubertine Auclert, who re-established Suffrage des Femmes in 1900, and pressed for the introduction of a suffrage bill in parliament by means of her old tactic of petitioning. In the first instance she demanded that the vote be given only to single women, including widows and divorcees, so as to meet the objection that the female vote was a potential threat to the unity of the family. Among her supporters was the independent republican deputy Paul Gautret, who agreed to transform her petition into his own suffrage bill, which he deposited in July 1901. The measure made no headway in parliament, having been sunk at the committee stage, but in any case it served to divide rather than unite French suffragists, many of whom were scandalised at the prospect of the exclusion of married women.

Auclert soon reverted to her original position in favour of integral suffrage, though another petition, this time submitted to the Conseil général of the Seine department, had no more success than previous ones. More successful was Jeanne Oddo-Deflou's idea of distributing a suffragist stamp alongside official stamps issued in 1901 to commemorate the Declaration of the Rights of Man, a document attacked by feminists as being insulting to women. Taken up with enthusiasm by Auclert and her group, this initiative proved to be a significant exercise in consciousness-raising, particularly in the French provinces. Recognising the importance of images, Suffrage des Femmes also mounted an extensive poster campaign in favour of votes for women. At a moment when even Durand and *La Fronde* still hesitated to throw their weight fully behind women's suffrage, Auclert once again emerged as the most prominent suffragist in France.[63]

Suffragism received a further stimulus from developments on both the international and the domestic fronts. The idea of building an international movement in favour of women's suffrage was one which appealed to Auclert but in the event it was once again American rather than French initiatives which were responsible for the creation of the International Woman Suffrage Alliance (IWSA). The prime mover was Carrie Chapman Catt of the International Council of Women, who, much to Auclert's indignation, proceeded to establish the new organisation at the ICW congress held in Berlin in 1904 without securing French participation and – even worse – appointing the German suffragist Kaethe Schirmacher to educate French feminists in the need to develop an effective suffrage organisation. Auclert's reversion to her militancy of the 1880s can be attributed in part at least to her determination to give the lie to Catt regarding the lack of commitment to women's suffrage to be found in France.

At the same time, the decision of the French government to celebrate the centenary of the Civil Code in 1904 galvanised Auclert and other militants into protesting against what they regarded as the very symbol of women's oppression. Marguerite Durand took the lead in organising a banquet for some 1000 people who wanted to express their indignation at the official celebrations. For Auclert and Caroline Kauffmann of Solidarité such a gesture did not go far enough: it was time, they argued, for French feminists to take to the streets, and some fifty of them did so on 29 October 1904 at the opening of the official commemoration. Only a handful, however, supported Auclert in her attempt to carry out a ritual burning of a copy of the Code in the Place Vendôme, which in any event was forestalled by the police, alerted to the plan by a spy from within the movement. Undaunted, Caroline Kauffmann attended a ceremony at the Sorbonne the following day and released a series of balloons which bore the message 'The Code crushes women', for which she was charged but not sentenced.[64] Such gestures may not have been spectacular, but cumulatively they gave the impression that French feminism was on the move and that better days lay ahead.

Days of hope: the push for suffrage, 1906–14

The momentum behind street action was maintained in 1906 to coincide with the parliamentary elections in May. In addition to a poster campaign bearing Auclert's slogan 'Women must vote', Suffrage des Femmes, along with Solidarité and the UFF, organised a decorous street demonstration in the form of a cortege of hired cars and trucks which toured Paris distributing suffrage propaganda – not, apparently, with any great success to judge by the hoots of derision from bystanders.[65] More striking was a gesture organised by Kauffmann and her younger colleague Madeleine Pelletier. Having obtained access to the spectators' gallery at the Chamber of Deputies in June, they terrified the parliamentarians by scattering leaflets which many thought were anarchist bombs of the kind unleashed by Auguste Vaillant in December 1893. Unwilling to create feminist martyrs or afford the movement the oxygen of publicity, the government decided not to prosecute, leaving Pelletier free to continue her protests from the streets. On two occasions she led a march of women to the Chamber to bring pressure to bear on the socialist deputies who, in theory at least, were supposed to be sympathetic to the cause of women's suffrage.[66]

Partly as a result of this pressure from the left of the women's movement, but also because of the startling developments on the right involving Marie Maugeret, who, as already related, had succeeded in manipulating a congress of Catholic women into passing a suffrage resolution in 1906, even the CNFF came round to accepting the necessity of committing itself to the struggle for the vote and, having established a suffrage section, invited Auclert to be its president. At this point feminist hopes were raised further by the introduction of a new suffrage bill by Paul Dussaussoy, deputy for the Pas-de-Calais and a member of the largely Catholic Action libérale party, who proposed that all women be given the right to vote in municipal and local elections as a prelude to full parliamentary suffrage. The bill's *rapporteur*, the Radical Ferdinand Buisson, unlike most members of his party, was known to be sympathetic to the cause. On the other hand, the parliamentary committee which was set up to examine the question attached far more importance to the issue of proportional representation than to women's suffrage and relegated the matter to the bottom of its agenda. And the fact that the Conseil général of the Seine, following yet another petition from Auclert, finally expressed its support for the Dussaussoy bill in November 1907 could not allay the frustrations of the radical suffragists, who now also had before them the example of the militancy practised by the British suffragettes. Auclert's flirtation with the moderates was therefore short-lived, and she and the few others who shared her views increasingly found themselves contemplating recourse to violence and what the anarchists called 'propaganda by the deed', or 'direct action'.[67]

In 1908 the radicals returned to the streets. During the municipal elections held in Paris in May 1908 a number supported the candidacy of Jeanne Laloë, a young woman journalist who worked for the Parisian daily *Le Matin* (though others were wary, suspicious that the anti-suffragist *Matin* was merely engaging in a publicity stunt). Then, on election day, 3 May 1908, Auclert, Kauffmann and Pelletier staged a street demonstration in which they and perhaps forty other women marched and chanted suffragist slogans. Auclert rounded off the day by entering a polling station and overturning the urn which contained the votes, trampling over them to express her disgust at their exclusively masculine provenance. At the age of 60 Auclert had become France's first suffragette. Once again, however, the government refused to make a martyr of her and she received only a nominal fine. The press likewise made light of the incident.[68] Nor were other feminists prepared to go down the suffragette road – except Madeleine Pelletier, Kauffmann's collaborator and successor in Solidarité and the founder in 1907 of a monthly review, *La Suffragiste*, whose title made explicit her programme. An admirer of the British suffragettes, she had no difficulty in rallying to Auclert's call for militant action and followed her lead in committing an illegal act in 1908 by smashing the window of a polling station, for which she too received a nominal fine.[69]

Anne 'Madeleine' Pelletier (1874–1939) was by far the most significant radical feminist in France under the Third Republic. Born into poverty (her parents were fruit-and-vegetable sellers, her father having formerly been a coachman and her mother a domestic servant), Pelletier survived a wretched childhood, during which she suffered sexual abuse at the hands of her father and witnessed terrible quarrels over religion between him and his fanatically Catholic wife, and succeeded against all the odds in qualifying as a doctor, specialising in the treatment of mental illness. Her extreme feminist positions reflected first and foremost her personal experience of struggle, from which she derived her sense of her own worth and her consciousness of herself as an individual of exceptional ability. A supreme individualist and radical non-conformist, she refused to accept the stereotypical role prescribed for women by bourgeois mores: it was her determination 'not to be a woman in the way society expects'. Her feminism emanated less from a preoccupation with improving women's collective lot than from challenging the entire set of conventions by which femininity was constructed. Political rights were important not as a means of extending feminine influence in society – as most French suffragists claimed – but as a means of allowing women to function in society as autonomous individuals.[70]

Pelletier totally rejected a feminine identity which, to her mind, meant acquiescing in institutionalised oppression. Unlike the bourgeois feminists, who claimed to be reinforcing the family, Pelletier sought its destruction: only this, she maintained, would set women free to choose their own destiny (and in the process emancipate men and children also).[71] Her action was motivated by her core belief that the social cell of the future should be the individual, not the family, for the individual was not made for society but society for the happiness of the individual. The only valid reason for marriage was to provide for the socialisation of children: but alternative, and better, arrangements could be made for this task. Sexual activity was only 'a physiological function, neither more noble nor more shameful than any other'. Women should be left to choose their partners with the same freedom that men already enjoyed to select their mistresses. Sex was for pleasure and could be profitably enjoyed from the age of about 16. Girls should be taught how to avoid pregnancies, and the concept of illegitimacy should be abolished to prevent any stigma being attached to children born out of wedlock or to their mothers (a conviction which sprang from Pelletier's recollection of the psychological damage visited upon her own mother, a peasant woman haunted by the knowledge of her own illegitimacy). There was no inherent reason why mothers should have to breast-feed their own children, who were better brought up collectively in any case.[72] Women who desired an abortion should be able to have one (almost certainly she herself performed clandestine abortions). Only women should decide whether or not to have children and there was no necessary law to say that they should, since they might be better able to serve society without them.[73]

Pelletier despised those feminists (Marguerite Durand was undoubtedly one) who made a virtue of their femininity while demanding sex equality. In her view, those who flaunted their bare arms and nude breasts, their powdered faces and their elaborate hairstyles, were in no position to claim equal treatment. Feminism, she insisted, had to renounce any kind of special favours or privileges for women: if this meant equality of duties such as the obligation to perform military service, then so be it.[74] If women wanted to be emancipated they had to renounce their servile habits and rid themselves of their traditionally 'feminine' attributes.[75] This was the reason for Pelletier's apparently eccentric practice of habitually dressing like a man. In a man's world, the only way to be equal was to be a man: or, in the words of Joan Scott, 'since individuality was figured as masculine, since masculinity was as close to universalism as one could get, the refusal of feminine difference became synonymous with an avowal of the masculine'.[76]

Politically, Pelletier was always a radical, but never a genuine democrat. She had nothing but contempt for the masses and considered that the last social category to accept the emancipation of women would be the male proletariat.[77] Having started out as a left-wing republican, she attempted without success to compel the Freemasons to accept women members of the lodges and thereafter continually derided their refractory attitude towards women.[78] Having become a revolutionary socialist and pacifist, she rose through the ranks of the Socialist Party (the SFIO) to become the first woman on its executive committee, where she represented the violently antimilitarist faction of Gustave Hervé. (After the Russian Revolution, she would for a time sympathise with communism, until a trip to the Soviet Union shattered her illusions, whereupon she reverted to the milieux frequented by anarchists and libertarians.)[79] Within feminism, Pelletier showed herself to be a shrewd tactician as well as a major theorist. For her, as for Hubertine Auclert – but for different reasons – full political equality with men was the most important right which women should demand. As long as women did not figure on the electoral roll, she argued, they would obtain nothing, since in a regime of universal suffrage the only people who mattered to the politicians were the voters. The argument that women's enfranchisement would pave the way to clericalism and reaction she dismissed as absurd, ridiculing the paradox by which the advocates of 'free thought' were prepared to deprive half of humanity of its rights on the pretext that women's thought differed from their own 'enlightened' views.[80]

To win the vote, however, it was necessary to organise: hence her counsel to women to create large-scale feminist organisations on the one hand, and to penetrate existing political parties on the other. Pelletier was a supreme individualist, but she knew that individuals alone could not effect major political transformations. Writing in 1908, she recognised that the fragmentation of French feminism was a serious weakness:

> At present it can be said that each feminist has her own brand of feminism; with organisation, feminism would become a solidly established doctrine. It is rightly said that revolutions have always been made by minorities; one must add that the minorities that have made them were organised minorities.

She also had a word of warning for feminists who embarked on the task of penetrating other political parties:

> Under no pretext should a feminist prefer the party she has entered to feminism itself, for while she serves the party, she belongs only to feminism and to no other cause. A woman, like any individual, may be a socialist, a republican, or a monarchist, according to her convictions, but before all else she should be a feminist. For under a monarchy, a republic, or socialism, she will not be counted unless the political equality of the sexes becomes a reality.[81]

Pelletier, then, was an integral feminist. There was no tension between her socialism and her feminism, as some historians have claimed, because Pelletier was a feminist first and last. She was a feminist, however, because she was both an individualist and an elitist who sought emancipation for women from the oppression of a socially constructed femininity and the levelling tendencies of mass politics.

In the France of the *belle époque*, Pelletier could not be other than an isolated figure. Among her few collaborators were some women who held views even more extreme than her own. One was Louise Deverly-Dupont (1845–1925), who called herself Mme Remember. A convert to feminism after discovering *La Fronde*, she wrote for Pelletier's *La Suffragiste* before founding her own journal *Le Féminisme intégral* in 1913, which she described as 'an organ of combat'. Harbouring a hatred of men which bordered on the pathological (the result, it would appear, of an unhappy marriage) she had two favourite themes, namely that the great majority of men were infected with syphilis and that women should at all times carry guns against the omnipresent threat of assault from the predatory male.[82] Still more extreme was Arria-Ly (Josephine Gondon, 1881–1934), who along with her mother campaigned for women's suffrage in their home town of Toulouse. From her youth both parents had instilled in her a revulsion against the flesh and sexuality. Something of a latter-day Cathar, she aspired to found a new cult of 'arrialysme' which would be a perfect expression of hatred of the male sex, whose ultimate extinction she envisaged by the practice of universal virginity on the part of women – a cause which did not endear her to the villagers of the Ariège where she regularly repaired for health reasons. Her short-lived newspaper *Le Combat féministe* had just forty-four subscribers and, following the death of her mother, whom she called 'sister', in 1934 she took her own life.[83]

Nelly Roussel (1878–1922) was a rather different representative of French radical feminism and on account of her open and attractive personality was one of the few on the left to retain links with the moderates of the CNFF. Widely regarded as one of the best orators in the movement, she was the principal speaker at the anti-Code banquet organised by Durand in 1904 and was frequently commissioned by different groups to give lecture tours in the French provinces. Having rejected her conventional middle-class background on marrying the aspiring sculptor Henri Godet, by whom she had three children, she moved in bohemian and leftist circles and became particularly active in the neo-Malthusian movement as a propagandist for birth control. Sharing Pelletier's belief that female emancipation required a sexual as well as a political dimension, she preached that the most important right for women was the freedom to control their own bodies. The dangers of multiple pregnancies and the horrors of large families were her staple discourse, in which woman figured as '*l'éternelle sacrifiée*', 'she who is eternally sacrificed'.[84]

An indubitable consequence of French radical feminism, however, was to confer on centrist, bourgeois-republican feminism the respectability sought by its leaders. The militant methods of an Auclert or a Pelletier could be repudiated, but their cause – women's suffrage – could be pursued by other, legitimate, means. Since the foundation of the CNFF a growing number of its leaders had come round to the need for the franchise: Avril de Sainte-Croix, for instance, stressed its importance in her book *Le féminisme*.[85] In 1908 the moderates held their first full congress since

1900 and placed suffrage at the top of their agenda. The issue was thoroughly aired before the 800 delegates, who unanimously passed a resolution calling for the speedy passage of the Dussaussoy bill through parliament to give women the vote in municipal elections. At the same time, violence was explicitly ruled out.[86] This remained the official position of the mainstream feminists right up to the First World War, many times reiterated in the pages of *La Française*, the semi-official organ of the movement. Jane Misme never tired of declaring that the claims of radical feminists to either full suffrage and/or sexual liberation could only put in jeopardy the more modest but more plausible goal of first securing the municipal franchise. It was all very well for the English to have suffragettes, she asserted, but France required only *suffragistes*.[87] Street demonstrations were in her view harmful to the movement's prestige. French women, she insisted, were much more discreet and reserved than the women of England or America and should never appear on the streets for the sole purpose of being seen. In any case, since France was a nation which respected intelligence, the feminist cause could be carried by words and arguments rather than by protests and demonstrations. The feminist congress was the best place to impress the validity of their arguments on the public.[88]

Having converted to suffragism, the moderates wasted no time in setting up their own national suffrage league, the Union française pour le Suffrage des Femmes (UFSF), which became the French branch of the IWSA. Headed in the first instance by Schmahl (president) and Misme (secretary-general), it had the support of the leading lights of the CNFF and included members of other feminist groups such as the LFDF and UFF on its executive committee. Not content with winning over support from the left, in the pursuit of unity Schmahl was keen to keep the door open to the right and persuaded the duchesse d'Uzès to be a vice-president.[89] The real driving force behind the new group, however, was Cécile Brunschwicg (1877–1946), *née* Cécile Kahn, the daughter of a rich Jewish industrialist and the wife of the well-known philosopher Léon Brunschwicg. Rapidly recognised as an organiser of outstanding ability, in 1909 she effectively ousted Schmahl as leader and aligned the UFSF with both moderate republicanism and the social feminism of the CNFF – a shift symbolised by the election of Marguerite de Witt-Schlumberger to the presidency.[90] By 1914 the CNFF numbered 100,000 members: and in a short time, the UFSF established itself as the principal organ of women's suffrage in France, boasting sixty-five groups and a membership of 12,000 by the same date.[91] On the eve of the First World War French feminists could legitimately claim to have established their cause as a mass movement.

What was particularly encouraging for the feminist leadership was the fact that the movement seemed to be gaining support in the French provinces. Three-quarters of the members of the UFSF were to be found in provincial France, many of them provincial schoolteachers belonging to the Fédération Féministe Universitaire (FFU), founded by Marie Guérin in 1907. Guérin had started a professional organisation for women primary teachers at Nancy in 1903 with the aim of obtaining parity of pay and conditions with *instituteurs*, and the group had quickly acquired a wider feminist orientation. Its success encouraged the formation of similar groups in other regions, notably the Isère, where the prime mover was Venise Pellat-Finet, and in due course this led to the establishment of the Federation, which had its own journal (*L'Action féministe*) and by 1909 numbered thirty groups, each with a membership of around 100–150.[92]

The importance of *institutrices* in developing a feminist presence in the provinces can scarcely be exaggerated. Apart from their membership of the FFU, they also joined other local feminist organisations founded by individual militants who had contacts with the Parisian movements. Thus in Lyon another journalist from *La Fronde*, Odette Laguerre (1860–1956), the daughter of a diplomat and a militant Radical-Socialist republican, founded L'Education et Action féministe (EAF), which in addition to schoolteachers recruited women workers and female free thinkers, such as Mme Desparmet-Ruello, the first woman to be the headmistress of a lycée. Laguerre's group, which had around 250 members and affiliated to the CNFF in 1905, made no secret of its anticlericalism, antimilitarism and socialism and espoused a feminism that included both political rights for women and the right to be an unmarried mother. Its success, however, was not sustained, since it folded in 1909, but other groups proved more durable. At Le Havre, Pauline Rebour, who had a degree in law and taught at a girls' secondary school, established a local feminist society and also headed the suffrage section of the CNFF. Numbers were small (never more than twenty-five) but with the strong support of her husband, Raoul, a high-ranking civil servant, the group was extremely active, running its own lecture series and publishing its own *Bulletin*. Other groups could be found at Nice, where Anne de Réal brought out *Le Féministe de Nice* between 1906 and 1911, at Bayonne-Biarritz, where the society started by Thérèse Elosu, the wife of an anarchist doctor, was affiliated to the UFF, and elsewhere.[93]

Between 1910 and 1914 the drive to create the female citizen was pursued in earnest. The parliamentary elections of 1910 were seen as another opportunity to raise the profile of the suffrage campaign, though militants and moderates continued to disagree about tactics. Marguerite Durand, impressed by the impact of Jeanne Laloë's campaign in 1908, now favoured Auclert's old ploy of fielding female candidates, while the LFDF leadership, under the influence of its rising star Maria Vérone, was keen to stage the kind of large-scale suffrage rally which suffragists in the UK had mounted. In March 1910 she and Maria Bonnevial succeeded in attracting a capacity audience of 2000 to a hall in Paris, with many more would-be participants having to be turned away. The moderates of the UFSF, however, with the support of the CNFF and smaller moderate groups like the UFF, were reluctant to endorse either female candidacies or monster rallies, preferring instead to work for the election of male deputies known to be sympathetic to their cause. In the end,

Durand's hopes of running a female candidate in every Parisian *arrondissement* were dashed, and only four women stood – herself, Auclert, Pelletier and Kauffmann, the latter two with the grudging support of the SFIO. All polled abysmally, as did provincial candidates Arria-Ly in Toulouse and Marie Denizard in Amiens, though Elisabeth Renaud, with the backing of local socialists and the feminists of the Isère, obtained an impressive 2869 votes (27.5% of the poll) in Vienne.[94]

Partly because of Renaud's score, and partly because there was less at stake, the UFSF was more amenable to women candidates in the municipal elections of 1912, and backed Elisabeth Renaud's campaign in the Odéon district of Paris, where she polled 482 votes, which, if a poor showing, was still more than twice as many obtained by her male predecessor as socialist candidate. Pelletier, again a candidate, obtained 306 votes in the seventh *arrondissement*.[95] But as the legislative elections of 1914 approached, a growing number of suffragists thought that the campaign for women's suffrage required the injection of new vigour. Symptomatic was Maria Vérone's call for greater militancy, stopping short of violence. Vérone (1874–1938) was one of the most energetic, interesting and colourful characters in the feminist movement. Raised on the doctrines of republicanism and free thought by her parents, she was obliged to renounce her educational ambitions on the death of her father and went to work with her mother in the artificial flower trade. Having qualified as a primary teacher, she was banned from the profession in 1897 because of her radical political views and for a brief period had to earn her living dancing in a chorus line, before marrying and finding work in journalism, first with Clemenceau's newspaper *L'Aurore* and then with *La Fronde*, where she wrote under the pseudonym Thémis and specialised in legal affairs. Increasingly committed to feminism, she joined the LFDF, though she remained a socialist party member also. As a divorcee and mother of two children, she began to study law and qualified for the French bar in 1907, rapidly establishing herself as a leading counsel in children's cases. With the support of her second husband and fellow barrister Georges Lhermitte, who shared her feminist convictions and became a vice-president of the LFDF, she advocated taking to the streets to raise the suffragist profile in 1914.[96]

At the same time a number of UFSF members – among them Hélène Brion, Marianne Rauze and Marguerite Martin – quit to establish a more militant suffragist society, the Ligue nationale pour le Vote des Femmes, which attracted support from the likes of Marguerite Durand, Vérone, Pelletier, Séverine and Nelly Roussel as well as from socialist women disillusioned by Louise Saumoneau's antipathy to bourgeois feminism, such as Mme Ducret-Metsu, who was elected president, and Fabienne Tisserand, secretary-general. Numbering around 250 adherents, the new society refused to be fobbed off with municipal suffrage and demanded the speedy introduction of integral suffrage.[97] In a speech which Nelly Roussel frequently delivered on its behalf, she enunciated the demand for full rights of citizenship:

We want to be 'citizens' the way you are 'citizens', Gentlemen, under the same conditions and for exactly the same reasons. We want to be *citizens* like you, because we are *workers* like you, *taxpayers* like you, and *subject to trial* like you ... We want to be citizens because we believe M. René Viviani was right when he said, 'Legislators make laws for those who make the legislators', in other words, *nobody who cannot vote counts in the eyes of the elected.*

Roussel also made it plain that municipal suffrage was not enough to satisfy the legitimate aspirations of women, and rejected the argument that this was a necessary step on the way to full suffrage rights. Nor did she accept that moderation alone would produce success:

Ladies and gentlemen, my view is completely the opposite: I believe that to obtain a little we must demand a lot. Let us leave prudence, moderation, and expediency to the members of the Legislature, for pity's sake.[98]

In 1914, the UFSF hierarchy was not prepared to go along with this line of reasoning. On the other hand, with some reluctance, the UFSF and *La Française* agreed to participate in a mock ballot organised by the Parisian daily newspaper *Le Journal*, which under Gustave Téry had become an ardent convert to the now almost fashionable cause of women's suffrage. Over ten days of the election period, it issued a ballot sheet on which all women who supported female suffrage were given an opportunity to demonstrate their feelings, either by depositing a vote in special booths erected on election day itself or by mailing the ballot to the newspaper's offices (these postal votes were to be accompanied by a stamped and addressed envelope to ensure authenticity). The response was enormous: by 3 May 1914 *Le Journal* claimed to have received 505,912 expressions of a desire to vote.[99]

A further sign of progress was a suffrage rally held on 5 July 1914 to honour the memory of Condorcet. The idea seems to have originated with Séverine, now a convert to suffrage, and even the CNFF and the UFSF found it difficult to disagree with a public display to commemorate an outstanding feminist pioneer who was at the same time fêted by the Third Republic as an illustrious founding father of the republican tradition. A crowd of over 5000 suffragists gathered at the Orangerie of the Tuileries Gardens and proceeded in orderly procession to the left bank of the Seine, where wreaths were laid before Condorcet's statue. The event was an impressive, if rare, demonstration of suffragist unity. The LFDF's Maria Vérone was a member of the planning committee, while Pauline Rebour of the UFSF was one of the main speakers at the rally. Another was Marguerite Durand, who, while stressing the need for non-violence, chastised French feminists for their excessive prudence.[100]

Gender relations in crisis?

In the summer of 1914 hopes were high among suffragists that women would be voting in France by 1916. Little did they realise that the Great War would soon be a serious setback to their cause and that they would have to wait another thirty years before they would obtain the right to vote.

Epilogue

France and feminism

When war broke out in August 1914 French feminists were justified in thinking that their cause had made enormous progress since the turn of the century. It had obtained a number of legal reforms. Avant-Courrière's campaign to allow women to be civil witnesses and to enable married women to keep their own earnings had led to legislation on these issues in 1897 and 1908. Feminist pressure, too, contributed to the enactment of the law of 27 March 1907, by which women were allowed to vote in elections to the Conseil de Prud'hommes (a kind of arbitration tribunal). Equally, the law of 1912 which introduced paternity suits had long been sought by the principal feminist organisations, even if it did not satisfy all their aspirations. Feminism itself had been transformed from a collection of small and disunited factions into a mass movement, and feminists could now envisage in a not-too-distant future the crowning of a decade of achievement with the introduction of women's suffrage.

The war, of course, made national survival rather than women's rights the essential priority, and the vast majority of feminists willingly suspended their activities in order to work for victory. In what developed into a 'total' war – one in which the civilian population at the 'rear' was mobilised to play its part in the war effort as much as the fighting men at the 'front' – the contribution of women in general was universally acknowledged to be massive, and this in turn served to reinforce the conviction of feminists that women would be 'rewarded' with the suffrage for all their sacrifices after the cessation of hostilities. In May 1919, the forecasts of an impending feminist victory appeared to be vindicated when the Chamber of Deputies finally debated the Dussaussoy bill and, following an eloquent speech from ex-Prime Minister and longtime suffragist René Viviani calling for the immediate introduction of the female franchise, voted in favour of the proposal by a majority of 344 to 97.

Feminist celebrations proved premature, however. Before the suffrage bill could become law it had to receive the approval of the second chamber, the Senate, and senators procrastinated until November 1922 before debating it. In the course of their deliberations, many of the hoary arguments against women's suffrage were once again rehearsed: the already dwindling powers of the husband and head of the

217

family would be undermined; women did not want the vote; women did not need the vote. As ever, the crucial argument, put by its *rapporteur* in the Senate, Alexandre Bérard, was that female suffrage was a threat to republican institutions and the instrument of clerical domination. As in the nineteenth century, so after the First World War and throughout the period between the wars the spectre of clericalism was raised to frustrate the best efforts of feminists to secure the political enfranchisement of women.[1]

Feminism, antifeminism and sexual difference

The failure of French women to obtain full political and civic equality prompts a series of reflections on the condition of women and the politics of gender over the long nineteenth century. The first concerns the context in which French feminists were obliged to operate, namely – despite all the political upheavals – in a basically stable and conservative society which was hostile to political innovation and experimentation. In 1914 France was still predominantly a peasant society. According to the census of 1911 some 56% of the population still lived in the countryside, and if 44% lived in towns it should be remembered that a town might have as few as 2000 inhabitants. In 1900 only 15.4% of the population lived in towns with more than 100,000 inhabitants (in England and Wales the comparable figure was 39%, in Scotland 30.8%), and Paris, with its three million inhabitants (most of them not native Parisians), was very much the exceptional metropolitan centre. Lyon and Marseille were the only other cities with more than 500,000 inhabitants. Few of the inhabitants of rural and small town France evinced any enthusiasm for social or political experimentation and in the provinces the cause of women's rights was viewed with indifference, if not outright hostility, in many quarters. In the popular mentality feminism was frequently associated with the excesses of the British suffragettes: hence, even after the Great War, local women might sympathise with the cause of suffrage but be afraid to identify with it openly.[2]

In this essentially conservative society, which nevertheless remained haunted by the nightmare of France's revolutionary past and fearful of the consequences of further political turmoil, the maintenance of a gender order based on sexual difference was widely regarded as fundamental to the preservation of social stability. As we have already seen, the image of the *tricoteuses* of the Revolution and of the *pétroleuses* of the Commune had been used to suggest women's unfitness for public life and fears continued to be expressed by antifeminists about the type of role which women might play if they were admitted to the political arena. Antifeminism, therefore, was always a factor with which feminists had to reckon, even if it was never constituted into an organised lobby comparable to, say, the Women's National Anti-Suffrage

League in Britain. Founded in 1908, the latter organisation grouped prominent male members of the Establishment such as Lords Curzon and Cromer, as well as women like Violet Markham, for whom the enfranchisement of women was 'a gamble with the future of womanhood'.[3] This was also the position of French antifeminists such as as Anna Lampérière, whose fundamental objection to feminism was its alleged confusing of masculine and feminine roles and its tendency to erode sexual difference.[4]

In France, the defence of 'true womanhood' was frequently mounted by well-known literary women, for whom feminism was the sworn enemy of femininity, above all because it sought to cultivate women's minds at the expense of their emotions. According to the popular novelist Colette Yver, feminists were over-educated intellectuals, or 'cervelines', in other words 'women whose brains have atrophied their hearts'. In her view, the ideal, chivalric, relations which should exist between the sexes had been fixed long ago by 'ancient laws'. As for votes for women, this was a fad promoted by an unrepresentative minority.[5] Léontine Zanta likewise believed in the long-term influence of courtly love on the psychology of the 'Latin' woman. Whereas the 'woman of the North' had never known 'the liberties of the heart', 'the Latin woman is too attached to love not to fear losing it by being displeasing to men'.[6] Another novelist, Mme Rachilde, explaining why she could never be a feminist, affirmed that she regretted not being a man, and had tried to emulate George Sand in acting above all as an individual. Like Yver, she accepted that women were intellectually inferior to men and deplored attempts to over-educate women, which could only lead to 'the end of what is called family life'.[7]

The charge that feminism in general and suffragism in particular were incompatible with the ideology of separate spheres and therefore with the 'true' mission of woman as wife and mother was put most forcefully by diehard misogynists, of whom a ferocious and prolific representative was the writer Théodore Joran. Vituperating against all attempts to blur the differences between the sexes, he echoed Nietzsche in claiming that feminists were ugly and that their doctrine made life uglier. Above all, feminism subverted the virtues of the family:

> A woman cannot at the same time love science and literature and the humdrum aspects of domestic occupations. In my childhood and in my region, women never entertained any destiny other than marriage. They humbly admitted that the man should earn a living for two, now they want to be obliged to no one but themselves. Female celibacy will be the inevitable consequence of all the madcap ideas of emancipation which haunt these unhinged brains. And also the false households of so-called free union.[8]

Such statements touched a sensitive nerve in at least some sections of French opinion, given the widespread concern with the spectre of depopulation. In pro-natalist and nationalist circles, the demand for women's emancipation could be represented not only as an abdication of women's natural role but as a threat to the security of the state itself. Hostility to women's rights in the *belle époque* was thus fuelled by the nationalist and xenophobic discourse which flourished in an era marked by a heightening of international tensions and war scares.[9] Thus, by the beginning of the twentieth century, a favourite antifeminist argument was that feminism was an un-French phenomenon, flourishing only in Protestant and Anglo-Saxon countries. The University of Paris awarded a doctorate in law for a thesis on the character of feminism which made this its central point.[10] According to Joran, feminism could flourish only in a Nordic country such as Sweden, where co-education was possible because of the coldness of the national temperament and an enthusiasm for sport which was fuelled by the need for robust young maidens to work in the fields. But, as far as France was concerned, 'Our mentality has nothing in common with the mentality of the Scandinavian race'.[11]

For Joran and his ilk, a further consideration was that feminism was both internationalist and pacifist: consequently, votes for women would lead straight to the disarmament of France and benefit only Germany. Abbé Henry Bolo, a supporter of 'Christian feminism' but the enemy of any other kind, saw feminism as having originated in the United States, 'a country known for its eccentricity where women, less protected by traditions, had more need to defend themselves'. From America, feminism reached Europe by way of England, 'where pauperism and drunkenness keep women of the popular classes locked up in the most abject misery, where two and a half million spinsters have declared war on men guilty of not having married them, and where even in the upper classes women were beaten like beasts'. Thereafter, feminism had found a home in the Protestant countries of Europe 'where the liberty given to fantasies of dogma undoubtedly diminishes the influence of evangelical legislation'.[12]

Arguably, the climate of public opinion in France was by no means conducive to the progress of the women's movement and the enactment of women's suffrage. Feminists might have reason, justice and logic on their side, but, contrary to their expectations, these were far from enough to carry the day. Quite apart from the accusations of being unpatriotic and 'un-French', they faced an uphill struggle to overcome the biggest obstacle in their path, namely a belief in sexual difference that permeated the whole of French society. Far from being confined to raving misogynists like Joran or to the female writers of romantic fiction (who might well be thought to have a vested interest in the view that women's lives were governed by the search for love)[13], the notion of sexual difference was backed by the best scientific opinion of the day and passed for one of society's universal truths – one of the more dubious achievements of the development of medical science since the days of the Enlightenment. By the turn of the century, the gendered medical view of women was being invoked in courts of law to explain or rationalise deviant female behaviour:

in 1914 it formed a key element in the defence of Mme Caillaux, whose trial for the murder of the newspaper editor Gaston Calmette obtained more press coverage than the assassination of the Austrian Archduke Franz Ferdinand at Sarajevo.[14] Other sciences such as phrenology taught that women were inferior because of their smaller brain sizes, a discovery which, according to the eminent sociologist Emile Durkheim, further predisposed them to 'affective functions' rather than to 'intellectual functions'. For Durkheim and Gustave Le Bon, pioneer of the study of crowd psychology, sexual difference was a product of the evolution of civilisation to a higher level. Only among primitive peoples were women alleged to be admitted to a political role.[15]

French feminists, therefore, were obliged to fight for women's rights in a less than propitious social and cultural environment. Indeed, the ultimate irony was that they themselves were obliged to acknowledge women's 'difference'. Denied full citizenship on the grounds of their 'difference' from men, they were frequently driven into the paradoxical position of claiming civic and political equality precisely in the name of the difference which they contested.[16] Nevertheless, it would be quite wrong to conclude that they were predestined to failure because of the contradictions of feminist discourse. As far as women's suffrage was concerned, whatever anti-suffragists might claim, it was not the case that the female franchise could not be enacted because of the weight of antifeminist pressure at the grass-roots. There is no evidence to suggest that anti-suffragists enjoyed any more popular support than suffragists. Nor was public opinion so exercised by the prospect of votes for women that the enactment of a suffrage bill was simply unthinkable. It is hardly sufficient to argue, as opponents of women's rights did, that women were not entitled to vote because there was insufficient demand for such a measure: after all, the same could be said about the introduction of manhood suffrage in 1848. And, when women did eventually receive the vote, in 1944, this was not in response to a widespread militant suffrage campaign: rather, as in other countries, it was because the political elite had come to accept that female suffrage was not a recipe for disorder, likely to disturb and confuse traditional gender roles, so that, in the context of establishing new constitutional arrangements, it was possible to accord women equal rights of citizenship from the beginning.

Feminism, then, was hardly the 'un-French' phenomenon which its opponents made it out to be. On the contrary, as we have seen, France had a vibrant feminist tradition dating back to the time of the French Revolution, and by 1914, French feminists could point to many achievements. Yet the ultimate prize of full civic and political rights continued to elude them and the question needs to be put as to whether they could – and should – have done even better.

A failure of feminism?

Was it the case that, by comparison with, say, the British suffragettes, French feminists did not do as much as they might have done to compel the politicians to take their cause seriously? The answer must be a qualified 'Yes'. On the one hand French feminism failed to carry the day before French public opinion, in part at least because of a refusal to adopt a more militant strategy in pursuit of its goals. At the same time, as we have seen, the movement was unable to transcend the ideological and political divisions at work in French society at large and replicated these in its own organisations.

To be sure, as already noted, French feminists made some impression on public opinion before 1914, as the mock ballot in *Le Journal* and the Condorcet rally demonstrated. At least in Paris, feminism gave rise to serious discussion in the press, in literature and in academia – an impressive number of the law theses submitted in the *belle époque* were devoted to aspects of the 'woman question'. It has been calculated that by 1914 at least a dozen of the leading daily newspapers in France, with a combined circulation of more than 1,700,000, were in favour of women's suffrage, whereas opponents could muster only half that number of newspapers, with a readership of just some 750,000. Moreover, press support came from all points on the political spectrum, and included the right-wing *Autorité* as well as the socialist organ *Humanité*.[17]

But it was only in Paris and in other towns that the feminists enjoyed success with their propaganda. Though they were able to establish societies and hold meetings in most regions of France they usually preached to the converted. Their newspapers were unknown to the reading public, appearing only in limited editions and available only by subscription. Even the celebrated *Fronde* was unable to attract a circulation of more than 5600 in its heyday.[18] Marguerite Durand reckoned it collapsed because it was 'judged too bourgeois by the socialists, too serious by the Parisians, too Parisian by the provinces'.[19] No doubt her explanation is over-facile but it does have the merit of pointing out the enormous difficulties confronting the French feminists in their attempts to strike a sympathetic chord among the general public. When the well-known journalist Louise Weiss attempted to relaunch the suffrage crusade in the 1930s, she encountered the same apathy and ignorance which had greeted the earlier campaigns. As she put it:

> In 1934 the peasants remain open-mouthed when I spoke to them about the vote, the workers laughed, women in commerce shrugged their shoulders and bourgeois women repulsed me in horror.[20]

The failure of French feminism to make a larger impact on public opinion certainly owed something to a conscious decision to repudiate militancy as a strategy. Whether militancy was entirely efficacious in the case of the British suffragettes is a moot point: some historians argue that suffragette outrages in fact set back the timetable for the introduction of the female franchise in Britain. On the other hand, there is no doubt that the presence of a more obviously militant wing brought considerable pressure to bear on governments and eventually made it easier for politicians to negotiate with those women whom they considered to be the more reasonable and moderate elements in the suffrage movement.[21] In France radicals like Madeleine Pelletier were always isolated, and could thus be safely ignored, while the moderates were almost certainly too moderate, and too easily fobbed off by weasel words of encouragement from cynical politicians.

The fundamental reason for the moderation of the mainstream republican feminist movement was not so much the bourgeois character of its membership – a factor, certainly, but no more true of France than of other countries – but its close ties to the Republican political establishment. Modern French feminism owed its very existence to a close association with the rising fortunes of republicanism. The first generation of feminists, headed by Deraismes and Richer, were not simply (or even primarily) feminists: first and foremost they were militant Republicans, anticlericals and Freemasons (Deraismes became the first woman Freemason in France). In the second generation, many of the mainstream leaders remained intimately linked with the male political class, either by birth, marriage or, more unusually, as in the case of Marguerite Durand, an extra-marital relationship (with René Viviani, who rose to the rank of Prime Minister). Julie Siegfried was the wife of the deputy Jules Siegfried. Marguerite de Witt-Schlumberger was likewise the daughter of a deputy. Louise Cruppi, *née* Crémieux, a head of section in the CNFF, came from a dynasty of radical politicians and married Jean Cruppi, a deputy and several times minister.

Similarly, Mme Pichon-Landry, active in both the CNFF and the UFSF, was married to Stephen Pichon, foreign minister in several governments. Another prominent figure in the UFSF, Valentine Thomson, was the daughter of another minister, Gaston Thomson. Mme Marie Georges-Martin, who presided over the suffrage section of the CNFF, was married to a radical senator. Cécile Brunschwicg moved in Radical-Socialist circles and joined the party in 1924, notwithstanding the role of so many of its members in frustrating the enactment of women's suffrage in parliament. Mme Avril de Sainte-Croix was the first woman to be appointed to an extra-parliamentary commission (that on morals in 1904). At the time of the Dreyfus Affair and its aftermath, which produced another spate of anticlerical legislation culminating in the separation of Church and state in 1905, most bourgeois feminists were on the side of Dreyfus, radicalism and anticlericalism. Even the more conservative feminists of the CNFF, who were more comfortable with moderate republican governments, never wavered in their commitment to either the regime or the principle of *laïcité*.

The republican connection had important consequences, not the least of which was that feminists adhered to the principles and priorities of the Republic as defined by the male political establishment. And, just as the masters of the Third Republic, whether moderate or radical Republicans, were bent on establishing a viable regime which would obliterate the connotations of republicanism with the violence and disorder of the Commune, the June Days and the Terror, so too the feminists were equally anxious to dispel memories of previous links between feminism and political and sexual radicalism. Intent on living down the past, republicans and feminists alike sought above all to establish their respectability. French mainstream feminism was developed on the premise that the emancipation of women was a cause which must never rock the Republican boat. For this reason bourgeois republican feminists were prepared first to delay the demand for women's suffrage, according it a lower priority than the legal and moral issues which preoccupied especially the women who came to feminism from the world of philanthropy, and who preferred to develop their own brand of 'social feminism', and then, once suffrage moved to the top of the agenda after 1900, to insist that the main reason women should have the vote was to bring a special feminine contribution to the conduct of public affairs.

The republican connection also explains why, from the outset, the movement opted for action that was both prudent and moderate – as they saw it – or merely timid, as it appeared to more radical contemporaries like Pelletier. It was the firm belief of the moderate leadership that progress would be made by engaging in rational discussion and winning favourable publicity for the dignified deliberations characteristic of their feminist congresses – a belief they clung to even after the First World War. Mainstream feminists were at pains to demonstrate their fidelity to the Republic and to act as good and loyal *citoyennes*, convinced that the best way to advance their cause was to make friends with leading politicians – hence their immense satisfaction at the presence of deputies, senators and academicians at their congresses. Such official recognition persuaded them that they were on their way to inclusion in the 'Republican synthesis' – to borrow the phrase of Stanley Hoffman – of those who identified with the regime.[22]

Only in the mid-1920s would some members of the UFSF openly begin to question the wisdom of their 'softly-softly' approach, and to accuse the political class of taking advantage of their peaceful disposition. Mme Odette Simon, a woman barrister, concluded that women in 'Latin' countries had been too decorous and too afraid of ridicule in their campaigns for the suffrage, and advocated that they follow the example of British and American women as regards the intensity, extent and tenacity of their propaganda, though she immediately qualified her remarks by adding that any 'complete imitation of the suffragettes would run the risk of damaging French women'.[23] Even Jane Misme came to admit that the movement lacked popular appeal and contained a large number of dilettantes, female intellectuals who were more often profiteers from, rather than supporters of, feminism.[24] Careerism was rampant and mainstream women contained too many coteries headed by society women who wished only to cut a name for themselves.

The bourgeois-republican orientation of mainstream feminism had further consequences. For one thing, it did not enhance the appeal of feminism for women who looked to the labour movement for decisive change in French society. Such, for instance, was the widow Gabrielle Petit, who moved in anarchist and libertarian circles, which were the principal outlet for her journal *La Femme affranchie* (1904–9). Like Louise Michel before her, she had little faith in the franchise either for women or for men, and as a Malthusian and committed antimilitarist she identified more readily with revolutionary syndicalism than with bourgeois feminism.[25] Even within the ranks of militant schoolteachers – who were the best hope for the creation of vibrant feminist networks in the provinces – not everyone agreed with Marie Guillot of the Schoolteachers Federation that the cause of feminism went hand in hand with the organisation of working women.[26] Marie Vidal depicted the CNFF as a bourgeois organisation fraught with dangers for the female proletariat. Its interest in class reconciliation was a plot to woo the working class away from the ideal of social revolution and its concentration on the suffrage was an attempt to make working women think that they were exploited by men rather than by capitalism.[27] A male member, true to the labour movement's lingering Proudhonist misogyny, suggested that there was no need to organise a society in which women would have equal rights since they would have no idea what to do with freedom if they had it.[28] Revolutionary syndicalists, as anti-parliamentarians, automatically rejected suffragism. In their eyes, political rights were illusory, whereas the real problem confronting women of the working class was the large size of their families. Birth control, rather than the vote, was what they needed to hear about, and they were hardly likely to learn about that from an organisation like the CNFF, which strongly supported the natality crusade.[29]

Socialist women were similarly troubled by the competing claims of class and gender. After the demise of the GFS, it was only at the beginning of 1913 that another group of socialist women was formed, the Groupe des Femmes socialistes. The initiative was taken by the wife of an army captain and UFSF militant Marianne Rauze (born Marie-Anne Rose Gaillarde) with the help of Elisabeth Renaud, who hoped somehow to exclude Louise Saumoneau. Saumoneau, however, outmanoeuvred them at the founding meeting held on 23 January 1913 by obtaining a consensus for the view that party membership of the SFIO was a prerequisite for membership of the group, which could not therefore recruit from outside the party. Since 1912 Saumoneau also had an outlet for her views in her newspaper *La Femme socialiste*, where she continued to preach that socialism was incompatible with bourgeois feminism. Wracked by factionalism, the group could not even stage a rally in 1913 to mark 'International Women's Day' which had been successfully promoted by German socialist women.[30]

In February 1913 Rauze started her own organ *L'Equité*, which provided a forum for debate and gave a further platform to women like Suzanne Lacore, a schoolteacher and secretary of the SFIO federation of the Dordogne, who were followers of Saumoneau. Feminism, she affirmed, was a deviation from the class struggle and failed to tackle the essential problem of the economic exploitation of the proletarian woman. Feminists might be educated and enlightened but they were most often bourgeois women who, if they obtained the right to vote, would undoubtedly use their ballots to bolster the capitalist system. Proletarian women could seek their salvation only through the party.[31] In reply, Hélène Brion (1882–1962), a primary teacher and socialist militant in the working-class Parisian suburb of Pantin and a close friend of Madeleine Pelletier, maintained that the difference between the sexes was more important than the difference between social classes. Women were slaves irrespective of social status: indeed the Proudhonist formula 'housewife or harlot', in Brion's view, would be more accurate were it changed to housewife *and* harlot, since many were the wives who were beaten and raped by their husbands. In seeking the vote, bourgeois women were beginning the process of feminine emancipation for all women, proletarians first and foremost.[32]

It was the Saumoneau faction which carried the day in the group, however, where the working-class militants, especially those who like Saumoneau herself worked in the garment trade, proved staunch allies. They also helped her to organise the first International Women's Day in France in March 1914, which was attended by a crowd of some 2000 of both sexes, who heard speeches from Saumoneau and prominent figures in the party, including the socialist deputies Compère-Morel and Bracke, and by Jean Longuet of *L'Humanité*. The feminist faction, including Marianne Rauze herself who had come to see the necessity of a separate feminine section within the socialist movement, had no alternative but to quit, and were confirmed in their resolution by Saumoneau's intransigent attitude in the Couriau affair, when she stood solidly behind the intransigent printers' union rather than be seen to side with bourgeois feminists.[33] There were no more militant opponents of women's suffrage and the feminism of the CNFF than diehard socialist women like Louise Saumoneau.

If republican feminism had little or no appeal for working-class women of the Left, it likewise failed to mobilise support on the Right from women of the Catholic bourgeoisie, who had an agenda of their own. In the period before 1914 even Maugeret's Catholic feminist group could not compete with the Ligue des Femmes françaises (LFF) and the Ligue patriotique des Françaises (LPF). The LFF was founded in 1901 in the city of Lyon by a group of Catholic women who wished to involve themselves in the campaign against the Republic's anticlerical legislation and had the idea of mustering support for right-wing candidates in the elections due to be held in 1902. Dissensions arose, however, as to which candidates were most deserving of the Ligue's support, since some of its members favoured royalists and others *ralliés* (Catholics who had headed the call of Pope Leo XIII in the 1890s to rally to the Republican regime). Personal antagonisms, along with rivalry between the committees in Paris and Lyon, added to the tensions and in May 1902 the Paris committee set up its own rival organisation, the LPF. Headed by the baronne de

Brigode and baronne Reille, the LPF maintained close links with Catholic politicians such as Jacques Piou and Albert de Mun of the Action Libérale Populaire (ALP), the political party of the *ralliés*, and represented their organisation as a French equivalent of the Primrose League in England, an association which had proved a useful source of support for the Conservative party. While publicly maintaining an apolitical stance, the LPF leadership saw no reason why women should not seek to influence the outcome of elections. Elections had consequences for the Church and women were part of the Church: they affected the *patrie* and women were part of the nation. As baronne Reille explained, because religion was affected by the men in power, it was up to women to bring pressure to bear on them to ensure that religion was not harmed. The hand of woman might not drop the suffrage into the ballot box, but it could guide the hand that did.

It is true that, after the poor performance of the ALP in the elections of 1902 and 1906, the LPF leadership tended to turn away from political action and to concentrate more on social work and purely religious activities like spiritual retreats and pilgrimages to Lourdes. Led by women of the aristocracy and the upper echelons of the bourgeoisie, the LPF recruited its militants mainly from the ranks of the Catholic middle classes, though it made no secret of its aspirations to win back the masses to Catholicism. As Mlle Frossard, one of the Ligue's principal orators, argued in 1906, 'social services give us influence and enable us to win the trust of the lower classes'. The alternative was to allow the working classes to be duped by 'our adversaries' (meaning anticlerical republicans, godless socialists and insurrectionary anarcho-syndicalists). Strongly supported by the clergy, the LPF expanded its membership to 585,000 by 1914 and gained international recognition as the model for female Catholic action in defence of religion. In practice, the movement was an important Catholic outlet for 'active citizenship', allowing Catholic women to make an important contribution to public life despite their lack of formal political rights. Nevertheless, in the years before 1914 most of these women were reluctant to follow Maugeret over the question of votes for women because it was known that the Vatican under Pius X was opposed to the female franchise. Later, in the aftermath of the First World War, the LPF was to furnish a mass base for the development of a Catholic suffrage movement which vastly outnumbered the mainstream movement of the Republicans — proof enough, in Radical eyes, that their darkest suspicions about the consequences of the introduction of female suffrage were entirely justified.[34]

Feminism, political culture and French 'singularity'

In the end, therefore, in order to explain the limited progress made by French feminists in the period before 1914 one ultimately comes back to the men in power. Whatever the shortcomings of the feminist movement, it is surely otiose to blame the victims for a situation not of their making. The failure to create the French female citizen rests squarely with the male political establishment and with a political culture which rejected sex equality on grounds of principle and expediency.

To be sure, from Condorcet through Victor Considérant and Victor Hugo and down to the likes of Raymond Poincaré, Ferdinand Buisson and René Viviani, the Republican tradition had produced men who championed the rights of women. In the years before 1914, the French socialist party, the SFIO, was the first political party to admit women members. Some of its leaders (notably Marcel Sembat and Ernest Tarbouriech) had close connections with the LFDF. Seventy-three out of seventy-six socialist deputies signed the Dussaussoy–Buisson suffrage bill. Moreover, a political tradition which was responsible for the reintroduction of divorce and a massive expansion in female education cannot be held to have been predisposed to the politics of misogyny.

On the other hand, as the case of the socialist party suggests, left-wing declarations of support for women's rights cannot always be taken at face value. In theory, socialists were the party most committed to women's suffrage: in practice, they did little to advance the cause. As Madeleine Pelletier discovered, they were less than welcoming to female militants.[35] Furthermore, as Charles Sowerwine has pointed out, the socialists were far more preoccupied with the question of proportional representation than with that of women's suffrage. In 1912, when PR seemed close to being realised, the socialists rejected feminist appeals to link this issue to that of the female franchise.[36] Socialist advocacy of votes for women was insincere and undertaken largely so as to give the party a progressive image.

Ultimately, however, the decisive factor which sealed the fate of feminism in France was the paramount importance which the republican movement attached to the issue of anticlericalism. For radical Republicans especially, anticlericalism was both the defining element of their political identity and the mainspring of their political action. In their eyes, the separation of Church and state in 1905 represented not only the culmination of the programme of 'laic laws' enacted since 1879 but the symbolic victory of the Republic over the enemies of the Revolution and modernity. To introduce the female franchise could only encourage the enemies of the Republic and imperil the safety of the regime. As Clemenceau put it in 1907: 'If the right to vote were given to women tomorrow, France would all of a sudden jump backwards into the Middle Ages'.[37]

Such rhetoric ought not to be taken literally. If such a thing as 'the clerical threat' ever existed, it had surely been dealt with by the Separation Law of 1905, the historic solution to the problem of Church–state relations which radical Republicans had long desired. To the riposte that such a threat did not disappear overnight, one need only point out that, from the Church's point of view, the years around the turn of the century represented the low water mark in French religious practice. At best some 30% of the French population as a whole could be counted as practising

Catholics, though there were huge regional variations.[38] Talk of a 'clerical threat' rings hollow in a situation in which churchmen struggled to stem the tide of dechristianisation. However much Republicans tried to blame 'clericalism' for their inability to act on the question of women's suffrage, the fact remains that after 1879 they were firmly in charge of their own creation, the Third Republic, and it was this anticlerical regime which resolutely set its face against the admission of women to full rights of citizenship.

Anticlericalism involved more than ideology and the politics of principle. It was also about the calculation of political interest and political advantage. For the French Radical party, attachment to the cause of anticlericalism testifies less to the reality of the clerical threat than to a desire to maintain the new post-1905 *status quo* in which Radicals emerged as the pivotal element in the Republic's coalition governments. In an immensely variegated, opportunist and undisciplined party (which even numbered a few spokesmen for women's rights though it excluded women from party membership until 1924), anticlericalism furnished the one banner to which all shades of Radical opinion could rally. It also served as an excuse to delay the implementation of political and social reforms which might jeopardise their place in the new political order. When the deputies and senators of the Radical party expressed concern about the consequences of enfranchising women, what they meant was that women could not be relied upon to vote the right way – that is, for themselves. One can be reasonably sure that, had they thought differently, they would not have hesitated to support the measure.

Despite the evidence presented here and in the course of this book, a number of French historians have shown themselves reluctant to identify the republican tradition in France as in any way hostile to women's rights, doubtless since this sits ill with the myth of the Republic as the mainspring of progress. Mona Ozouf, for instance, has reacted strongly to the idea that the French Revolution was responsible for the subordination of French women, dismissing it as a fiction fabricated by 'des historiennes américaines'. If feminine political power was regarded with suspicion by the revolutionaries, she maintains, this was understandable on account of its associations with both the Ancien Régime and the counter-revolution. At the same time, the revolutionaries had no desire to obliterate sexual difference completely, which would create a dreary civilisation without sexes. Desiring to unite rather than to exclude, and ardent believers in the union of man and woman, they devised the happy invention of the patriotic 'republican mother' as the perfect complement to the male individual citizen and patriot, thus giving women their own particular stake in the new democratic order.[39] The triumph of Republicanism under the Third Republic perpetuated the Jacobin legacy. Hence, even in the *belle époque*, women continued to be viewed by the new masters of France not as individuals but as wives and mothers. For this very reason, according to Pierre Rosanvallon, women could not be given full rights of citizenship: rights were abstract and could be exercised only by the autonomous individual, who by definition was male. French universalism precluded the utilitarian approach characteristic of 'Anglo-Saxon' countries where rights could be conferred on groups which represented particular interests.[40]

It may be, as Ozouf and Rosanvallon contend, that the universalist vision of the political and social order enshrined in the rhetoric of the revolutionary tradition furnishes evidence of the radicalism of French democracy rather than of its timidity, and thus provides an explanation for the sluggishness of the political response to women's rights which reinforces rather than undermines the myth of French progressivism. An alternative – and more plausible – interpretation would be that republican rhetoric skilfully played on the theme of difference versus equality to produce a distinctively Gallic rationale for sexism and women's subordination. Either way, the victory of the republican political tradition proved to be an immense stumbling block for French feminists since it defined democracy in such a way as to exclude women from formal citizenship and perpetuated France as an exception to the democratic norm in the years after the First World War.

Notes

1 Defining womanhood

1   E. and J. de Goncourt, *La femme au xviiie siècle: la société, l'amour et le mariage* (Paris, Flammarion, n.d.). For a wide-ranging survey of the social condition of women in eighteenth-century France, L. Abensour, *La femme et le féminisme avant la Révolution* (Paris, 1923; Geneva, Slatkine reprints, 1977).

2   C. Fairchilds, 'Women and the family', in S. Spencer (ed.) *French Women and the Age of Enlightenment* (Bloomington, Indiana University Press, 1984), p. 101.

3   E. and J. de Goncourt, *La femme au xviiie siècle*, p. 7.

4   For a summary of medieval and early modern ideas on women see M.E. Wiesner, *Women and Gender in Early Modern Europe* (Cambridge, Cambridge University Press, 1993), Chapter 1. Also useful are O. Hufton, *The Prospect Before Her: A History of Women in Western Europe*: Vol. 1 *1500–1800* (London, HarperCollins, 1995) and I. MacLean, *The Renaissance Notion of Woman: A Study in the Fortunes of Scholasticism and Medical Science in European Intellectual Life* (Cambridge, Cambridge University Press, 1980). For early feminists, see J. Kelly, 'Early feminist theory and the *Querelle des Femmes*, 1400–1789', in J. Kelly, *Women, History and Theory* (Chicago, Chicago University Press, 1984).

5   On women and the Scientific Revolution, see C. Merchant, *The Death of Nature: Women, Ecology and the Scientific Revolution* (New York, Harper and Row, 1980), and L. Schiebinger, *The Mind Has No Sex? Women in the Origins of Modern Science* (Cambridge, Massachusetts, Harvard University Press, 1989).

6   Bossuet, *XIe Elévation sur les mystères*, quoted in P. Hoffmann, *La femme dans la pensée des lumières* (Paris, Editions Orphys, 1977), p. 18.

7   François de Sales, *Prière de la femme enceinte*, quoted ibid.

8   G. de Piaggi, *La sposa perfetta: educazione e condizione della donna nella famiglia frances del Rinascimento e della Controriforma* (Abano Terme, 1979).

9   Père J. Desmothes, S.J., *Les devoirs des filles chrétiennes pour une vie chaste et vertueuse dans le monde* (Paris, 3rd edn, 1719).

10 J-J. Duguet, *Conduite d'une dame chrétienne pour vivre sainement dans le monde* (Paris, 1725), pp. 204–5.

11 For a good introduction, E. Fox-Genovese, 'Women and the Enlightenment', in R. Bridenthal, C. Koonz and S. Stuard (eds) *Becoming Visible: Women in European History* (Boston, Houghton Mifflin Company, 2nd edn, 1987), pp. 251–77. See also D. Outram, *The Enlightenment* (Cambridge, Cambridge University Press, 1995), Chapter 6, and J. Rendall, *The Origins of Modern Feminism: Women in Britain, France and the United States 1780–1860* (London, Macmillan, 1985), Chapter 1. For more specialised studies, Spencer (ed.) *French Women and the Age of Enlightenment*; E. Jacobs et al. (eds) *Women and Society in Eighteenth-Century France: Essays in*

Notes

Honour of John Stephenson Spink (London, Athlone Press, 1979); and S. Tomaselli, 'The Enlightenment debate on women', History Workshop, 20, 1985, pp. 101–25.

12 The literature on women, the Enlightenment and medicine is now considerable. In addition to Schiebinger, The Mind Has No Sex?, see L.J. Jordonova, 'Natural facts: a historical perspective on science and sexuality', in C. MacCormack and M. Strathern (eds) Nature, Culture and Gender (Cambridge, Cambridge University Press, 1980); Y. Knibiehler and C. Fouquet, La femme et les médecins: analyse historique (Paris, Hachette, 1983); G. Fraisse, Muse de la raison: la démocratie exclusive et la différence des sexes (Paris, Alinéa, 1989), Chapter 3; E.A. Williams, The Physical and the Moral: Anthropology, Physiology and Philosophical Medicine in France 1750–1850 (Cambridge, Cambridge University Press, 1994); and L. Wilson, Women and Medicine in the Age of the Enlightenment: The Debate over Maladie des Femmes (Baltimore and London, Johns Hopkins University Press, 1993). For a long-term perspective, T. Laqueur, Making Sex: Body and Gender from the Greeks to Freud (Cambridge, Massachusetts, Harvard University Press, 1990).

13 J-J. Virey, De l'éducation publique et privée des Français (Paris, 1802), cited by Fraisse, Muse de la raison, p. 102.

14 P-J-G. Cabanis, Rapports du physique et du moral de l'homme (Paris, 1802; Geneva, Slatkine reprints, 1980), p. 282.

15 D. Diderot, 'On women', in Dialogues (London, George Routledge and Sons, 1827; first published 1772), pp. 185–96, esp. pp. 190–1.

16 P. Roussel, Système physique et moral de la femme (Paris, 1775).

17 J-J. Virey, cited by Fraisse, Muse de la raison, p. 87.

18 Schiebinger, The Mind Has No Sex?, pp. 191–200.

19 Wilson, Women and Medicine in the Age of the Enlightenment.

20 Jaucourt, 'Femme (Droit Naturel)', in D. Diderot and J. d'Alembert (eds) L'Encyclopédie, ou Dictionnaire raisonné des sciences, des arts et des métiers, 17 vols (Paris, 1751–65), vol. 6. For further comment on the ideas of the philosophes concerning women, see A.R. Kleinbaum, 'Women in the Age of Light', in R. Bridenthal and C. Koonz (eds) Becoming Visible: Women in European History (Boston, Houghton Mifflin Company, 1977), pp. 217–35, and D. Julia, Les trois couleurs du tableau noir – la Révolution (Paris, Belin, 1981), pp. 310–85.

21 E.M. Benabou, La prostitution et la police des moeurs au xviiie siècle (Paris, Perrin, 1987), p. 394; and E.J. Gardiner, 'The philosophes and women: sensationalism and sentiment', in Jacobs et al. (eds) Women and Society in Eighteenth-Century France, p. 19.

22 Demahis, 'Femme (Moralité)', L'Encyclopédie, vol. 6.

23 Barthez, 'Femme (Anthropologie)', ibid.

24 S.E.P. Malueg, 'Women and the Encyclopédie', in Jacobs et al. (eds) Women and Society in Eighteenth-Century France, p. 19.

25 Hoffmann, La femme dans la pensée des lumières.

26 A. Thomas, An Account of the Character, the Manners, and the Understanding of Women, in Different Ages, and Different Parts of the World (London, J. Dodsley, 1800).

27 Diderot, 'On Women'.

28 D. Diderot, 'Supplément au voyage de Bougainville', in Ouvres complètes, 20 vols (Paris, 1875–77), vol. 2. See also R. Niklaus, 'Diderot and women' and E. Jacobs, 'Diderot and the education of girls', both in Jacobs et al. (eds) Women and Society in Eighteenth-Century France.

29 For a biography, see P.N. Furbank, Diderot: A Critical Biography (New York, Alfred A. Knopf, 1992). Also, Niklaus, 'Diderot and women', and Jacobs, 'Diderot and the education of girls'.

30 J. Kelly-Gadol, 'Did women have a Renaissance?', in Bridenthal and Koonz (eds) Becoming Visible, pp. 137–64.

31 E.G. Bodek, 'Salonnières and Bluestockings: educational obsolescence and germinating feminism', Feminist Studies, 3, nos 3/4 Spring/Summer 1976, pp. 185–99, and especially the articles of D. Goodman, 'Enlightenment salons: the convergence of female and philosophic ambitions', Eighteenth-Century Studies, 22, 1989, pp. 329–50, and 'Public sphere and private life: towards a synthesis of current historiographical approaches to the Old Regime', History and Theory, 31, 1992, pp. 1–20. See also D. Goodman, The Republic of Letters. A Cultural History of the French Enlightenment (Ithaca, Cornell University Press, 1994).

Notes

32 On the seventeenth century, see C. Lougee, *Le Paradis des Femmes: Women, Salons and Social Stratification in Seventeenth-Century France* (Princeton, Princeton University Press, 1977).

33 In addition to the work of Goodman, see for instance B. Craveri, *Madame du Deffand and Her World* (London, Peter Halban, 1994).

34 N-E. Rétif (or Restif) de la Bretonne, *Les Gynographes, ou Idées de deux honnêtes femmes sur un projet de règlement proposé à toute l'Europe pour mettre les femmes à leur place et opérer le bonheur des deux sexes* (The Hague, 1777; Geneva, Slatkine reprints, 1988).

35 The literature on Rousseau is enormous. Among the most relevant studies are J. Schwartz, *The Sexual Politics of Jean-Jacques Rousseau* (Chicago, Chicago University Press, 1984); C. Piau-Gillot, 'Le discours de Jean-Jacques Rousseau sur les femmes et sa réception critique', *XVIIIe Siècle*, 1981, pp. 317–33; and V.G. Wexler, 'Made for man's delight: Rousseau as antifeminist', *American Historical Review*, 81, 1976, pp. 266–91.

36 J-J. Rousseau, *A Letter of M. Rousseau of Geneva, to M. d'Alembert of Paris, Concerning the Effects of Theatrical Entertainments on the Manners of Mankind* (London, 1759).

37 J-J. Rousseau, *Emile* (London, Dent, 1911).

38 R. Darnton, *The Literary Underground of the Old Regime* (Cambridge, Massachusetts, Harvard University Press, 1982), and 'The High Enlightenment and the low life of literature in pre-Revolutionary France', *Past and Present*, 51, 1971, pp. 81–115.

39 L. Hunt, 'The many bodies of Marie Antoinette: political pornography and the problem of the feminine in the French Revolution', in L. Hunt (ed.) *Eroticism and the Body Politic* (Baltimore, Johns Hopkins University Press, 1990), pp. 108–31; L. Hunt, *The Family Romance of the French Revolution* (Berkeley, Los Angeles and London, University of California Press, 1992), esp. Chapters 4 and 5; and C. Thomas, *La reine scélérate: Marie-Antoinette dans les pamphlets* (Paris, Le Seuil, 1989).

40 M-A. Gacon-Dufour, *Mémoire pour le sexe féminin contre le sexe masculin* (Paris and London, 1787).

41 N.R. Gelbart, *Feminism and Opposition Journalism in Old Regime France: Le Journal des Dames* (Berkeley, University of California Press, 1987).

42 Cf. M. Legates, 'The cult of womanhood in eighteenth-century thought', *Eighteenth-Century Studies*, 10, no. 1 Fall 1976, pp. 21–39.

43 Comtesse de Genlis, *Adelaide and Theodore: Or Letters on Education*, 3 vols (London, 1783).

44 N.R. Gelbart, 'The *Journal des Dames* and its female editors: politics, censorship and feminism in the Old Regime press', in J. Censer and J.D. Popkin (eds) *Press and Politics in Pre-Revolutionary France* (Berkeley, Los Angeles and London, University of California Press, 1987).

45 Jordonova, 'Natural facts', pp. 58–59; P.O. Jimack, 'The paradox of Sophie and Julie: contemporary responses to Rousseau's ideal wife and ideal mother', in Jacobs *et al. Women and Society in Eighteenth-Century France*; and B.C. Pope, 'The influence of Rousseau's ideology of domesticity', in M.J. Boxer and J.H. Quataert (eds) *Connecting Spheres: Women in the Western World, 1500 to the Present* (Oxford, Oxford University Press, 1987), pp. 136–45.

46 For Condorcet, K.M. Baker, *Condorcet, from Natural Philosophy to Social Mathematics* (Chicago, University of Chicago Press, 1975); and B. Brookes, 'The feminism of Condorcet and Sophie de Grouchy', *Studies on Voltaire and the Eighteenth Century*, 189, 1980, pp. 297–361.

47 M.J.A.N. Marquis de Condorcet, *Lettres d'un bourgeois de New Haven à un citoyen de Virginie* (1787), in A.C. O'Connor and M.F. Arago (eds) *Oeuvres de Condorcet*, 12 vols (Paris, 1847), vol. 9, pp. 1–123.

48 Ibid., *Essai sur la constitution et les fonctions des assemblées provinciales* (1788), ibid., vol. 8.

49 M. Gutwirth, *The Twilight of the Goddesses: Women and Representation in the French Revolutionary Era* (New Brunswick, Rutgers University Press, 1992).

50 J. Landes, *Women in the Public Sphere in the Age of the French Revolution* (Ithaca, Cornell University Press, 1988).

2 The rights of man and the rights of woman

1   For the transformation in political culture, see the essays in K.M. Baker (ed.) *The French Revolution and the Creation of Modern Political Culture*: Vol. 1 *The Political Culture of the Old Regime* (Oxford, Pergamon Press, 1987); C. Lucas (ed.) *The French Revolution and the Creation of Modern Political Culture*: Vol. 2 *The Political Culture of the French Revolution* (Oxford, Pergamon Press, 1988); F. Furet and M. Ozouf (eds) *The French Revolution and the Creation of Modern Political Culture*: Vol. 3 *The Transformation of Political Culture, 1789–1848* (Oxford, Pergamon Press, 1990); and K.M. Baker (ed.) *The French Revolution and the Creation of Modern Political Culture*: Vol. 4 *The Terror* (Oxford, Pergamon Press, 1994).

2   Condorcet, *Essai sur l'admission des femmes au droit de la cité* (1790), in O'Connor and Arago (eds) *Oeuvres de Condorcet*, vol. 10, pp. 119–30. Translated as 'Condorcet's plea for the citizenship of women', in J. Morley, *Critical Miscellanies* (London, 1871), pp. 367–72.

3   'Petition of the women of the Third Estate to the King', in D.G. Levy, H.B. Applewhite and M.D. Johnson (eds) *Women in Revolutionary Paris 1789–1795. Selected Documents Translated with Notes and Commentary* (Urbana, Chicago and London, University of Illinois Press, 1979), pp. 18–21. For another useful documentary collection, see *Cahiers des doléances et autres textes* (Paris, Editions des femmes, 1981).

4   Mme B.B., *Cahier des doléances et réclamations des femmes*, quoted by P-M. Duhet, *Les femmes et la Révolution* (Paris, Gallimard/Julliard, 1971), pp. 35–39.

5   Ibid., p. 41.

6   For de Gouges, O. Blanc, *Olympe de Gouges* (Paris, Syros, 1981); on Marie-Antoinette, E. Colwill, 'Just another *citoyenne*? Marie-Antoinette on trial', *History Workshop Journal*, 28, 1989, pp. 63–87.

7   For the text of the Declaration, see Levy, Applewhite and Johnson (eds) *Women in Revolutionary Paris*, pp. 87–96.

8   J.W. Scott, *Only Paradoxes to Offer: French Feminists and the Rights of Man* (Cambridge, Massachusetts, Harvard University Press, 1996), Chapter 2.

9   J. Abray, 'Feminism in the French Revolution', *American Historical Review*, 80, 1975, pp. 43–62; A. Dessens, *Les revendications des droits de la femme au point de vue politique, civil, économique pendant la Révolution* (Law thesis, Toulouse, 1905); and A. Soprani, *La Révolution et les femmes de 1789 à 1796* (Paris, MA Editions, 1988).

10 O. Ernst, *Théroigne de Méricourt, D'après des documents inédits tirés des archives secrètes de la Maison d'Autriche* (Paris, Payot, 1935); and E. Roudinesco, *Théroigne de Méricourt: A Melancholic Woman during the French Revolution* (New York, Verso, 1991).

11 P. Léon, *Adresse individuelle à l'Assemblée nationale par des citoyennes de la Capitale, le 6 mars 1791* (Paris, n.d.). English translation in Levy, Applewhite and Johnson (eds) *Women in Revolutionary Paris*, pp. 72–74.

12 Ibid., p. 73.

13 On traditional protest, O. Hufton, *Women and the Limits of Citizenship in the French Revolution* (Toronto, Buffalo and London, University of Toronto Press, 1992), Chapters 2 and 3.

14 S. Desan, 'Crowds, community and ritual in the work of E.P. Thompson and Natalie Davis', in L. Hunt (ed.) *The New Cultural History* (Berkeley, Los Angeles and London, University of California Press, 1989), pp. 47–71, and *Reclaiming the Sacred: Lay Religion and Popular Politics in Revolutionary France* (Ithaca, Cornell University Press, 1991), Chapter 5.

15 D.G. Levy and H.B. Applewhite, 'Women and political revolution in Paris', in R. Bridenthal, C. Koonz and S. Stuard (eds) *Becoming Visible* (Boston, Houghton Mifflin Company, 2nd edn, 1987), pp. 279–306.

16 This account is based on S. Schama, *Citizens: A Chronicle of the French Revolution* (London, Penguin Books, 1989), p. 456ff.

17 On these petitions, Duhet, *Les femmes et la Révolution*, pp. 54–56.

18 On the club movement, M. de Villiers, *Histoire des clubs des femmes et des légions d'Amazones (1793–1848–1871)* (Paris, 1910), Chapter 2; I. Bourdin, *Les sociétés populaires à Paris pendant la Révolution* (Paris, 1937); H. Giroux, 'Les femmes clubistes à Dijon (1791–1793)', *Annales*

Notes

de Bourgogne, 57, 1985, pp. 23–45; and S. Desan, ' "Constitutional amazons": Jacobin women's clubs in the French Revolution', in B.T. Ragan, Jr and E.A. Williams (eds) *Re-creating Authority in Revolutionary France* (New Jersey, Rutgers University Press, 1992), pp. 11–35.

19 On sans-culotte women, the essential work is now D. Godineau, *Citoyennes tricoteuses: les femmes du peuple à Paris pendant la Révolution française* (Aix-en-Provence, Editions Alinéa, 1988). For a shorter, English-language distillation, D. Godineau, 'Masculine and feminine political practice during the French Revolution, 1793 – Year III', in H.B. Applewhite and D.G. Levy (eds) *Women and Politics in the Age of the Democratic Revolution* (Ann Arbor, Michigan University Press, 1993), pp. 61–80. See also D.G. Levy and H.B. Applewhite, 'Women, radicalization and the fall of the French monarchy', ibid., pp. 81–107, and the documents printed in *Women in Revolutionary Paris*, Part 4.

20 On the Society of Revolutionary Republican Women, in addition to Godineau, see M. Cerati, *Le club des citoyennes révolutionnaires* (Paris, Editions sociales, 1966); S.H. Lyttle, 'The second sex (September 1793)', *Journal of Modern History*, 27, 1955, pp. 14–26; R.B. Rose, *The Enragés: Socialists of the Revolution?* (Melbourne, Melbourne University Press, 1965); and R.C. Cobb, *A Second Identity* (Oxford, Oxford University Press, 1989), pp. 168–76. See also the documents in *Women in Revolutionary Paris*, Part 4.

21 Roudinesco, *Théroigne de Méricourt*.

22 Godineau, *Citoyennes tricoteuses*, pp. 337–40.

23 For more on the fashion aspect, see L. Hunt, 'The unstable boundaries of the French Revolution', in P. Ariès and G. Duby (eds) *A History of Private Life*: Vol. 4 *From the Fires of Revolution to the Great War*, ed. M. Perrot (Cambridge, Massachusetts and London, The Belknap Press of Harvard University Press, 1990; original French edn, 1987), pp. 16–21.

24 D Godineau, 'Formation d'un mythe contre-révolutionnaire, les "tricoteuses" ', in *L'Image de la Révolution française. Communications présentées lors du Congrès Mondial pour le Bicentenaire de la Révolution française (Sorbonne, Paris, 6–12 juillet, 1989)*, 4 vols (Paris, 1989), vol. 3, pp. 2278–85.

25 Hufton, *Women and the Limits of Citizenship*, pp. 92–142; O. Hufton, 'The reconstruction of a church 1796–1801', in G. Lewis and C. Lucas (eds) *Beyond the Terror. Essays in French Regional and Social History, 1794–1815* (Cambridge, Cambridge University Press, 1983), pp. 21–52; and Desan, *Reclaiming the Sacred*.

26 S. Desan, 'The role of women in religious riots during the French Revolution', *Eighteenth-Century Studies*, 22, 1989, pp. 451–68.

27 T. Tackett, 'Women and men in counter-revolution: the Sommières riot, 1791', *Journal of Modern History*, 59, December 1987, pp. 680–704.

28 R.C. Cobb, *The People's Armies* (New Haven and London, Yale University Press, 1987).

29 Desan, *Reclaiming the Sacred*, pp. 209–10.

30 Hufton, 'The reconstruction of a church'.

31 F. Giroud (ed.) *Les femmes de la Révolution de Michelet* (Paris, Editions Carrere, 1988), p. 157.

32 Talleyrand, *Rapport sur l'instruction publique fait au nom du Comité de Constitution les 10, 11 et 19 septembre 1791* (Paris, 1791), pp. 116–17, quoted in Julia, *Les trois couleurs du tableau noir*, p. 311.

33 Mirabeau, *Travail sur l'éducation publique trouvé dans les papiers de Mirabeau l'aîné, publié par P.J.G. Cabanis* (Paris, 1791), pp. 36–38, quoted ibid., p. 312.

34 C-L. Masuyer, *Discours sur l'organisation de l'instruction publique et de l'éducation nationale en France. Examen et réfutation du système proposé par les citoyens Condorcet et G. Romme* (Paris, 1793), quoted ibid., p. 313.

35 L-M. Prudhomme, in *Révolutions de Paris*, 19–26 Jan. 1793, quoted in Desan, ' "Constitutional amazons" ', p. 31.

36 Ibid., p. 68.

37 Colwill, 'Just another *citoyenne?*'.

38 The quotation is from D. Outram, *The Body and the French Revolution* (New Haven and London, Yale University Press, 1989), p. 126. See also D. Outram, '*Le langage mâle de la vertu*: women and the discourse of the French Revolution', in P. Burke and R. Porter (eds) *The Social History*

of Language (Cambridge, Cambridge University Press, 1987), pp. 120–35; L. Hunt, *The Family Romance of the French Revolution* (Berkeley and Los Angeles, University of California Press, 1992), p. 158ff.; and C. Blum, *Rousseau and the Republic of Virtue: The Language of Politics in the French Revolution* (Ithaca, Cornell University Press, 1986).

39 L-M. Prudhomme, in *Révolutions de Paris*, 12 Feb. 1791, cited by E. Badinter, *Paroles d'hommes* (Paris, POL, 1989), pp. 72–73.

40 The interpretation offered here differs significantly from that advanced by M. Ozouf, *Les mots des femmes: essai sur la singularité française* (Paris, Fayard, 1995) and is in line with that of Desan, ' "Constitutional amazons" '.

41 Hufton, *Women and the Limits of Citizenship*, pp. 37–38.

42 The text of Amar's speech can be found in translation in *Women in Revolutionary Paris*, pp. 212–17.

43 Chaumette's speech is cited ibid., pp. 219–20.

3 Revolutionary aftermath

1 *A History of Private Life*, vol. 4, pp. 13–16.

2 L. Hunt, *Politics, Culture and Class in the French Revolution* (Berkeley and Los Angeles, University of California Press, 1984).

3 See relevant texts in Levy, Applewhite and Johnson (eds) *Women in Revolutionary Paris*, pp. 197–208.

4 This and the following paragraph are based on J.F. Traer, *Marriage and the Family in Eighteenth-Century France* (Ithaca and London, Cornell University Press, 1980), esp. Chapters 5 and 6. See also B. Schnapper, 'Liberté, égalité, autorité: la famille devant les assemblées révolutionnaires (1790–1800)', in M-F. Lévy (ed.) *L'Enfant, la famille et la Révolution française* (Paris, Olivier Orban, 1990), pp. 325–40.

5 On the divorce law, see Traer, *Marriage and the Family*, Chapter 4, and R. Phillips, *Putting Asunder: A History of Divorce in Western Society* (Cambridge, Cambridge University Press, 1988), pp. 175–85. For regional studies, R. Phillips, *Family Breakdown in Late Eighteenth-Century France: Divorces in Rouen, 1792–1803* (Oxford, Oxford University Press, 1980), and D. Dessertine, *Divorcer à Lyon sous la Révolution et l'Empire* (Lyon, Presses Universitaires de Lyon, 1981).

6 Traer, *Marriage and the Family*, p. 132.

7 Phillips, *Putting Asunder*, p. 184.

8 On Josephine and the circle of the 'Merveilleuses', see E. Bruce, *Napoleon and Josephine: An Improbable Marriage* (London, Weidenfeld and Nicolson, 1995), esp. Chapters 5 and 7.

9 Ibid., p. 155.

10 On de Stael, H. Guillemin, *Madame de Stael, Benjamin Constant et Napoléon* (Paris, Plon, 1959).

11 Bruce, *Napoleon and Josephine*, p. 162.

12 Traer, *Marriage and the Family*, Chapter 6. For further comment on the Code, M. Ostrogorski, *The Rights of Women* (London, 1893) and M. Ancel (ed.) *La condition de la femme mariée dans la société contemporaine* (Paris, 1938).

13 Phillips, *Putting Asunder*, p. 275.

14 Quoted by N. Arnaud-Duc, 'The law's contradictions', in G. Duby and M. Perrot (eds) *A History of Women in the West*: Vol. 4 *Emerging Feminism from the Revolution to the Great War*, eds G. Fraisse and M. Perrot (Cambridge, Massachusetts and London, The Belknap Press of Harvard University Press, 1995; original Italian edn, 1995), p. 98.

15 Ibid., p. 100.

16 H.D. Lewis, 'The legal status of women in nineteenth-century France', *Journal of European Studies*, 10, 1980, pp. 178–88; J. Monnet, *Le contrat de mariage et son utilité* (Paris, 1924); and P. Moissinac, *Le contrat de mariage de séparation de biens* (Paris, 2nd edn, 1924).

17 Lewis, 'The legal status of women', and A. Eyquem, *Le régime dotal: son histoire, son évolution et ses transformations au dix-neuvième siècle sous l'influence de la jurisprudence et du notariat* (Paris, 1903).

Notes

P. Granotier, *L'Autorité du mari sur la personne de la femme et la doctrine féministe* (Law thesis, Grenoble, 1909).
19 A. Damez, *Le libre salaire de la femme mariée et le mouvement féministe* (Law thesis, Paris, 1905).
20 R. Dereux, *Le budget matrimonial* (Law thesis, Lille, 1923), pp. 68–69.
21 Moissinac, *Le contrat de mariage*, p. 1ff.
22 Granotier, *L'Autorité du mari*, p. 169ff.
23 H. de Balzac, *The Physiology of Marriage* (London, 1904), pp. 48–49.
24 L. Fiaux, *La femme, le mariage et le divorce. Etude de psychologie et de sociologie* (Paris, 1880), p. 306.
25 K. Thomas, 'The double standard', *Journal of the History of Ideas*, 20, 1959, pp. 195–216.
26 Mme Romieu, *La femme au dix-neuvième siècle* (Paris, 1859), p. 13.
27 For a summary of the evolution of French political culture, J.F. McMillan, 'France', in R. Eatwell (ed.) *European Political Cultures: Conflict or Convergence?* (London, Routledge, 1997).
28 On Charlotte Robespierre, see M. Yalom, *Blood Sisters: The French Revolution in Women's Memory* (New York, Basic Books, 1993). On the transmission of the feminine revolutionary tradition, D. Barry, *Women and Political Insurgency: France in the Mid-Nineteenth Century* (Basingstoke, Macmillan, 1996), p. 13.
29 K. Offen, 'Retrospective of the French Revolution. Women's memory and women's action: the first centennial, 1889', in M-F. Brive (ed.) *Les femmes et la Révolution française*: Vol. 3 *L'Effet 89* (Toulouse, Presses Universitaires du Mirail, 1991), pp. 221–34.
30 Yalom, *Blood Sisters*.
31 Vicomtesse de Fars Fausslaundry, quoted in Yalom, *Blood Sisters*.
32 Marquise de la Rochejaquelein, *Mémoires de la Marquise de la Rochejaquelein, 1772–1857* (Paris, Mercure de France, 1984).
33 For a typical formulation, J. Simon, *La femme au vingtième siècle* (Paris, 1892), p. 67.
34 *Le Ménagier de Paris*, ed. and transl. E. Power as *The Goodman of Paris*, c.1393 (London, 1928).
35 P. Le Moyne, *La galerie des femmes fortes* (Paris, 1647), cited by Lougee, *Le Paradis des Femmes*, p. 63.
36 The critical importance of the Revolutionary experience is emphasised, for example, by Desan, ' "Constitutional amazons" ', pp. 11–35, and M. Gutwirth, '*Citoyens, citoyennes*: cultural regression and the subversion of female citizenship in the French Revolution', in R. Waldinger, P. Dawson and I. Woloch (eds) *The French Revolution and the Meaning of Citizenship* (Westport, Connecticut and London, Greenwood Press, 1993), pp. 17–28.
37 J-M. de Maistre, *Les soirées de Saint-Petersbourg: ou entretiens sur le gouvernement temporel de la providence* (Paris, 1821).
38 Vicomte de Bonald, *Du divorce considéré au dix-neuvième siècle relativement à l'Etat public de société* (Paris, 1818), esp. pp. 65–66.
39 This is contested by Ozouf, *Les mots des femmes*.
40 For an introduction to 'Republican motherhood', see D. Godineau, 'Daughters of liberty and revolutionary citizens', in *A History of Women in the West*, vol. 4, pp. 29–32.
41 M. Darrow, 'French noblewomen and the new domesticity, 1750–1850', *Feminist Studies*, 5, no. 1 Spring 1979, pp. 41–65.
42 Marquise de La Tour du Pin, *Memoirs of Madame de la Tour du Pin*, ed. F. Harcourt (London, Harvill Press, 1969).
43 Cited by Darrow, 'French noblewomen'.

4 'Angels of the hearth'?

1 For an excellent overview, see P. McPhee, *A Social History of France 1780–1880* (London, Routledge, 1992). For an interesting case study see D. Garrioch, *The Formation of the Parisian Bourgeoisie 1690–1830* (Cambridge, Massachusetts, Harvard University Press, 1996).
2 E. Goblot, *La barrière et le niveau* (Paris, 1925).
3 On high society, see A. Martin-Fugier, *La vie élégante: ou la formation du Tout-Paris* (Paris, Fayard,

Notes

1990), and A. Daumard, *La vie de salon en France dans la première moitié du xixe siècle*, in *Sociabilité et société bourgeoise en France, en Allemagne et en Suisse (1750–1850)* (Paris, Editions Recherches sur les Civilisations, 1986), pp. 81–94.

4 E-F. Bayle-Mouillard (Mme Celnart), *Manuel de la bonne compagnie, ou guide de la politesse et de la bienséance* (Paris, 1834). Extract cited and translated in E.O. Hellerstein, L.P. Hume and K.M. Offen (eds) *Victorian Women: A Documentary Account of Women's Lives in Nineteenth-Century England, France and the United States* (Brighton, The Harvester Press, 1981), pp. 96–97.

5 Cf. Perrot (ed.) *A History of Private Life*, vol. 4.

6 Ibid., pp. 126–28.

7 H. Le Bras and E. Todd, *L'Invention de la France* (Paris, Pluriel, 1981). Cf. M. Darrow, *Revolution in the House* (Princeton, Princeton University Press, 1989).

8 On arranged marriages, see for instance the comment of the comtesse d'Agoult that marriage for the French is 'an arrangement, a calculation' in *Mémoires, souvenirs et journaux de la comtesse d'Agoult (Daniel Stern)*. Présentation et notes de C.F. Dupèchez, 2 vols (Paris, Mercure de France, 1990; original edn, 1877), vol. 1, p. 172.

9 The phrase is that of E. Shorter in *The Making of the Modern Family* (London, Fontana, 1977).

10 R. Pillorget, *La tige et le rameau. Familles anglaises et françaises 16–18e siècle* (Paris, Calmann-Lévy, 1979).

11 Cf. C. de Ribbe, *La vie domestique, ses modèles et ses règles d'après des documents originaux* (Paris, 1877), p. 165ff. See also R. Deniel, *Une image de la famille et de la société sous la Restauration (1815–1830), étude de la presse catholique* (Paris, Les Editions Ouvrières, 1965).

12 The relevant extract of d'Agoult's memoirs is cited in translation in Hellerstein, Hume and Offen (eds) *Victorian Women*, p. 63.

13 B. Smith, *Ladies of the Leisure Class: The Bourgeoises of Northern France in the Nineteenth Century* (Princeton, Princeton University Press, 1981), p. 57.

14 Romieu, *La femme au dix-neuvième siècle*, p. 21.

15 Well into the twentieth century marriage was viewed as the most important financial decision of the bourgeois man's life. Cf. P. Bureau, *L'Indiscipline des moeurs* (Paris, 1927), and T. Zeldin, *France 1848–1945*, 2 vols (Oxford, Clarendon Press, 1973–77), vol. 1, p. 288ff.

16 For examples, A. Tolédano, *La vie de famille sous la Restauration et la Monarchie de juillet* (Paris, 1943), pp. 94–95.

17 Perrot (ed.) *A History of Private Life*, vol. 4, p. 140.

18 Cited by Maria Martin in *La Fronde*, 23 February 1898.

19 B.C. Pope, 'Maternal education in France, 1815–1848', *Proceedings of the Western Society for French History*, 3, 1976, pp. 368–77.

20 Cited by H. Mills, 'Negotiating the divide: women, philanthropy and the "public sphere" in nineteenth-century France', in F. Tallett and N. Atkin (eds) *Religion, Society and Politics in France since 1789* (London and Rio Grande, The Hambledon Press, 1991), pp. 29–54, quotation at p. 40.

21 L. Aimé-Martin, *De l'éducation des mères de famille, ou de la civilisation du genre humain par les femmes* (Paris, 1834).

22 E. Legouvé, *Histoire morale des femmes* (Paris, 1st edn, 1848; Paris, 7th edn, 1882), pp. 358–59. On Legouvé, see K. Offen, 'Ernest Legouvé and the doctrine of "equality in difference" for women: a case study of male feminism in nineteenth-century French thought', *Journal of Modern History*, 58, 1986, pp. 452–84.

23 On Necker de Saussure, see C.C. Orr, 'A republican answers back: Jean-Jacques Rousseau, Albertine Necker de Saussure and forcing little girls to be free', in C.C. Orr (ed.) *Wollstonecraft's Daughters: Womanhood in England and France 1780–1920* (Manchester and New York, Manchester University Press, 1996), pp. 61–78, quotation at p. 70.

24 A. Necker de Saussure, *The Study of the Life of Woman* (Philadelphia, 1844; Paris, original French edn, 1838).

25 Mme de Rémusat, *Essai sur l'éducation des femmes* (Paris, 1824).

26 P. Guizot, *Lettres de famille sur l'éducation* (Paris, 1824).

27 C. Duprat, 'Le silence des femmes: associations féminines du premier xixe siècle', in A. Corbin,

Notes

J. Lalouette and M. Riot-Sarcey (eds) *Femmes dans la cité 1815–1871* (Paris, Créaphis, n.d.), pp. 79–100.

28 For example, E. Lejeune-Resnick, *Femmes et associations (1830–1880): vraies démocrates ou dames patronnesses?* (Paris, Publisud, 1991).

29 J-P. Chaline, 'Sociabilité féminine et "maternalisme": les sociétés de charité maternelle au xixe siècle', in *Femmes dans la cité*, pp. 69–78.

30 Lejeune-Resnick, *Femmes et associations*, p. 155ff.

31 Ibid., p. 127ff.

32 H. Mills, '*Saintes soeurs* and *femmes fortes*: alternative accounts of the route to womanly civic virtue, and the history of French feminism', in Orr (ed.) *Wollstonecraft's Daughters*, pp. 135–50.

33 The point is developed by J.F. McMillan, 'Religion and gender in modern France: some reflections', in Tallett and Atkin (eds) *Religion, Society and Politics*, pp. 55–66.

34 Cf. R. Gibson, *A Social History of French Catholicism 1789–1914* (London, Routledge, 1989), p. 180ff.

35 G. Cholvy and Y-M. Hilaire, *Histoire religieuse de la France contemporaine*: Vol. 1 *1800–1880* (Toulouse, Privat, 1985), esp. Chapter 5.

36 P. Boutry, *Prêtres et paroisses au pays du curé d'Ars* (Paris, Editions du Cerf, 1986).

37 Cf. Gibson, *A Social History of French Catholicism*, Chapter 8.

38 C. Langlois, *Le Catholicisme au féminin. Les congrégations à supérieure générale au xixe siècle* (Paris, Editions du Cerf, 1984).

39 C. Langlois and P. Wagret, *Structures religieuses et célibat féminin au xixe siècle* (Lyon, 1972).

40 Mills, 'Negotiating the divide'.

41 Zeldin, *France 1848–1945*, vol. 2, p. 867.

42 Ibid., p. 993.

43 D. Barry, 'Hermance Lesguillon: the diversity of French feminism in the nineteenth century', *French History* (in press). I am grateful to Dr Barry for allowing me to see an unpublished version of this article.

44 Jean Baubérot, 'The Protestant woman', in *A History of Women in the West*, vol. 4, pp. 198–212.

45 On Niboyet, see M. Riot-Sarcey, *La démocratie à l'épreuve des femmes. Trois figures critiques du pouvoir 1830–1848* (Paris, Albin Michel, 1994).

46 Martin-Fugier, *La vie élégante*.

47 N. Dauphin, 'Les salons de la Restauration. Une influence spécifique sur les milieux dirigeants', in *Femmes dans la cité*, pp. 251–60.

48 C-I. Brelot, 'De la tutelle à la collaboration: une femme de la noblesse dans la vie politique (1814–1830)', ibid., pp. 237–50.

49 S. Aprile, 'Bourgeoise et républicaine, deux termes inconciliables', ibid., pp. 211–24.

50 Mme Louise d'Alq, cited by Zeldin, *France 1848–1945*, vol. 2, pp. 669–71.

51 Romieu, *La femme au dix-neuvième siècle*, pp. 28–29.

52 Perrot (ed.) *A History of Private Life*, vol. 4, p. 253. See also A. Farge and C. Klapisch-Zuber (eds) *Madame ou mademoiselle? Itinéraires de la solitude féminine xviie–xx siècle* (Paris, Editions Montalba, 1984).

53 M. Sonnet, *L'Education des filles au temps des lumières* (Paris, Editions du Cerf, 1987); and F. Mayeur, *L'Education des filles au dix-neuvième siècle* (Paris, Hachette, 1979).

54 Julia, *Les trois couleurs du tableau noir*.

55 E. Charrier, *L'Evolution intellectuelle féminine* (Paris, 1931).

56 A. Prost, *Histoire de l'enseignement en France, 1800–1967* (Paris, Colin, 1968), and R.D. Anderson, *Education in France, 1848–1870* (Oxford, Oxford University Press, 1975), p. 158.

57 L.L. Clark, *Schooling the Daughters of Marianne: Textbooks and the Socializing of Girls in Modern France 1848–1870* (Albany, State University of New York Press, 1984).

58 Ibid., p. 9, quoting Lucille Sauvan, *Cours national des institutrices primaires, ou Directions relatives à l'éducation physique, morale et intellectuelle, dans les écoles primaires* (Paris, 2nd edn, 1840), p. 26.

59 Smith, *Ladies of the Leisure Class*.

60 Barry, 'Hermance Lesguillon'.

Notes

61 Cf. her novel *Lui* (1859) and her *Poème de la femme*.
62 C. Planté, *La petite soeur de Balzac* (Paris, Editions du Seuil, 1989).
63 Barry, 'Hermance Lesguillon'.
64 Lejeune-Resnick, *Femmes et associations*, p. 127ff.
65 E. Sullerot, *Histoire de la presse féminine en France des origines à 1848* (Paris, Colin, 1966).
66 L. Adler, *A l'aube du féminisme. Les premières journalistes (1830–1850)* (Paris, Payot, 1979).
67 Ibid., p. 103ff.
68 On these female singers see J. Warrack and F. West (eds) *The Oxford Dictionary of Opera* (Oxford, Oxford University Press, 1992).
69 See her memoirs, *Souvenirs de ma vie* (Paris, 1835–37).
70 Her most famous picture, *The Horse Fair* (1853), is in the Metropolitan Museum of Art, New York.
71 A. Higonnet, *Berthe Morisot's Images of Women* (Cambridge, Massachusetts, Harvard University Press, 1992).

5 Labouring women

1 Quoted by J. Simon, *L'Ouvrière* (Paris, 1861 edn), p. iv.
2 J. Simon, *La femme au vingtième siècle* (Paris, 1892).
3 S.L. Kaplan and C.J. Koepp (eds) *Work in France. Representations, Meaning, Organization, and Practice* (Ithaca, Cornell University Press, 1986).
4 On the 'family economy', L. Tilly and J. Scott, *Women, Work and Family* (London, Holt, Reinhart and Winston, 1978). On 'proto-industrialisation', H. Medick, 'The proto-industrial family economy: the structural function of household and family during the transition from peasant society to industrial capitalism', *Social History*, 1, 1976, pp. 291–316. The view that industrialisation was inimical to family life was advanced by Frédéric Le Play and his disciples: see F. Le Play, *La réforme sociale en France, déduite de l'observation comparée des peuples européens*, 2 vols (Tours, 1878).
5 'Optimistic' contemporaries included A. Audiganne, *Les populations ouvrières et les industries de la France*, 2 vols (Paris, 1860), and L. Reybaud, *Rapport sur la condition morale, intellectuelle et matérielle des ouvriers qui vivent de l'industrie de coton* (Paris, 1863). Among historians who stress the continuities between 'pre-industrial' and industrial society, see Y. Lequin, *Les ouvriers de la région lyonnaise (1848–1914)*, 2 vols (Lyon, Presses Universitaires de Lyon, 1977), and L. Moch, *Paths to the City: Regional Migration in Nineteenth-Century France* (Beverly Hills, Sage Publications, 1983).
6 Cf. G. Gullickson, *Spinners and Weavers of Auffay: Rural Industry and the Sexual Division of Labour in a French Village* (Cambridge, Cambridge University Press, 1986). See also Tessie P. Liu, *The Weaver's Knot: The Contradictions of Class Struggle and Family Solidarity in Western France, 1750–1914* (Ithaca, Cornell University Press, 1994), Introduction. For British comparisons, see C.F. Sabel and J. Zeitlin, 'Historical alternatives to mass production: politics, markets and technology in nineteenth-century industrialisation', *Past and Present*, 108, August 1985, pp. 133–76, and M. Berg and P. Hudson, 'Rehabilitating the Industrial Revolution', *Economic History Review*, 45, 1992, pp. 24–50.
7 Tilly and Scott, *Women, Work and Family*.
8 M. Guilbert and V. Isambert-Jamati, *Travail féminin et travail à domicile* (Paris, CNRS, 1956).
9 O. Hufton, 'Women and the family economy in eighteenth-century France', *French Historical Studies*, 9, Spring 1975, pp. 1–22.
10 J.M. Merriman (ed.) *French Cities in the Nineteenth Century* (London, Hutchinson, 1982).
11 On the economy, C. Trebilcock, *The Industrialization of the Continental Powers 1780–1914* (London, Addison-Wesley/Longman, 1981); F. Caron, *An Economic History of Modern France* (London, Methuen, 1979); and A. Broder, *L'Economie française au xixe siècle* (Paris, Ophrys, 1993).

Notes

12 R. Magraw, *A History of the French Working Class*, 2 vols (Oxford, Blackwell, 1992): Vol. 1 *The Age of Artisan Revolution 1815–1871*, pp. 11–12.

13 W. Walton, 'Working women, gender and industrialization in nineteenth-century France: the case of Lorraine embroidery manufacturing', *Journal of Women's History*, 2, Fall 1990, pp. 42–65.

14 W.R. Reddy, 'Family and factory: French linen workers in the Belle Epoque', *Journal of Social History*, 8, Winter 1975, pp. 102–12.

15 A. Cottereau, 'The distinctiveness of working-class cultures in France, 1848–1900', in I. Katznelson and A.R. Zolberg (eds) *Working-Class Formation: Nineteenth-Century Patterns in Western Europe and the United States* (Princeton, Princeton University Press, 1986); and R. Aminzade, *Class, Politics and Early Industrial Capitalism: A Study of Mid-Nineteenth-Century Toulouse* (Albany, State University of New York Press, 1981).

16 E. Accampo, *Industrialization, Family Life and Class Relations: Saint-Chamond 1815–1914* (London, University of California Press, 1989).

17 The fundamental work on women in French rural society is M. Segalen, *Love and Power in the Peasant Family* (Oxford and Chicago, Basil Blackwell and the University of Chicago, 1983). See also T.P. Liu, '*Le patrimoine magique*: reassessing the power of women in rural households in nineteenth-century France', *Gender and History*, 6, 1994, pp. 13–36.

18 Liu, *The Weaver's Knot*.

19 Segalen, *Love and Power*, p. 139.

20 Cf. J. Coffin, *The Politics of Women's Work: The Paris Garment Trades 1750–1915* (Princeton, Princeton University Press, 1996), Chapter 1.

21 M. Sonenscher, *Work and Wages: Natural Law, Politics and Eighteenth-Century French Trades* (Cambridge, Cambridge University Press, 1989).

22 Hufton, 'Women and the family economy'.

23 On women's work in late nineteenth-century Paris, see Godineau, *Citoyennes tricoteuses*, p. 70ff.

24 K.A. Lynch, *Family, Class and Ideology in Early Industrial France: Social Policy and the Working-Class Family 1825–1848* (Madison, University of Wisconsin Press, 1988), p. 71.

25 J. Scott and L. Tilly, 'Women's work and the family in nineteenth-century Europe', *Comparative Studies in Society and History*, 17, 1975, pp. 36–64.

26 Accampo, *Industrialization, Family Life and Class Relations*.

27 Tilly and Scott, *Women, Work and Family*, pp. 84–85.

28 Lynch, *Family, Class and Ideology*, esp. Chapter 3.

29 L. Chevalier, *Labouring Classes and Dangerous Classes in Paris during the First Half of the Nineteenth Century* (London, Routledge and Kegan Paul, 1973).

30 E. Shorter, *The Making of the Modern Family* (London, Fontana, 1977); and J.M. Phayer, *Sexual Liberation and Religion in Nineteenth-Century Europe* (London, Croom Helm, 1977).

31 P. Branca, *Women in Europe since 1750* (London, Croom Helm, 1978), p. 90.

32 M. Frey, 'Du mariage et du concubinage dans les classes populaires à Paris (1846–1847)', *Annales ESC*, 33, 1978, pp. 803–29.

33 Lynch, *Family, Class and Ideology*, p. 91.

34 Cf. H. Leyret, *En plein faubourg (Moeurs ouvrières)* (Paris, 1895), p. 122ff.

35 W.M. Reddy, *The Rise of Market Culture: The Textile Trade and French Society, 1750–1900* (Cambridge, Cambridge University Press, 1984), p. 163ff.

36 L. Strumingher, *Women and the Making of the Working Class: Lyon 1830–1870* (St Albans, Vermont, Eden Press, 1979).

37 On the supposed incapacity of the lower orders for 'affective individualism', L. Stone, *The Family, Sex and Marriage in England 1500–1800* (London, Weidenfeld and Nicolson, 1977).

38 Cf. Leyret, *En plein faubourg*.

39 Reddy, *The Rise of Market Culture*, p. 163.

40 Strumingher, *Women and the Making of the Working Class*.

41 Accampo, *Industrialization, Family Life and Class Relations*.

Notes

42   M. Perrot, 'La femme populaire rebelle', in C. Dufrancatel *et al.* (eds) *L'Histoire sans qualités* (Paris, Editions Galilée, 1979), pp. 123–56.
43   D. Barry, *Women and Political Insurgency*, pp. 15–16, 31–32.
44   Ibid., pp. 69–70.
45   Ibid., Chapter 2.
46   M. Pointon, 'Liberty on the barricades: women, politics and sexuality in Delacroix', in S. Reynolds (ed.) *Women, State and Revolution: Essays on Power and Gender in Europe since 1789* (Brighton, Wheatsheaf Books, 1986), pp. 25–43.
47   These paragraphs on 1848 are heavily indebted to Barry, *Women and Political Insurgency*, Chapters 3 and 4.
48   P. McPhee, *The Politics of Rural Life: Political Mobilization in the French Countryside 1846–52* (Oxford, Oxford University Press, 1992), p. 188.
49   Barry, *Women and Political Insurgency*, Chapter 6.

6 *Femmes nouvelles*

1   M. Riot-Sarcey, *La démocratie à l'épreuve des femmes. Trois figures critiques du pouvoir, 1830–1848: Désirée Véret, Eugénie Niboyet, Jeanne Deroin* (Paris, Albin Michel, 1994).
2   O. Krakovitch, 'Les pétitions, seul moyen d'expression laissé aux femmes. L'exemple de la Restauration', in *Femmes dans la cité*, pp. 347–72.
3   C.G. Moses, *French Feminism in the Nineteenth Century* (Albany, State University of New York Press, 1984), p. 98ff. Also Sullerot, *Histoire de la presse féminine en France*.
4   H. de Saint-Simon, *Le nouveau christianisme et les écrits sur la religion. Textes choisis et présentés par H. Desroche* (Paris, Le Seuil, 1969).
5   S.K. Grogan, *French Socialism and Sexual Difference: Women and the New Society* (Basingstoke and London, Macmillan, 1992). Some older studies are still valuable. See esp. M. Thibert, *Le féminisme dans le socialisme français de 1830 à 1850* (Paris, M. Giard, 1926); C. Patureau-Mireaud, *De la femme et de son rôle dans la société d'après les écrits saint-simoniens, exposé analytique* (Politics thesis, Limoges, 1910); and C. Thiébaux, *Le féminisme et les socialistes depuis Saint-Simon jusqu'à nos jours* (Law thesis, Paris, 1906).
6   C.G. Moses, 'Saint-Simonian men/Saint-Simonian women: the transformation of feminist thought in 1830s France', *Journal of Modern History*, 54, 1982, pp. 240–67. For the enthusiastic response of women, see M. Riot-Sarcey (ed.) *De la liberté des femmes. Lettres des dames au Globe (1831–1832)* (Paris, Côté-Femmes, 1992).
7   C.G. Moses and L.W. Rabine (eds) *Feminism, Socialism and French Romanticism* (Bloomington, Indiana University Press, 1993), p. 174.
8   C. Démar, *Appel d'une femme au peuple sur l'affranchissement de la femme* (Paris, 1833).
9   C. Démar, *Ma loi d'avenir* (Paris, 1834).
10   S. Voilquin, *Souvenirs d'une fille du peuple, ou la Saint-simonienne en Egypte* (Paris, François Maspéro, 1978).
11   C. Fourier, *Théorie des quatre mouvements et des destinées générales. Prospectus et annonce de la découverte* (Paris, Jean-Jacques Pauvert, 1967).
12   Moses and Rabine (eds) *Feminism, Socialism and French Romanticism*, p. 75.
13   On Fourierism, see J. Beecher and R. Bienvenu (eds) *The Utopian Vision of Charles Fourier: Selected Texts on Work, Love and Passionate Attraction* (London, Cape, 1972).
14   For Niboyet, see esp. Riot-Sarcey, *La démocratie á l'épreuve des femmes*. Also E. Niboyet, *Le vrai livre des femmes* (Paris, 1863).
15   The literature on Tristan is extensive. Still valuable is J. Puech, *La vie et l'oeuvre de Flora Tristan, 1803–1844* (Paris, Librairie Marcel Rivière et Cie, 1925). More recent studies include S.K. Grogan, *Flora Tristan: Life Stories* (London, Routledge, 1998); M. Cross and T. Gray, *The Feminism of Flora Tristan* (Oxford, Berg, 1992); and S. Michaud (ed.) *Un fabuleux destin: Flora Tristan* (Dijon, Editions Universitaires de Dijon, 1985). A selection from her writings is extracted in

Notes

F. Gordon and M. Cross (eds) *Early French Feminisms 1830–1940* (Cheltenham, Edward Elgar, 1996).

16   On Deroin, see esp. Riot-Sarcey, *La démocratie à l'épreuve des femmes*. Also J.W. Scott, 'The duties of the citizen: Jeanne Deroin in the Revolution of 1848', in *Only Paradoxes to Offer*, pp. 57–89. By Deroin herself, see in particular J. Deroin, *Almanach des femmes* (London and Jersey, 1852, 1853, 1854), extracts from which, along with other writings, are translated in Gordon and Cross (eds) *Early French Feminisms*.

17   E. Thomas, *Pauline Roland: socialisme et féminisme au xixe siècle* (Paris, Marcel Rivière, 1956), and B. Groult, *Pauline Roland, ou comment la liberté vint aux femmes* (Paris, Robert Laffont, 1991).

18   E. Sullerot, 'Journaux féminins et lutte ouvrière (1848–1849)', in *Société d'histoire de la Révolution de 1848* (Paris, CNRS, 1966), pp. 88–122, and Moses, *French Feminism*, Chapter 6.

19   Text cited and translated in Gordon and Cross (eds) *Early French Feminisms*, p. 68.

20   Quoted by Moses, *French Feminism*, p. 141.

21   Ibid., pp. 143–44.

22   Scott, 'The duties of the citizen'.

23   Moses, *French Feminism*, p. 135.

24   J. Tixerant, *Le féminisme à l'époque de 1848 dans l'ordre politique et dans l'ordre économique* (Law thesis, Paris, 1908).

25   Gordon and Cross (eds) *Early French Feminisms*, p. 71.

26   Ibid., p. 65.

27   Ibid., p. 83.

28   Moses, *French Feminism*, pp. 147–48.

29   On the crackdown on republicans, see J. Merriman, *The Agony of the Republic: The Repression of the Left in Revolutionary France 1848–1851* (New Haven and London, Yale University Press, 1978).

30   Gordon and Cross (eds) *Early French Feminisms*, p. 90.

31   T. Moreau, *Le sang de l'histoire. Michelet, l'histoire et l'idée de la femme au xixe siècle* (Paris, Flammarion, 1982).

32   J. Michelet, *Du prêtre, de la femme, de la famille* (Paris, 1845). Extract translated in S.G. Bell and K.M. Offen, *Women, the Family and Freedom: The Debate in Documents*, vol. 1, p. 171.

33   P.J. Proudhon, *Système des contradictions économiques, ou philosophie de la misère*: Vol. 2 *La propriété* (Paris, 1846), p. 197.

34   J.R. Kist, *Daumier, Eyewitness of an Epoch* (London, Victoria and Albert Museum, 1976).

35   L.S. Strumingher, 'The Vésuviennes: images of women warriors in 1848 and their significance for French history', *History of European Ideas*, 8, 1987, pp. 451–88.

36   Offen, 'Ernest Legouvé and the doctrine of "equality in difference" for women'.

37   Legouvé, *Histoire morale des femmes*.

7 Femininity

1   Quoted by Clark, *Schooling the Daughters*, p. 10.

2   Prost, *Histoire de l'enseignement en France*; Anderson, *Education in France*.

3   Clark, *Schooling the Daughters*, p. 11.

4   K. Auspitz, *The Radical Bourgeoisie: The Ligue de L'Enseignement and the Origins of the Third Republic, 1866–1885* (Cambridge, Cambridge University Press, 1982).

5   J. Ferry, *Discours sur l'éducation: l'égalité d'éducation* (Paris, 1870).

6   E. Acomb, *The French Laic Laws: The First Anticlerical Campaign of the French Third Republic* (New York, Octagon, 1967; originally pub. New York, Columbia University Press, 1941).

7   Clark, *Schooling the Daughters*, pp. 22–23.

8   McPhee, *France 1780–1880*, p. 251.

9   Dossiers on the Duruy experiment can be consulted in AN F17 8753–55. See also C. Sée, *Lycées et collèges de jeunes filles* (Paris, 1884), pp. 6–7, and S.V. Horvath, 'Victor Duruy and the

controversy over secondary education for girls', *French Historical Studies*, 9, Spring 1975, pp. 83–104.

10 Mgr F. Dupanloup, *M. Duruy et l'éducation des filles: lettre à un de ses collègues* (Paris, 1867), pp. 15–16.

11 Mgr F. Dupanloup, *Seconde lettre sur M. Duruy et l'éducation des filles* (Paris, 1867), p. 19.

12 AN F17 8753.

13 Sée, *Lycées et collèges*, p. 60.

14 Ibid., and AN F17 8753.

15 AN F17 8755. Duruy approved a speech along these lines given by the mayor of Saint Mihiel.

16 O. Faure, *Les Français et leur médecine au xixe siècle* (Paris, Belin, 1993).

17 G.D. Sussman, 'The wet-nursing business in nineteenth-century France', *French Historical Studies*, 9, 1975, pp. 304–28; F. Fay-Sallois, *Les nourrices à Paris au xixe siècle* (Paris, Payot, 1980).

18 O. Moscucci, *The Science of Woman: Gynaecology and Gender in England 1800–1929* (Cambridge, Cambridge University Press, 1990).

19 A. Chéreau, *Mémoires pour servir à l'étude des maladies des ovaires* (Paris, 1844).

20 Moreau, *Le sang de l'histoire*, p. 93ff.

21 E. Georget, *De la folie, considérations sur cette maladie* (Paris, 1820), quoted in Y. Ripa, *Women and Madness: The Incarceration of Women in Nineteenth-Century France* (Cambridge, Polity Press, 1990), p. 119.

22 Ibid., pp. 123–24.

23 Ibid., p. 131. Also R. Harris, *Murder and Madness: Medicine, Law, and Society in the Fin de Siècle* (Oxford, Oxford University Press, 1989).

24 J. Gillais, *Crimes of Passion: Dramas of Private Life in Nineteenth-Century France* (Cambridge, Polity Press, 1990).

25 A. Dumas *fils*, *L'Homme-femme. Réponse à M. Henri d'Ideville* (Paris, 1872).

26 A-L. Shapiro, *Breaking the Codes: Female Criminality in Fin-de-Siècle Paris* (Stanford, Stanford University Press, 1996), Chapter 4.

27 *La Gazette des Tribunaux*, 5–6, 7, 8. April 1880.

28 Guillais, *Crimes of Passion*, pp. 16–17.

29 *La Gazette des Tribunaux*, 26 June 1847.

30 *La Gazette des Tribunaux*, 4 February 1880.

31 *La Gazette des Tribunaux*, 11 March 1880.

32 J-L. Flandrin, *Families in Former Times: Kinship, Household and Sexuality* (Cambridge, Cambridge University Press, 1979).

33 J. Guerber, *Le ralliement du clergé français à la morale liguorienne: l'abbé Gousset et ses précurseurs (1785–1832)* (Rome, Università Gregoriana, 1973).

34 Le Père Féline, *Catéchisme des gens mariés* (Paris, 1880); and J. Hoppenot, S.J., *Petit catéchisme du mariage* (Paris, 1920). On the theology of marriage, see also J.T. Noonan, *Contraception: A History of its Treatment by the Catholic Theologians and Canonists* (Cambridge, Massachusetts, Harvard University Press, 1965).

35 Fiaux, *La femme, le mariage, et le divorce*.

36 A. Debay, *Hygiène et physiologie du mariage* (1848; Paris, 153rd edn, 1880): extracts in Hellerstein, Hume and Offen (eds) *Victorian Women*, pp. 175–77.

37 Dr Villemont, *L'Amour conjugal* (Paris, 1885), p. 265.

38 L. Adler, *Secrets d'alcôve: histoire du couple* (Paris, Hachette, 1983), p. 94.

39 G. Droz, *Monsieur, madame et bébé* (Paris, 1866).

40 J. Stengers, 'Les pratiques anticonceptionnelles dans le mariage au xixe siècle: problèmes humains et attitudes religieuses', *Revue Belge de Philologie et d'Histoire*, xlix (2), 1971/72, pp. 403–81. R. Gibson, *A Social History of French Catholicism 1789–1914* (London, Routledge, 1989).

41 A-J-B. Parent-Duchâtelet, *De la prostitution dans la ville de Paris considéré sous le rapport de l'hygiène publique, de la morale et de l'administration*, 2 vols (Paris, 1836).

42 Ibid. See also J. Harsin, *Policing Prostitution in Nineteenth-Century Paris* (Princeton, Princeton University Press, 1985); A. Corbin, *Women for Hire: Prostitution and Sexuality in France after 1850*

(Cambridge, Massachusetts, Harvard University Press, 1990); and J. Termeau, *Maisons closes de province* (Paris, Editions Cénomane, 1986).

43 J. Butler, *Personal Reminiscences of a Great Crusade* (London, 1896).
44 Y. Guyot, *La prostitution* (Paris, 1880).
45 L. Andrieux, *Souvenirs d'un préfet de police*, 2 vols (Paris, 1885).
46 Corbin, *Women for Hire*, p. 21ff.
47 E. Zola, *Nana* (Paris, 1880).
48 Dr O. Commenge, *La prostitution clandestine à Paris* (Paris, 1897), p. 338.
49 Ibid.

8 Representations of the *ouvrière*

1 J. Scott, 'The woman worker', in *A History of Women*, vol. 4, pp. 399–426.
2 A. de Villeneuve-Bargemont, *Economie politique chrétienne, ou recherches sur la nature et les causes du paupérisme en France et en Europe, et sur les moyens de le soulager et de le prévenir*, 3 vols (Paris, 1834). See also J.B. Duroselle, *Les débuts du catholicisme social en France, 1822–1870* (Paris, 1951).
3 Baron C. Dupin, *Forces productives et commerciales de la France*, 2 vols (Paris, 1827).
4 J. Scott, ' "L'ouvrière! Mot impie, sordide…". Women workers in the discourse of political economy, 1840–1860', in *Gender and the Politics of History* (New York, Columbia University Press, 1988), pp. 139–62.
5 L-R. Villermé, *Tableau de l'état physique et morale des ouvriers employés dans les manufactures de coton, de laine et de soie*, 2 vols (Paris, 1840).
6 Reddy, *The Rise of Market Culture*, p. 171ff.
7 Audiganne, *Les populations ouvrières*, vol. 1, quotes at pp. 69, 93 and 102.
8 Scott, ' "L'ouvrière! Mot impie, sordide…" '.
9 Simon, *La femme au vingtième siècle*, p. 67.
10 Scott, ' "L'ouvrière! Mot impie, sordide…" '.
11 Ibid.
12 J. Scott, 'A statistical representation of work. La Statistique de l'Industrie à Paris 1847–1848', in *Gender and the Politics of History*, pp. 113–38.
13 *L'Atelier*, 30 December 1842. Quoted in translation in Bell and Offen (eds) *Women, the Family and Freedom*, vol. 1, pp. 204–8.
14 Magraw, *History of the French Working Class*, vol. 1, pp. 73–75.
15 Quoted by J. Rabaut, *Histoire des féminismes français* (Paris, Stock, 1978), p. 157.
16 Quoted in Hellerstein, Hume and Offen (eds) *Victorian Women*, p. 397.
17 Ibid.
18 Quoted by Rabaut, *Histoire des féminismes français*, pp. 156–57.
19 C. Sowerwine, *Sisters or Citizens? Women and Socialism in France since 1876* (Cambridge, Cambridge University Press, 1982), pp. 22–23.
20 Ibid., p. 26.
21 Deroin, *Almanach des femmes*. Quoted in Gordon and Cross (eds) *Early French Feminisms*, p. 135.
22 BMD, dossier Daubié.
23 J. Daubié, *La femme pauvre au xixe siècle* (Paris, 1866).
24 Scott, ' "L'ouvrière! Mot impie, sordide…" '.
25 BMD, dossier Daubié.
26 P. Minck, quoted and translated in Hellerstein, Hume and Offen (eds) *Victorian Women*, pp. 398–400, quotation at p. 399.
27 L. Klejman and F. Rochefort, *L'Egalité en marche: le féminisme sous la Troisième République* (Paris, Presses de la Fondation Nationale des Sciences Politiques/des femmes, 1989), pp. 41–44.
28 Sowerwine, *Sister or Citizens?*, p. 22.
29 Ibid., p. 23.

Notes

9 Reformulating the 'woman question'

1 J.F. McMillan, *Napoleon III* (Harlow, Longman, 1991).
2 For an introduction to the rise of Republicanism, see P.M. Pilbeam, *Republicanism in Nineteenth-Century France, 1814–1871* (Basingstoke and London, Macmillan, 1995).
3 P.-J. Proudhon, *De la justice dans la Révolution et dans l'Eglise* (Paris, 1858).
4 Quoted by Moses, *French Feminism*, p. 157.
5 P.-J. Proudhon, *La pornocratie, ou les femmes dans les temps modernes* (Paris, 1875).
6 Giroud (ed.) *Les femmes de la Révolution de Michelet*, p. 157.
7 Moreau, *Le sang de l'histoire*, p. 95.
8 Cited ibid.
9 J. Michelet, *L'Amour* (Paris, 1859).
10 On Lamber, see W. Stephens, *Madame Adam Juliette Lamber. La Grande Française, from Louis Philippe until 1917* (New York, E.P. Dalton and Co., 1917).
11 J. Lambert (Mme Adam), *Idées anti-proudhonniennes sur l'amour, la femme et le mariage* (Paris, 2nd edn, 1861).
12 Moses, *French Feminism*, p. 168.
13 J. d'Héricourt, *La femme affranchie: réponse à MM. Michelet, Proudhon, E. de Girardin, A. Comte et autres novateurs modernes*, 2 vols (Brussels, 1860).
14 Ibid.
15 On Audouard, Moses, *French Feminism*, pp. 178–79, and P.K. Bidelman, *Pariahs Stand Up! The Founding of the Liberal Feminist Movement in France 1859–1889* (Westport, Connecticut and London, Greenwood Press, 1982), pp. 40–41.
16 A. Audouard, *Guerre aux hommes* (Paris, 1866).
17 A. Audouard, *La femme dans le mariage, la séparation et le divorce, conférence faite le 28 février 1870* (Paris, 1870).
18 On Léo, Klejman and Rochefort, *L'Egalité en marche*, pp. 41–42.
19 Moses, *French Femininsm*, p. 167.
20 Bidelman, *Pariahs Stand Up!*, pp. 38–39.
21 A. Dalotel (ed.) *Paule Minck, communarde et féministe, 1839–1901* (Paris, Syros, 1981).
22 E. Thomas, *Louise Michel* (Paris, Gallimard, 1971).
23 BMD: dossier Potonié -Pierre.
24 Horvath, 'Victor Duruy and the controversy over secondary education for girls', pp. 83–104.
25 Klejman and Rochefort, *L'Egalité en marche*, p. 42.
26 BMD: dossier Deraismes; APP B/a 1031 dossier Deraismes.
27 M. Deraismes, *La femme et le droit*, in M. Deraismes, *Oeuvres complètes*, vol. 2 (Paris, 1895), p. 137.
28 Bidelman, *Pariahs Stand Up!*, p. 78.
29 BMD: dossier Richer; BHVP, fonds Richer; Bidelman, *Pariahs Stand Up!*, p. 91ff.
30 *Le Droit des Femmes*, 10 April 1869.
31 Moses, *French Feminism*, p. 187.
32 *Le Droit des Femmes*, 24 April 1870.
33 S. Edwards, *The Paris Commune 1871* (London, Eyre and Spottiswoode, 1971).
34 K. Marx and F. Engels, *Writings on the Paris Commune*, ed. H. Draper (New York, Monthly Review Press, 1971).
35 See, in general, E. Thomas, *Les pétroleuses* (Paris, Gallimard, 1963), translated as *The Women Incendiaries* (New York, George Brazillier, 1966). Also Thomas, *Louise Michel*.
36 On the club movement, see esp. Barry, *Women and Political Insurgency*.
37 Ibid.
38 Quoted ibid., p. 127.
39 G.L. Guillickson, *Unruly Women of Paris: Images of the Commune* (Ithaca, Cornell University Press, 1996).
40 Bidelman, *Pariahs Stand Up!*, p. 94ff.

41   M. Deraismes, *France et progrès* (Paris, 1873).

42   L. Richer, *La femme libre* (Paris, 1877).

43   M. Deraismes, *Eve contre Monsieur Dumas fils* (Paris, 1872).

44   *Congrès International du Droit des Femmes. Compte rendu des séances plénières* (Paris, 1878).

45   H. Auclert, *Le droit politique des femmes: question qui n'est pas traitée au Congrès International des Femmes* (Paris, 1878).

46   The fullest treatment of Auclert is S. Hause, *Hubertine Auclert: The French Suffragette* (New Haven and London, Yale University Press, 1987).

10 A new Eve?

1   For a useful introduction, see E.A. Accampo, R.G. Fuchs and M.L. Stewart (eds) *Gender and the Politics of Social Reform in France, 1870–1914* (Baltimore and London, Johns Hopkins University Press, 1995), esp. pp. 10–11.

2   C. Dyer, *Population and Society in Twentieth-Century France* (London, Hodder and Stoughton, 1978).

3   K. Offen, 'Depopulation, nationalism and feminism in fin-de-siècle France', *American Historical Review*, 89, 1984, pp. 648–76.

4   A. Maugue, *L'Identité masculine en crise au tournant du siècle, 1871–1914* (Paris, Editions Rivages, 1987). See also Maugue, 'The new Eve and the old Adam', in *A History of Women*, vol. 4, pp. 515–32.

5   C. Cosnier, *Marie Bashkirtseff: un portrait sans retouche* (Paris, Pierre Horay, 1985).

6   H. Ibsen, *A Doll's House and Two Other Plays* (London, Dent, 1910).

7   J. Bois, *L'Eve nouvelle* (Paris, 1913).

8   F. de Céez, *En attendant l'avenir: aux jeunes filles* (Paris, 1905), p. 3.

9   M. Prévost, *Les demi-vierges* (Paris, 1894).

10   Maugue, *L'Identité masculine en crise*.

11   D.L. Silverman, *Art Nouveau in Fin-de-Siècle France: Politics, Psychology and Style* (Berkeley, Los Angeles and London, University of California Press, 1989), esp. Chapter 4.

12   Ibid.

13   Cf. *L'Assiette au Beurre*. Both of the cartoons mentioned are reproduced in G. Racine, *Entre hommes: regards sur les femmes 1880–1930* (Paris, Flammarion, 1994), pp. 134–35.

14   *Gil Blas Illustré*, 1893. Reproduced in Silverman, *Art Nouveau*, p. 64.

15   *Le Rire*, 1903. Reproduced in Racine, *Entre hommes*, p. 89.

16   On the impact of sport generally, see the pioneering work of R. Holt, *Sport and Society in Modern France* (London, Macmillan, 1981).

17   On department stores, M. Miller, *The Bon Marché: Bourgeois Culture and the Department Store, 1869–1920* (Princeton, Princeton University Press, 1981), and R. Williams, *Dream Worlds* (Berkeley, Los Angeles and London, University of California Press, 1982).

18   Zeldin, *France 1848–1945*, vol. 2, p. 153.

19   Tilly and Scott, *Women, Work and Family*, p. 178.

20   Sée, *Lycées et collèges de jeunes filles*, pp. 157ff, 192.

21   AN F17 8777. Académie d'Aix: Rector to Minister of Education, 21 July 1885.

22   AN F17 14187. Le Mans: Report of mayor to municipal council, 24 December 1900.

23   AN F17 8770. Académie de Toulouse: Inspector to Rector, 2 August 1886.

24   AN F17 8758. Académie d'Aix: Inspector to Minister of Education, 16 August 1886.

25   AN F17 8763. Académie de Douai: Rector to Minister of Education, 14 August 1886.

26   AN F17 14187. Letter of Minister, 20 March 1888, with note of 1887.

27   F. Mayeur, *L'Enseignement secondaire des jeunes filles sous la Troisième République* (Paris, Presses de la Fondation Nationale des Sciences Politiques, 1977).

28   Ibid.

Notes

29 G. Coireault, *Les cinquantes premières années de l'enseignement secondaire féminin, 1880–1930* (Thèse complémentaire pour le doctorat ès lettres, Poitiers, 1940), p. 29.

30 Ibid., pp. 129–30.

31 Charrier, *L'Evolution intellectuelle féminine*, p. 143ff.

32 L. Weiss, *Mémoires d'une Européenne 1893–1919* (Paris, Payot, 1968), vol. 1, pp. 139–41.

33 Ibid., p. 13.

34 R. Reid, *Marie Curie* (London, 1974).

35 S. Hause with A.R. Kenney, *Women's Suffrage and Social Politics in the French Third Republic* (Princeton, Princeton University Press, 1984), p. 125.

36 Clark, *Schooling the Daughters*, pp. 13–14.

37 V. Leroux-Hugon, *Des saintes laïques: les infirmières à l'aube de la Troisième République* (Paris, Sciences en Situation, 1992).

38 Phrase used by Aline Valette, *La Fronde*, 17 February 1898.

39 F. Clark, *The Position of Women in Contemporary France* (London, 1937).

40 J. Bouvier, *Histoire des dames dans les postes, télégraphes et téléphones de 1714 à 1929* (Paris, 1940).

41 M. Guilbert, 'L'Evolution des effectifs du travail féminin en France depuis 1866', *Revue Française du Travail*, September 1947, p. 768.

42 Mlle T. Razous, *Guide pratique des femmes et des jeunes filles dans le choix d'une profession* (Paris, 1910), pp. 311–12.

43 Guilbert, 'L'Evolution des effectifs', p. 768.

44 A. Bonnefoy, *Place aux femmes! Les carrières féminines administratives et libérales* (Paris, 1914), pp. 89–91.

45 P. Kergomard, 'La féminisation de l'enseignement primaire', *La Fronde*, 18 February 1898.

46 *Autorité*, 16 April 1893 (cutting in AN F17 9399).

47 I. Berger, *Lettres d'institutrices rurales d'autrefois, rédigées à la suite de l'enquête de Fracisque Sarcey en 1897* (Paris, n.d.), pp. 1–11. This is a marvellous collection of autobiographical statements.

48 *La Fronde*, 25 December 1897.

49 J. Ozouf, 'Les instituteurs de la Manche au début du vingtième siècle', *Revue d'Histoire Moderne et Contemporaine*, 13, 1966, pp. 95–114.

50 Berger, *Lettres d'institutrices*, pp. 54–57.

51 *La Fronde*, 25 December 1897.

52 G. Vincent, 'Les professeurs de l'enseignement secondaire dans la société de la belle époque', *Revue d'Histoire Moderne et Contemporaine*, 13, 1966, pp. 49–86.

53 Mayeur, *L'Enseignement secondaire des jeunes filles*. For more on women secondary teachers, see J.B. Margadant, *Madame le Professeur: Women Educators in the Third Republic* (Princeton, Princeton University Press, 1990).

54 Mme G. Regnal, *Comment la femme peut gagner sa vie* (Paris, 1908).

55 Razous, *Guide pratique*, p. ii.

56 A. Rouast, 'La transformation de la famille en France depuis la Révolution', in *Sociologie comparée de la famille contemporaine* (Paris, CNRS, 1955); M. Rouquet, *L'Evolution du droit de la famille vers l'individualisme* (Paris, 1909).

57 Phillips, *Putting Asunder*, pp. 423–24.

58 A. Naquet, *Religion, propriété, famille* (Paris, 1869).

59 Phillips, *Putting Asunder*, pp. 424–25.

60 P. Margueritte, 'L'Evolution de la morale et de l'amour', *La Revue*, 1 August 1907, pp. 329–37. See also F. Ronsin, *Les divorciaires: affrontements politiques et conceptions du mariage dans la France du xixe siècle* (Paris, Editions Aubier, 1992).

61 Phillips, *Putting Asunder*, p. 428.

62 A. Valensi, *L'Application de la loi du divorce en France* (Law thesis, Montpellier, 1905).

63 *La Gazette des Tribunaux*, 19 February 1914.

64 J.T. Noonan, *Power to Dissolve: Lawyers and Marriages in the Courts of the Roman Curia* (Cambridge, Massachusetts, Harvard University Press, 1972).

Notes

65   *La Gazette des Tribunaux*, 14 March and 3 April 1914.

66   *La Gazette des Tribunaux*, 27 and 28 April 1914.

67   *La Gazette des Tribunaux*, 14 March 1914.

68   Abbé de Gibergues, *Les devoirs des hommes envers les femmes, instructions aux hommes du monde prêchées à Saint-Philippe du Roule et à Saint Augustin* (Paris, 1903).

69   *Plan d'éducation d'une mère chrétienne* in A. de Ségur, *Vie de l'abbé Bernard* (Paris, 1882). Extract quoted and translated in Hellerstein, Hume and Offen (eds) *Victorian Women*, p. 248.

70   J. Ferry, *Discours sur l'éducation: l'égalité d'éducation* (Paris, 1870).

71   P. Grimanelli, *La femme et le positivisme* (Paris, 1905).

72   Simon, *La femme au vingtième siècle*, p. 67.

73   Cited by Zeldin, *France 1848–1945*, vol. 2, pp. 668–69.

74   D. Lesueur, *L'Evolution féminine: ses résultats économiques* (Paris, 1900), p. 5.

75   *L'Assiette au Beurre*, 15 October 1912.

76   Branca, *Women in Western Europe since 1750*, p. 89.

77   See, for instance, the plays of Augier and Scribe, usefully discussed by S.B. John in *French Literature and its Background*: Vol. 5 *The Late Nineteenth Century*, ed. J. Cruickshank (London, 1969).

78   Bureau, *L'Indiscipline des moeurs*, p. 60. See also Zeldin, *France 1848–1945*, vol. 1, p. 288ff. for a discussion of financial arrangements in marriage. According to one authority, of the 287,179 marriages which were celebrated in 1898, 82,346 had some form of contract (Moissinac, *Le contrat de mariage*, pp. 5–6).

79   M. Deraismes, 'Comment on se marie aujourd'hui', *Le Nain Jaune*, 14 March 1866.

80   Cf. *L'Assiette au Beurre*, 12 March 1904.

81   *La Fronde*, 4 March 1898.

82   A. Corbin, in *A History of Private Life*, vol. 4, p. 598ff.

83   Cited ibid.

84   L. Blum, *Du mariage* (Paris, 1907).

85   On the neo-Malthusians, D.V. Glass, *Population Policies and Movements in Europe* (London, 1940), and F. Ronsin, 'La classe ouvrière et le néo-malthusianisme: l'exemple français avant 1914', *Le Mouvement Social*, 106, January–May 1979, pp. 85–117. For Roussel, see N. Roussel, 'La liberté de la maternité', in *Trois conférences* (Paris, 1930).

86   *A History of Private Life*, vol. 4, p. 596.

87   A. MacLaren, *Sexuality and Social Order: The Debate over the Fertility of Women and Workers in France, 1770–1920* (New York, Holmes and Meier, 1983).

88   *A History of Private Life*, vol. 4, p. 593.

89   AN F7 12652: publications obscènes.

90   M. Prévost, *Lettres à Françoise* (Paris, 1902), pp. 192–93.

91   de Céez, *En attendant l'avenir*, pp. 47–48.

92   Y. Delatour, *Les effets de la guerre sur la situation de la Française d'après la presse féminine, 1914–1918* (Paris, maîtrise, 1965), p. 13.

93   *La Gazette des Tribunaux*, 24 July 1913.

94   *La Gazette des Tribunaux*, 20 March 1914.

95   *La Gazette des Tribunaux*, 2, 3–4 January 1914.

96   Cf. *La Fronde*, 22 January 1898, 24 February 1898.

97   L. Fiaux, *La police des moeurs devant la commission extra-parlementaire du régime des moeurs*, 3 vols (Paris, 1907–10).

98   Corbin, *Women for Hire*, p. 310ff.

99   F.C. Sautman, 'Invisible women: lesbian working-class culture in France, 1880–1930', in J. Merrick and B.T. Ragan, Jr (eds) *Homosexuality in Modern France* (Oxford and New York, Oxford University Press, 1996), pp. 177–201.

Notes

11 Gender at work

1   Caron, *An Economic History of Modern France*.
2   J. Daric, *L'Activité professionnelle des femmes en France* (Paris, PUF, 1947).
3   Ibid.
4   Ibid., p. 154.
5   Scott and Tilly, 'Women's work and the family in nineteenth-century Europe'.
6   M. Gemähling, *Le salaire féminin* (Paris, 1912), pp. 35–36.
7   Ibid.
8   Daric, *L'Activité professionnelle*, p. 80.
9   P. Stearns, *Lives of Labour: Work in a Maturing Industrial Society* (London, Croom Helm, 1975), p. 80.
10   *Cost of Living in French Towns. Report of an Enquiry by the Board of Trade into Working Class Rents, Housing and Retail Prices, together with the Rates of Wages in Certain Occupations in the Principal Industrial Towns of France* (London, 1909) p. xvi.
11   Tilly and Scott, *Women, Work and Family*, pp. 91–92.
12   Ibid., p. 167.
13   Ibid.
14   A. MacLaren, 'Abortion in France: women and the regulation of family size 1800–1914', *French Historical Studies*, 10, Spring 1978, pp. 461–85.
15   Ronsin, 'La classe ouvrière et le néo-malthusianisme: l'exemple français avant 1914', pp. 85–117.
16   Tilly and Scott, *Women, Work and Family*, p. 123.
17   Guilbert and Isambert-Jamati, *Travail féminin et travail à domicile*. Also G. Mény, *La lutte contre le sweating-system* (Law thesis, Paris, 1910), p. 21.
18   Miller, *The Bon Marché*.
19   Coffin, *The Politics of Women's Work*, Chapters 3 and 4.
20   Liu, *The Weaver's Knot*.
21   Coffin, *The Politics of Women's Work*.
22   *Enquête sur le travail à domicile dans l'industrie de la lingerie*: Vol. 1 *Paris* (Paris, Office du Travail, 1907), pp. 648–49.
23   *Enquête sur le travail à domicile dans l'industrie de la fleur artificielle* (Paris, Office du Travail, 1913).
24   R. Guillou, *La Française dans ses quatre âges* (Paris, 3rd edn, 1911), pp. 83–84.
25   F. de Donville, *Guide pour les professions des femmes* (Paris, 1894), p. 18.
26   Charrier, *L'Evolution intellectuelle féminine*, p. 242ff.; P. Kergomard, 'Les écoles professionelles de filles', *La Fronde*, 20 May 1898.
27   Liu, *The Weaver's Knot*.
28   Accampo, *Industrialization, Family Life and Class Relations*.
29   J. Bouvier, *Mes mémoires: ou 59 années d'activité industrielle, sociale et intellectuelle d'une ouvrière* (Paris, 1936), quotation at p. 27.
30   P. Hilden, *Working Women and Socialist Politics in France 1880–1914: A Regional Study* (Oxford, Clarendon Press, 1986).
31   L. and M. Bonneff, *Les métiers qui tuent: enquête auprès des syndicats ouvriers sur les maladies professionnelles* (Paris, n.d.), p. 35.
32   C. Milhaud, *L'Ouvrière en France* (Paris, 1907), pp. 41–42. Cf. AN F22 514: reports of factory inspectors on the temperature in factories, plus related pamphlets, esp. P. Boulin, *Les milieux chauds et humides dans l'industrie textile* (n.d.).
33   Milhaud, *L'Ouvrière en France*, pp. 42–43.
34   Hilden, *Working Women and Socialist Politics*.
35   K. Schirmacher, 'Le travail des femmes en France', *Musée Social, Mémoires et Documents*, May 1902.
36   Milhaud, *L'Ouvrière en France*, pp. 27–28.
37   M. Guilbert, *Les femmes et l'organisation syndicale avant 1914* (Paris, CNRS, 1966), p. 21.

38 Coffin, *The Politics of Women's Work*.
39 O. Uzanne, *La femme à Paris, nos contemporaines* (Paris, 1894), pp. 93–94. Cf. Bouvier, *Mes mémoires*, pp. 60–61.
40 'Le travail féminin à Paris, avant et depuis la guerre dans les industries du vêtement', *Bulletin du Ministère du Travail (BMT)*, October–December 1925, p. 349.
41 Bouvier, *Mes mémoires*, p. 52.
42 'Le travail féminin à Paris', *BMT*, January–March 1926, p. 7.
43 Ibid., pp. 1–24.
44 C. Benoist, *Les ouvriers de l'aiguille à Paris* (Paris, 1895).
45 Ibid., pp. 114–15.
46 'Le travail féminin à Paris', *BMT*, January–March 1926, p. 10.
47 Bouvier, *Mes mémoires*, pp. 53–54.
48 A. Lainé, *Les demoiselles de magasin à Paris* (Law thesis, Paris, 1911).
49 Ibid., pp. 58–59.
50 Ibid., pp. 79–81.
51 Ibid., quoting C. Cheysson, 'Du rôle et de l'avenir de la petite et de la grande industrie', *Journal des Economistes*, November 1884, p. 314.
52 Ibid., pp. 92–93.
53 *Enquête sur le travail à domicile dans l'industrie de la lingerie*: Vol. 1 *Paris*, pp. 648–49.
54 Ibid., pp. 649–50.
55 Ibid., pp. 658–59.
56 Ibid., pp. 661–62.
57 Ibid., p. 727ff.
58 *Enquête sur le travail à domicile dans l'industrie de la lingérie*: Vol. 2 *Cher, Allier, Loir-et-Cher, Indre, Maine-et-Loire, Sarthe* (Paris, Office du Travail, 1908), pp. 234–36.
59 Ibid., pp. 362–63.
60 Ibid., p. 651.
61 *Enquête sur le travail à domicile dans l'industrie de la lingérie*: Vol. 3 *Seine-Inférieure, Oise, Aisne, Somme, Pas-de-Calais, Nord, Meuse, Meurthe-et- Moselle, Vosges* (Paris, Office du Travail, 1909).
62 L. Bonnevay, *Les ouvrières lyonnaises travaillant à domicile* (Paris, 1896), pp. 78–80.
63 Mény, *La lutte contre le sweating-system*, p. 97.
64 M. Boxer, 'Women in industrial homework: the flowermakers of Paris in the Belle Epoque', *French Historical Studies*, 17, Spring 1983.
65 *Enquête sur le travail à domicile dans l'industrie de la fleur artificielle* (Paris, Office du Travail, 1913).
66 L. Chevalier, *Les Parisiens* (Paris, 1967).
67 E. Zola, *Au bonheur des dames* (Paris, 1871). See also F. Parent-Lardeur, *Les demoiselles de magasin* (Paris, 1970) and C. Lesellier, 'Employées de grands magasins à Paris avant 1914', *Le Mouvement Social*, October–December 1978.
68 Cited by Lainé, *Les demoiselles de magasin*, pp. 51–52.
69 Zeldin, *France 1848–1945*, vol. 2, p. 943.
70 M. Cusenier, *Les domestiques en France* (Law thesis, Paris, 1912), p. 17.
71 T. McBride, *The Domestic Revolution: The Modernization of Household Service in England and France, 1820–1920* (London, Croom Helm, 1976), pp. 34–35.
72 Contrast McBride, *The Domestic Revolution* with M. Mittre, *Des domestiques en France dans leurs rapports avec l'économie sociale, le bonheur domestique, les lois civils* (Paris, 1867), p. 50.
73 Uzanne, *La femme à Paris*, p. 63ff.
74 Cusenier, *Les domestiques en France*, p. 165ff.
75 Bouvier, *Mes mémoires*, p. 34.
76 Mittre, *Des domestiques*, p. 25.
77 Romieu, *La femme au dix-neuvième siècle*, p. 165.
78 F. Fournier, *Des domestiques d'aujourd'hui* (Paris, 1877), pp. 2–3. Cf. E. Legouvé, 'Les domestiques d'autrefois et ceux d'aujourd'hui', *Revue des cours littéraires*, 13 March 1869; C. de Ribbe, *Les domestiques dans la famille* (Paris, 1862), p. 14.

Notes

79 Legouvé, 'Les domestiques d'autrefois'.

80 Cusenier, *Les domestiques en France*, pp. 84, 90–92.

81 Bouvier, *Mes mémoires*, pp. 38–39.

82 Fournier, *Des domestiques d'aujourd'hui*, pp. 18–19.

83 O. Mirbeau, *Le journal d'une femme de chambre* (Paris, 1900).

84 Cusenier, *Les domestiques en France*, p. 304ff. Also E. Chauvet, *Le travail: études morales: les domestiques* (Caen, 1896).

85 Cusenier, *Les domestiques en France*, p. 123ff.

86 Uzanne, *La femme à Paris*.

87 Simon, *L'Ouvrière*, pp. 84–87.

88 Uzanne, *La femme à Paris*.

89 See in particular M.L. Stewart, *Women, Work and the French State: Labour Protection and Social Patriarchy 1879–1919* (London, McGill-Queen's University Press, 1989). Also Accampo, Fuchs and Stewart (eds) *Gender and the Politics of Social Reform in France*, and J.F. Stone, *The Search for Social Peace: Reform Legislation in France, 1890–1914* (Albany, State University of New York Press, 1985).

90 Stewart, *Women, Work and the French State*, p. 29ff.

91 Maria Pognon, 'La loi néfaste de 1892', *La Fronde*, 20 December 1899. Quoted and translated in Bell and Offen (eds) *Women, the Family and Freedom*, vol. 2, pp. 211–13.

92 Accampo, *Industrialization, Family Life and Class Relations*, p. 157.

93 P.J. Hilden, 'Women and the labour movement in France, 1869–1914', *The Historical Journal*, 29, 1986, pp. 809–32.

94 Milhaud, *L'Ouvrière en France*, p. 17.

95 Ibid., pp. 79–81.

96 Ibid. See also J. Vallier, *Le travail des femmes dans l'industrie française* (Law thesis, Grenoble, 1899).

97 Milhaud, *L'Ouvrière en France*, pp. 79–81.

98 'Le travail féminin à Paris', *BMT*, October–December 1925, p. 349.

99 Milhaud, *L'Ouvrière en France*, pp. 79–81.

100 'Le travail féminin à Paris', *BMT*, October–December 1925, pp. 351–52.

101 Ibid.

102 AN F22 439: report of Mme Maître, 13 June 1911.

103 'Le travail féminin à Paris', *BMT*, October–December 1925, p. 352.

104 Milhaud, *L'Ouvrière en France*, pp. 70, 74.

105 Ibid., pp. 75–76. Also AN F22 512/3: hygiène des travailleurs.

106 *Journal officiel (Chambre des députés)*, 17 February 1914.

107 J. Lupiac, *La loi du 10 juillet 1915 pour la protection des ouvrières dans l'industrie du vêtement* (Law thesis, Paris, 1918), and E. and F. Combat, *Le travail des femmes à domicile. Textes officiels, avec commentaire explicatif et étude générale sur les salaires féminins* (Paris, 1916). See also M.J. Boxer, 'Protective legislation and home industry: the marginalization of women workers in late nineteenth–early twentieth century France', *Journal of Social History*, Fall 1986, pp. 45–66.

108 Perrot, 'La femme populaire rebelle'.

109 L.A. Tilly, 'Women's collective action and feminism in France, 1870–1914', in C. Tilly and L. Tilly (eds) *Class Conflict and Collective Action* (Beverly Hills, Sage Publications, 1981), pp. 207–31.

110 Ibid.

111 R.A. Jonas, *Industry and Politics in Rural France: Peasants of the Isère 1870–1914* (Ithaca, Cornell University Press, 1994), pp. 157–58.

112 The fundamental study remains Guilbert, *Les femmes et l'organisation syndicale avant 1914*.

113 M-H. Zylberberg-Hocquard, 'Les ouvrières d'Etat (tabac-allumettes) dans les dernières années du xixe siècle', *Le Mouvement Social*, 105, October–December 1978, p. 93.

114 Guilbert, *Les femmes et l'organisation syndicale*.

115 M. Perrot, *Les ouvriers en grève: France 1871–1890*, 2 vols (Paris, Mouton, 1974).

116 Guilbert, *Les femmes et l'organisation syndicale*, p. 29.
117 M. Turmann, *Le syndicalisme chrétien en France* (Paris, 1929).
118 Guilbert, *Les femmes et l'organisation syndicale*.
119 Hilden, *Working Women and Socialist Politics*.
120 Cf. J.F. McMillan, *Housewife or Harlot: The Place of Women in French Society* (Brighton, The Harvester Press, 1981), p. 156.
121 A. Chirac, quoted by Guilbert, *Les femmes et l'organisation syndicale*, p. 407.
122 E. Berth, 'Le centenaire de Proudhon', *Le Mouvement Socialiste*, 1 January 1909.
123 A. Rosmer, quoted by Guilbert, *Les femmes et l'organisation syndicale*, p. 410.
124 P. Gemähling, *Travailleurs au rabais. La lutte contre les sous-concurrences ouvrières* (Paris, 1910), p. 150ff.
125 C. Sowerwine, 'Workers and women in France before 1914: the debate over the Couriau Affair', *Journal of Modern History*, 55, 1983, pp. 411–41.
126 BMD: dossier typographes.
127 BMD: dossier Congrès du Travail féminin.
128 Cf. Pierre Monatte, writing in *La Vie Ouvrière*, 5 July 1913.
129 Cf. A. Rosmer, 'La femme à l'atelier', *La Bataille Syndicaliste*, 28 September 1913.
130 McMillan, *Housewife or Harlot*, p. 156.
131 R. Stuart, 'Whores and angels: women and the family in the discourse of French Marxism, 1882–1905', *European History Quarterly*, 27, 1997, pp. 339–70. See also R. Stuart, ' "Calm, with a grave and serious temperament, rather male". French Marxism, gender and feminism, 1882–1905', *International Review of Social History*, 41, 1996, pp. 57–82.
132 E.J. Hobsbawm, 'Man and woman in socialist iconography', *History Workshop*, 6, Autumn 1978, pp. 121–38.
133 C. Dufrancatel, 'La femme imaginaire des hommes: politique, idéologie et imaginaire dans le mouvement ouvrier', in Dufrancatel *et al.* (eds) *L'Histoire sans qualités*, pp. 157–86.
134 Chevalier, *Labouring Classes and Dangerous Classes*.
135 A. MacLaren, 'Sex and socialism: the opposition of the French Left to birth control in the nineteenth century', *Journal of the History of Ideas*, 37, 1976, pp. 475–92. See also Ronsin, 'La classe ouvrière et le néo-malthusianisme: l'exemple français avant 1914'.

12 In search of citizenship

1 *La Citoyenne*, 13 February 1881. See also H. Auclert, *Le vote des femmes* (Paris, 1908), and H. Auclert, *Les femmes au gouvernail* (Paris, 1923).
2 Hause, *Hubertine Auclert*, p. 68ff.
3 Ibid., pp. 78–79.
4 Bidelman, *Pariahs Stand Up!*, p. 116ff.
5 *La Citoyenne*, 6 February 1881.
6 J.W. Scott, 'The rights of the "social": Hubertine Auclert and the politics of the Third Republic', in *Only Paradoxes to Offer*, p. 109ff., and Auclert, *Le vote des femmes*; *La Citoyenne*, 27 March 1881.
7 Hause, *Hubertine Auclert*, p. 106ff.
8 Ibid., p. 81ff.
9 Ibid., p. 95.
10 APP B/a 885: dossier Auclert, report of 29 April 1880.
11 Bidelman, *Pariahs Stand Up!*, p. 129.
12 Ibid., p. 73ff.
13 *Le Droit des Femmes*, 20 May 1888.
14 Bidelman, *Pariahs Stand Up!*, p. 156ff.
15 *Actes du Congrès International des Oeuvres et Institutions Féminines, 1889* (Paris, 1890).
16 Bidelman, *Pariahs Stand Up!*, p. 177ff.
17 *Congrès Français et International du Droit des Femmes* (Paris, 1889).

Notes

18   Hause with Kenney, *Women's Suffrage and Social Politics*, p. 55.
19   BMD: dossiers Pognon and Bonnevial.
20   BMD: dossier Chéliga-Loevy.
21   BMD: dossier Schmall.
22   BMD: dossier Le Groupe Français d'Etudes Féministes; J. Oddo-Deflou, *Le sexualisme* (Paris, 1906).
23   BMD: dossier Vincent.
24   BMD: dossier Potonié-Pierre.
25   BMD: dossier Kauffmann.
26   BMD: dossier Martin.
27   Hause, *Hubertine Auclert*, p. 149ff.
28   Thomas, *Louise Michel*, p. 322.
29   Bidelman, *Pariahs Stand Up!*, p. 141.
30   Sowerwine, *Sisters or Citizens?*, pp. 36–41.
31   Ibid., pp. 59–66.
32   (A. Valette and P. Bonnier), *Socialisme et sexualisme: programme du Parti socialiste français* (Paris, 1893).
33   Sowerwine, *Sisters or Citizens?*, p. 62ff.
34   BMD: dossier Monod; I. Bogelot, *Trente ans de solidarité 1877–1906* (Paris, 1906).
35   J.F. McMillan, 'Wollstonecraft's daughters, Marianne's daughters and the daughters of Joan of Arc: Marie Maugeret and Catholic feminism in the French Belle Epoque', in Orr (ed.) *Wollstonecraft's Daughters*, pp. 186–98. See also BHVP, Fonds Bouglé, dossier 523, Marie Maugeret, and issues of *Le Féminisme chrétien*.
36   Comtesse Marie de Villermont, *Le mouvement féministe: ses causes, son avenir, solution chrétienne*, 2 vols (Paris, Bloud, 1900–4), vol. 2, p. 34.
37   S. Hause and A.R. Kenney, 'The development of the Catholic women's suffrage movement in France, 1886–1922', *Catholic Historical Review*, 67, 1981, pp. 11–30.
38   Hause with Kenney, *Women's Suffrage and Social Politics*, pp. 40–41.
39   Sowerwine, *Sisters or Citizens?*, p. 60.
40   *Voeux adoptés par le Congrès Féministe International, tenu à Paris en 1896 pendant les journées 8 au 12 avril* (Paris, n.d.).
41   BMD: dossier Congrès 1896; BHVP, Fonds Bouglé, dossier Congrès; C. Dissard, *Opinions féministes à propos du congrès féministe de 1896* (Paris, 1896).
42   BMD: dossier Durand.
43   Hause with Kenney, *Women's Suffrage and Social Politics*, p. 289, footnote 20.
44   Li Dzeh-Djen, *La presse féministe en France de 1869 à 1914* (Paris, Rodstein, 1934).
45   BHVP, Fonds Bouglé, dossier Maugeret.
46   *Deuxième Congrès International des Oeuvres et Institutions féminines, tenu au Palais des Congrès de l'Exposition Universelle de 1900: compte rendu des travaux par Madame Pégard*, 4 vols (Paris, 1902).
47   M. Durand (ed.) *Congrès International de la Condition et des Droits des Femmes* (Paris, 1901).
48   On these individuals and groups, see Klejman and Rochefort, *L'Egalité en marche*, pp. 182–85.
49   BMD: dossier Misme.
50   BMD: dossier Conseil National des Femmes.
51   BMD: dossiers Monod and Siegfried.
52   BMD: dossier Avril de Sainte-Croix.
53   BMD: dossier de Witt-Schlumberger; Bogelot, *Trente ans de solidarité*.
54   The concept was developed by W.L. O'Neill in *Everyone was Brave: A History of Feminism in America* (Chicago, Quadrangle Books, 1971; original edn, 1969).
55   BMD: dossier CNFF.
56   McMillan, 'Wollstonecraft's daughters'.
57   BMD: dossier *Action sociale de la Femme*. Also J.F. McMillan, 'Women in social Catholicism in late nineteenth and early twentieth-century France', in W.J. Sheils and D. Wood (eds) *Women and the Church (Studies in Church History* no. 27) (Oxford, Blackwell, 1990), pp. 467–80, and S.

Notes

Fayet-Scribe, *Associations féminines et catholicisme: de la charité à l'action sociale xixe–xxe siècle* (Paris, Les Editions Ouvrières, 1990).

58 L'Abbé Naudet, *Pour la femme: études féministes* (Paris, 1903), Preface; A.D. Sertillanges, *Féminisme et christianisme* (Paris, 1908), and C. Turgeon, *Le féminisme français*, 2 vols (Paris, 1902).

59 Turgeon, *Le féminisme français*, vol. 1, Chapter 2, esp. pp. 71 and 73.

60 Hause and Kenney, 'The development of the Catholic women's suffrage movement'.

61 Sowerwine, *Sisters or Citizens?*, pp. 81–97.

62 C. Sowerwine, 'The organization of French socialist women 1880–1914: a European perspective for women's movements', *Historical Reflexions*, 3, 1976, pp. 3–24.

63 Hause, *Hubertine Auclert*, Chapter 9.

64 Ibid., p. 183ff.

65 Hause with Kenney, *Women's Suffrage and Social Politics*, pp. 77–78, and Auclert, *Les femmes au gouvernail*, p. 71.

66 Hause with Kenney, *Women's Suffrage and Social Politics*, pp. 79–81.

67 Ibid., pp. 94–96.

68 Hause, *Hubertine Auclert*, p. 194ff., and Auclert, *Le vote des femmes*.

69 BMD: dossier Pelletier. The literature on Pelletier is now extensive. See in particular F. Gordon, *The Integral Feminist: Madeleine Pelletier, 1874–1939* (Cambridge, Polity Press, 1990); C. Sowerwine and C. Maignien, *Madeleine Pelletier: une féministe dans l'arène politique* (Paris, Les Editions Ouvrières, 1992); C. Bard, (ed.) *Madeleine Pelletier (1874–1939): logiques et infortunes d'un combat pour l'égalité* (Paris, Côté-Femmes, 1992); M. Boxer, 'When radical and socialist feminism were joined: the extraordinary failure of Madeleine Pelletier', in J. Slaughter and R. Kern (eds) *European Women of the Left: Socialism, Feminism and the Problems Faced by Political Women, 1880 to the Present* (Westport, Connecticut and London, Greenwood Press, 1981), pp. 51–74; and J.W. Scott, 'The radical individualism of Madeleine Pelletier', in *Only Paradoxes to Offer*, pp. 125–60.

70 Scott, 'The radical individualism of Madeleine Pelletier'.

71 M. Pelletier, *L'Emancipation sexuelle de la femme* (Paris, 1911) and *La désagrégation de la famille* (Paris, n.d.).

72 M. Pelletier, *L'Amour et la maternité* (Paris, n.d.).

73 M. Pelletier, *Le droit à l'avortement* (Paris, 2nd edn, 1913).

74 M. Pelletier, *La femme en lutte pour ses droits* (Paris, 1906).

75 M. Pelletier, 'Les femmes et le féminisme', *La Revue Socialiste*, January 1906, pp. 37–45.

76 Scott, 'The radical individualism of Madeleine Pelletier', p. 135.

77 M. Pelletier, *Philosophie sociale: les opinions, les partis, les classes* (Paris, 1912), p. 142.

78 M. Pelletier, *L'Admission des femmes dans la franc-maçonnerie* (Paris, 1905).

79 M. Pelletier, *Mon voyage aventureux en Russie* (Paris, 1922).

80 Pelletier, *La femme en lutte pour ses droits*. Also, M. Pelletier, 'La question du vote des femmes', *La Revue Socialiste*, September–October 1908, pp. 193–206.

81 M. Pelletier, 'La tactique féministe', *La Revue Socialiste*, April 1908. Quoted in Bell and Offen (eds) *Women, the Family and Freedom*, vol. 2, pp. 105–6.

82 BMD: dossier Remember; *La Suffragiste*, October and November 1911.

83 BMD: dossier Arria-Ly; BHVP, Fonds Bouglé, papers of Arria-Ly; *Le Combat féministe*, July 1914.

84 BMD: dossier Roussel; N. Roussel, *L'Eternelle sacrifiée*, eds D. Armogathe and M. Albistur (Paris, 1979). English translation in J. Waelti-Walters and S.C. Hause (eds) *Feminisms of the Belle Epoque: A Historical and Literary Anthology* (Lincoln, Nebraska and London, University of Nebraska Press, 1994), pp. 18–41.

85 Avril de Sainte-Croix, *Le féminisme* (Paris, 1907).

86 BMD: dossier Congrès National des Droits Civils et du Suffrage des Femmes; *Congrès National des Droits Civils et du Suffrage des Femmes, 26–28 juin 1908, compte-rendu par Mme Oddo-Deflou* (Paris, 1911).

87 *La Française*, 16 May 1914.

Notes

88 *La Française*, 4 April 1914.
89 BMD: dossier Union française pour le Suffrage des Femmes.
90 BMD: dossier Brunschwicg.
91 BMD: dossier Conseil National des Femmes Françaises; *La Française*, 7 February 1914.
92 BMD: dossier Groupements femmes; L'Action féministe.
93 Hause with Kenney, *Women's Suffrage and Social Politics*, pp. 124–28.
94 Ibid., pp. 145–51. For Renaud's campaign in the Isère, see also Sowerwine, *Sisters or Citizens?*, pp. 124–26.
95 Sowerwine, *Sisters or Citizens?*, p. 126.
96 BMD: dossier Vérone.
97 APP B/a 1651: Le mouvement féministe (1880–1914), report of 6 July 1914.
98 N. Roussel, *Créeons la citoyenne* (Paris, 1914), in *Trois conférences* (Paris, 1930). English translation in Waelti-Walters and Hause (eds) *French Feminisms*, pp. 278–91, quotation at p. 279.
99 *La Française*, 9 May 1914.
100 APP B/a 1651: report of 6 July 1914.

Epilogue

1 McMillan, *Housewife or Harlot*, pp. 178–79.
2 *Minerva*, 5 July 1925.
3 B. Harrison, *Separate Spheres: The Opposition to Women's Suffrage in Britain* (London, Croom Helm, 1978).
4 A. Lampérière, *Le rôle social de la femme* (Paris, 1898).
5 C. Yver, *Dans le jardin du féminisme* (Paris, 1920). For an (unconvincing) attempt to represent Yver as a 'closet feminist', see J. Waelti-Walters, *Feminist Novelists of the Belle Epoque: Love as a Lifestyle* (Bloomington and Indianapolis, Indiana University Press, 1990).
6 L. Zanta, *Psychologie du féminisme* (Paris, 1922).
7 Mme Rachilde, *Pourquoi je ne suis pas féministe* (Paris, 1928).
8 T. Joran, *Le mensonge du féminisme* (Paris, 1905), quoted in Racine, *Entre hommes*, pp. 123–25.
9 Offen, 'Depopulation, nationalism and feminism'.
10 A. Leclère, *Le vote des femmes en France: les causes de l'attitude particulière à notre pays* (Law thesis, Paris, 1929).
11 T. Joran, 'Le féminisme à l'heure actuelle', *Revue Internationale de Sociologie*, May 1907, pp. 321–36. See also his *Au coeur du féminisme* (Paris, 1908).
12 Abbé H. Bolo, *La femme et le clergé* (Paris, 1902).
13 See Waelti-Walters, *Feminist Novelists of the Belle Epoque*.
14 E. Berenson, *The Trial of Madame Caillaux* (Berkeley and Oxford, University of California Press, 1992).
15 Cf. Harris, *Murder and Madness*, and J. Goldstein, *Console and Classify: The French Psychiatric Profession in the Nineteenth Century* (Cambridge, Cambridge University Press, 1987).
16 Scott, *Only Paradoxes to Offer*.
17 Hause with Kenney, *Women's Suffrage and Social Politics*, p. 153.
18 AN F7 12544: report of 7 October 1904.
19 Quoted by E. Sullerot, *La presse féminine* (Paris, 1963), p. 43.
20 L. Weiss, *Mémoires d'une Européenne*: Vol. 2 *Années de lutte pour le droit du suffrage, 1934–1939* (Paris, Julliard, 1946), p. 22.
21 The literature on British suffragism is now enormous. A good introduction is S.S. Holton, 'Women and the vote', in *Women's History: Britain, 1850–1945* (London, UCL Press, 1995), pp. 277–306.
22 S. Hoffman (ed.) *France: Change and Tradition* (London, Gollancz, 1963).
23 *La Française*, 5 May 1923.
24 Article in *L'Oeuvre*, quoted by F. Golland, *Les féministes françaises* (Paris, 1925), p. 177.
25 Hilden, *Working Women and Socialist Politics*, p. 165.

Notes

26 See, in general, M-H. Zylberberg-Hocquard, *Féminisme et syndicalisme en France avant 1914* (Paris, Anthropos, 1978). For Guillot's views, *L'Ecole Emancipée*, 4 February and 22 April 1911.

27 *L'Ecole Emancipée*, 25 February 1911.

28 *L'Ecole Emancipée*, 19 November 1910.

29 *L'Ecole Emancipée*, 1 April and 17 June 1911.

30 Sowerwine, *Sisters or Citizens?*, pp. 129–39.

31 Ibid., pp. 132–33.

32 *L'Equité*, 15 August and 15 November 1913. See also H. Bouchardeau, *Hélène Brion, la voie féministe* (Paris, Syros, 1978).

33 Sowerwine, *Sisters or Citizens?*, pp. 138–39.

34 J.F. McMillan, 'Women, religion and politics: the case of the Ligue Patriotique des Françaises', in W. Roosen (ed.) *Proceedings of the Annual Meeting of the Western Society for French History* (Flagstaff, Arizona, 1988), vol. 15, pp. 355–64. In addition, see O. Sarti, *The Ligue Patriotique des Françaises 1902–1933: A Feminine Response to the Secularization of French Society* (New York and London, Garland Publishing Inc., 1992).

35 Pelletier, *La femme en lutte pour ses droits*, p. 60.

36 Sowerwine, *Sisters or Citizens?*, p. 110.

37 G. Clemenceau, *La "Justice" du sexe fort* (Paris, 1907).

38 M. Larkin, *Church and State after the Dreyfus Affair: The Separation Issue in France* (London, Macmillan, 1974), p. 7.

39 Ozouf, *Les mots des femmes*.

40 P. Rosanvallon, *Le sacre du citoyen: histoire du suffrage universel en France* (Paris, Gallimard, 1992).

Bibliography

Unpublished primary sources

1. Archives Nationales (AN)

Series F7 is particularly useful for police files and press cuttings on feminist organisations and meetings. F17 is indispensable for information on the progress of girls' education. F22 has rich documentation on work and the application of labour legislation. See in particular:

Sous-série F7: Police générale

F7: 12652: Publications obscènes: traite des blanches (1910)
      13266: Assemblée Nationale de Versailles

Sous-série F17: Instruction publique

F17: 8753–84: Enseignement secondaire des jeunes filles; lycées et cours secondaires (1867–97)
       8754–56: Dossiers classés par académies (1867–68)
       8757–70: Dossiers classés par académies (1879–86)
       8771–78: Cours secondaires de jeunes filles transformés ou supprimés (ordre alphabétique des noms de villes) (1881–86)
       8779–80: Affaires diverses (1880–85)
       8781–83: Etats de traitements (1886–90)
       8784: Affaires diverses
       8785–99: Certificat d'aptitude à l'enseignement secondaire des jeunes filles: agrégation dudit enseignement
       8800–07: Diplôme de fin d'études secondaires des jeunes filles (1893–95)
       8808–14: Ecole Normale de Sèvres (1882–96)
       9398: Articles de journaux (1880–95)
       9399: Articles de journaux (1880–1901)
       12440–41: Application de la loi du 16 juin 1881 sur les écoles de jeunes filles
       14187: Ecole Normale de Sèvres
       14201–05: Agrégation et certificat d'aptitude (CAP): procès-verbaux et listes d'admissibles (1894–98)

Sous-série F22: Travail et prévoyance sociale

F22: 438–43: Travail des femmes et des enfants (1886–1937)

438: Législation, enquêtes, jugements (1886–1930)

439: Infractions à la législation (1894–1931)

440: Application du décret du 28 déc. 1909 sur les surcharges imposées aux femmes et aux enfants (1910–14)

441: Application des décrets du 13 mai 1893 et 21 mars 1914 (1893–1930)

442–43: Travail de nuit des femmes (1894–1937)

444–48: Protection de la maternité

458–61: Travail des femmes et des enfants: commissions départementales du travail et comités de patronage (1872–1938)

462–72: Travail des femmes et des enfants (1898–1922)

512–14: Hygiène des travailleurs (1902–29)

2. Archives de la Préfecture de Police (APP)

More police files on individual feminists and meetings of groups.

B/a 885: dossier Auclert

1031: dossier Deraismes

1651: Le mouvement féministe

1660: dossier Séverine

3. Bibliothèque Marguerite Durand (BMD)

A marvellous collection of materials relating to all aspects of the history of women and the feminist movement. Particularly useful are the dossiers compiled on individual feminist leaders and on different women's organisations, as well as runs of feminist newspapers.

4. Institut Français d'Histoire Sociale (IFHS)

The Fonds Hélene Brion has an extraordinary collection of materials amassed by Helene Brion with the purpose of bringing out a feminist encyclopaedia. 14 ASP 337 and 14 ASP 338 contain collections of feminist (and other) newspapers.

5. Bibliothèque Historique de la Ville de Paris (BHVP)

This contains the vast array of unpublished papers and printed sources collected in the Fonds Marie-Louise Bouglé.

6. Bibliothèque de l'Arsenal

Houses the Fonds Enfantin, the main source for the history of Saint-Simonian women.

Published primary sources

1. Feminist newspapers and periodicals

La Tribune des Femmes, La Voix des Femmes, La Politique des Femmes, L'Opinion des Femmes, L'Almanach des Femmes, Le Droit des Femmes, La Citoyenne, Le Journal des Femmes, La Fronde, La Française, La Suffragiste, L'Equité, L'Action féministe, Le Combat féministe, Le Féminisme intégral, La Femme affranchie, La Femme Socialiste, L'Action sociale de la Femme, Le Féminisme chrétien.

2. Other newspapers and journals

L'Assiette au Beurre, Gil Blas Illustré, Le Rire, La Vie Ouvrière, La Bataille Syndicaliste, La Revue Socialiste, L'Ecole Emancipée, La Gazette des Tribunaux, La Revue.

3. Contemporary books, pamphlets and articles

Abram, P. *L'Evolution du mariage* (Paris, 1908).

Acker, P. *Oeuvres sociales de femmes* (Paris, 1908).

Aftalion, A. *Le développement de la fabrique et le travail à domicile dans les industries de l'habillement* (Paris, 1906).

d'Agoult, Comtesse. *Mémoires, souvenirs et journaux de la comtesse d'Agoult (Daniel Stern)*. Présentation et notes de C.F. Dupêchez, 2 vols (Paris, Mercure de France, 1990).

Aimé-Martin, L. *De l'éducation des mères de famille, ou de la civilisation du genre humain par les femmes* (Paris, 1834).

Andrieux, L. *Souvenirs d'un préfet de police*, 2 vols (Paris, 1885).

Auclert, H. *Le droit politique des femmes: question qui n'est pas traitée au Congrès International des Femmes* (Paris, 1878).

—— *Le vote des femmes* (Paris, 1908).

—— *Les femmes au gouvernail* (Paris, 1923).

Audiganne, A. *Les populations ouvrières et les industries de la France*, 2 vols (Paris, 1860).

Audouard, A. *Guerre aux hommes* (Paris, 1866).

—— *La femme dans le mariage, la séparation et le divorce, conférence faite le 28 février 1870* (Paris, 1870).

Avigdor, P. *Examen critique des tendances modernes dans le mariage et vers l'union libre* (Paris, 1909).

Avril de Sainte-Croix. *Le féminisme* (Paris, 1907).

Bader, C. *La femme française dans les temps modernes* (Paris, 1883).

Baggio, C. *Petit catéchisme socialiste ou la conquête des femmes au socialisme* (Paris, 1888).

de Balzac, H. *The Physiology of Marriage* (London, 1904).

Barbey d'Aurevilly, J. *Les bas-bleus* (Paris, 1878).

Bastien, P. *Les carrières de la jeune fille* (Paris, 1903).

Bayle-Mouillard, E-F. (Mme Celnart). *Manuel de la bonne compagnie, ou guide de la politesse et de la bienséance* (Paris, 1834).

Benoist, C. *Les ouvrières de l'aiguille à Paris* (Paris, 1895).

Berth, E. 'Le centenaire de Proudhon', *Le Mouvement Socialiste*, 1 January 1909.

Blum, L. *Du mariage* (Paris, 1907).

Bibliography

Bogelot, I. *Trente ans de solidarité 1877–1906* (Paris, 1906).

Bois, J. *L'Eve nouvelle* (Paris, 1913).

Bolo, Abbé H. *La femme et le clergé* (Paris, 1902).

Bonald, Vicomte de. *Du divorce considéré au dix-neuvième siècle relativement à l'etat public de la société* (Paris, 1818).

Bonnecase, J. *Le féminisme et le régime dotal* (Law thesis, Toulouse, 1905).

Bonneff, L. and M. *Les métiers qui tuent: enquête auprès des syndicats ouvriers sur les maladies professionnelles* (Paris, n.d.).

Bonnefoy, A. *Place aux femmes! Les carrières féminines administratives et libérales* (Paris, 1914).

Bonnevay, L. *Les ouvrières lyonnaises travaillant à domicile* (Paris, 1896).

Bonnier, C. *La femme et le socialisme* (Lille, 1893).

—— *La question de la femme* (Paris, 1897).

Bouvier, Abbé C. *Le besoin d'une éducation supérieure chez les femmes* (Paris, 1909).

Bouvier, J. *Mes mémoires: ou 59 années d'activité industrielle, sociale et intellectuelle d'une ouvrière* (Paris, 1936).

Braun, L. *Le problème de la femme* (Paris, 1908).

Bridel, L. *Questions féministes* (Paris, 1896).

—— *Mélanges féministes: questions de droit et de sociologie* (Paris, 1897).

Buisson, F. *Rapport: le droit de vote des femmes* (Paris, 1909).

Bureau, P. *L'Indiscipline des moeurs* (Paris, 1927).

Buret, E. *De la misère des classes laborieuses en Angleterre et en France* (Paris, 1840).

Butler, J. *Personal Reminiscences of a Great Crusade* (London, 1896).

Cabanis, P-J-G. *Rapports du physique et du moral de l'homme en France* (Paris, 1802; Geneva, Slatkine reprints, 1980).

Cadet, E. *Le mariage en France* (Paris, 1870).

Cahen, G. 'L'Ouvrière en chambre à Paris', *La Revue Bleue*, 19 May 1906, pp. 636–39.

Caron, M. *Le mariage de l'ouvrier* (Law thesis, Poitiers, 1901).

de Céez, F. *En attendant l'avenir: aux jeunes filles* (Paris, 1905).

Cetty, H. *Le mariage dans les classes ouvrières* (Action populaire, 4th series, no. 74) (Paris, 1905).

Chauvet, E. *Le travail: études morales: les domestiques* (Caen, 1896).

Chéliga, M. 'Les hommes féministes', *Revue Encyclopédique Larousse*, 1896, pp. 825–31.

Chéreau, A. *Mémoires pour servir à l'étude des maladies des ovaires* (Paris, 1844).

Choquenay, A. *L'Emancipation de la femme au commencement du vingtième siècle* (Paris, 1902).

Cinquante ans de féminisme 1870–1921 (Paris, LFDF, 1921).

Clamorgan, P. *Le travail de la femme et la bien faisance privée à Paris* (Law thesis, Paris, 1908).

Combat, E. and F. *Le travail des femmes à domicile. Textes officiels, avec commentaire explicatif et étude générale sur les salaires féminins* (Paris, 1916).

Commenge, Dr O. *La prostitution clandestine à Paris* (Paris, 1897).

Condorcet, M.J.A.N. Marquis de. *Lettres d'un bourgeois de New Haven à un citoyen de Virginie* (1787), in A.C. O'Connor and M.F. Arago (eds) *Oeuvres de Condorcet*, 12 vols (Paris, 1847), vol. 9.

—— *Essai sur la constitution et les fonctions des assemblées provinciales* (1788), ibid., vol. 8.

—— *Essai sur l'admission des femmes au droit de la cité* (1790), ibid., vol. 10.

Cusenier, M. *Les domestiques en France* (Law thesis, Paris, 1912).

Damez, A. *Le libre salaire de la femme mariée et le mouvement féministe* (Law thesis, Lyon, 1905).

Dangennes, B. *Ce que toute femme moderne doit savoir* (Paris, n.d.).

—— *La jeune fille et l'émancipation* (Paris, n.d.).

—— *Mariée ou non, la femme doit être indépendante* (Paris, n.d.).

Daubié, J. *La femme pauvre au dix-neuvième siècle* (Paris, 1866).

Bibliography

—— L'émancipation de la femme (Paris, 1871).

Debay, A. Hygiène et physiologie du mariage (Paris, 1848).

Deherme, G. Le pouvoir social des femmes (Paris, 1914).

Delzons, L. La famille française et son évolution (Paris, 1913).

Démar, C. Appel d'une femme au peuple sur l'affranchissement de la femme (Paris, 1833).

—— Ma loi d'avenir (Paris, 1834).

Deraismes, M. La femme et le droit, in M. Deraismes, Oeuvres complètes, 3 vols (Paris, 1895–96), vol. 2.

—— Eve contre M. Dumas fils (Paris, 1872).

—— France et progrès (Paris, 1873).

Dereux, R. Le budget matrimonial (Law thesis, Lille, 1923).

Deroin, J. Almanach des femmes (London and Jersey, 1852, 1853, 1854).

Desmothes, Père J., S.J. Les devoirs des filles chrétiennes pour une vie chaste et vertueuse dans le monde (Paris, 3rd edn, 1719).

Diderot, D. 'On women', in Dialogues (London, George Routledge and Sons, 1827; first published 1772).

Dissard, C. Opinions féministes à propos du congrès féministe de 1896 (Paris, 1896).

de Donville, F. Guide pour les professions de femmes (Paris, 1894).

Droz, G. Monsieur, madame et bébé (Paris, 1866).

Dubois, R. De la condition juridique des domestiques (Law thesis, Paris, 1907).

Duguet, J-J. Conduite d'une dame chrétienne pour vivre sainement dans le monde (Paris, 1725).

Dumas fils, A. L'Homme-femme. Réponse à M. Henri d'Ideville (Paris, 1872).

—— Les femmes qui tuent et les femmes qui votent (Paris, 1880).

Dupanloup, Mgr F. M. Duruy et l'éducation des filles: lettre à un de ses collègues (Paris, 1867).

—— Seconde lettre sur M. Duruy et l'éducation des filles (Paris, 1867).

—— Lettres sur l'éducation des filles et sur l'education qui conviennent aux femmes dans le monde (Paris, 2nd edn, 1879).

Dupin, Baron C. Forces productives et commerciales de la France, 2 vols (Paris, 1827).

L'Encyclopédie, ou Dictionnaire raisonné des sciences, des arts et des métiers, eds D. Diderot and J. d'Alembert, 17 vols (Paris, 1751–65), esp. vol. 6.

Eyquem, A. Le régime dotal: son historie, son évolution et ses transformations au dix-neuvième siècle sous l'influence de la jurisprudence et du notariat (Paris, 1903).

Fabre, A. Le féminisme: ses origines et son avenir (Paris, 1897).

Faguet, E. Le féminisme (Paris, 1907).

Féline, Le Père. Catéchisme des gens mariés (Paris, 1880).

Ferry, J. Discours sur l'éducation: l'egalité d'éducation (Paris, 1870).

Fiaux, L. La femme, le mariage et le divorce. Etude de psychologie et de sociologie (Paris, 1880).

—— La police des moeurs devant la commission extra-parlementaire du régime des moeurs, 3 vols (Paris, 1907–10).

Fletcher, M. Christian Feminism: A Charter of Rights and Duties (London, 1915).

Fouin, L-J. De l'état des domestiques en France et des moyens propres à les moraliser (Paris, 1837).

Fourier, C. Théorie des quatre mouvements et des destinées générales. Prospectus et annonce de la découverte (Paris, Jean-Jacques Pauvert, 1967).

Fournier, F. Des domestiques d'aujourd'hui (Paris, 1877).

Gacon-Dufour, M-A. Mémoire pour le sexe féminin contre le sexe masculin (Paris and London, 1787).

Gemahling, M. Le salaire féminin (Paris, 1912).

Gemahling, P. Travailleurs au rabais. La lutte contre les sous-concurrences ouvrières (Paris, 1910).

Genlis, Comtesse de. Adelaide and Theodore: Or Letters on Education, 3 vols (London, 1783).

Bibliography

Gibergues, Abbé de. *Les devoirs des hommes envers les femmes, instructions aux hommes du monde prêchées à Saint-Philippe du Roule et à Saint-Augustin* (Paris, 1903).

Gibon, F. *Employées et ouvrières* (Paris, 1906).

de Girardin, E. *L'Egale de l'homme* (Paris, 1881).

Goblot, E. *La barrière et le niveau* (Paris, 1925).

Golland, F. *Les féministes françaises* (Paris, 1925).

Gonnard, R. *La femme dans l'industrie* (Paris, 1906).

Granotier, P. *L'Autorité du mari sur la personne de la femme et la doctrine féministe* (Law thesis, Grenoble, 1909).

Gréard, O. *Education et instruction: enseignement secondaire*, vol. 1 (Paris, 1887).

Grimanelli, P. *La femme et le positivisme* (Paris, 1905).

Guillou, R. *La Française dans ses quatre âges* (Paris, 3rd edn, 1911).

Guizot, P. *Lettres de famille sur l'education* (Paris, 1824).

Guyot, Y. *La prostitution* (Paris, 1880).

Haussonville, Comte d'. *Salaires et misèrs de femmes* (Paris, 1900).

d'Héricourt, J. *La femme affranchie: réponse à MM Michelet, Proudhon, E. de Girardin, A. Comte et autres novateurs modernes*, 2 vols (Brussels, 1860).

Hoppenot, J., S.J. *Petit catéchisme du mariage* (Paris, new edn, 1920).

Jeannel, Dr J. *De la prostitution dans les grandes villes au dix-neuvième siècle* (Paris, 1868).

Joran, T. *Autour du féminisme* (Paris, 1906).

—— 'Le féminisme à l'heure actuelle', *Revue Internationale de Sociologie*, May 1907, pp. 321–36.

—— *Au coeur du féminisme* (Paris, 1908).

Lacour, L. *Les origines du féminisme contemporain: trois femmes de la Révolution: Olympe de Gouges, Théroigne de Méricourt et Rose Lacombe* (Paris, 1912).

Lafargue, P. *La question de la femme* (Paris, 1904).

Lainé, A. *Les demoiselles de magasin à Paris* (Law thesis, Paris, 1911).

Lambert, J. (Mme Adam). *Idées anti-proudhoniennes sur l'amour, la femme et le mariage* (Paris, 2nd edn, 1861).

Lampérière, A. *Le rôle social de la femme* (Paris, 1898).

Lamy, E. *La femme de demain* (Paris, 1901).

de Lanessan, J-L. *L'Education de la femme moderne* (Paris, 1908).

Lapie, P. *La femme dans la famille* (Paris, 1908).

La Tour du Pin, Marquise de. *Memoirs of Madame de La Tour du Pin*, ed. F. Harcourt (London, Harvill Press, 1969).

Leclère, A. *Le vote des femmes en France: les causes de l'attitude particulière à notre pays* (Law thesis, Paris, 1929).

Lecour, C.J. *La prostitution à Paris et a Londres 1789–1871* (Paris, 1877).

Legouvé, E. *Histoire morale des femmes* (Paris, 1848).

—— 'Les domestiques d'autrefois et ceux d'aujourd'hui', *Revue des cours littéraires*, 13 March 1869.

Legrand, L. *Le mariage et les moeurs en France* (1879).

Le Play, F. *L'Organisation de la famille* (Paris, 1870).

—— *La réforme sociale en France, déduite de l'observation comparée des peuples européens*, 2 vols (Tours, 1878).

Leroy-Beaulieu, P. *Le travail des femmes au dix-neuvième siècle* (Paris, 1873).

Lesueur, D. *L'Evolution féminine: ses résultats économiques* (Paris, 1900).

Letourneau, C. *L'Evolution du mariage et de la famille* (Paris, 1888).

Leyret, H. *En plein faubourg (Moeurs ouvrières)* (Paris, 1895).

Loria, A. 'Le féminisme au point de vue sociologique', *Revue Internationale de Sociologie*, January 1907, pp. 5–17.

Bibliography

Lupiac, J. *La loi du 10 juillet 1915 pour la protection des ouvrières dans l'industrie du vêtement* (Law thesis, Paris, 1918).

de Maistre, J-M. *Les soirées de Saint-Petersbourg: ou entretiens sur le gouvernement temporel de la providence* (Paris, 1821).

Margueritte, P. 'L'Evolution de la morale et de l'amour', *La Revue*, 1 August 1907, pp. 329–37.

Marion, H. *L'Education des jeunes filles* (Paris, 1902).

Marx, K. and Engels, F. *Writings on the Paris Commune*, ed. H. Draper (New York, Monthly Review Press, 1971).

Mény, G. *La lutte contre le sweating-system* (Law thesis, Paris, 1910).

Mercier, T. *Le rôle de la femme dans la société* (Paris, 1908).

Michel, L. *Mémoires* (Paris, 1886).

Michelet, J. *Du prêtre, de la femme, et de la famille* (Paris, 1845).

—— *L'Amour* (Paris, 1858).

—— *La femme* (Paris, 1860).

—— *Les femmes de la Révolution de Michelet*, ed. F. Giroud (Paris, Editions Carrere, 1988).

Milhaud, C. *L'Ouvrière en France* (Paris, 1907).

Mireur, Dr H. *La prostitution à Marseille* (Paris, 1882).

Mittre, M. *Des domestiques en France dans leurs rapports avec l'économie sociale, le bonheur domestique, les lois civils* (Paris, 1837).

Moissinac, P. *Le contrat de mariage de séparation de biens* (Paris, 2nd edn, 1924).

Moll-Weiss, A. *Le livre du foyer* (Paris, 1912).

Monnet, J. *Le contrat de mariage et son utilité* (Paris, 1924).

Monnier, M.F. *De l'organisation du travail manuel des jeunes filles: les internats industriels* (Paris, 1869).

Naquet, A. *Religion, propriété, famille* (Paris, 1869).

Naudet, L'Abbé. *Pour la femme: études féministes* (Paris, 1903).

Necker de Saussure, A. *The Study of the Life of Woman* (Philadelphia, 1844; Paris, original French edn, 1838).

Niboyet, E. *Le vrai livre des femmes* (Paris, 1863).

Nikitine, Mme. 'La prétendue infériorité de la femme', *La Réforme Economique*, 1 August and 1 September 1880.

Oddo-Deflou, J. *Le sexualisme* (Paris, 1906).

Ollivier, E. *Le féminisme: conférence faite dans une assemblée des dames de l'Action sociale de la Femme*, 31 May 1902 (Paris, 1902).

Ostrogorski, M. *The Rights of Women* (London, 1893).

Paquier, J-B. *L'Enseignement professionnel en France* (Paris, 1908).

Parent-Duchâtelet, A-J-B. *De la prostitution dans la ville de Paris considéré sous le rapport de l'hygiène publique, de la morale et de l'administration*, 2 vols (Paris, 1836).

Pelletier, M. *L'Admission des femmes dans la franc-maçonnerie* (Paris, 1905).

—— *La femme en lutte pour ses droits* (Paris, 1906).

—— 'Les femmes et le féminisme', *La Revue Socialiste*, January 1906.

—— 'La tactique féministe', *La Revue Socialiste*, April 1908.

—— 'La question du vote des femmes', *La Revue Socialiste*, September–October 1908.

—— *L'Emancipation sexuelle de la femme* (Paris, 1911).

—— *Philosophie sociale: les opinions, les partis, les classes* (Paris, 1912).

—— *Le droit à l'avortement* (Paris, 2nd edn, 1913).

—— *Mon voyage aventureux en Russie* (Paris, 1922).

—— *La désagrégation de la famille* (Paris, n.d.).

—— *L'Amour et la maternité* (Paris, n.d.).

Bibliography

Perennes, F. *De la domesticité avant et depuis 1789* (Paris, 1844).

Pléven, C. *La semaine anglaise à l'étranger et en France. Son application dans le département du Finistère* (Law thesis, Rennes, Dinan, 1914)

Pottecher, T. *Le mouvement féministe en France* (*La Grande Revue*, 1910, *Pages Libres*).

Power, E. (ed. and transl.) *The Goodman of Paris* (London, 1928) [*Le Ménagier de Paris* (c.1393].

Prévost, M. *Lettres à Françoise* (Paris, 1902).

Proudhon, P.J. *Système des contradictions économiques, ou philosophie de la misère*: Vol. 2 *La propriété* (Paris, 1846).

—— *De la justice dans la Révolution et dans l'Eglise* (Paris, 1858).

—— *La pornocratie, ou les femmes dans les temps modernes* (Paris, 1875).

Rachilde, Mme. *Pourquoi je ne suis pas féministe* (Paris, 1928).

Razous, Mlle M-Th. *Guide pratique des femmes et des jeunes filles dans le choix d'une profession* (Paris, 1910).

Regnal, Mme G. *Comment la femme peut gagner sa vie* (Paris, 1908).

de Rémusat, Mme. *Essai sur l'éducation des femmes* (Paris, 1824).

Restif de la Bretonne, N-E. *Les Gynographes, ou Idées de deux honnêtes femmes sur un projet de règlement proposé à toute l'Europe pour mettre les femmes à leur place et opérer le bonheur des deux sexes* (The Hague, 1777; Geneva, Slatkine reprints, 1988).

Reybaud, L. *Rapport sur la condition morale, intellectuelle et matérielle des ouvriers qui vivent de l'industrie de coton* (Paris, 1863).

de Ribbe, C. *Les domestiques dans la famille* (Paris, 1862).

—— *La vie domestique, ses modèles et ses règles d'après des documents originaux*, 2 vols (Paris, 1877).

Richer, L. *La femme libre* (Paris, 1877).

Rivière, E. *Le travail de la femme dans l'industrie typographe (étude sur le salaire)* (Paris, 1898).

Robert, E. *Les domestiques: étude de moeurs et d'histoire* (Paris, 1825).

Rochejaquelein, Marquise de la. *Mémoires de la Marquise de la Rochejaquelein 1772–1857* (Paris, Mercure de France, 1984).

Romieu, Mme. *La femme au dix-neuvième siècle* (Paris, 1859).

Rouquet, M. *L'Evolution du droit de famille vers l'individualisme* (Law thesis, Montpellier, 1909).

Rousseau, J-J. *A Letter of M. Rousseau of Geneva, to M. d'Alembert of Paris, Concerning the Effects of Theatrical Entertainments on the Manners of Mankind* (London, 1759).

—— *Julie: ou la nouvelle Heloïse* (1761).

—— *Emile* (London, Dent, 1911).

Roussel, N. *Créons la citoyenne* (Paris, 1914), in *Trois conférences* (Paris, 1930).

—— *L'Eternelle sacrificiée*, eds D. Armogathe and M. Albistur (Paris, 1979).

Roussel, P. *Système physique et moral de la femme* (Paris, 1775).

Rozier, P.M. *De la condition sociale des femmes* (Paris, 2nd edn, 1842).

de Saint-Simon, H. *Le nouveau christianisme et les écrits sur la religion. Textes choisis et présentés par H. Desroche* (Paris, Le Seuil, 1969).

Schirmacher, K. 'Le travail des femmes en France', *Musée Social, Mémoires et Documents*, May 1902.

Schuyten, M-C. *L'Education de la femme* (Paris, 1908).

Sée, C. *Lycées et collèges de jeunes filles: documents, rapports et discours à la Chambre des Députés et au Sénat: decrets, arrêtés, circulaires, etc. relatifs à la loi sur l'enseignement secondaire des filles* (Paris, 1884).

Sertillanges, A.D. *Féminisme et christianisme* (Paris, 1908).

Simon, J. *L'Ouvrière* (Paris, 1861).

—— *La femme au vingtième siècle* (Paris, 1892).

Staffe, Baronne. *Usages du monde: règles de savoir-vivre dans la société moderne* (Paris, 1889).

Stanton, T. *The Woman Question in Europe* (New York, 1884).

Thomas, A. *An Account of the Character, the Manners, and the Understanding of Women, in Different Ages, and Different Parts of the World* (London, J. Dodsley, 1800).
Tristan, F. *Pérégrinations d'une paria: Dieu, franchise, liberté*, 2 vols (Paris, 1838).
—— *L'Union ouvrière* (Paris, 1843).
Turgeon, C. *Le féminisme français*, 2 vols (Paris, 1902).
Turmann, M. *Le syndicalisme chrétien en France* (Paris, 1929).
Uzanne, O. *La femme à Paris, nos contemporaines* (Paris, 1894).
Valensi, A. *L'Application de la loi du divorce en France* (Law thesis, Montpellier, 1905).
(Valette, A. and Bonnier, P.) *Socialisme et sexualisme: programme du Parti socialiste français* (Paris, 1893).
Vallier, J. *Le travail des femmes dans l'industrie française* (Law thesis, Grenoble, 1899).
Vérone, M. *La femme et la loi* (Paris, n.d.).
Villemont, Dr. *L'Amour conjugal* (Paris, 1885).
Villemot, A. *Enseignement secondaire: documents, publications et ouvrages relatifs à l'éducation secondaire des jeunes filles* (Paris, 1889).
de Villeneuve-Bargemont, A. *Economie politique chrétienne, ou recherches sur la nature et les causes du paupérisme en France et en Europe, et sur les moyens de le soulager et de le prévenir*, 3 vols (Paris, 1834).
Villermé, L-R. *Tableau de l'état physique et morale des ouvriers employés dans les manufactures de coton, de laine et de soie*, 2 vols (Paris, 1840).
Villermont, Comtesse Marie de. *Le mouvement féministe: ses causes, son avenir, solution chrétienne*, 2 vols (Paris, Bloud, 1900–4).
Virey, J-J. *De l'éducation publique et privée des Français* (Paris, 1802).
Voilquin, S. *Souvenirs d'une fille du peuple, ou la Saint-simonienne en Egypte* (Paris, Francois Maspéro, 1978).
Weiss, L. *Années de lutte pour le droit de suffrage: ce que femme veut, 1934–1939* (Paris, Julliard, 1946).
—— *Mémoires d'une Européenne 1893–1919* (Paris, Payot, 1968).
Yver, C. *Dans le jardin du féminisme* (Paris, 1920).
Zanta, L. *Psychologie du féminisme* (Paris, 1922).

4. Proceedings of feminist congresses

Congrès International du Droit des Femmes. Compte rendu des séances plénières (Paris, 1878).
Actes du Congrès International des Oeuvres et Institutions Féminines, 1899 (Paris, 1890).
Congrès Français et International du Droit des Femmes (Paris, 1889).
Voeux adoptés par le Congrès Féministe International, tenu à Paris en 1896 pendant les journées 8 au 12 avril (Paris, n.d.).
Congrès International de la Condition et des Droits des Femmes, ed. M. Durand (Paris, 1901).
Deuxième Congrès International des Oeuvres et Institutions féminines, tenu au Palais des Congrès de l'Exposition Universelle de 1900: compte rendu des travaux par Madame Pégard, 4 vols (Paris, 1902).
Congrès National des Droits Civils et du Suffrage des Femmes, 26–28 juin 1908, compte-rendu par Mme Oddo-Deflou (Paris, 1911).
Dixième Congrès International des Femmes, Oeuvres et Institutions, Droit des Femmes (Paris, 1914).

5. Official sources

Cost of Living in French Towns. Report of an Enquiry by the Board of Trade into Working Class Rents, Housing and Retail Prices, together with the Rates of Wages in Certain Occupations in the Principal Industrial Towns of France (London, 1909).

Bibliography

Publications of the Office du Travail

Enquête sur le travail à domicile dans l'industrie de la lingerie, 4 vols (Paris, 1907–11): Vol. 1 *Paris* (1907); Vol. 2 *Cher, Allier, Loir-et-Cher, Indre, Maine-et-Loire, Sarthe* (1908); Vol. 3 *Seine-Inférieure, Oise, Aisne, Somme, Pas-de-Calais, Nord, Meuse, Meurthe-et-Moselle, Vosges* (1909); Vol. 4 *Rhône, Loire, Isère, Bouches-du Rhône, Gard, Hérault, Aude, Haute-Garonne* (1911).

Enquête sur le travail à domicile dans l'industrie de la fleur artificielle (Paris, 1913).

Enquête sur la réduction de la durée du travail le samedi (semaine anglaise) (Paris, 1913).

Enquête sur le travail à domicile dans l'industrie de la chaussure (Paris, 1914).

'Le travail féminin à Paris, avant et depuis la guerre dans les industries du vêtement', *Bulletin du Ministère du Travail*, October–December 1925 and January–March 1926.

6. Collections of documents and texts

Badinter, E. *Paroles d'hommes* (Paris, POL, 1989).

Beecher, J. and Bienvenu, R. (eds) *The Utopian Vision of Charles Fourier: Selected Texts on Work, Love and Passionate Attraction* (London, Cape, 1972).

Bell, S.G. and Offen, K.M. (eds) *Women, the Family and Freedom: The Debate in Documents*, 2 vols: Vol. 1 *1750–1880*; Vol. 2 *1880–1950* (Stanford, Stanford University Press, 1983).

Berger, I. *Lettres d'institutrices rurales d'autrefois, rédigées à la suite de l'enquête de Fracisque Sarcey en 1897* (Paris, n.d.).

Cahiers des doléances et autres textes (Paris, Éditions des femmes, 1981).

Duhet, P-M. *Les femme et la Révolution, 1789–1794* (Paris, Gallimard/Julliard, 1971).

Gordon, F. and Cross, M. (eds) *Early French Feminisms 1830–1940* (Cheltenham, Edward Elgar, 1996).

Hellerstein, E.O., Hume, L.P. and Offen, K.M. (eds) *Victorian Women: A Documentary Account of Women's Lives in Nineteenth-Century England, France and the United States* (Brighton, The Harvester Press, 1981).

Julia, D. *Les trois couleurs du tableau noir – la Révolution* (Paris, Belin, 1981).

Levy, D.G., Applewhite, H.B. and Johnson, M.D. (eds) *Women in Revolutionary Paris 1789–1795. Selected Documents Translated with Notes and Commentary* (Urbana, Chicago and London, University of Illinois Press, 1979).

Moses, C.G. and Rabine, L.W. (eds) *Feminism, Socialism and French Romanticism* (Bloomington, Indiana University Press, 1993).

Ozouf, J. (ed.) *Nous les maîtres d'école: autobiographies d'instituteurs de la belle époque présentées par Jacques Ozouf* (Paris, Gallimard, Collection Archives, 1967).

Riot-Sarcey, M. (ed.) *De la liberté des femmes. Lettres des dames au Globe (1831–1832)* (Paris, Côté-Femmes, 1992).

Waelti-Walters, J. and Hause, S.C. (eds) *Feminisms of the Belle Epoque: A Historical and Literary Anthology* (Lincoln, Nebraska and London, University of Nebraska Press, 1994).

Secondary sources

Abensour, L. *Histoire générale du féminisme des origines à nos jours* (Geneva, Slatkine reprints, 1977).

Abray, J. 'Feminism in the French Revolution', *American Historical Review*, 80, 1975, pp. 43–62.

Accampo, E. *Industrialization, Family Life and Class Relations: Saint-Chamond 1815–1914* (London, University of California Press, 1989).

Accampo, E.A., Fuchs, R.G. and Stewart, M.L. (eds) *Gender and the Politics of Social Reform in France, 1870–1914* (Baltimore and London, Johns Hopkins University Press, 1995).

Bibliography

Acomb, E.M. *The French Laic Laws 1879–1889* (New York, Columbia University Press, 1941; Octagon, 1967).

Adler, L. *A l'aube du féminisme. Les premières journalistes (1830–1850)* (Paris, Payot, 1979).

—— *Secrets d'alcôve: histoire du couple* (Paris, Hachette, 1983).

Albistur, M. and Armogathe, D. *Histoire du féminisme français* (Paris, Editions des femmes, 1977).

Aminzade, R. *Class, Politics and Early Industrial Capitalism: A Study of Mid-Nineteenth-Century Toulouse* (Albany, State University of New York Press, 1981).

Ancel, M. (ed.) *La condition de la femme mariée dans la société contemporaine* (Paris, 1938).

Anderson, R.D. *Education in France, 1848–1870* (Oxford, Oxford University Press, 1975).

Applewhite, H.B. and Levy, D.G. (eds) *Women and Politics in the Age of the Democratic Revolution* (Ann Arbor, Michigan University Press, 1993).

Ariès, P. *Centuries of Childhood: A Social History of Family Life* (New York, Knopf, 1962).

—— *Histoire des populations françaises et de leurs attitudes devant la vie depuis le xviiie siècle* (Paris, 1971).

Auspitz, K. *The Radical Bourgeoisie: The Ligue de l'Enseignement and the Origins of the Third Republic, 1866–1885* (Cambridge, Cambridge University Press, 1982).

Baker, K.M., Lucas, C., Furet, F. and Ozouf, M. (eds) *The French Revolution and the Creation of Modern Political Culture*, 4 vols (Oxford, Pergamon Press, 1987–94).

Bard, C. (ed.) *Madeleine Pelletier (1874–1939): logiques et infortunes d'un combat pour l'égalité* (Paris, Côté-Femmes, 1992).

Barry, D. *Women and Political Insurgency: France in the Mid-Nineteenth Century* (Basingstoke, Macmillan, 1996).

—— 'Hermance Lesguillon: the diversity of French feminism in the nineteenth century', *French History* (in press).

Benabou, E.M. *La prostitution et la police des moeurs au xviii siècle* (Paris, Perrin, 1987).

Berenson, E. *The Trial of Madame Caillaux* (Berkeley and Oxford, University of California Press, 1992).

Bidelman, P.K. *Pariahs Stand Up! The Founding of the Liberal Feminist Movement in France 1859–1889* (Westport, Connecticut and London, Greenwood Press, 1982).

Blanc, O. *Olympe de Gouges* (Paris, Syros, 1981).

Blum, C. *Rousseau and the Republic of Virtue: The Language of Politics in the French Revolution* (Ithaca, Cornell University Press, 1986).

Bodek, E.G. 'Salonnières and Bluestockings: educational obsolescence and germinating feminism', *Feminist Studies*, 3, nos 3/4 Spring/Summer 1976, pp. 185–99.

Boiron, N-M. *La prostitution dans l'histoire, devant le droit, devant l'opinion* (Paris, 1926).

Bouchardeau, H. *Hélène Brion, la voie féministe* (Paris, Syros, 1978).

Bourdin, I. *Les sociétés populaires à Paris pendant la Révolution* (Paris, 1937).

Bouvier, J. *Histoire des dames dans les postes, télégraphes et téléphones de 1714 à 1929* (Paris, 1940).

Boxer, M. 'When radical and socialist feminism were joined: the extraordinary failure of Madeleine Pelletier', in J. Slaughter and R. Kern (eds) *European Women of the Left: Socialism, Feminism and the Problems Faced by Political Women, 1880 to the Present* (Westport, Connecticut and London, Greenwood Press, 1981), pp. 51–74.

—— 'Women in industrial homework: the flowermakers of Paris in the Belle Epoque', *French Historical Studies*, 17, Spring 1983.

—— 'Protective legislation and home industry: the marginalization of women workers in late nineteenth–early twentieth century France', *Journal of Social History*, Fall 1986, pp. 45–66.

Boxer, M.J. and Quataert, J.H. (eds) *Connecting Spheres: Women in the Western World, 1500 to the Present* (Oxford, Oxford University Press, 1987).

Branca, P. *Women in Europe since 1750* (London, Croom Helm, 1978).

Bibliography

Bridenthal, R. and Koonz, C. (eds) *Becoming Visible: Women in European History* (Boston, Houghton Mifflin Company, 1977).

Bridenthal, R., Koonz, C. and Stuard, S. (eds) *Becoming Visible: Women in European History* (Boston, Houghton Mifflin Company, 2nd edn, 1987).

Brive, M.F. (ed.) *Les femmes et la Révolution française*, 3 vols (Toulouse, Presses Universitaires du Mirail, 1991).

Broder, A. *L'Economie française au xixe siècle* (Paris, Ophrys, 1993).

Brookes, B. 'The feminism of Condorcet and Sophie de Grouchy', *Studies on Voltaire and the Eighteenth Century*, 1980, pp. 297–361.

Bruce, E. *Napoleon and Josephine: An Improbable Marriage* (London, Weidenfeld and Nicolson, 1995).

Caron, F. *An Economic History of Modern France* (London, Methuen, 1979).

Cerati, M. *Le club des citoyennes révolutionnaires* (Paris, Editions sociales, 1966).

Charrier, E. *L'Evolution intellectuelle féminine* (Paris, 1931).

Chevalier, L. *Les Parisiens* (Paris, 1967).

—— *Labouring Classes and Dangerous Classes in Paris during the First Half of the Nineteenth Century* (London, Routledge and Kegan Paul, 1973).

Cholvy, G. and Hilaire, Y-M. *Histoire religieuse de la France contemporaine*: Vol. 1 *1800–1880* (Toulouse, Privat, 1985).

Clark, F. *The Position of Women in Contemporary France* (London, 1937).

Clark, L.L. *Schooling the Daughters of Marianne: Textbooks and the Socializing of Girls in Modern France 1848–1870* (Albany, State University of New York Press, 1984).

Cobb, R.C. *A Second Identity* (Oxford, Oxford University Press, 1969).

—— *The People's Armies* (New Haven and London, Yale University Press, 1987).

Coffin, J. *The Politics of Women's Work: The Paris Garment Trades 1750–1915* (Princeton, Princeton University Press, 1996).

Coireault, G. *Les cinquante premières années de l'enseignement secondaire féminin, 1880–1930* (Thèse complémentaire pour le doctorat ès lettres, Poitiers, 1940).

Colwill, E. 'Just another *citoyenne?* Marie-Antoinette on trial', *History Workshop Journal*, 28, 1989, pp. 63–87.

Corbin, A. *Women for Hire: Prostitution and Sexuality in France after 1850* (Cambridge, Massachusetts, Harvard University Press, 1990).

Corbin, A., Lalouette, J. and Riot-Sarcey, M. (eds) *Femmes dans la cité 1815–1871* (Paris, Créaphis, n.d.).

Cosnier, C. *Marie Bashkirtseff: un portrait sans retouche* (Paris, Pierre Horay, 1985).

Cottereau, A. 'The distinctiveness of working-class cultures in France, 1848–1900', in I. Katznelson and A.R. Zolberg (eds) *Working-Class Formation: Nineteenth-Century Patterns in Western Europe and the United States* (Princeton, Princeton University Press, 1986).

Craveri, B. *Madame du Deffand and Her World* (London, Peter Halban, 1994).

Cross, M. and Gray, T. *The Feminism of Flora Tristan* (Oxford, Berg, 1992).

Dalotel, A. (ed.) *Paule Minck, communarde et féministe, 1839–1901* (Paris, Syros, 1981).

Daric, J. *L'Activité professionnelle des femmes en France* (Paris, PUF, 1947).

Darrow, M. 'French noblewomen and the new domesticity, 1750–1850', *Feminist Studies*, 5, no. 1 Spring 1979, pp. 41–65.

Daumard, A. *La bourgeoisie parisienne de 1815 à 1848* (Paris, SEVPEN, 1963).

—— 'La vie de salon en France dans la première moitié du xix siècle', in *Sociabilité et société bourgeoise en France, en Allemagne et en Suisse (1750–1850)* (Paris, Editions Recherches sur les Civilisations, 1986), pp. 81–94.

Bibliography

Delatour, Y. *Les effets de la guerre sur la situation de la Française d'après la presse féminine, 1914–1918* (Paris, maîtrise, 1965).

Deniel, R. *Une image de la famille et de la société sous la Restauration (1815–1830), étude de la presse catholique* (Paris, Les Editions Ouvrières, 1965).

Desan, S. 'The role of women in religious riots during the French Revolution', *Eighteenth-Century Studies*, 22, 1989, pp. 451–68.

—— 'Crowds, community and ritual in the work of E.P. Thompson and Natalie Davis', in L. Hunt (ed.) *The New Cultural History* (Berkeley, Los Angeles and London, University of California Press, 1989), pp. 47–71.

—— *Reclaiming the Sacred: Lay Religion and Popular Politics in Revolutionary Paris* (Ithaca, Cornell University Press, 1991).

—— ' "Constitutional amazons": Jacobin women's clubs in the French Revolution', in B.T. Ragan, Jr and E.A. Williams (eds) *Re-creating Authority in Revolutionary France* (New Jersey, Rutgers University Press, 1992), pp. 11–35.

Dessens, A. *Les revendications des droits de la femme au point de vue politique, civil, économique pendant la Révolution* (Law thesis, Toulouse, 1905).

Dessertine, D. *Divorcer à Lyon sous la Révolution et l'Empire* (Lyon, Presses Universitaires de Lyon, 1981).

Dufrancatel, C. *et al.* (eds) *L'Histoire sans qualités* (Paris, Editions Galilée, 1979).

Duplessis-Le Guélinel, G. *Les mariages en France* (Paris, Cahier de la Fondation Nationale de la Recherche Scientifique no. 53, 1954).

Duroselle, J.B. *Les débuts du catholicisme social en France, 1822–1870* (Paris, 1951).

Dyer, C. *Population and Society in Twentieth-Century France* (London, Hodder and Stoughton, 1978).

Edwards, S. *The Paris Commune 1871* (London, Eyre and Spottiswoode, 1971).

Ernst, O. *Théroigne de Méricourt, D'après des documents inédits tirés des archives secrètes de la Maison d'Autriche* (Paris, Payot, 1935).

Farge, A. and Klapisch-Zuber, C. (eds) *Madame ou mademoiselle? Itinéraires de la solitude féminine xviie–xx siècle* (Paris, Editions Montalba, 1984).

Fauré, C. *Democracy without Women: Feminism and the Rise of Liberal Individualism in France* (Bloomington, Indiana University Press, 1991).

Faure, O. *Les Français et leur médecine au xixe siècle* (Paris, Belin, 1993).

Fay-Sallois, F. *Les nourrices à Paris au xixe siècle* (Paris, Payot, 1980).

Fayet-Scribe, S. *Associations féminines et catholicisme: de la charité à l'action sociale xixe–xxe siècle* (Paris, Les Editions Ouvrières, 1990).

Flandrin, J-L. *Families in Former Times: Kinship, Household and Sexuality* (Cambridge, Cambridge University Press, 1979).

Fraisse, G. *Muse de la raison: la démocratie exclusive et la différence des sexes* (Paris, Alinéa, 1989).

Fraisse, G. and Perrot, M. (eds) *Emerging Feminism from the Revolution to the Great War*: Vol. 4 of G. Duby and M. Perrot (eds) *A History of Women in the West* (Cambridge, Massachusetts and London, The Belknap Press of Harvard University Press, 1995).

Frey, M. 'Du mariage et du concubinage dans les classes populaires à Paris (1846–1847)', *Annales ESC*, 33, 1978, pp. 803–29.

Gelbart, N.R. *Feminism and Opposition Journalism in Old Regime France:* Le Journal des Dames (Berkeley, Los Angeles and London, University of California Press, 1987).

—— 'The *Journal des Dames* and its female editors: politics, censorship and feminism in the Old Regime Press', in J. Censer and J.D. Popkin (eds) *Press and Politics in Pre-Revolutionary France* (Berkeley, Los Angeles and London, University of California Press, 1987).

Gibson, R. *A Social History of French Catholicism 1789–1914* (London, Routledge, 1989).

Giroux, H. 'Les femmes clubistes à Dijon (1791–1793)', *Annales de Bourgogne*, 57, 1985, pp. 23–45.

Bibliography

Glass, D.V. *Population Policies and Movements in Europe* (London, 1940).

Godineau, D. *Citoyennes tricoteuses: les femmes du peuple à Paris pendant la Révolution française* (Aix-en-Provence, Editions Alinéa, 1988).

—— 'Formation d'un mythe contre-révolutionnaire, les "tricoteuses" ', in *L'Image de la Révolution française. Communications présentées lors du Congrès Mondial pour le Bicentenaire de la Révolution française (Sorbonne, Paris, 6–12 juillet, 1989)*, 4 vols (Paris, 1989), vol. 3, pp. 2278–85.

—— 'Masculine and feminine political practice during the French Revolution, 1793 – Year III', in H.B. Applewhite and D.G. Levy (eds) *Women and Politics in the Age of the Democratic Revolution* (Ann Arbor, Michigan University Press, 1993), pp. 61–80.

de Goncourt, E. and J. *La femme au xviiie siècle: la société, l'amour et le mariage* (Paris, Flammarion, n.d.).

Goodman, D. 'Enlightenment salons: the convergence of female and philosophic ambitions', *Eighteenth-Century Studies*, 22, 1989, pp. 329–50.

—— 'Public sphere and private life: towards a synthesis of current historiographical approaches to the Old Regime', *History and Theory*, 31, 1992, pp. 1–20.

—— *The Republic of Letters. A Cultural History of the French Enlightenment* (Ithaca, Cornell University Press, 1994).

Gordon, F. *The Integral Feminist: Madeleine Pelletier, 1874–1939* (Cambridge, Polity Press, 1990).

Grinberg, S. *Histoire du mouvement suffragiste depuis 1848* (Paris, 1926).

—— *Historique du mouvement suffragiste depuis 1848* (Paris, Goulet, 1927).

Grogan, S.K. *French Socialism and Sexual Difference: Women and the New Society* (Basingstoke and London, Macmillan, 1992).

—— *Flora Tristan: Life Stories* (London, Routledge, 1998).

Groult, B. *Pauline Roland, ou comment la liberté vint aux femmes* (Paris, Robert Laffont, 1991).

Guélaud-Léridon, F. *Le travail des femmes en France* (Paris, INED cahier no. 42, 1964).

Guerber, J. *Le ralliement du clergé à la morale liguorienne: l'abbé Gousset et ses précurseurs (1785–1832)* (Rome, Università Gregoriana, 1973).

Guilbert, M. 'L'Evolution des effectifs du travail féminin en France depuis 1866', *Revue Française du Travail*, September 1947.

—— *Les femmes et l'organisation syndicale avant 1914* (Paris, CNRS, 1966).

—— *Les fonctions des femmes dans l'industrie* (Paris, Mouton et Cie, 1966).

Guilbert, M. and Isambert-Jamati, V. *Travail féminin et travail à domicile* (Paris, CNRS, 1956).

Guillais, J. *Crimes of Passion: Dramas of Private Life in Nineteenth-Century France* (Cambridge, Polity Press, 1990).

Guillemin, H. *Madame de Staël, Benjamin Constant et Napoléon* (Paris, Plon, 1959).

Gullickson, G.L. *Spinners and Weavers of Auffay: Rural Industry and the Sexual Division of Labour in a French Village* (Cambridge, Cambridge University Press, 1986).

—— *Unruly Women of Paris: Images of the Commune* (Ithaca, Cornell University Press, 1996).

Gutwirth, M. *The Twilight of the Goddesses: Women and Representation in the French Revolutionary Era* (New Brunswick, Rutgers University Press, 1992).

—— 'Citoyens, citoyennes: cultural regression and the subversion of female citizenship in the French Revolution', in R. Waldinger, P. Dawson and I. Woloch (eds) *The French Revolution and the Meaning of Citizenship* (Westport, Connecticut and London, Greenwood Press, 1993), pp. 17–28.

Harris, R. *Murder and Madness: Medicine, Law and Society in the Fin de Siècle* (Oxford, Oxford University Press, 1989).

Harrison, B. *Separate Spheres: The Opposition to Women's Suffrage in Britain* (London, Croom Helm, 1978).

Harsin, J. *Policing Prostitution in Nineteenth-Century Paris* (Princeton, Princeton University Press, 1990).

Bibliography

Hause, S. *Hubertine Auclert: The French Suffragette* (New Haven and London, Yale University Press, 1987).

Hause, S. and Kenney, A.R. 'The development of the Catholic women's suffrage movement in France, 1886–1922', *Catholic Historical Review*, 67, 1981, pp. 11–30.

Hause, S. with Kenney, A.R. *Women's Suffrage and Social Politics in the French Third Republic* (Princeton, Princeton University Press, 1984).

Higonnet, A. *Berthe Morisot's Images of Women* (Cambridge, Massachusetts, Harvard University Press, 1992).

Hilden, P. *Working Women and Socialist Politics in France 1880–1914: A Regional Study* (Oxford, Clarendon Press, 1986).

—— 'Women and the labour movement in France, 1869–1914', *The Historical Journal*, 29, 1986, pp. 809–32.

Hobsbawm, E.J. 'Man and woman in socialist iconography', *History Workshop*, 6, Autumn 1978, pp. 121–38.

Hoffmann, P. *La femme dans la pensée des lumières* (Paris, Editions Orphys, 1977).

Holt, R. *Sport and Society in Modern France* (London, Macmillan, 1981).

Horvath, S.V. 'Victor Duruy and the controversy over secondary education for girls', *French Historical Studies*, 9, Spring 1975, pp. 83–104.

Hufton, O. 'Women in Revolution, 1789–1796', *Past and Present*, 53, 1971, pp. 90–108.

—— 'Women and the family economy in eighteenth-century France', *French Historical Studies*, 9, Spring 1975, pp. 1–22.

—— 'The reconstruction of a church, 1796–1801', in G. Lewis and C. Lucas (eds) *Beyond the Terror: Essays in French Regional and Social History, 1789–1815* (Cambridge, Cambridge University Press, 1983), pp. 21–52.

—— *Women and the Limits of Citizenship in the French Revolution* (Toronto, Buffalo and London, University of Toronto Press, 1992).

—— *The Prospect Before Her: A History of Women in Western Europe*: Vol. 1 *1500–1800* (London, HarperCollins, 1995).

Hunt, L. *Politics, Culture and Class in the French Revolution* (Berkeley and Los Angeles, University of California Press, 1984).

—— (ed.) *Eroticism and the Body Politic* (Baltimore, Johns Hopkins University Press, 1990).

—— *The Family Romance of the French Revolution* (Berkeley, Los Angeles and London, University of California Press, 1992).

Institut National d'Etudes Démographiques. *La prévention des naissances dans la famille: ses origines dans les temps modernes* (Travaux et documents, cahier no. 35, 1960).

Jacobs, E. *et al.* (eds) *Women and Society in Eighteenth-Century France: Essays in Honour of John Stephenson Spink* (London, Athlone Press, 1979).

Jonas, R.A. *Industry and Politics in Rural France: Peasants of the Isère 1870–1914* (Ithaca, Cornell University Press, 1994).

Kaplan, S.L. and Koepp, C.J. (eds) *Work in France. Representations, Meaning, Organization and Practice* (Ithaca, Cornell University Press, 1986).

Kelly, J. *Women, History and Theory* (Chicago, Chicago University Press, 1984).

Klejman, L. and Rochefort, F. *L'Egalité en marche: le féminisme sous la Troisième République* (Paris, Presses de la Fondation Nationale des Sciences Politiques/des Femmes, 1989).

Kniebiehler, Y. and Fouquet, C. *La femme et les médecins: analyse historique* (Paris, Hachette, 1983).

Landes, J. *Women in the Public Sphere in the Age of the French Revolution* (Ithaca, Cornell University Press, 1988).

Bibliography

Langlois, C. *Le Catholicisme au féminin. Les congrégations à supérieure générale au xixe siècle* (Paris, Editions du Cerf, 1984).

Langlois, C. and Wagret, P. *Structures religieuses et célibat féminin au xixe siècle* (Lyon, 1972).

Laqueur, T. *Making Sex: Body and Gender from the Greeks to Freud* (Cambridge, Massachusetts, Harvard University Press, 1990).

Legates, M. 'The cult of womanhood in eighteenth-century thought', *Eighteenth-Century Studies*, 10, no. 1 Fall 1976, pp. 21–39.

Lejeune-Resnick, E. *Femmes et associations (1830–1880): vraies démocrates ou dames patronnesses?* (Paris, Publisud, 1991).

Lequin, Y. *Les ouvriers de la région lyonnaise (1848–1914)*, 2 vols (Lyon, Presses Universitaires de Lyon, 1977).

Leroux-Hugon, V. *Des saintes laïques: les infirmières à l'aube de la Troisième République* (Paris, Sciences en Situation, 1992).

Lesellier, C. 'Employées de grands magasins à Paris avant 1914', *Le Mouvement Social*, October–December 1978.

Lewis, H.D. 'The legal status of women in nineteenth-century France', *Journal of European Studies*, 10, 1980, pp. 178–88.

Li Dzeh-Djen. *La presse féministe en France de 1869 à 1914* (Paris, Rodstein, 1934).

Liu, T.P. *The Weaver's Knot: The Contradictions of Class Struggle and Family Solidarity in Western France, 1750–1914* (Ithaca, Cornell University Press, 1994).

—— '*Le patrimonie magique*: reassessing the power of women in rural households in nineteenth-century France', *Gender and History*, 6, 1994, pp. 13–36.

Lougee, C. *Le Paradis des Femmes: Women, Salons and Social Stratification in Seventeenth-Century France* (Princeton, Princeton University Press, 1977).

Lynch, K.A. *Family, Class and Ideology in Early Industrial France: Social Policy and the Working-Class Family 1825–1848* (Madison, The University of Wisconsin Press, 1988).

Lytle, S.H. 'The second sex (September 1793)', *Journal of Modern History*, 27, 1955, pp. 14–26.

McBride, T. *The Domestic Revolution: The Modernization of Household Service in England and France, 1820–1920* (London, Croom Helm, 1976).

MacCormack, C. and Strathern, M. (eds) *Nature, Culture and Gender* (Cambridge, Cambridge University Press, 1980).

MacLaren, A. 'Sex and socialism: the opposition of the French Left to birth control in the nineteenth century', *Journal of the History of Ideas*, 37, 1976, pp. 475–92.

—— 'Abortion in France: women and the regulation of family size 1800–1914', *French Historical Studies*, 10, Spring 1978, pp. 461–85.

—— *Sexuality and Social Order: The Debate over the Fertility of Women and Workers in France, 1770–1920* (New York, Holmes and Meier, 1983).

MacLean, I. *The Renaissance Notion of Woman: A Study in the Fortunes of Scholasticism and Medical Science in European Intellectual Life* (Cambridge, Cambridge University Press, 1980).

McMillan, J.F. *Housewife or Harlot: The Place of Women in French Society 1870–1940* (Brighton, The Harvester Press, 1981).

—— 'Clericals, anticlericals and the women's movement in France under the Third Republic', *The Historical Journal*, 24, 1981, pp. 361–76.

—— 'Women, religion and politics: the case of the Ligue Patriotique des Françaises', in W. Roosen (ed.) *Proceedings of the Annual Meeting of the Western Society for French History* (Flagstaff, Arizona, 1988), vol. 15, pp. 355–64.

273

Bibliography

—— 'Women in social Catholicism in late nineteenth and early twentieth-century France', in W.J. Sheils and D. Wood (eds) *Women and the Church* (*Studies in Church History* no. 27) (Oxford, Blackwell, 1990), pp. 467–80.

—— *Napoleon III* (Harlow, Longman, 1991).

—— 'Religion and gender in modern France: some reflections', in F. Tallett and N. Atkin (eds) *Religion, Society and Politics in France since 1789* (London and Rio Grande, The Hambledon Press, 1991), pp. 29–54.

—— 'Wollstonecraft's daughters, Marianne's daughters and the daughters of Joan of Arc: Marie Maugeret and Christian feminism in the French Belle Epoque', in C.C. Orr (ed.) *Wollstonecraft's Daughters: Womanhood in England and France 1780–1920* (Manchester and New York, Manchester University Press, 1996), pp. 186–98.

—— 'France', in R. Eatwell (ed.) *European Political Cultures: Conflict or Convergence?* (London, Routledge, 1997), pp. 69–87.

McPhee, P. *A Social History of France 1780–1880* (London, Routledge, 1992).

—— *The Politics of Rural Life: Political Mobilization in the French Countryside 1846–52* (Oxford, Oxford University Press, 1992).

Magraw, R. *A History of the French Working Class*, 2 vols (Oxford, Blackwell, 1992).

Margadant, J.B. *Madame le Professeur: Women Educators in the Third Republic* (Princeton, Princeton University Press, 1990).

Martin-Fugier, A. *La vie élégante: ou la formation du Tout-Paris* (Paris, Fayard, 1990).

Mauge, A. *L'Identité masculine en crise au tournant du siècle, 1871–1914* (Paris, Editions Rivages, 1987).

Mayeur, F. *L'Enseignement secondaire des jeunes filles sous la Troisième République* (Paris, Presses de la Fondation Nationale des Sciences Politiques, 1977).

—— *L'Education des filles au dix-neuvième siècle* (Paris, Hachette, 1979).

Medick, H. 'The proto-industrial family economy: the structural function of household and family during the transition from peasant society to industrial capitalism', *Social History*, 1, 1976, pp. 291–316.

Merchant, C. *The Death of Nature: Women, Ecology and the Scientific Revolution* (New York, Harper and Row, 1980).

Merriman, J.M. *The Repression of the Left in Revolutionary France 1848–1851* (New Haven and London, Yale University Press, 1978).

—— (ed.) *French Cities in the Nineteenth Century* (London, Hutchinson, 1982).

Michaud, S. (ed.) *Un fabuleux destin: Flora Tristan* (Dijon, Editions Universitaires de Dijon, 1985).

—— *Muse et Madone. Visages de la femme de la Révolution française aux apparitions de Lourdes* (Paris, Le Seuil, 1986).

Miller, M. *The Bon Marché: Bourgeois Culture and the Department Store, 1869–1920* (Princeton, Princeton University Press, 1981).

Mills, H. 'Negotiating the divide: women, philanthropy and the "public sphere" in nineteenth-century France', in F. Tallett and N. Atkin (eds) *Religion, Society and Politics in France since 1789* (London and Rio Grande, The Hambledon Press, 1991), pp. 29–54.

—— 'Saintes soeurs and femmes fortes: alternative accounts of the route to womanly civic virtue, and the history of French feminism', in C.C. Orr (ed.) *Wollstonecraft's Daughters: Womanhood in England and France 1780–1920* (Manchester and New York, Manchester University Press, 1996), pp. 55–66.

Moch, L. *Paths to the City: Regional Migration in Nineteenth-Century France* (Beverly Hills, Sage Publications, 1983).

Moreau, T. *Le sang de l'histoire. Michelet, l'histoire et l'idée de la femme au xixe siècle* (Paris, Flammarion, 1982).

Bibliography

Moscucci, O. *The Science of Woman: Gynaecology and Gender in England 1800–1929* (Cambridge, Cambridge University Press, 1990).

Moser, F. *Vie et aventures de Céleste Mogador, fille publique, femme de lettres, et comtesse (1824–1909)* (Paris, 1935).

Moses, C.G. 'Saint-Simonian men/Saint-Simonian women: the transformation of feminist thought in 1830s France', *Journal of Modern History*, 54, 1982, pp. 240–67.

—— *French Feminism in the Nineteenth Century* (Albany, State University of New York Press, 1984).

Noonan, J.T. *Contraception: A History of its Treatment by the Catholic Theologians and Canonists* (Cambridge, Massachusetts, Harvard University Press, 1965).

—— *Power to Dissolve: Lawyers and Marriages in the Courts of the Roman Curia* (Cambridge, Massachusetts, Harvard University Press, 1972).

Offen, K. 'The Second Sex and the Baccalaureat in Republican France, 1880–1924', *French Historical Studies*, 13, Fall 1983, pp. 252–86.

—— 'Depopulation, nationalism and feminism in fin-de-siècle France', *American Historical Review*, 89, 1984, pp. 648–76.

—— 'Ernest Legouvé and the doctrine of "equality in difference" for women: a case study of male feminism in nineteenth-century French thought', *Journal of Modern History*, 58, 1986, pp. 452–84.

—— 'Women, citizenship and suffrage with a French twist, 1789–1993', in C. Daley and M. Nolan (eds) *Suffrage and Beyond: International Feminist Perspectives* (New York, New York University Press, 1994), pp. 151–70.

O'Neill, W.L. *Everyone was Brave: A History of Feminism in America* (Chicago, Quadrangle Books, 1971; original edn, 1969).

Orr, C.C. (ed.) *Wollstonecraft's Daughters: Womanhood in England and France 1780–1920* (Manchester and New York, Manchester University Press, 1996).

Outram, D. '*Le langage mâle de la vertu*: women and the discourse of the French Revolution', in P. Burke and R. Porter (eds) *The Social History of Language* (Cambridge, Cambridge University Press, 1987), pp. 120–35.

—— *The Body and the French Revolution* (New Haven and London, Yale University Press, 1989).

—— *The Enlightenment* (Cambridge, Cambridge University Press, 1995).

Ozouf, J. 'Les instituteurs de la Manche au début du vingtième siècle', *Revue d'Histoire Moderne et Contemporaine*, 13, 1966, pp. 95–114.

Ozouf, M. *L'Ecole, l'Eglise et la République* (Paris, 1963).

—— *Les mots des femmes: essai sur la singularité française* (Paris, Fayard, 1995).

Parent-Lardeur, F. *Les demoiselles de magasin* (Paris, 1970).

Patureau-Miraud, C. *De la femme et de son rôle dans la société d'après les écrits saint-simoniens* (Politics thesis, Limoges, 1910).

Paulin, V. 'Le travail à domicile en France: ses origines, son évolution, son avenir', *La Revue Internationale du Travail*, February 1938, pp. 205–40.

Perrot, M. *Enquêtes sur la condition ouvrière en France au xixe siècle* (Paris, Microéditions Hachette, 1972).

—— *Les ouvriers en grève: France 1871–1890*, 2 vols (Paris, Mouton, 1974).

—— (ed.) *From the Fires of Revolution to the Great War*: Vol. 4 of P. Ariès and G. Duby (eds) *A History of Private Life* (Cambridge, Massachusetts and London, The Belknap Press of Harvard University Press, 1990).

Phayer, J.M. *Sexual Liberation and Religion in Nineteenth-Century Europe* (London, Croom Helm, 1977).

Phillips, R. *Family Breakdown in Late Eighteenth-Century France: Divorces in Rouen, 1792–1803* (Oxford, Oxford University Press, 1980).

—— *Putting Asunder: A History of Divorce in Western Society* (Cambridge, Cambridge University Press, 1988).

de Piaggi, G. *La sposa perfetta: educazione e condizione della donna nella famiglia frances del Rinascimento e della Controriforma* (Abano Terme, 1979).

Piau-Gillot, C. 'Le discours de Jean-Jacques Rousseau sur les femmes et sa réception critique', *XVIIIe Siècle*, 1981, pp. 317–33.

Pilbeam, P.M. *Republicanism in Nineteenth-Century France, 1814–1871* (Basingstoke and London, Macmillan, 1995).

Pillorget, R. *La tige et le rameau. Familles anglaises et françaises 16–18e siècles* (Paris, Calmann-Lévy, 1979).

Planté, C. *La petite soeur de Balzac* (Paris, Editions du Seuil, 1989).

Pope, B.C. 'Maternal education in France, 1815–1848', *Proceedings of the Western Society for French History*, 3, 1976, pp. 368–77.

Prigent, R. *Renouveau des idées sur la famille* (Paris, INED cahier no. 18, 1954).

Prost, A. *Histoire de l'enseignement en France, 1800–1967* (Paris, Colin, 1968).

Puech, J-L. *La vie et l'oeuvre de Flora Tristan* (Paris, Librairie Marcel Rivière et Cie, 1925).

Rabaut, J. *Histoire des féminismes français* (Paris, Stock, 1978).

Reddy, W.R. 'Family and factory: French linen workers in the Belle Epoque', *Journal of Social History*, 8, Winter 1975, pp. 102–12.

—— *The Rise of Market Culture: The Textile Trade and French Society* (Cambridge, Cambridge University Press, 1984).

Rendall, J. *The Origins of Modern Feminism: Women in Britain, France and the United States 1780–1860* (London, Macmillan, 1985).

Reynolds, S. (ed.) *Women, State and Revolution* (Brighton, Wheatsheaf Books, 1986).

Riot-Sarcey, M. *La démocratie à l'épreuve des femmes. Trois figures critiques du pouvoir 1830–1848: Désirée Veret, Eugénie Niboyet, Jeanne Deroin* (Paris, Albin Michel, 1994).

Ripa, Y. *Women and Madness: The Incarceration of Women in Nineteenth-Century France* (Cambridge, Polity Press, 1990).

Ronsin, F. 'La classe ouvrière et le néo-malthusianisme: l'exemple français avant 1914', *Le Mouvement Social*, 106, January–May 1979, pp. 85–117.

—— *Les divorciaires: affrontements politiques et conceptions du mariage dans la France du xixe siècle* (Paris, Editions Aubier, 1992).

Rosanvallon, P. *Le sacre du citoyen: histoire du suffrage universel en France* (Paris, Gallimard, 1992).

Rose, R.B. *The Enragés: Socialists of the Revolution?* (Melbourne, Melbourne University Press, 1965).

Rouast, A. 'La transformation de la famille en France depuis la Révolution', in *Sociologie comparée de la famille contemporaine* (Paris, CNRS, 1955).

Roudinesco, E. *Théroigne de Méricourt: A Melancholic Woman during the French Revolution* (New York, Verso, 1991).

Sarti, O. *The Ligue Patriotique des Françaises 1902–1933: A Feminine Response to the Secularization of French Society* (New York and London, Garland Publishing Inc., 1992).

Sautman, F.C. 'Invisible women: lesbian working-class culture in France, 1880–1930', in J. Merrick and B.T. Ragan, Jr (eds) *Homosexuality in Modern France* (Oxford and New York, Oxford University Press, 1996), pp. 177–201.

Schama, S. *Citizens: A Chronicle of the French Revolution* (London, Penguin Books, 1989).

Schiebinger, L. *The Mind Has No Sex? Women in the Origins of Modern Science* (Cambridge, Massachusetts, Harvard University Press, 1989).

276

Bibliography

Schnapper, B. 'Liberté, égalité, autorité: la famille devant les assemblées révolutionnaires (1790–1800)', in M-F. Lévy (ed.) *L'Enfant, la famille et la Révolution française* (Paris, Olivier Orban, 1990), pp. 325–40.

Schwartz, J. *The Sexual Politics of Jean-Jacques Rousseau* (Chicago, Chicago University Press, 1984).

Scott, J.W. *Gender and the Politics of History* (New York, Columbia University Press, 1988).

—— *Only Paradoxes to Offer: French Feminists and the Rights of Man* (Cambridge, Massachusetts, Harvard University Press, 1996).

Scott, J.W. and Tilly, L. 'Women's work and the family in nineteenth-century Europe', *Comparative Studies in Society and History*, 17, 1975, pp. 36–64.

Segalen, M. *Love and Power in the Peasant Family* (Oxford and Chicago, Basil Blackwell and the University of Chicago, 1983).

Servais, J-J. and Laurend, J-P. *Histoire et dossier de la prostitution* (Paris, 1965).

Shapiro, A-L. *Breaking the Codes: Female Criminality in Fin-de-Siècle Paris* (Stanford, Stanford University Press, 1996).

Shorter, E. *The Making of the Modern Family* (London, Fontana, 1977).

Silverman, D.L. *Art Nouveau in Fin-de-Siècle France: Politics, Psychology and Style* (Berkeley, Los Angeles and London, University of California Press, 1989).

Smith, B. *Ladies of the Leisure Class: The Bourgeoises of Northern France in the Nineteenth Century* (Princeton, Princeton University Press, 1981).

Sonnenscher, M. *Work and Wages: Natural Law, Politics and Eighteenth-Century French Trades* (Cambridge, Cambridge University Press, 1989).

Soprani, A. *La Révolution et les femmes de 1789 à 1796* (Paris, MA Editions, 1988).

Sowerwine, C. 'The organization of French socialist women 1880–1914: a European perspective for women's movements', *Historical Reflexions*, 3, 1976, pp. 3–24.

—— *Sisters or Citizens? Women and Socialism since 1876* (Cambridge, Cambridge University Press, 1982).

—— 'Workers and women in France before 1914: the debate over the Couriau Affair', *Journal of Modern History*, 55, 1983, pp. 411–41.

Sowerwine, C. and Maignien, C. *Madeleine Pelletier: une féministe dans l'arène politique* (Paris, Les Editions Ouvrières, 1992).

Spencer, S. (ed.) *French Women and the Age of Enlightenment* (Bloomington, Indiana University Press, 1984).

Spengler, J.J. *France Faces Depopulation* (London, 1938).

Stearns, P. *Lives of Labour: Work in a Maturing Industrial Society* (London, Croom Helm, 1975).

Stengers, J. 'Les pratiques anticonceptionnelles dans le mariage au xixe siècle: problèmes humains et attitudes religieuses', *Revue Belge de Philologie et d'Histoire*, xlix (2), 1971/72, pp. 403–81.

Stephens, W. *Madame Adam Juliette Lamber. La grande Française, from Louis Philippe until 1917* (New York, E.P. Dalton and Co., 1917).

Stewart, M.L. *Women, Work and the French State: Labour Protection and Social Patriarchy 1879–1919* (London, McGill-Queen's University Press, 1989).

Stone, J.F. *The Search for Social Peace: Reform Legislation in France, 1890–1914* (Albany, State University of New York Press, 1985).

Strumingher, L. *Women and the Making of the Working-Class: Lyon 1830–1870* (St Albans, Vermont, Eden Press, 1979).

—— 'The Vésuviennes: images of women warriors in 1848 and their significance for French history', *History of European Ideas*, 8, 1987, pp. 451–88.

Stuart, R. 'Whores and angels: women and the family in the discourse of French Marxism, 1882–1905', *European History Quarterly*, 27, 1997, pp. 339–70.

Bibliography

—— ' "Calm with a grave and serious temperament, rather male." French Marxism, gender and feminism, 1882–1905', *International Review of Social History*, 41, 1996, pp. 57–82.

Sullerot, E. *La presse féminine* (Paris, 1963).

—— *Histoire de la presse féminine en France des origines à 1848* (Paris, Colin, 1966).

—— 'Journaux féminins et lutte ouvrière (1848–1849)', in *Société d'histoire de la Révolution de 1848* (Paris, CNRS, 1966), pp. 88–122.

—— *Histoire et sociologie du travail féminin* (Paris, 1968).

Sussman, G.D. 'The wet-nursing business in nineteenth-century France', *French Historical Studies*, 9, 1975, pp. 304–28.

Tackett, T. 'Women and men in counter-revolution: the Sommières riot, 1791', *Journal of Modern History*, 59, 1987, pp. 680–704.

Tallett, F. and Atkin, N. (eds) *Religion, Society and Politics in France since 1789* (London and Rio Grande, The Hambledon Press, 1991).

Termeau, J. *Maisons closes de province* (Paris, Editions Cénomane, 1986).

Thibert, M. *Le féminisme dans le socialisme français de 1830 à 1850* (Paris, M. Giard, 1926).

Thiébaux, C. *Le féminisme et les socialistes depuis Saint-simon à nos jours* (Law thesis, Paris, 1906).

Thomas, C. *La reine scélérate: Marie-Antoinette dans les pamphlets* (Paris, Le Seuil, 1989).

Thomas, E. *Les femmes de 1848* (Paris, PUF, 1948).

—— *Pauline Roland: Socialisme et féminisme au xixe siècle* (Paris, Marcel Rivière, 1956).

—— *Les pétroleuses* (Paris, Gallimard, 1963), translated as *The Women Incendiaries* (New York, George Brazillier, 1966).

—— *Louise Michel* (Paris, Gallimard, 1971).

Thomas, K. 'The double standard', *Journal of the History of Ideas*, 20, 1959, pp. 195–216.

Thuillier, G. *Pour une histoire du quotidien en Nivernais au xixe siècle* (Paris, Mouton, 1977).

Tilly, L.A. 'Women's collective action and feminism in France, 1870–1914', in C. Tilly and L. Tilly (eds) *Class Conflict and Collective Action* (Beverly Hills, Sage Publications, 1981), pp. 207–31.

Tilly, L. and Scott, J. *Women, Work and Family* (London, Holt, Reinhart and Winston, 1978).

Tixerant, J. *Le féminisme à l'époque de 1848* (Law thesis, Paris, 1908).

Tolédano, A-D. *La vie de famille sous la Restauration et la Monarchie de juillet* (Paris, 1943).

Tomaselli, S. 'The Enlightenment debate on women', *History Workshop*, 20, 1985, pp. 101–25.

Traer, J.F. *Marriage and the Family in Eighteenth-Century France* (Ithaca and London, Cornell University Press, 1980).

Trebilcock, C. *The Industrialization of the Continental Powers 1780–1914* (London, Addison-Wesley/ Longman, 1981).

Vanier, H. *La mode et ses métiers: frivolités et luttes de classes, 1830–70* (Paris, Colin, 1960).

Verdier, Y. *Façons de dire, façons de faire. La Laveuse, la couturière, la cuisinière* (Paris, Gallimard, 1979).

de Villiers, M. *Histoire des clubs des femmes et des légions d'Amazones (1793–1848–1871)* (Paris, 1910).

Vincent, G. 'Les professeurs de l'enseignement secondaire dans la sociéte de la belle époque', *Revue d'Histoire Moderne et Contemporaine*, 13, 1966, pp. 49–86.

Waelti-Walters, J. *Feminist Novelists of the Belle Epoque: Love as a Lifestyle* (Bloomington and Indianapolis, Indiana University Press, 1990).

Walton, W. 'Working women, gender and industrialization in nineteenth-century France: the case of Lorraine embroidery manufacturing', *Journal of Women's History*, 2, 1990, pp. 42–65.

Wexler, V.G. 'Made for man's delight: Rousseau as antifeminist', *American Historical Review*, 81, 1976, pp. 266–91.

Wiesner, M.E. *Women and Gender in Early Modern Europe* (Cambridge, Cambridge University Press, 1993).

Bibliography

Williams, E.A. *The Physical and the Moral: Anthropology, Physiology and Philosophical Medicine in France 1750–1850* (Cambridge, Cambridge University Press, 1994).

Williams, R. *Dream Worlds* (Berkeley, Los Angeles and London, University of California Press, 1982).

Wilson, L. *Women and Medicine in the Age of the Enlightenment: The Debate over Maladie des Femmes* (Baltimore and London, Johns Hopkins University Press, 1993).

Yalom, M. *Blood Sisters: The French Revolution in Women's Memory* (New York, Basic Books, 1993).

Zeldin, T. *France 1848–1945*, 2 vols (Oxford, Clarendon Press, 1973–77).

Zylberberg-Hocquard, M-H. *Féminisme et syndicalisme en France avant 1914* (Paris, Anthropos, 1978).

—— 'Les ouvrières d'Etat (tabac-allumettes) dans les dernières années du xixe siècle', *Le Mouvement Social*, 105, October–December 1978.

279

Index

Index

Index

Index

Index

Index